Ampara
2007

MAKING
MONEY
MATTER
Financing America's Schools

Committee on Education Finance

Helen F. Ladd and Janet S. Hansen, *Editors*

Commission on Behavioral and Social Sciences and Education

National Research Council

NATIONAL ACADEMY PRESS
Washington, D.C.

NATIONAL ACADEMY PRESS • 2101 Constitution Avenue, N.W. • Washington, D.C. 20418

NOTICE: The project that is the subject of this volume was approved by the Governing Board of the National Research Council, whose members are drawn from the councils of the National Academy of Sciences, the National Academy of Engineering, and the Institute of Medicine. The members of the committee responsible for the volume were chosen for their special competences and with regard for appropriate balance.

This volume was supported by Contract No. RF95194001 between the National Academy of Sciences and the U.S. Department of Education. Any opinions, findings, conclusions, or recommendations expressed in this publication are those of the author(s) and do not necessarily reflect the view of the organizations or agencies that provided support for this project.

Library of Congress Cataloging-in-Publication Data

Making money matter : financing America's schools / Helen F. Ladd and
Janet S. Hansen, editors ; Committee on Education Finance, Commission on
Behavioral and Social Sciences and Education, National Research Council.
    p. cm.
Includes bibliographical references and index.
    ISBN 0-309-06528-3 (casebound)
    1. Education—United States—Finance. 2. Educational
productivity—United States. 3. Educational equalization—United
States. 4. Educational change—United States. I. Ladd, Helen F. II.
Hansen, Janet S. III. National Research Council (U.S.). Committee on
Education Finance.
    LB2825+
    379.1'1'0973—dc21
                 99-050424

Suggested citation:
National Research Council (1999). *Making Money Matter: Financing America's Schools.* Committee on Education Finance, Helen F. Ladd and Janet S. Hansen, editors. Commission on Behavioral and Social Sciences and Education. Washington, DC: National Academy Press.

Additional copies of this volume are available from:
National Academy Press
2101 Constitution Avenue N.W.
Washington, D.C. 20418
Call 800-624-6242 or 202-334-3313 (in the Washington Metropolitan Area).

This volume is also available on line at **http://www.nap.edu**

Printed in the United States of America
Copyright 1999 by the National Academy of Sciences. All rights reserved.

THE NATIONAL ACADEMIES

National Academy of Sciences
National Academy of Engineering
Institute of Medicine
National Research Council

The **National Academy of Sciences** is a private, nonprofit, self-perpetuating society of distinguished scholars engaged in scientific and engineering research, dedicated to the furtherance of science and technology and to their use for the general welfare. Upon the authority of the charter granted to it by the Congress in 1863, the Academy has a mandate that requires it to advise the federal government on scientific and technical matters. Dr. Bruce M. Alberts is president of the National Academy of Sciences.

The **National Academy of Engineering** was established in 1964, under the charter of the National Academy of Sciences, as a parallel organization of outstanding engineers. It is autonomous in its administration and in the selection of its members, sharing with the National Academy of Sciences the responsibility for advising the federal government. The National Academy of Engineering also sponsors engineering programs aimed at meeting national needs, encourages education and research, and recognizes the superior achievements of engineers. Dr. William A. Wulf is president of the National Academy of Engineering.

The **Institute of Medicine** was established in 1970 by the National Academy of Sciences to secure the services of eminent members of appropriate professions in the examination of policy matters pertaining to the health of the public. The Institute acts under the responsibility given to the National Academy of Sciences by its congressional charter to be an adviser to the federal government and, upon its own initiative, to identify issues of medical care, research, and education. Dr. Kenneth I. Shine is president of the Institute of Medicine.

The **National Research Council** was organized by the National Academy of Sciences in 1916 to associate the broad community of science and technology with the Academy's purposes of furthering knowledge and advising the federal government. Functioning in accordance with general policies determined by the Academy, the Council has become the principal operating agency of both the National Academy of Sciences and the National Academy of Engineering in providing services to the government, the public, and the scientific and engineering communities. The Council is administered jointly by both Academies and the Institute of Medicine. Dr. Bruce M. Alberts and Dr. William A. Wulf are chairman and vice chairman, respectively, of the National Research Council.

PANEL ON SPECIAL EDUCATION FINANCE

DAVID W. BRENEMAN *(Chair)*, Curry School of Education, University of
Virginia
MARY-BETH FAFARD, Northeast and Island Regional Educational
Laboratory, Brown University
MARGARET E. GOERTZ, Consortium for Policy Research in Education,
University of Pennsylvania
MARGARET J. McLAUGHLIN, Institute for the Study of Exceptional
Children and Youth, University of Maryland
THOMAS B. PARRISH, Center for Special Education Finance, American
Institutes for Research, Palo Alto, California

Acknowledgments

Many people contributed in important ways to the completion of this report; and we are most grateful for their efforts. First, we appreciate the support provided by the study's sponsor, the U.S. Department of Education, and the individuals within the Office of Education Research and Improvement with whom we worked during the project: Kent McGuire, assistant secretary, James Fox, and Duc-Le To.

The committee was assisted in its review of the voluminous literature related to education finance by a number of individuals who prepared background papers. We previously published eight of these papers related to issues in equity and adequacy.[1] Authors (who were not also committee or staff members) included Melissa C. Carr, William D. Duncombe, William N. Evans, Margaret E. Goertz, Sheila E. Murray, Richard Rothstein, Leanna Stiefel, and John M. Yinger. These papers, plus the comments of reviewers selected by the National Research Council (NRC) in accordance with its report review procedures, were extremely helpful in preparing the analysis in this report. We again thank the reviewers of the previous volume: John Augenblick, Dominic Brewer, William Buss, David Figlio, Eric Hanushek, David Monk, Richard Murnane, Lawrence Picus, Andrew Reschovsky, Julie Underwood, and Arthur Wise.

Unpublished background papers that also greatly assisted us in our work were prepared by Ronald Fisher, Kenneth Godwin, Laura Hamilton, Jane

---

[1]National Research Council, *Equity and Adequacy in Education Finance: Issues and Perspectives*, Committee on Education Finance. Washington, DC: National Academy Press, 1999.

viii ACKNOWLEDGMENTS

Hannaway, Jennifer Hochschild, Jack Jennings, Frank Kemerer, Therese McGuire, Michele McLaughlin, and Cecilia Rouse.

In addition to the many scholars whose written work informed our deliberations and is acknowledged in the report's reference list, many individuals met with us to extend our understanding of specific issues.

A technical panel on special education, set up by the committee, met four times over a year to review the particular issues involved in financing education for students with disabilities. We thank panel chair David Breneman and members Mary-Beth Fafard, Margaret E. Goertz, Margaret J. McLaughlin, and Thomas B. Parrish for their hard work and excellent analysis.

We also benefited from the advice of 23 researchers and practitioners who joined us for a one-day workshop to discuss data needs related to education finance. Participants included John Augenblick, Dominic Brewer, Jay Chambers, Matthew Cohen, Thomas Downes, Jerry Fastrup, David Figlio, Pascal Forgione, William Fowler, Jr., Michael Garet, David Grissmer, Nancy Heiligman, Linda Hertert, Philip Kaufman, David Monk, Martin Orland, Lauri Peternick, Lawrence Picus, Paul Planchon, Richard Rothstein, Leanna Steifel, Duc-Le To, and Eugenia Toma. In addition, William Clune, Ronald Ferguson, Christopher Jencks, and William Taylor joined the committee to discuss issues of adequacy and equity and student achievement.

The report was reviewed in draft form by individuals chosen for their diverse perspectives and technical expertise, in accordance with procedures approved by the NRC's Report Review Committee. The purpose of this independent review is to provide candid and critical comments that will assist the institution in making the published report as sound as possible and to ensure that the report meets institutional standards for objectivity, evidence, and responsiveness to the study charge. The review comments and draft manuscript remain confidential to protect the integrity of the deliberative process.

We wish to thank the following individuals for their participation in the review of this report: Christopher Cross, Council for Basic Education, Washington, D.C.; William H. Danforth, Chairman, Board of Trustees, Washington University, St. Louis; G. Alfred Hess, Jr., School of Education and Social Policy, Northwestern University; Caroline Hoxby, Department of Economics, Harvard University; James A. Kelley, National Board for Professional Teaching Standards, Southfield, Michigan; Cora Marrett, Vice Chancellor for Academic Affairs and Provost, University of Massachusetts, Amherst; David H. Monk, Dean of the College of Education, Pennsylvania State University; Anita A. Summers, Wharton School, University of Pennsylvania; David Tyack, School of Education, Stanford University; and James H. Wyckoff, Rockefeller College of Public Affairs and Policy, University at Albany, New York.

Although the individuals listed above have provided constructive comments and suggestions, it must be emphasized that responsibility for the final content of this report rests entirely with the authoring committee and the institution.

Finally, we wish to express our appreciation for the efforts of the staff at the NRC in supporting the committee's deliberations and in preparing this report for publication. Alexandra Wigdor, director of the Division on Education, Labor, and Human Performance, provided valuable guidance throughout the project. Rosemary Chalk served as staff for the technical panel on special education as well as chief editor of the previously published volume of papers on education equity and adequacy. Neal Finkelstein, Thomas Husted, and Paul Minorini provided analytical support on school finance, economic, and legal issues, respectively. Anne Marie Finn brought her incomparable organizational skills to the important tasks of organizing and managing the project library, preparing briefing notes for the committee, checking the accuracy of facts and references in the report, and overseeing final preparation of the manuscript for publication. Sharon Vandivere and later Nat Tipton provided administrative support for the committee, both in arranging its meetings and in preparing this and the earlier published volume. The report also benefited from the editorial attention of Christine McShane. The committee extends its sincere thanks and appreciation to all those who assisted us in our work.

Helen F. Ladd, *Cochair*
Thomas Sobol, *Cochair*
Janet S. Hansen, *Study Director*
Committee on Education Finance

Contents

xi

MAKING
MONEY
MATTER

Executive Summary

A national desire to ensure that all children learn and achieve to high standards now poses fundamental challenges to almost every facet of business as usual in American education. Policy makers and educators are searching for better ways to provide today's schoolchildren with the knowledge and skills they will need to function effectively as citizens and workers in a future society that promises to be increasingly complex and globally interconnected. A key component of this quest involves school finance and decisions about how the $300 billion the United States spends annually on public elementary and secondary education can most effectively be raised and used.

A new emphasis on raising achievement for all students poses an important but daunting challenge for policy makers: how to harness the education finance system to this objective. This challenge is important because it aims to link finance directly to the purposes of education. It is daunting because making money matter in this way means that school finance decisions must become intertwined with an unprecedented ambition for the nation's schools: never before has the nation set for itself the goal of educating all children to high standards.

This report argues that money can and must be made to matter more than in the past if the nation is to reach its ambitious goal of improving achievement for all students. There are, however, no easy solutions to this challenge, because values are in conflict, conditions vary widely from place to place, and knowledge about the link between resources and learning is incomplete. Moreover, without societal attention to wider inequalities in social and economic opportunities, it is unrealistic to expect that schools alone, no matter how much money they receive or how well they use it, will be able to overcome serious disadvantages that affect the capacity of many children to gain full benefit from what education has to offer.

❖ **Taking full account of conflicting values, wide variation in educational contexts, and strengths and limitations of existing knowledge, the Committee on Education Finance concludes that money can and should be used more effectively than it traditionally has been to make a difference in U.S. schools. To promote the achievement of a fair and productive educational system, finance decisions should be explicitly aligned with broad educational goals.** In the past, finance policy focused primarily on availability of revenues or disparities in spending, and decisions were made independently of efforts to improve the educational system's performance. Although school finance policy must not ignore the continuing facts of revenue needs and spending disparities, it also should be a key component of education strategies designed to foster higher levels of learning for all students and to reduce the nexus between student achievement and family background.

❖ **To this end, the emerging concept of funding adequacy, which moves beyond the more traditional concepts of finance equity to focus attention on the sufficiency of funding for desired educational outcomes, is an important step.** The concept of adequacy is useful because it shifts the focus of finance policy from revenue inputs to spending and educational outcomes and forces discussion of how much money is needed to achieve what ends. It also could drive the education system to become more productive by focusing attention on the relationship between resources and outcomes.

❖ **Applying an adequacy standard to school finance is at present an art, not a science. Misuse of the concept can be minimized if adequacy-based policies are implemented with appropriate recognition of the need for policy judgments and of the incomplete knowledge about the costs of an adequate education.** Efforts to define and measure adequate funding are in their infancy. A number of technical challenges remain, including the determination of how much more it costs to educate children from disadvantaged backgrounds than those from more privileged circumstances. Beyond these, some fundamental questions about educational adequacy (such as how broad and how high the standards should be) are ultimately value judgments and are not strictly technical or mechanical issues. A key danger is that political pressures may result in specifying adequacy at so low a level as to trivialize the concept as a meaningful criterion in setting finance policy, or at so high a level that it encourages unnecessary spending. Another is that policy makers will fail to account for the higher costs of educating disadvantaged students.

❖ **Making money matter more requires more than adequate funding. It also requires additional finance strategies, such as investing in the capacity of the education system, altering incentives to ensure that performance counts, and empowering schools or parents or both to make decisions about the uses of public funds.** For money to matter more, it must be used in ways that ensure that schools will have the capacity to teach all students to higher standards as well as the incentive to do so. Policy options involve choices among individual finance strategies and combinations of strategies; policy decisions will depend partially on philosophical outlook but can also be informed by careful attention to evidence from research and practice. Attention to context is important as well, as educational and political conditions diverge widely from place to place and individual policy options will often vary in effectiveness depending on local circumstances.

❖ **Educational challenges facing districts and schools serving concentrations of disadvantaged students are particularly intense, and social science research provides few definitive answers about how to improve educational outcomes for these youngsters.** While pockets of poverty and disadvantage can be found in all types of communities, the perceived crisis in urban education is especially worrisome. Ongoing reform efforts should be encouraged and evaluated for effectiveness. At the same time, systematic inquiry is needed into a range of more comprehensive and aggressive reforms in urban schools. Piecemeal reform efforts in the past have not generated clear gains in achievement, and generations of at-risk schoolchildren have remained poorly served by public education. Because the benefits of systematic inquiry will extend beyond any one district or state, the federal government should bear primary responsibility for initiating and evaluating bold strategies for improving education for at-risk students.

❖ **Improving the American system of education finance is complicated by deeply rooted differences in values about education, the role of parents in guiding the development of their children, and the role of individuals and governments in a democratic society. In addition, there are serious shortcomings in knowledge about exactly how to improve learning for all students. Education policy cannot ignore these facts. Instead, the challenges are to balance differing values in a thoughtful and informed manner and continuously to pursue bold, systematic, and rigorous inquiry to improve understanding about how to make money matter more in achieving educational goals.** The committee is convinced that these challenges can be met and that the nation can improve the way it raises and spends money so that finance decisions contribute more directly to making American education fair and effective.

THE COMMITTEE'S CHARGE AND APPROACH

The Committee on Education Finance was established under a congressional mandate to the U.S. Department of Education to contract with the National Academy of Sciences for a study of school finance. In fleshing out the brief mandate assigned from Congress, the department charged the committee to evaluate the theory and practice of financing elementary and secondary education by federal, state, and local governments in the United States. The key question posed to the committee was: *How can education finance systems be designed to ensure that all students achieve high levels of learning and that education funds are raised and used in the most efficient and effective manner possible?* In carrying out its study, the committee was further charged to give particular attention to issues of educational equity, adequacy, and productivity.

The committee translated these key questions into three goals for education finance systems. This translation provided objectives against which to evaluate the performance of existing arrangements and the likely effects of proposed changes:

Goal 1: education finance systems should facilitate a substantially higher level of achievement for all students, while using resources in a cost-efficient manner.

Goal 2: education finance systems should facilitate efforts to break the nexus between student background characteristics and student achievement.

Goal 3: education finance systems should generate revenue in a fair and efficient manner.

Finance policy and practice, especially now that they are being linked to the nation's highest ambitions for schools, touch on virtually all facets of education. Inevitably, therefore, finance is controversial; education policy is one of the most contentious items on the public policy agenda because it is deeply enmeshed in competing public values. Widespread support for equality of educational opportunity masks disagreement over the extent to which high levels of fiscal equality among students or between school districts is required and over the extent to which it is appropriate for parents to spend some of their resources to benefit their own children in preference to others. The division of powers in U.S. government and a traditional emphasis on local control make changes in the dispersion of responsibilities for raising and spending education dollars difficult and slow. Americans' deep belief in the value of efficiency becomes complicated to act on when it encounters limited knowledge about what efficient solutions are in education, disagreements about what the ends of education should be, and belief that the educational system should be democratically governed and responsive to a variety of local, state, and national needs and views. It is thus hard for schools to be both democratic institutions and to have the focused and durable goals that are viewed by some as necessary for an efficient system.

Education policy in general and finance policy more specifically raise difficult questions that require both moral wisdom and empirical research. Experts, such as the members of the Committee on Education Finance, can contribute to policy making by examining evidence and by rationally and objectively clarifying the values and objectives at stake. They cannot resolve all disagreements, but they can render some views more reasonable and others less so.

The committee's inquiry into education finance takes place against the backdrop of a highly decentralized and diverse system of U.S. education that makes description and generalization difficult. The existing finance system is broadly characterized by delegation of significant responsibility for education to the local level, by an average division of funding responsibilities roughly even between state and local governments (with the federal government providing only about 7 percent of education revenues available to schools), and by great variation from place to place in the funds available for education and the level of government that provides them. Education is not mentioned in the federal Constitution and therefore has been viewed as a power reserved to the states, most of whose constitutions specify the provision of education as a key state obligation.

Another backdrop for the committee's deliberations is its assessment of the current condition of education as it relates to the three goals. Regarding goal 1—promoting higher achievement for all students—and goal 2—reducing the nexus between student achievement and family background—the committee concluded that although schools are not failing as badly as some people charge, they are not sufficiently challenging all students to achieve high levels of learning and are poorly serving many of the nation's most disadvantaged children. The continuing correlation between measures of student achievement and student background characteristics, such as ethnic status and household income, looms ever more serious as global economic changes have increasingly tied the economic well-being of individuals to their educational attainment and achievement. Particularly troublesome is the perceived crisis in education in many big-city school systems, a condition that has concerned policy makers since the 1960s but has been too often stubbornly resistant to improvement.

Regarding goal 3—raising revenue fairly and efficiently—the United States is unique in its heavy reliance on revenue raising by local school districts, the extensive use of the local property tax, and the small federal role. Despite significant amounts of state financial assistance to local school districts, spending levels vary greatly among districts within states and also across states, a situation that many people believe is unfair. Moreover, the local property tax is not always administered equitably and may generate a greater burden on taxpayers with low income than on those with high income. Efforts to increase fairness, however, must be balanced by sensitivity to possible effects on the efficiency with which funds are raised.

FAIRNESS AND PRODUCTIVITY IN SCHOOL FINANCE

Fairness in the distribution of education dollars has long been an objective of school finance reformers, but one that has frequently been thwarted by the political realities of an education system that allocates much of the responsibility for funding and operating schools to local governments. Concern about how funding policies and practices affect the performance of schools is a more recent development, but one that is becoming ever more central to school finance decision making.

In the aftermath of *Brown v. Board of Education*, 347 U.S. 483 (1954), the United States awoke from its historical indifference to the problem of unequal educational opportunities and began to address them. Beginning about 1970, the nation entered a notably vigorous period of school finance reform aimed at making the distribution of education dollars more fair. Litigants in a number of states succeeded in having state finance systems overturned in court on the grounds that they violated state constitutional equal protection provisions or education clauses. In the wake of these court decisions, virtually all states, whether under court order or not, substantially changed their finance systems. State and federal governments also created a number of categorical programs directing resources to students with special education needs and to some extent compensating for funding inequities at the local level.

Despite these changes, U.S. education continues to be characterized by large disparities in educational spending. While within-state funding disparities decreased in some states, especially those subject to court-mandated reform, large disparities persist. Moreover, disparities continue to mirror the economic circumstances of district residents; districts with lower-income residents spend less than districts whose residents have higher incomes. In some districts, this pattern is repeated in school-to-school spending differences. Nationwide, over half of the disparity in district per-pupil spending is the result of differences in spending between states rather than within states.

Particularly in the last decade, the concept of fairness as it applies to school finance has taken on a new emphasis, spawning another round of litigation and reform. The pursuit of fairness has moved beyond a focus on the relative distribution of educational inputs to embrace the idea of educational adequacy as the standard to which school finance systems should be held.

Despite the success of adequacy arguments in several prominent school finance court decisions, there is as yet no consensus on its meaning and only limited understanding about what would be required to achieve it. Adequacy is an evolving concept, and major conceptual and technical challenges remain to be overcome if school finance is to be held to an adequacy standard. Earlier concepts of equity posed similar challenges in their infancy, although over time much progress was made in defining and measuring them. Similar progress may be expected here. In the meantime, awareness of the shortcomings in current understanding of adequacy is important for all who would use the concept in either policy making or in research.

In part, efforts to use finance policies to achieve educational adequacy depend centrally on understanding how to translate dollars into student achievement. In fact, however, knowledge about improving productivity in education is weak and contested. The concept itself is elusive and difficult to measure. There is as yet no generally accepted theory to guide finance reforms. Instead multiple theories, each of which is incomplete, compete for attention. Empirical studies seeking to determine the best ways to direct resources to improve school performance have produced inconsistent findings.

Equality of Educational Opportunity, the famous study of the mid-1960s known as the Coleman Report, found that, after family background factors were statistically controlled, school resource variation did not explain differences in student achievement. The Coleman report ushered in decades of productivity research attempting to understand (and perhaps discredit) that counterintuitive result. For many years, the inability of researchers to speak consistently on how to improve schools has frustrated scientists and policy makers alike. While there is still a great deal of uncertainty about how to make schools better or how to deploy resources effectively, the committee's review of the last several decades of research and policy development on educational productivity makes us more optimistic than our predecessors regarding the prospects for making informed school finance choices. Thirty years' worth of insights have generated a host of ideas about how to use school finance to improve school performance, and researchers have learned to ask better questions and to use improved research designs that yield more trustworthy findings. Knowledge is growing and will continue to grow. One major implication of this fact for school finance is that good policy will reflect both the best knowledge available to date *and* the need to continue experimenting and evolving as new knowledge emerges.

Even while understanding is becoming more sophisticated, knowledge about how to improve educational productivity will always be contingent and tentative, in part because the characteristics and needs of key actors—the students—differ greatly from place to place. Therefore, solutions to the challenge of improving school performance are unlikely ever to apply to all schools and students in all times and places. Policy makers and the public will have to consider evidence and analysis about the strengths and weaknesses of strategies for change as they also weigh differing values about what Americans want their schools to be and to do.

STRATEGIES FOR MEETING THE GOALS

Four generic strategies can be used to make money matter more for U.S. schools and to propel the education system in desirable directions:

- Reduce funding inequities and inadequacies;
- Invest more resources (either new or reallocated from other uses) in developing capacity;

- Alter incentives to make performance count (within the existing governance structure); and
- Empower schools and parents to make decisions about the use of public funds (thereby altering governance and management relationships).

Reducing funding inequities and inadequacies includes options such as reducing disparities in funding across schools, districts, or states; ensuring that all schools or districts have funding sufficient to provide an adequate level of education to the students they serve; and raising revenue more fairly without neglecting efficiency. Investing more resources in developing capacity refers not only to the capacity of the formal education system to provide services but also to the capacity of students to learn. Hence, it includes investments in inputs, such as teacher quality and technology, and in programs, such as preschool for disadvantaged students. Altering incentives embraces changes in incentives designed to operate primarily within the existing system of school governance and includes policies such as restructuring teacher salaries, use of school-based incentive programs, and changes to the incentives built into financing formulas for students with special needs. Empowering schools and parents refers to policies that would decentralize significant authority over the use of public funds, to schools in the form of site-based management or charter schools, and to parents in the form of significant additional parental choice over which schools (public and perhaps private as well) their children will attend.

In reality, policy makers do not and should not consider strategies in isolation. Finance policies ought to reflect the interrelatedness of the various facets of the finance system and the possibility that complementary changes may be required for reform to be successful. Indeed, some visions of overall education reform explicitly call for a set of intertwined finance strategies.

Our decision to examine the strategies separately is useful for analytical purposes, but it also reflects the important fact that strategies can be combined in different ways. It is important to emphasize, however, that not all strategies are compatible. For example, a centrally (i.e., state or school district) managed program of investment in capacity would not fit naturally with a program that empowers parents and schools to make decisions about the kind of capacity in which they wish to invest.

For each of the three goals for an education finance system, we evaluate a variety of policy options employing these strategies and weigh the evidence on how effective they are likely to be in helping meet the objectives.

Achieving Goal 1:
Promoting Higher Achievement for All Students in a Cost-Efficient Way

- Adequate funding (sufficient funding for efficiently operating schools to generate higher achievement levels) is clearly essential for meeting goal 1. Although we do not know how to identify this level with precision, it is important to try. But providing adequate funding by itself may do little to foster significant improvements in overall student achievement. Thus, while funding adequacy may be a necessary part of any education reform effort—and is likely to be especially crucial for districts or schools serving disproportionate numbers of disadvantaged students—it is at most part of an overall program for increasing student achievement in a cost-efficient way.

- Teaching all students to higher standards makes unprecedented demands on teachers and requires changes in traditional approaches to teacher training and retraining. In addition to nonfinance policies for investing in the capacity of teachers (e.g., reforming teacher preparation and licensing), finance options might include raising teacher salaries and investing in the professional development of teachers once they are on the job. Given schools' need to hire 2 million new teachers over the coming decade, raising salaries—especially for new hires— may be needed to ensure sufficient numbers of qualified people in classrooms. Professional development that is aligned with curriculum reform and teaching objectives offers the promise of changing teaching practice in ways likely to improve student performance. But neither approach is likely to be effective in achieving goal 1 unless it is aligned with appropriate incentives throughout the education system to make performance count.

- Altering incentives responds to the fact that the school finance system historically has operated almost in isolation from educational performance, in that educational goals and desired outcomes have seldom been reflected in pay for teachers and budgets for schools. Traditional teacher salary schedules provide higher pay for experience and postgraduate degrees, neither of which appears to be systematically linked with student achievement. Skill and knowledge-based pay shows greater promise for making teachers more effective in the classroom but remains to be tested. School-based accountability and incentive systems are increasingly popular and seem to contribute to desired student outcomes. To be fully effective, however, they require adequate funding for schools and attention to capacity building.

- Empowering schools or parents to make decisions about public funds (via enhanced site-based management, charter schools or contract schools, or vouchers, for example) has been justified as a strategy for improving student achievement in a cost-efficient way based on a variety of different arguments: some contend that local control will enhance innovation at the school level; some believe that schools with a strong sense of community perform better; and some believe that the introduction of competition and the possibility of losing students (and their associated funding) will encourage schools to be more productive than under the current monopoly situation. Although positive effects for children using vouchers have been reported from several sites where vouchers have been tried, the small scale of current programs leaves many important questions unanswered.

Achieving Goal 2:
Reducing the Nexus Between Student Achievement and
Family Background Characteristics

• As money is made to matter more in education, funding disparities will become increasingly worrisome, because their effects on achievement will be magnified to the detriment of children in underfunded schools, many of whom are likely to be from disadvantaged backgrounds. The new focus on funding adequacy has the potential to help disadvantaged students, but it will do so only to the extent that school funding formulas are appropriately adjusted for the additional costs of educating youngsters from disadvantaged backgrounds.

• Achieving goal 2 will also require attention to increasing both the capacity of children to learn and of schools to teach. Children raised in economically and socially impoverished environments or suffering from physical disabilities often come to school less ready to learn than their more advantaged counterparts. Schools must deal with these problems, even though they alone will not be able to solve them. A strong consensus has emerged among policy makers, practitioners, and researchers about the importance of increasing investments in the capacity of at-risk children to learn, by focusing on the school-readiness of very young children and by linking education to other social services, so that the broad range of educational, social, and physical needs that affect learning are addressed. Programs providing early childhood interventions and school-community linkages give evidence of both promise and problems, suggesting that there is still much to learn about making these investments effectively.

• That more investment is needed in the capacity of schools to educate concentrations of disadvantaged students would seem to be obvious given the dismal academic performance of many of these students, but as yet we have only incomplete answers to the question of which types of investments are likely to be the most productive and how to structure them to make them effective. The quality of teachers is likely to be a key component; reducing class size might help under certain conditions; whole-school restructuring may have significant potential; and the dilapidated state of school buildings in many older urban areas suggests that reform of facilities financing must also be attended to. Again, the effectiveness of any individual policy change may depend on how it is linked to an interconnected set of strategies for improving school performance, and some critics question whether these most troubled of U.S. schools can be reformed through strategic investments and related strategies, or whether they require much more fundamental structural change, such as might be brought about by a voucher program.

• Most federal and some state aid flows to schools via categorical programs tied to the special needs of certain groups of disadvantaged students. Title I compensatory education grants and special education funding are the chief examples. Questions have been raised about the extent to which the incentives deliberately or inadvertently created by categorical programs serve educationally desirable purposes and whether and to what extent it continues to be appropriate to treat children with special needs separately in an educational system increasingly oriented toward fostering higher levels of learning for all students. Our findings suggest that previously defined sharp distinctions between students with special educational needs and other students have compromised educational effectiveness and that current efforts to move toward more integrated school programs should be facilitated by the finance system.

• Arguments for dramatic changes in school governance (by empowering schools or parents to make decisions about public funds) may be more compelling in urban areas with large numbers of disadvantaged students than in the educational system in general for a number of reasons. The size of many urban districts and the continuing fact of racial and economic segregation offer many urban residents much less choice over where and how to educate their children than suburban residents have. Moreover, urban residents have arguably benefited least from prior school reforms. Some economic models suggest that, among choice options, charter schools and vouchers, rather than interdistrict and intradistrict choice programs, are the approaches most worthy of further exploration as vehicles for improving poor-performing schools. At present, however, little is known about the effects of either. Extensive evaluation is needed of the many charter efforts currently under way. Vouchers, both publicly and privately funded, are being tried in a number of cities, but the existing small-scale efforts are unlikely to provide adequate information to assuage the concerns of those who question the need for so dramatic a break with traditional school finance policies.

Achieving Goal 3:
Raising Revenue Fairly and Efficiently

• Shifting away from local revenue raising to greater reliance on state revenues and/or increasing significantly the federal role in revenue provision for elementary and secondary education would foster the goal of raising revenues fairly. Both, however, have to be considered in light of trade-offs and complementarities with the other two goals of a good financing system and with attention to maintaining some local control over managerial decisions.

• A larger federal role in providing education revenues could be justified either on the grounds that is fair and appropriate for the federal government to take responsibility for disproportionate needs of students who are poor, who have disabilities, or are otherwise educationally disadvantaged, or on the grounds of ensuring that all states can provide adequate education funding. Fully funding federal compensatory education programs would be consistent with past federal policy and is likely to be the more politically viable of the two approaches. The

alternative of a new federal foundation aid program based on an adequacy justification would entail a significant change in federal policy and would raise many
of the same analytical, conceptual, and political issues that arise in the formula-
tion of adequacy programs at the state level.

Finally, the report draws attention to the nation's need for better and more
focused education research to help strengthen schools and bring about substantial
improvements in student learning. Acknowledging the especially challenging
conditions facing many big-city educators, the committee proposes three new
substantial research initiatives in urban areas (without specifying the priority
among them): (1) an experiment on capacity-building that would tackle the
challenges of developing and retaining well-prepared teachers; (2) systematic
experimentation with incentives designed to motivate higher performance by
teachers and schools; and (3) a large and ambitious school voucher experiment,
including the participation of private schools. Meeting the nation's education
goals will depend in part on continuously and systematically seeking better knowledge about how to improve educational outcomes, through new research initiatives such as these along with more extensive evaluation of the many reform
efforts already under way.

Part I

Introduction

1

Introduction

In 1994 the United States Congress adopted legislation declaring that "all students can learn and achieve to high standards and must realize their potential if the United States is to prosper" (Goals 2000: Educate America Act, P.L. 103-227, Section 301(1)). Enactment of this legislation marked the culmination of an extraordinary set of events that began with the first-ever education summit between the president and the governors of the nation's states and territories in 1989. For the first time, federal and state leaders joined together to establish common goals for the improvement of American elementary and secondary schools.

Ensuring that all students learn and achieve to high standards has posed fundamental challenges to almost every aspect of business as usual in American education. From curriculum reform and the development of national and state standards for learning to the management structures of individual schools and school districts, traditional ways of organizing and delivering education are being questioned and changed. Policy makers and educators are urgently searching for better ways to provide today's schoolchildren with the knowledge and skills they will need to function effectively as citizens and workers in a future that promises to be increasingly complex and globally interconnected.

A key component of this quest centers on money. The nation spends roughly $300 billion annually on public elementary and secondary education, the second-largest target of governmental expenditures after national defense. If schools are to meet the nation's high expectations of them, it is imperative that this huge financial resource be invested well.

How best to raise and spend money for education is a difficult and contentious question, one that bedevils policy makers at all governmental levels. Although the federal government is a junior partner to states and local jurisdictions in financing education, Congress, too, becomes caught up in the complex issues involved each time it considers funding decisions related to new and continuing federal programs. In late 1994, after passing Goals 2000 and then undertaking an especially fractious debate in the course of authorizing the Improving America's Schools Act, Congress included in the appropriations bill for the U.S. Departments of Education, Labor, and Health and Human Services provision for a study to be conducted by the National Academy of Sciences on education finance.

CHARGE TO THE COMMITTEE

In response to this request from Congress, the National Research Council (the operating arm of the National Academy of Sciences and the National Academy of Engineering) established the Committee on Education Finance to carry out a study under the auspices of the U.S. Department of Education. In fleshing out the brief mandate assigned from Congress, the department charged the committee to evaluate the theory and practice of financing elementary and secondary education by federal, state, and local governments in the United States.

The key question posed to the committee was: How can education finance systems be designed to ensure that all students achieve high levels of learning and that education funds are raised and used in the most efficient and effective manner possible? In answering this question, the committee was further charged to:

- give particular attention to issues of equity, adequacy, and productivity;
- be sensitive to the legal and constitutional context and constraints surrounding school finance;
- examine the relationship between incentive structures and education resources;
- clarify, to the extent it could, the relationships between expenditures and performance;
- identify data needed to give policy makers a better understanding of resource allocations, expenditures, and outcomes; and
- consider developing funding models that would display policy options for consideration by elected officials, educators, judges, and other interested parties.

The committee translated this key question into three goals for education finance systems, a translation that provides objectives against which to evaluate the performance of existing arrangements and the likely effects of proposed changes:

Goal 1: education finance systems should facilitate a substantially higher level of achievement for all students, while using resources in a cost-efficient manner.

Goal 2: education finance systems should facilitate efforts to break the nexus between student background characteristics and student achievement.

Goal 3: education finance systems should generate revenues in a fair and efficient manner.

The first two of these goals speak to different aspects of ensuring that all students achieve high levels of learning. The best way to explain these two aspects is with reference to the current distribution of students along some spectrum of achievement. Goal 1 says that as a nation we are dissatisfied with the existing level of achievement and that we want all students to do better. In other words, we want the entire distribution to shift upward. At the same time, goal 1 acknowledges that raising student achievement is not just (or even necessarily) a matter of increasing the amount of resources devoted to education but also of ensuring that resources are used well and not wasted. Goal 2 says that the nation also is dissatisfied with the differences, or variance, in the distribution of student achievement, especially because the differences are linked to background characteristics like race and wealth that American society does not regard as legitimate explanations for achievement gaps.

Goal 3 embraces the belief that in raising revenues for schools, as well as in spending, school finance systems should operate fairly and efficiently.

SHIFTING EXPECTATIONS OF SCHOOL FINANCE

Goal 1 marks a crucial change in expectations about education finance policies. In the past, finance focused mainly on how and at which levels of government money to support public schools should be raised. Most finance debates in the 20th century have revolved around the extent to which state and later federal aid should be used to overcome the fiscal disparities that have resulted from the 19th century's dependence on local funding of education.

School finance in the 21st century faces a more important but more daunting challenge: how to harness the financing system to promote greater student achievement. This challenge is more important because it aims to link finance directly to the purposes of education. It is more daunting because in linking finance with education's purposes it becomes intertwined with an unprecedented ambition: never before has the nation set for itself the goal of educating all children to high standards.

Despite the "intense faith in education—almost a secular religion" that Americans have had and their belief that reforming the public schools would improve not just education but society (Tyack and Cuban, 1995:1), it is only in the last quarter of the 20th century that we have truly set our sights on giving all children—including the poor, all racial and ethnic groups, immigrants, those with disabilities, and those who family and neighborhood circumstances pose serious barriers to learning—the opportunity to reach high standards of learning. On some dimensions, the accomplishments of the public education in the 20th century are impressive. At the same time, the achievement of American students appears mediocre by international standards and has not improved despite significant increases in educational spending. The nation's past willingness to tolerate low levels of achievement for many students is no longer acceptable, given the demands that a complex democratic society makes on the knowledge, skills, understanding, and tolerance of its citizens. Moreover, low achievement (whether perceived or real) leaves schools open to attacks that threaten public confidence in and support for public education.

The recent and amazingly vigorous and sustained period of educational reform, which has held the attention of policy makers, educators, and the public for almost two decades, attests to the depth of the desire to improve education for all students. The successes, failures, and uncertain results of reform efforts, however, make it clear that educational change is slow (Elmore and McLaughlin, 1988; Tyack and Cuban, 1995) and its ultimate shape and outcome are still very unclear. Figuring out how to improve learning for all students is an evolving story. A key question about education finance is how to design it to evolve alongside and in support of the work in progress of broader school reform.

Finance policies not only should address this new challenge but also should face up to past challenges that have gone unmet. The most compelling of these is embraced in goal 2. Almost a century after the first school finance reforms using state aid to reduce fiscal disparities among local school districts, almost 50 years after *Brown v. Board of Education*, 347 U.S. 483 (1954), made segregated schools illegal, 35 years after the nation launched a "war on poverty" that made equalizing educational opportunities one of its main targets, 30 years after the first successful court cases overturning state education financing policies that made the educational resources available to children dependent on where they happened to live: after all this time and effort, the United States still has an education finance system supporting schools that in many places are separate and unequal. Racial segregation between blacks and whites in metropolitan areas remains very high, especially in older cities of the North and North Central regions (Jargowsky, 1997; Massey, 1998), thus consigning many black children to inner-city urban schools that face enormous bureaucratic and political obstacles in addressing the needs of their students.

Basic fairness compels attention to continuing inequities in American education. So does the fact that changes in the relationship between education and work mean that it is no longer possible for the poorly educated to earn a living wage (Jencks and Phillips, 1998; Murnane et al., 1995; Blank, 1997). Finally, social peace may be at stake, given the nation's rapidly shifting racial and ethnic demographics. The Bureau of the Census estimates that if recent demographic trends continue, Asians, non-Hispanic blacks, Hispanics, and American Indians together will approach 50 percent of the population by the year 2050 (Council of Economic Advisers, 1998). These changes are likely to place even more than the usual strain on the challenge of "maintaining a humane, harmonious pluralistic society" (Miller, 1995:xiii), making it increasingly important that justice seems to be done and that we as a society take seriously failures to remedy the race-based inequities of the past.

Schools face limits in breaking the nexus between student background characteristics and student achievement. Achievement is influenced not only by the resources provided by the school but also by the resources devoted by the family. Family resources vary widely from child to child, even more than school resources do. Miller (1995), following James Coleman and others, has borrowed the concept of capital from economics to describe the different forms of education-relevant resources possessed by families, schools, and other societal institutions that can be invested in children. Human capital is largely acquired via formal schooling. Social, health, financial, and polity capital are largely the product of broader institutional arrangements and societal conditions. These institutional arrangements and societal conditions constitute an educational opportunity structure; they "heavily influence the ability of groups to acquire and use education-relevant resources to improve their educational performance, both absolutely and relative to other groups over time" (Miller, 1995:96).

Disparities (which are correlated with racial/ethnic and socioeconomic status) in the access of children and their families to various kinds of education-relevant resources and capital mean that goal 2 cannot reasonably be achieved by schools alone. Too often in the past, "millennial thinking about schooling has . . . been a favored solution to social and economic problems. . . . [T]he utopian tradition of social reform through schooling has often diverted attention from more costly, politically controversial, and difficult societal reforms" (Tyack and Cuban, 1995:2-3). The fact that this committee, in following its charge, focuses its attention on schools does not diminish our view that it is imperative that society acknowledge the limited role of schools in addressing these larger social and economic problems.

At the same time, we wish to avoid the danger of using these larger problems as an excuse for schools to tolerate large differences in the academic achievement of children that are related to characteristics such as race or income. Kenneth Clark warned of this kind of danger over a quarter of a century ago, when he argued that a book like *Inequality* (Jencks et al., 1972) did a disservice to children from minority and poverty backgrounds because, in stressing the impotence of schools in the face of societal problems, it enabled school officials to shift their responsibility to the society at large (Clark, 1973).

We argue in this report that schools can make a difference and, to give ourselves a manageable task, we accept that the main focus of our investigation into goal 2 must be on the school's role in breaking the nexus between students' background characteristics and their academic achievement.

Goal 3 complements the first two goals of a good education finance system by focusing attention on how revenues are generated. For historical reasons, the United States has relied much more heavily on state and local revenue sources than have most other countries. While such a decentralized financing system clearly promotes certain values that Americans hold dear, such as the value of local control, the continuing reliance in many states on locally generated revenue may be unfair in a world in which some households are increasingly able to move with ease from one area to another. That middle- and upper-income households can move out of high-taxation areas makes it possible for them to avoid sharing the burden of financing the local share of education for those left behind. In particular, as households and firms have moved out of central cities in search of lower land prices in the suburbs or more favorable business conditions in other states or countries, they have often left behind them smaller tax bases and concentrations of economically disadvantaged and difficult-to-educate students. The result is widening disparities among the capacities of school districts to generate local funds to meet the educational needs of their students at the same time that graduating students are increasingly having to compete for jobs in a national and global marketplace. While assistance from the federal and state governments helps to offset these disparities, large differences remain, both within and across states.

Moreover, the property tax has been a mainstay of education finance and historically has been a productive generator of revenue, but many people believe it imposes unfair burdens. The burdens may be unfair because the tax is poorly administered or because a local property tax may end up putting a disproportionately greater burden on low-income taxpayers than on higher-income taxpayers. Ensuring that revenues are raised in a fair way is important not only for its own sake but also to ensure support for education. However, any changes designed to increase fairness must also be sensitive to their impacts on the efficiency with which funds are raised and in how education is delivered.

The importance of rethinking how educators can raise and spend money efficiently and fairly as they strive to meet goals 1 and 2 is underscored by the drumbeat of criticism that has been directed at American education in recent years, with its threat of diminished support for public schools. In part the criticism has been motivated by concerns over the performance of the system, in both an overall sense and in terms of how well it meets the needs of particular groups of students. In part it reflects dislike of the main tax (the local property tax) that pays for education.

Attacks on public schools (which, it should be noted, have never been absent) seemed to grow steadily louder beginning in the late 1960s—perhaps not coincidentally the same time when the Vietnam War and then Watergate and the economic shocks initiated by the Arab oil embargo punctured the post-World

War II bubble of American self-confidence and prosperity. Surely the tendency to see schools as the pathway to societal improvement helps explain why the loss of faith in larger institutions inevitably embraced education as well.

But other forces are also at work. For a time, academic achievement as measured by widely publicized test scores did indeed decline. Moreover, international comparisons indicated that American students performed less well on tests than students in many other countries. While concerns over academic achievement (as well as worries about the educational environment, such as drugs and discipline) were reflected in polls showing declining confidence in public education, there also began to be evidence of a "culture of resistance" to existing public schools by groups who saw themselves as oppressed by the dominant society and who opposed subjecting their children to the standards of that society. Ogbu (1978, 1982) documented this phenomenon for certain black subcommunities; Cremin (1989) observed it also among working-class families in some communities and ethno-religious minority families in others. It also became clearer, especially for low-income black Americans, that the existing system of school finance and governance effectively denied them the same degree of choice over their children's education that more economically advantaged and nonblack groups were able to exercise primarily through residential mobility and, to a lesser extent, through the option of paying for private education.

These forces help explain the attention being given to a variety of changes in the way American schools have traditionally operated: standards-based reforms attempting to align the entire educational system around common objectives, school-level policies emphasizing greater flexibility in the way services are offered, and efforts to give parents the ability to exercise more choice over the kinds of schools their children attend.

That such reforms elicit passionate debate and reveal deep divisions can be explained in part because they are taking place at a time in American history when key understandings about how a democratic society can best improve the education and social welfare of its citizens are more than usually in dispute. The downfall of communism, the inefficiencies that have been exposed in European postwar welfare states, and the uneven successes of American social policies in addressing the needs of the disadvantaged have fostered a worldwide debate on the relative role of governments and private markets in meeting society's needs and fostering economic prosperity (Yergin and Stanislaw, 1998). In the United States, policy makers at all levels are examining previously unexamined assumptions about how to deliver publicly financed services and are moving away from an exclusive focus on uniform public provision to public financing with various forms of provision, including private-sector provision. In education, this can be seen across the country as states and districts are experimenting with charter schools, the contracting of educational services, and more parental choice for public and in some cases private schools. The desirability of breaking the virtual monopoly that public schools have had on the provision of publicly funded education for the past century and a half will not be decided on the merits of the education issues alone, nor indeed on the basis of social science evidence, but also in the context of the broader societal debate over the proper balance to be struck in a democratic society between public and private interests and mechanisms.

These changes in the social and economic climate in which schools are embedded reinforce both the importance and the complexity of aligning school finance policies with the goals the committee is charged to address. They also explain why, in interpreting these goals, we adopt a broad definition of education finance systems, including within them governance as well as money-raising and resource allocation policies. This definition reflects our view that understanding and evaluating finance arrangements depends on considering them simultaneously with the governance or authority systems within which they are embedded, which in turn reflect political and historical influences that determine how decisions about education in the United States are made and carried out. Understanding these interconnections is crucial to assessing the possibilities for and likely effects of change.

EDUCATION, VALUES, AND THE ROLE OF EXPERTISE

Education policy making is as much concerned with central public values as it is with schools per se, and central values that Americans hold dear may conflict. Widespread support for equality of educational opportunity masks disagreement over the extent to which high levels of fiscal equality among students or between school districts are required and over the extent to which it is appropriate for parents to spend some of their resources to benefit their own children in preference to others. American political traditions complicate consideration of such issues because of their emphasis on the separation of powers and local government. Any changes in the dispersion of responsibilities for raising and spending education dollars across different levels of government and different jurisdictions, which may be called for to reduce funding disparities, inevitably must disturb the balance between these levels and jurisdictions and the balance between the values each serves. Changing these balances will be difficult and contentious.

Americans are also great believers in efficiency, both in the overall sense used by economists that resources should be allocated in line with consumer preferences, and in the sense that education should be provided in a cost-efficient way.[1] Efficiency in the first sense provides a strong justification for financing decisions to be made by local school districts so that local communities can make

---

[1]Economists refer to these two concepts as allocative efficiency and productive efficiency, respectively.

their own decisions about how much to spend on education. Efficiency in the second sense requires a shared view about the ends of education—which does not always exist. Furthermore, the value placed on efficiency may need to be accommodated to the value placed on legitimate governance, since schools, as public agencies and not private corporations, are expected to be democratically governed and to respond to a variety of needs and views as well as to ongoing public debate. It is thus hard for schools to be both democratic institutions and to have goals that are focused and durable.

These cross-pressures explain why decisions about the finance of schools will seldom be clear-cut, but rather must be made against a background of moral and factual ambiguity that frequently engenders passionate debate. Education policy, especially when it concerns matters of complexity such as school finance, raises difficult questions that require both moral wisdom and empirical research. Such questions can benefit from the illumination offered by social scientists examining relevant evidence, but in a democratic society professionals are not policy makers. Rational deliberation and empirical research cannot resolve all disagreements, but they can render some views more reasonable and others less. They can contribute to the resolution of moral as well as empirical disagreements, by clarifying the values and objectives at stake.

In a democratic society, public deliberation is essential to the resolution of policy disagreements. Public deliberation is also an educational tool: it is a means by which the rule of the many can also be the rule of the wise. Scientists thus need to conceive of their role not only as one of discovery, but also as a matter of education and of informing a process of public deliberation. Finally, public deliberation is especially important when policy debates are rooted in central public values.

In approaching the task of informing a process of public deliberation, the committee undertook as the major objective to review the state of knowledge about how to achieve the goals for education finance systems as specified in our charge. Recognizing that science is only one among a number of sources of authority or knowledge about how a system should go about reaching its goals,[2] we acknowledge that in the first instance "social science research can best be

---

[2]Among the diverse sources of authority in education are (1) moral philosophy, ethics, and religions; (2) history, tradition, and precedent; (3) constitutional, statutory, and case law; (4) common sense and professional lore, which are constituted of uncodified and codified ideas about education; (5) the exercise of discretion (individual and group), which may reveal not only the aims of education but also a theory of how to achieve them; and (6) science. As Wise (1976) has pointed out, the problem with most of these sources of authority is that their implicit or explicit hypotheses about how to achieve the aims of education may not be correct. Only science seeks to confirm hypotheses systematically (including those generated by other sources of authority); in doing so it also seeks to make the assumptions and empirical evidence used in drawing conclusions transparent. Its value to policy makers is that it is potentially a way to reduce the uncertainties in decision making.

used to frame the issues and their consequences rather than to obtain conclusive evidence on what is right and what is to be done" (Levin, 1976:140). Concomitantly, we have the responsibility, as Levin pointed out, to consider where, along with social science research, aspects of the world that cannot be quantified or analyzed in a social science setting should also be considered. Ultimately, given our charge, we also have the responsibility to advise policy makers—on the basis of both our review of the evidence and our judgment—if and when a strong case can be made for changes in the educational finance system to make it more effective, efficient, and fair.

While it is appropriate for a committee such as ours to evaluate school finance in light of the knowledge that can be gained from formal research and the testing of scientific hypotheses, it is important to make explicit our opposition to substituting scientific authority for other forms of authority when circumstances do not justify that response.

The danger that a school finance report grounded in scientific authority will be misunderstood or misused is perhaps greater at a time, such as the present, when there is a strong desire to harness finance to the task of improving school performance but uncertain knowledge about how best to accomplish this. Some (e.g., Wise, 1976) argue that a sobering example of what can happen can be seen in the history of school finance in the aftermath of the 1966 report, *Equality of Educational Opportunity* (Coleman et al., 1966). This famous 1960s presentation of social science research found little connection between school resources and the educational achievement of students and a much stronger relationship between student achievement and family circumstances. As it and subsequent research along the same lines came to be used in the policy and legal arenas, the absence of a relationship between resources and achievement frequently became an argument against putting more resources into schools or reducing the wide disparities in spending on students across and within states and school districts. As Wise (1976:xiv) described it, school finance disputes were "transformed by the use of social science into an educational reform effort. As the school-effectiveness question is raised, it has appeared that school finance reform cannot proceed unless educational reform is guaranteed." Rather than use the results of research as an excuse for inaction, the appropriate response to the absence of clear guidance from science may well consist of invoking other sources of legitimate authority as touchstones for evaluating finance reform proposals—for example, an appeal to ideas about what constitutes basic fairness in a just society.

By focusing attention on scientific authority as a guide to education finance reform, we do not intend to prejudge the extent to which the use of this authority is warranted. Indeed, another objective of this report is to inform policy makers and others about how the present state of research can and cannot serve as a useful source of knowledge for action.

OVERVIEW OF THE REPORT

This report has three parts. Following this introductory chapter, Part I includes a chapter setting the stage for the committee's evaluation of school finance reform by clarifying and elaborating the goals being sought and the nature of the finance system as it exists today. Part II examines efforts to improve the fairness of school finance systems over the last 30 years and explores how the concept of fairness is increasingly and inextricably tied to questions about how to improve school performance. Part III evaluates various ways that the education finance system might be reformed to foster the three goals identified.

Needed improvements in data related to education finance are briefly discussed in an appendix.

2

Setting the Stage

This chapter describes basic features of the existing education governance and finance system, since current arrangements mark the starting point for change. In it we also examine the meaning of and the assumptions behind the three goals for education finance systems implied by the committee's charge, in order to clarify the concerns we are attempting to address. Finally, we identify a set of generic strategies through which finance systems can be aligned with the goals. These strategies provide the organizing framework for our evaluation of specific policy options later in the report.

ROLES AND RESPONSIBILITIES
IN AMERICAN EDUCATION

Education governance, and with it patterns of resource allocation, varies significantly across the United States. Because education is not mentioned in the Constitution, it has historically been viewed as a responsibility reserved to the states. While state constitutions almost all specifically call on the states to provide a public education system, most states have delegated much of the responsibility for financing and providing schools to local governments. States have come to play a larger role in recent years, although the extent of state responsibility varies significantly from place to place.

Elementary and Secondary Education in the United States

In school year 1996-97, 45,592,213[1] students attended 88,223 public elementary and secondary schools in 14,883 school districts (these and the following statistics in this section, unless otherwise noted, come from U.S. Department of Education, 1999a: *Digest of Education Statistics, 1998*). Another 5,783,000 students were enrolled in an estimated 27,600 private elementary and secondary schools. In 1997-98, total expenditures of public elementary and secondary educational institutions were $324.3 billion or 4 percent of the nation's gross domestic product (GDP). Total expenditures of elementary and secondary educational institutions (public and private) were $351.3 billion in 1997-98 or 4.3 percent of GDP.

Elementary and secondary education is a major item in state and local budgets, but a minor one in the federal budget. Together state and local governments raise over 90 percent of the revenue for elementary and secondary schools. Although variation among states is considerable, in 1997 states on average spent 22 percent of their budgets on K-12 education. This exceeds the 20 percent share for Medicaid and the 11 percent share for higher education, the other leading categories of state spending (National Association of State Budget Officers, 1998: Table 3). Local governments on average directed 36 percent of their total expenditures to education in 1995 (Bureau of the Census, 1998: Table 519).

In 1995-96, the federal government provided $19 billion in revenues for public elementary and secondary schools, or 6.6 percent of total revenues the schools received. This amount, which accounts for only 1 percent of federal outlays for all purposes, is delivered mainly through Department of Education programs. The largest of these by far is the Title I compensatory education program, which provides grants to districts and state education agencies for educating disadvantaged students; this program was funded at $8.0 billion in fiscal year 1998. Education for students with disabilities ($3.8 billion in FY 1998) and for vocational and adult education ($1.3 billion) are the other large Department of Education programs. Not necessarily counted among revenues for public schools, but still representing sizeable federal investments in elementary and secondary education, are other large programs such as the child nutrition programs of the Department of Agriculture ($8.8 billion in FY 1998), the Head Start programs of the Department of Health and Human Services ($4.4 billion in FY 1998), and the education component of training programs sponsored by the Department of Labor ($3.8 billion in FY 1998) (*1998 Digest of Education Statistics* and U.S. Department of Education budget web site: http://www.ed.gov/offices/OUS/budget.html).

---

[1] A tiny but growing number of these students are enrolled in prekindergarten programs; the number of pre-K students in public schools rose from approximately 106,000 in fall 1982 to about 674,000 in fall 1996 (U.S. Department of Education, 1999a: Table 43).

Diversity: Legacy of Local Control

A unique feature of U.S. education is the degree of control that has been granted to local governments. Governance arrangements (both formal and informal) matter because they determine who is in a position to decide what interests and objectives will receive priority and to influence the allocation of resources in accordance with those priorities. Given their power to raise revenue for schools, district school boards have historically played a crucial role within the governance structure. While too much local control of education may be detrimental to the educational interests of some students, it is also true that local control generates at least one key benefit worth preserving: it keeps the country from making wholesale major errors. While particular districts or states may make errors, these errors are typically remediable in a short time frame because they occur on a small scale.

Education governance has not been static; the system has been flexible and has changed incrementally over time to adjust to changing conditions. School districts have been consolidated, declining in number from 127,531 in 1932 to 16,960 in 1973 (Tyack and Cuban, 1995:19) and slightly under 15,000 today. States increased their role in financing, from 16.5 percent of revenues in 1919-20 to 47.5 percent in 1995-96 (Table 2-1). However, during the final 25 years of that period, the state share remained relatively constant despite large increases in some western states such as California (from 35 to 56 percent), Idaho (from 38 to 64 percent) and Montana (from 24 to 49 percent) (U.S. Department of Health, Education, and Welfare, 1972; U.S. Department of Education, 1999a). Through legislative action in 1993, Michigan reversed the roles of the state and local governments almost overnight. Before the reform, about two-thirds of the rev-

TABLE 2-1 Revenues for Public Elementary and Secondary Schools, by Source of Funds (percentage of total), Selected Years, 1919-1996

Date	Federal	State	Local
1919-20	0.3	16.5	83.2
1929-30	0.4	16.9	82.7
1939-40	1.8	30.3	68.0
1949-50	2.9	39.8	57.3
1959-60	4.4	39.1	56.5
1969-70	8.0	39.9	52.1
1979-80	9.8	46.8	43.4
1989-90	6.1	47.1	46.8
1995-96	6.6	47.5	45.9

SOURCE: U.S. Department of Education, 1999a: Table 157.

enue was generated by the local property tax. After the reform, the state took responsibility for about two-thirds of the revenue in the form of a statewide property tax and increased reliance on the state sales tax. In addition to taking on more responsibility for financing, states have also increased their role in setting educational policy (witness current efforts at establishing state learning standards).

The federal government has become a noticeable though still junior financing partner, providing 6.6 percent of revenues in 1995-96, up from virtually nothing in the early 20th century and peaking at 9.8 percent in 1979-80 (Table 2-1). It is a significant influence in the areas of its particular concerns (such as compensatory education for special populations and national standards) through the mandates and rules accompanying these funds.

In addition to government, parents are gaining more influence as they push for charter schools and various forms of school choice, and private contractors have been hired to perform many of the functions of schools. The changes have been incremental, but not inconsequential.

Nevertheless, the legacy of local government control of U.S. schools is an educational system characterized by enormous diversity across states and districts in sources of revenue and in spending levels (Table 2-2). School districts obtain revenues for education primarily through local property taxes[2] and intergovernmental aid. Districts that have large property tax bases tend to rely more on local sources. Districts with low property wealth typically rely more heavily on aid from the state (Howell and Miller, 1997:40).

In 1995-96, the local government shares of education revenues ranged from 0.4 percent in Hawaii (a one-district state) and 12 percent in New Mexico to 87 percent in New Hampshire (Table 2-2). The mirror image of these patterns are the state shares, which ranged from 90 percent in Hawaii to 7 percent in New Hampshire.

In addition to balancing responsibilities differently among state and local governments, states also differ widely in the amount they spend from all sources on a per-pupil basis. Table 2-2 indicates that average current expenditure per pupil in 1995-96 ranged from $3,867 in Utah to $9,955 in New Jersey.[3] Within states, large disparities exist in spending from district to district and even from school to school within districts. In Vermont, for example, a state that has recently revamped its school finance system to reduce disparities, 1995 per-pupil spending in Stowe was $8,585, whereas Bennington spent just $4,526 (National

---

[2]Only in three states—Kentucky, Louisiana, and Pennsylvania—does the local property tax account for less than 90 percent of local taxes for school districts.

[3]Current expenditures include salaries, transportation, schoolbooks, materials, and energy costs but not capital outlays or interest on school debt. The average state expenditure levels reported here have not been adjusted to reflect geographic cost-of-living differences or differences in student need.

TABLE 2-2 Percentage of School Revenues from Local, State, and Federal
Sources, 1995-96

State	Local Funds	State Funds	Federal Funds	Current Expenditure Per Pupil[a]
Alabama	21.0%	61.3%	9.2%	$ 4,716
Alaska	20.2	66.1	11.1	9,012
Arizona	44.6	44.1	9.0	4,860
Arkansas	26.3	60.0	8.5	4,710
California	34.2	55.8	8.9	5,108
Colorado	47.6	43.8	5.3	5,521
Connecticut	55.5	38.0	3.7	8,817
Delaware	25.2	66.6	6.7	7,267
District of Columbia	91.5	—	8.1	9,565
Florida	40.2	48.6	7.4	5,894
Georgia	39.4	51.9	6.8	5,377
Hawaii	0.4	89.8	7.8	6,051
Idaho	26.9	64.3	7.1	4,465
Illinois	64.3	27.3	6.1	6,128
Indiana	37.3	54.3	5.2	6,040
Iowa	40.6	49.0	5.1	5,772
Kansas	34.7	57.3	5.4	5,971
Kentucky	25.6	65.3	8.3	5,545
Louisiana	34.9	50.3	12.1	4,988
Maine	46.4	47.0	5.6	6,546
Maryland	53.7	38.2	4.9	7,382
Massachusetts	55.4	38.3	4.7	7,613
Michigan	25.1	66.8	6.1	7,166
Minnesota	33.7	58.2	4.3	6,162
Mississippi	25.2	57.8	13.7	4,250
Missouri	49.8	40.2	6.0	5,626
Montana	37.2	48.6	9.9	5,847
Nebraska	56.9	31.6	5.6	6,083
Nevada	59.8	32.0	4.5	5,320
New Hampshire	87.1	7.0	3.3	5,958
New Jersey	55.7	38.6	3.4	9,955
New Mexico	11.8	73.9	12.2	4,587
New York	53.5	39.7	5.8	9,549
North Carolina	25.4	64.5	7.2	5,090
North Dakota	41.0	42.1	11.5	4,979
Ohio	49.0	40.7	6.3	6,266
Oklahoma	25.8	59.3	9.3	4,881
Oregon	35.8	54.1	6.5	6,615
Pennsylvania	52.9	39.8	5.5	7,492
Rhode Island	52.2	41.5	5.1	7,936
South Carolina	34.4	52.9	8.3	5,096
South Dakota	57.3	29.7	9.8	4,780
Tennessee	36.9	47.9	8.6	4,548
Texas	47.2	42.9	7.2	5,473

TABLE 2-2 Continued

State	Local Funds	State Funds	Federal Funds	Current Expenditure Per Pupil[a]
Utah	29.6	58.6	6.7	3,867
Vermont	64.9	27.8	4.7	6,837
Virginia	60.2	31.1	5.3	5,433
Washington	23.1	68.0	5.8	6,044
West Virginia	27.4	63.0	8.0	6,325
Wisconsin	50.6	42.9	4.3	7,094
Wyoming	40.8	51.3	6.2	6,243
U.S.	43.2	47.5	6.6	6,146

[a]Current expenditure per pupil in average daily attendance.

SOURCE: U.S. Department of Education, 1999a: Tables 158 and 167.

Center for Education Statistics: www.nces.ed.gov./edfin). In California, disparities across schools within a district were highlighted in a 1992 court case (*Rodriguez v. Los Angeles Unified School District*, Consent Decree, No. C611358, May 5), which found that this large district spent as much as $400 per year less per pupil in elementary schools serving mainly minority students than in elementary schools serving nonminority students. Guthrie (1998) cited data on intradistrict per-pupil spending differences in 1992-93 for the 24 largest districts of an unnamed midwestern state. Intradistrict differences averaged $1,074 for elementary schools and $779 for secondary schools. The largest intradistrict per-pupil difference among elementary schools was $2,092; for high schools it was $1,475.

Intradistrict spending disparities have received much less attention than interdistrict disparities among both school finance reformers and analysts, in part because until quite recently little effort was being devoted to developing reliable data systems about financial and nonfinancial resources available at the school level (Stiefel et al., 1998). While generalizations are therefore difficult, it is clear that at least in some places there is substantial variation in fiscal resources across schools within districts, and that within districts schools with higher levels of student poverty sometimes receive lower allocations of both money and other educational resources (e.g., Rubenstein, 1998).

In sum, the large variations across states and the recent changes in some states indicate, first, the absence of a single generally accepted model of education finance in the United States and, second, the potential for states to change their finance systems. That is, despite the large role that a state's history and culture may play in influencing how it finances education, no state system is fully set in concrete and unable to change. Court pressure has often been the most effective catalyst for change, and political considerations make some states more amenable to change than others.

The Paradox of Concentration Amid Decentralization

Although American education is characterized by a multiplicity of school districts, many of which enroll fewer than a thousand students, about half of all students attend schools in districts with enrollments of more than 10,000.

Table 2-3 shows the enormous range of size in American school districts. Just 226 large school districts (1.5 percent) account for more than 31 percent of the pupils in American schools. Almost half of the students (49.8 percent) are enrolled in 5.3 percent of school districts. At the other end of the size spectrum, about 7,000 school districts enrolling fewer than 1,000 students each provide education for 6.1 percent of American students.

The appearance of fragmentation and decentralization in American education is further attenuated by the realization that 24 super-size districts enroll more than 100,000 pupils each (Table 2-4). As Table 2-4 indicates, this is frequently (though not always) a big-city phenomenon. Some of these super-size districts are counted among the nation's most troubled—e.g., New York, Chicago, Detroit—although others are usually counted among the nation's best—e.g., Fairfax County, Virginia.

The districts at the two ends of the size spectrum—large urban and small rural—have frequently been the objects of special concern when it comes to education financing issues. Urban schools often must carry out their educational

TABLE 2-3 Public School Districts and Enrollment, by Size of District, 1996-97

Enrollment Size	Number of Districts	Percent of Districts	Percent of Students
Total	14,841	100.0 %	100.0 %
25,000 or more	226	1.5	31.1
10,000 to 24,999	569	3.8	18.7
5,000 to 9,999	1,024	6.9	15.5
2,500 to 4,999	2,069	13.9	15.9
1,000 to 2,499	3,536	23.8	12.7
600 to 999	1,772	11.9	3.1
300 to 599	2,066	13.9	2.0
1 to 299	3,160	21.3	1.0
Size not reported	419	2.8	—

SOURCE: U.S. Department of Education, 1999a: Table 91.

TABLE 2-4 Enrollment of Public School Districts Greater than 100,000, Fall 1996

School District	State	Rank	Enrollment
New York City	NY	1	1,063,561
Los Angeles Unified	CA	2	667,305
City of Chicago	IL	3	469,098
Dade County	FL	4	341,117
Broward County	FL	5	218,608
Philadelphia	PA	6	212,150
Houston ISD	TX	7	209,375
Hawaii Public Schools	HI	8	187,653
Detroit Public Schools	MI	9	182,316
Clark County	NV	10	179,106
Dallas ISD	TX	11	154,847
Hillsborough County	FL	12	147,826
Fairfax County	VA	13	143,266
Palm Beach County	FL	14	137,585
San Diego City Unified	CA	15	133,687
Orange County School Board	FL	16	129,143
Duval County	FL	17	126,118
Prince George's County	MD	18	125,198
Montgomery County	MD	19	122,505
Memphis City	TN	20	111,156
Baltimore City	MD	21	108,759
Pinellas County	FL	22	107,060
Baltimore County	MD	23	104,073
Milwaukee City	WI	24	101,007

SOURCE: U.S. Department of Education, 1999a: Table 95.

mission in an environment in which social conditions have deteriorated badly. Urban populations are typically characterized by comparatively high poverty rates, greater percentages of children with poorly educated parents, greater percentages of students with limited English proficiency, and high rates of student mobility. Rural schools face their own set of educational challenges, most notably poverty and sparse population spread out over large areas. Student achievement in urban schools lags that in more affluent suburbs, with student achievement in rural schools somewhere in between.

The Starting Point

This great diversity represents the starting point for changes to the education finance system. We seek a finance system that facilitates higher achievement for all students in a cost-efficient manner; that breaks, or at least reduces, the nexus between student background and student achievement; and that raises revenues fairly and efficiently. We now examine the meaning and significance of these goals.

GOAL 1: FACILITATING HIGHER LEVELS OF ACHIEVEMENT FOR ALL STUDENTS IN A COST-EFFICIENT MANNER

A popular view, especially since *A Nation at Risk* (National Commission on Excellence in Education, 1983), is that American public schools are "failing": failing to prepare students for the challenges of the next century and, what is worse, failing even to provide today's students with the same quality of education that their parents and grandparents got (e.g., see Finn, 1991, Itzkoff, 1994; Sykes, 1995). Meanwhile, other voices (e.g., Berliner and Biddle, 1996) see this dire portrait of the nation's schools as a "manufactured crisis" that greatly exaggerates problems with student achievement.

In our view, while schools may not be failing miserably, neither are they performing satisfactorily. In particular, they are not doing enough to challenge all students to achieve the high levels of learning that they will increasingly need to succeed in the new globally competitive economic environment. The "failure" argument neglects the quite extraordinary gains in educational attainment that have been realized over the 20th century and overstates the conclusions that should be drawn from available measures of student achievement. At the same time, there are numerous indications that the average achievement levels of American students have at best been stagnant over many years, and, moreover, that they are on average mediocre by international standards, although there are certainly pockets of excellence.

What Does Student Achievement Mean and Why Does It Matter?

The nation is increasingly committed to fostering high levels of learning for all students. Student learning has generally been gauged both by measuring the educational attainment of students (e.g., completion of high school or post-secondary education) and by how much students show that they know on tests of subject-matter knowledge. There is much controversy over how well these tests measure academic achievement; furthermore, academic achievement is only one among a number of objectives that Americans believe schools should pursue. Nevertheless, few would disagree with the proposition that academic achievement is an important objective of education, and public judgments about the quality of schooling frequently rest on how well students perform on available tests of their knowledge and skills.

Why does academic achievement matter? Until recently, one of the most politically potent arguments was that high educational achievement was essential for the economic prosperity of the country. However, that argument has been questioned in light of the current economic boom and has now been replaced by a different argument that is better supported by the evidence: namely, that a changing relationship between education and employment means that an *individual's* future economic well-being is increasingly tied to educational attainment and achievement. The restructuring of the U.S. economy that occurred in response to the decline in the rate of productivity growth, which began in the early 1970s, resulted in remarkable strides in efficiency (by the mid-1990s, the United States had regained its position as the most competitive economy in the world), but it exacted a stiff price among workers with the fewest skills and the least education (Blank, 1997; McMurrer and Sawhill, 1998; Murnane and Levy, 1996; Murnane et al., 1995). Prior to the early 1970s, wages rose roughly proportionately for all skill groups as productivity increased. Incomes then began to diverge across groups with different levels of education. Basic cognitive skills are increasingly important predictors of wage and career opportunities, as the nature of work changes (especially for the least skilled), from jobs emphasizing strong muscles to jobs that demand much more than limited literacy and numeracy.

The effects of economic change can be seen in the widening gap between the earnings of workers with college and high school educations. The "wage premium paid to workers with a college degree relative to those with a high school degree . . . increased steadily between 1979 and 1995, from 27 percent to 44 percent for men and from 31 percent to 52 percent for women" (McMurrer and Sawhill, 1998:66). This gap reflected the fact that wages for less-skilled workers actually fell for much of the last quarter-century. Economic recoveries no longer mean rising wages for all workers (Blank, 1997). Moreover, jobs have always been harder to find for the less skilled; and the nature of economic change suggests this situation will persist, if not worsen.

Murnane and Levy (1996) point out that wage and employment gaps between college graduates and those with less education do not necessarily mean that college is essential for everyone. Rather, they observe that students who go on to college demonstrate greater skills than those who don't, even when both groups are high school seniors. Thus, "as high-wage employers increasingly search for new workers with strong basic skills they tend to bypass high school graduates who did not go to college, because so many of them lack those skills" (Murnane and Levy, 1996:8). Improving the skills of high school graduates, they suggest, would give more of them access to jobs in the changing economy.

The toll that economic change has wrought on workers has been particularly high for minorities and those from disadvantaged backgrounds, whose educational levels and performance on measures of academic achievement have typically lagged their more advantaged peers. Moreover, these are precisely the groups for whom education has been held out as offering the best route to social and economic opportunity.

Thus, the mixed picture painted in the next section about educational attainment and achievement, while not entirely justifying the school-bashing that has been so frequent in recent years, does lead to the conclusion that schools can do better and must do better so that all students receive the education they will need to prosper in a complex and rapidly changing world.

Educational Attainment and Achievement

The 20th century has seen remarkable progress in enrolling and retaining students in school. At the turn of the century, 72 percent of children ages 5 to 17 were enrolled in school. This figure has continually improved, reaching 78 percent by 1920, 83 percent by 1950, and moving above 90 percent after 1990 (U.S. Department of Education, 1999a: Table 39). In 1910, 24 percent of people age 25 and over had completed less than five years of elementary school, and 14 percent had completed 4 years of high school or more. In 1997, the comparable percentages were 1.7 percent and 82 percent. For younger adults (ages 25 to 29), the comparable percentages were 0.8 percent and 87 percent (U.S. Department of Education, 1999a: Table 8).

Less clear is what has happened to student achievement levels as enrollments have expanded to encompass virtually all young people. Given the inclusion of populations who in earlier times would not have stayed in school to graduate and who might therefore be less academically inclined or motivated than students of earlier generations, one might expect to see achievement decline even if school quality had not, but in fact students seem to perform roughly as well as ever on the imperfect measures available of academic achievement.

Rothstein (1998) indicates that anecdotal stories of declining student achievement have characterized virtually all periods in American education. They cannot be proven or disproven with empirical evidence, since there are virtually no long-term testing programs that would permit scientifically valid "then and now" comparisons before 1968.

Concern about the declining quality of American education received a great boost in the 1970s because of widely publicized drops in scores on the SAT, a test designed for colleges to use in making admission decisions. Average scores declined from 980 (out of a possible 1600) in 1963 to 890 in 1980. They have risen irregularly and slightly since then (the average in 1997 was 915) (Rothstein, 1998:52-53). The SAT, though widely known, is not a particularly good instrument for tracking the health of American education, however, because it is taken by a self-selected group of college-bound students, and it is difficult to untangle the compositional effects of successive test-taking groups on changing test scores. It appears that some part of the score decline can be attributed to changes in the pool of test takers and another part to the quality of the education received by those students (Rothstein, 1998; Stedman, 1998).

A better instrument for measuring student performance over time (and the only instrument that is based on a nationally representative sample of students) is the National Assessment of Educational Progress (NAEP), which was explicitly designed to monitor academic achievement. It did not begin, however, until 1969. For political reasons, NAEP was originally designed to track performance only at the national level and among certain groups of students (e.g., urban versus rural). Only since 1990 have state NAEP scores been calculated, and the testing program is still not designed to permit the calculation of scores at the substate (e.g., district, school, or student) level. While it provides important trend data on the academic performance of elementary and secondary students in key subject areas, it was never intended to measure all aspects of student achievement (for aspects not covered, see Chapter 4 and National Research Council, 1999b).

NAEP scores in math and science show declines in the early 1970s followed by improved performance; reading and writing results have been more mixed (Campbell et al., 1997:iii). In no case, however, are there overall score declines that would justify the wide pessimism frequently expressed about the quality of American schools compared with their counterparts 20 or 30 years ago. In a number of instances, gains can be cited, especially for black students. The performance of black students on NAEP achievement tests in reading, mathematics, and science improved substantially between the early 1970s and the mid-1990s, both in terms of absolute achievement levels and in comparison with whites, although some slippage occurred in the 1990s.

The perception that school quality is poor and/or getting poorer, while not supported by NAEP test scores, was probably reinforced by a new method of reporting these scores. Beginning in 1992, in addition to reporting average scores on a 500 point scale, the U.S. Department of Education has reported NAEP results in terms of the percentage of students performing at various levels: below basic, basic, proficient, or advanced. Scores reported in this way have been alarming (for example, only 21 percent of fourth graders were judged to have proficient or advanced achievement on the 1996 NAEP mathematics test, and 36 percent were judged to be below basic (U.S. Department of Education, 1999a: Table 123). A recent National Research Council (NRC) evaluation (National Research Council, 1999b:7), however, determined that "the current process for setting NAEP achievement levels is fundamentally flawed" and that "the achievement level results do not appear to be reasonable compared with other external information about students' achievement."

While an empirical case is difficult to make that the quality of American education is worse than it used to be, there is stronger evidence that it is lower than many international counterparts. Forty-one countries tested half a million students as part of the Third International Mathematics and Science Study in the mid-1990s. Achievement results were reported for three student populations (roughly 4th graders, 8th graders, and students enrolled in their final year of secondary education). U.S. 4th graders performed above the international average in mathematics and near the top in science. U.S. 8th graders, however, scored somewhat below the international average in mathematics and only somewhat higher than the international average in science. And 12th graders performed below the international average and among the lowest of the 21 countries that tested students at this grade level in both mathematics and science (National Center for Education Statistics, 1996, 1997, 1998).

Opinion polls show that public attitudes about schools are roughly in line with these international results. The annual Gallup poll of public attitudes toward public schools, sponsored by the *Phi Delta Kappan* (and cited in U.S. Department of Education, 1999a: Table 22), shows adults giving the schools a grade somewhere around C or C+. Adults with no children in school assign a lower grade than do public school parents; not surprisingly, the lowest grades for the public schools come from parents with children in private schools. Schools in the local community and local neighborhood of the poll respondents get higher grades than do schools nationally.

Despite the fact that criticism of public schools has been loud and sustained for the past 15 years or so, the grades given the schools in the annual polls haven't changed noticeably for a quarter of a century. Moreover, there is no evidence that parents are fleeing public education. The percentage of students enrolled in private schools, which was 8 percent in 1910, actually peaked in 1959 at about 14 percent and has hovered around 10 to 11 percent since 1970 (calculations based on data from U.S. Department of Education, 1999a: Table 3).[4]

In the face of this evidence of, at worst, stagnation but not decline in educational achievement and in public attitudes, what else might contribute to the sense that public schools are not living up to expectations? Another key aspect of educational performance that has drawn increasing criticism concerns the efficiency of educational spending.

Spending, Spending Growth, and the Efficiency of Public Schools

The U.S. investment of over $300 billion annually in public precollegiate education exceeds its investment in any other public service except national defense and international relations. Citizens reasonably want to know whether these resources are being used in ways that yield the maximum possible results for the expenditures involved.

The efficiency of American education has been called into question by observers (e.g., Hanushek et al., 1994) who point to rapidly rising expenditures at the same time that academic achievement appears at best to have remained flat. To some, this combination of trends suggests that schools do not use their financial resources well and that adding increased resources to these inefficient enterprises would be unwise public policy. Others disagree with this policy conclusion,

---

[4]Beginning in fall 1980, the Department of Education included an expanded universe of private schools in its data collection. Therefore, private school enrollment figures before and after 1980 are not strictly comparable.

pointing out that the observed rise in spending overstates the rise in resources available to schools and that the challenges facing schools have increased because of the shifting demographics of the school-age population and of new legal requirements about educating children who are more expensive to educate, such as those with disabilities or whose first language is not English.

Growth in Educational Expenditures since 1970

Both total and per-pupil current expenditures for public primary and secondary education have grown rapidly in the United States over the past quarter-century.[5] Real current expenditures increased about 93 percent from $146 billion in academic year 1969-70 to $282 billion in 1997-98. (These figures are adjusted for inflation using the consumer price index or CPI with 1997-98 as the base year, adjusted to a school year basis.)

Because student enrollment in public elementary and secondary schools remained virtually the same between 1970 and 1997, growth in current expenditures increased spending per pupil: from $3,430 in 1970-71 to $6,131 in 1997-98 (constant 1997-98 dollars). Enrollment changes occurred unevenly, with declines in the 1970s and early 1980s (from 46 million students in 1971 to 40 million students in 1985) and then increases beginning in 1986 (growing to over 46 million students in 1997). Increases in per-pupil spending also occurred unevenly, growing 27 percent in the 1970s and 37 percent in the 1980s, but leveling off to 3.6 percent between 1991 and 1998.

Even in periods when student enrollments declined, the number of teachers increased, growing from about 2 million in 1970 to 2.7 million in 1997. The result was a substantially lower pupil-teacher ratio in 1997 (17 pupils per teacher) than in 1970 (22 pupils per teacher). This change is one of the factors frequently cited as proof of the inefficiency of public schools, which failed to translate more teacher resources per pupil into gains in student improvement. Skeptics (e.g., Hanushek and Rivkin, 1996) also note that the growth in all staff exceeded that of teachers alone. Staff includes—besides classroom teachers—principals, assistant principals, curriculum specialists, library specialists, guidance counselors, psychological personnel, and other professionals. The pupil-staff ratio fell from 13-to-1 in 1970 to 9-to-1 in 1996.

Changes in total expenditures reflect not only enrollment and staffing trends, but also trends in salaries. Salaries and benefits for teachers and others who provide instruction represent over 55 percent of current expenditures. Average teacher salaries (adjusted for inflation, with 1997-98 as the base year) increased

---

[5]Current expenditures include salaries, transportation, school books, materials, and energy costs. They exclude capital outlays and interest on school debt. Unless otherwise indicated, data are taken from the *Digest of Education Statistics, 1998* (U.S. Department of Education, 1999a).

just 4.4 percent between 1970-71 and 1997-98, from $37,735 to $39,385. Teacher salaries are usually tied to years of experience, among other things; over the same period, the American Federation of Teachers reports that the average experience of teachers increased from 11.2 to 16.0 years (Nelson and Schneider, 1997: Table II-4).

Understanding Expenditure Growth

A number of factors complicate the interpretation of the growth in education spending over time and make it difficult draw conclusions from data on spending growth about the production efficiency of schools (Ladd, 1996; Rothstein and Miles, 1995; Consortium on Productivity in the Schools, 1995).

Adjusting for Changes in Costs

One problem is how to account for changes in the price of educational resources or inputs over time, in order to distinguish between the growth in spending caused by cost increases and the growth that represents real change in the amounts of input being used.

Analysts disagree about the proper method for accounting for cost changes in education. Some analysts believe that commonly used general prices indices, such as the CPI or the deflator the gross domestic product, understate the rising costs of educational inputs. This understatement occurs because the indices do not take into account the fact that education and many other service sectors have to raise salaries to compete successfully with other sectors for workers, yet these sectors do not benefit as much as the rest of the economy from technological changes that lead to productivity improvements (see Baumol, 1993). Because the CPI understates the rise in costs, adjusting spending by the CPI leads to an overestimate of the growth rate of real resources.

Some analysts argue for using a cost index specifically designed to take account of the education sector's reliance on inputs whose productivity cannot grow very fast. Rothstein and Miles (1995), for example, develop and use an index that measures inflation in service sectors other than rent/shelter and health care in their recent study of the growth of school spending. Based on this inflation index, they conclude that real per-pupil spending increased by 61 percent between 1967 and 1991, or about 40 percent less than real per-pupil expenditure growth based on the CPI. An alternative cost index specifically developed for primary and secondary education is available for the academic year (AY) 1974-75 to AY 1994-95. Using this index, real per-pupil current expenditures grew 36 percent between AY 1974-75 and AY 1994-95 in comparison to the 51 percent increase as calculated with the CPI adjustment. Using either of these indices would lead to the conclusion that while real per-pupil expenditures in public primary and secondary education did rise between 1970 and 1995, the actual growth in real resources required to maintain a given level of education was not as large as has been measured using more conventional inflation indices. Other analysts question the use of an index specifically designed for education. Hanushek and Rivkin (1996:5) point out that these indices are difficult to adjust for changes in the quality of labor, "a key concern in the consideration of teachers" whose wages comprise a large proportion of education costs. Moreover, there has been a profound shift in the overall labor market for women in the last half-century that has resulted in a lessening of barriers to women in the general labor market and a decrease in the attractiveness of teaching. Such labor market shifts are also difficult to capture through standard wage indices or through deflators based on service industries. While there is some validity to these objections, the issue remains a real one: the use of the CPI to deflate growth in spending leads to an inflated estimate of how much growth there has been in the real resources available to provide educational services.

Special Education

A major concern of both practitioners and scholars has been the growth in expenditures on educating students with disabilities—called special education—since passage of the Education for All Handicapped Children Act in 1975 (P.L. 94-142; hereafter EHA). This federal law requires school districts to provide a "free and appropriate" education to children with disabilities, in accordance with an individualized education program (IEP) developed for each affected child. The federal government partially reimburses districts for the costs of special education, but federal aid is estimated to cover only 7 percent of these expenses (U.S. Department of Education, 1997).

Since passage of EHA, the number of students ages 0 to 21 classified as disabled grew from 3.7 million pupils in 1976-77 to 5.9 million in 1996-97 (U.S. Department of Education, 1999a: Table 53). Of this 5.9 million, 5.2 million were ages 6 to 21; this represented 10 percent of all children enrolled in public and private elementary and secondary schools (U.S. Department of Education, 1998). The average cost of educating a special education student has been estimated at 1.9 to 2.3 times the cost of providing education to a student in "regular" education (Chaikind et al., 1993). Total costs for special education are currently estimated at $32 to $36 billion annually.[6] The growing costs of special education have alarmed education practitioners, raised fears that mandated special education expenditures were "crowding out" funds for regular education, and have led to

---

[6]The cost estimates are marginal costs; that is, what was spent on special education over and above what these children would have cost if they were regular students enrolled in regular classrooms. Cost estimates for special education in particular are notoriously imprecise, for reasons discussed in Chapter 7.

disagreements among analysts about how much of the increase in overall education expenditures should be attributed to new special education requirements.

Hanushek and Rivkin (1996) conclude that spending on special education had a disproportionate effect on the growth in education costs in the 1980s, but they doubt that increased resources for special education can be blamed for the largest portion of the recent increases in per-pupil spending. They attribute about 18 percent of the per-pupil expenditure growth during the 1980s to spending on special education and estimate that increases in special education spending accounted for less than one-third of the fall in the pupil-teacher ratio during the 1980s.[7] They cite in support of their position the small percentage of students classified as having disabilities of the total student population. They also observe that the general increase in per-pupil spending as well as the decrease in pupil-teacher ratios is pervasive across heterogeneous school districts with varying proportions of students with disabilities.

Other studies place a greater portion of the responsibility for expenditure growth on increased expenses for special education. Lankford and Wyckoff (1995) estimate an average of 30 percent of the increased real spending on education in the major school districts in the state of New York between 1980 and 1992 was the direct result of teaching students with disabilities. The impact was disproportionate in New York City, where special education accounted for 60 percent of the increase. Lankford and Wyckoff also showed that spending requirements under EHA have a greater impact during times of state fiscal downturns; they estimate that although spending on teaching students with disabilities accounted for 26 percent of the growth in spending between 1980 and 1989, it accounted for about 85 percent of the growth between 1989 and 1992. Hanushek and Rivkin also recognize that the contribution of special education costs to expenditure growth cannot be considered in isolation from constraints on state budgets.

Rothstein and Miles (1995) examined changes in the growth and composition of education spending in nine "representative" school districts across the nation between 1967 (pre-EHA) and 1991. After adjusting for inflation using their service-sector index, they estimate that the share of total per-pupil spending on special education increased from 3.7 percent in 1967 to 17 percent in 1991. Moreover, spending on special education accounted for the largest share of net new money (38 percent) between 1967 and 1991 in these nine school districts. Rothstein and Miles find that the share of total per-pupil spending going to

---

[7]In 1994, Helen Ladd reexamined the numbers used by Hanushek and Rivkin in their calculation of the contribution of special education to the decline in the public school pupil-teacher ratio (Ladd, unpublished data, Terry Sanford Institute of Public Policy, Duke University). Using data from the *Digest of Education* and the *Annual Report to Congress on the Implementation of the EHA*, she calculates that over 50 percent of the decline of the pupil-teacher ratio is attributable to the expansion of special education between 1980 and 1990.

regular education in these nine districts declined from 80 percent in 1967 to 59 percent in 1991.

The absence of reliable nationwide data makes it difficult to determine just how much of the increase can be accounted for by state and federal requirements that schools provide educational services to all children with disabilities. Nonetheless, it is clear that a significant part of the growth in education spending over the last quarter-century can be attributed to the growth in special education.

Changes in Student Backgrounds

Children whose home backgrounds deprive them of economic, social, and health "capital" come to school less ready to learn than their more advantaged peers. To the extent that the number of children from disadvantaged backgrounds has been growing, costs of education might be expected to have grown as schools attempted to provide compensating educational services.

It is impossible to determine what proportion of the last quarter-century's overall increase in educational expenditures should be attributed to such changes, although the impact in some districts has undoubtedly been large. On one hand, some of the factors generally thought to make children more expensive to educate have become more prevalent in the school-age population, but on the other, certain changes in families' circumstances may have enhanced children's learning ability. For example, the percentage of children younger than 18 living in families with incomes below the poverty level increased from 15 percent in 1970 to 21 percent in 1992. There has also been a significant and consistent growth in the incidence of children living in single-parent families since 1969; in 1992, around 45 percent of poor children and 80 percent of black children lived with a female head of household. More mothers now work; the proportion of wives in married couples in the paid labor force increased from 40 percent of married women in 1970 to 58 percent in 1990. Working in the other direction, the educational attainment of parents has gone up, as has the real median family income of families with children, average family size has gone down, and the percentage of children with some preprimary education increased in the 1980s (Bureau of the Census, 1992).

The precise relationship between the changing socioeconomic status of students and the growth of education costs is not clear. Related research, however, provides some information on how these changes have affected student achievement between 1970 and 1990. Grissmer et al. (1994) conclude that the improvements described above in parental education, family size, and family income, as well as an increase in the age of the mother when the child was born, have had a greater impact on student achievement (in a positive direction) than have changes in family circumstances that are associated with decreases in achievement. Findings from other studies support in part the results from the Grissmer et al. study. Powell and Steelman (1996) found a strong positive relationship between parents' education and average state SAT scores. Blake (1989) finds a positive relationship between smaller family size and higher achievement. The evidence of the effect of working mothers on student achievement is mixed. Milne et al. (1986) found a negative effect on achievement from living in a single-parent family or having a mother in paid employment. However, in a critique of the research by Milne et al., Heyns and Catsambis (1986) found a weaker link between mother's employment and student achievement.

In summary, it is difficult to evaluate how the changing background characteristics of students have affected their achievement or the associated costs of the educational system as a whole. It appears that the aggregate effect of changing family characteristics on the growth of education costs is probably small and of undetermined direction. In areas of increasing concentration of poverty, however, such changes are likely to have a large and significant adverse impact on student achievement or educational costs or both.

Improving Achievement While Using Money Well

Our evaluation of the evidence leads us to conclude that school performance and public confidence have not deteriorated as much as the rhetoric surrounding schools suggests, and the achievements of American schools in the 20th century have perhaps been too seldom acknowledged in recent years. At the same time, both public opinion and available national and international achievement measures indicate that the nation has a long way to go in educating all students to high standards. The fact that schools have undergone almost constant efforts at reform over the past century (Elmore and McLaughlin, 1988; Tyack and Cuban, 1995), with no evidence that academic achievement has been significantly boosted as a result, indicates the difficulty of the task and the importance of reviewing in this report what is known and unknown about improving school performance and about possible strategies for aligning school finance with this objective. The unsettled debate over the efficiency of schools further suggests that how school finance strategies do or could encourage desirable efficiencies must also be an important topic for investigation.

GOAL 2: BREAKING THE NEXUS BETWEEN STUDENT BACKGROUND CHARACTERISTICS AND STUDENT ACHIEVEMENT

The increasing importance of education to success in the labor market highlights the significance of disparities in educational opportunity. Of particular concern are continuing gaps in academic achievement related to the background characteristics of students, such as race and family income. Although many factors beyond schooling contribute to these gaps, it is important to determine the extent to which education finance strategies currently exacerbate those gaps and to explore what school finance reforms might reduce them.

Gaps in Attainment and Achievement

One of the most persistent and troublesome indicators of unequal opportunity in American schools has been the difference in academic attainment and achievement among groups of students defined by such background characteristics as race and income. Upon close study, the achievement picture is complicated, with signs of real progress as well as reasons for continuing concern.

A major accomplishment has been the near parity reached between black and white Americans in educational attainment at the high school level. In 1920, 45 percent of blacks ages 25-29 had less than five years of elementary school education, compared with 13 percent of whites, and only 6 percent of blacks had four years of high school or more, compared to 22 percent of whites. By 1997, near parity had been achieved: 87 percent of non-Hispanic blacks ages 25-29 had four years of high school or more compared with 93 percent with their white non-Hispanic counterparts. Most of this progress in black educational attainment took place after 1960. Separate figures for Hispanics have been reported only since 1980. Here the news is not so good: in 1997, only 62 percent of people ages 25-29 had attained four years of high school or more, an increase of only 4 percentage points from the 1980 figure (U.S. Department of Education, 1999a: Table 8). This signifies some but not a great deal of progress.

Much attention has been focused over the years on test score gaps among students from different racial/ethnic groups, with the black-white test score gap the most prominent and intensely studied. Introducing a recent collection of research papers on the subject, Jencks and Phillips (1998:1) summarize the issue: "African Americans currently score lower than European Americans on vocabulary, reading, and mathematics tests, as well as on tests that claim to measure scholastic aptitude and intelligence. This gap appears before children enter kindergarten, and it persists into adulthood. It has narrowed since 1970, but the typical American black still scores below 75 percent of American whites on most standardized tests. On some tests the typical American black scores below more than 85 percent of whites."

Test scores in reading and mathematics on NAEP increased for black children in the 1970s and 1980s and the gap between black and white test takers' scores diminished by about half (Campbell et al., 1997). Since the late 1980s, though, the trend toward smaller gaps between black and white students' scores has partially reversed as black student scores have dropped somewhat. Hispanic students' scores show a similar pattern, with an overall narrowing of the gap with white students' scores since the mid-1970s and some recent slippage backward.

NAEP scores also differ by place of residence, with "urban fringe" students performing at higher levels than their rural or central-city counterparts (U.S.

Department of Education, 1994, 1996). Recent trend data by place of residence are not available, nor does NAEP collect data on the income levels of test takers' families. Numerous other studies, though, beginning with the Coleman report in the mid-1960s, have consistently shown that test scores and family income levels are directly related (Coleman et al., 1966). Since 1986 NAEP has measured the level of school poverty for tested students. Recent unpublished tabulations prepared for the National Assessment of Title I (U.S. Department of Education, 1999b) indicate that NAEP reading scores for 9-year-old public school students in high-poverty schools (more than 75 percent of students eligible for free or reduced price lunch) dropped by 2 points between 1988 and 1996, and mathematics scores improved by 9 points or about one grade level.

Educational Achievement and School Spending

As Jencks and Phillips' (1998) recent volume exploring the causes and possible remedies for the black-white test score gap vividly illustrates, the relationship between test scores and student background characteristics is complex and only partially understood. Of particular interest to us as a committee on education finance are the relationships between family income and student achievement on one hand and between family income and district-level spending on the other. Given the large disparities in spending across districts already mentioned and the causes that are examined in much more detail in the next chapter, one important question is the extent to which these disparities are related to variations in the income levels of families residing in different school districts.

Several U.S. Department of Education reports (Parrish et al., 1995, 1998; Parrish, 1996a, 1996b) use data for academic years 1989-90 and 1991-92 to examine variations among school districts and across states in the revenues available for educational programs and services and their relationship to family and community characteristics. Looked at from a national perspective, families living in the poorest districts—those with the highest poverty levels and the lowest median incomes (where income levels have been adjusted for differences across districts in the cost of living)—had lower per-pupil revenues than those in the richest districts (Table 2-5). For example, in 1991-92, districts with 25 percent or more of their school-age children in poverty had average total per-pupil revenues only 89 percent of the average total per-pupil revenues of districts with less than 8 percent of school-age children in poverty. Similarly, districts with median household income of less than $22,000 had average per-pupil revenues only 81 percent as large as the average revenues per pupil of districts with cost-adjusted median household incomes of $38,000 or more. Urban districts had just slightly more revenue per pupil than suburban districts and 18 percent more than rural districts, while districts with the lowest minority enrollments had 7 percent less revenue per pupil than districts with the highest level (50 percent or more) minority enrollments.

When district revenue figures were adjusted to reflect costs and student needs (described in the notes to Table 2-5), the comparative situation of urban and high-minority-enrollment districts changed. Reflecting the fact that high-minority and urban districts are often high-cost areas, the cost and need-adjusted revenues per pupil for urban areas were 97 percent of the suburban districts, and the high-minority-enrollment districts had per-pupil revenues that were 96 percent of low-minority-enrollment districts. Race itself does not appear to be the key demographic variable explaining the difference in spending between low-minority and high-minority districts, however. When race was considered simultaneously with other factors, the poverty of families, rather than their race, was the variable that correlated more with the buying power of education dollars in different districts. Poorer families lived in districts that spend less. These nationwide differences understate differences that are seen within some individual states (Table 2-6) and, because commonly used measures to adjust for student needs are presently quite imperfect, they may well understate the costs faced by districts with large enrollments of at-risk students.

These figures suggest that student background characteristics like race and income that are correlated with lower student test scores are also correlated with lower spending on schools. They signal the importance of examining what is known about the relationship between educational spending and student achievement, an issue taken up in Chapter 5.

The Condition of Children and Education in Cities

We have seen that student achievement as measured by test scores is lower for children living in central cities than for their suburban and rural counterparts. This is one manifestation of a widely perceived crisis in urban education. As *Education Week* put it in introducing a massive special issue on the "urban challenge," "it's hard to exaggerate the education crisis in America's cities. . . . When people talk about the problems in public education, they're usually not talking about suburbs or small towns. They're talking about big-city schools—specifically the ones that serve poor children" (*Education Week*, 1998:6,9).

Achieving the goal of breaking the nexus between family background and student achievement requires special attention to this urban challenge. Minorities and poor people are heavily concentrated in cities. In 1990, 57 percent of all blacks and 52 percent of all Hispanics lived in central cities (National Research Council, 1999a: Table 2-3); 60 percent of individuals in metropolitan areas living in households below the poverty line lived in central cities rather than in suburbs (National Research Council, 1999a).

Moreover, residential racial segregation is extraordinarily high in most U.S. metropolitan areas, a feature of cities with special implications for education. Because school attendance is largely based on residential patterns, school segregation is also very high. In 1991-92, 66 percent of all black students and 73

TABLE 2-5 Total Revenues per Student, 1991-92

	Percentage of All Students Enrolled
Revenues by School-Age Children in Poverty	
Less than 8%	22.2%
8-<15%	23.6
15-<25%	27.7
25% or more	26.6
Revenues by Minority Enrollment	
Less than 5%	21.5
5-<20%	24.9
20-<50%	26.6
50% or more	27.0
Revenues by Metropolitan Status	
Urban/central cities	26.9
Suburban/metropolitan	48.8
Rural	24.3
Revenues by Median Household Income (cost-adjusted)	
Less than $22,000	16.8
$22,000-<$26,000	26.9
$26,000-<$30,000	22.1
$30,000-<$38,000	21.4
$38,000 or more	12.8

[a]Education revenues are expressed in cost-adjusted terms to reflect variations in real education resources, as opposed to nominal dollars. The cost-adjustments used are based on the teacher cost index (TCI) developed by Chambers (1995), which measures variations in the costs of comparable teachers across geographic locations.

[b]Student-need adjustments reflect the varying needs of three categories of special needs students, which were weighted to equal more than one student. Special education students are given a weight

percent of all Hispanic students attended schools that were predominantly minority, and 34 percent of each group attended schools that were 90-100 percent minority (Orfield et al., 1993). Residential segregation declined, but only slightly, between 1970 and 1990. Similarly, there have been modest declines since 1968 in the proportion of blacks and Hispanics attending predominantly minority schools and massive drops in the percentage of blacks attending 90-100 percent minority schools from 64 percent in 1968 to 34 percent in 1991; however, the percentage of Hispanics attending such schools grew from 23 to 34 percent over the same period. Virtually all of the improvement occurred in the early years of that period, and school segregation has increased slightly since the late 1980s

Revenues per Student

Actual	Cost-Adjusted[a]	Need-Adjusted[b]	Cost- and Need-Adjusted
$6,266	$5,863	$5,427	$5,080
5,273	5,289	4,506	4,521
5,162	5,409	4,339	4,547
5,600	5,557	4,587	4,554
5,425	5,558	4,631	4,739
5,598	5,541	4,794	4,741
5,353	5,454	4,527	4,610
5,797	5,538	4,786	4,574
5,781	5,539	4,788	4,593
5,748	5,533	4,915	4,730
4,894	5,477	4,111	4,597
5,391	5,707	4,417	4,677
5,407	5,389	4,498	4,489
5,189	5,339	4,390	4,518
5,566	5,374	4,780	4,617
6,650	6,113	5,785	5,321

of 2.3, compensatory education students a weight of 1.2, and limited-English-proficient (LEP) students a weight of 1.2. To apply this adjustment, the counts of special needs students in each district are then multiplied by their weights to calculate a total weight count.

SOURCE: Parrish et al., 1998: Tables II-1,II-2, II-6 and II-7.

(Orfield et al., 1993). The residential racial segregation of blacks is not simply a by-product of economic segregation; high-income blacks live in areas nearly as segregated as do low-income blacks. The level of income segregation is markedly lower than the level of racial segregation.

The concentration in cities of minority residents is worrisome because "many metropolitan areas are . . . characterized by a set of problems so severe that some see them as threatening the long-term viability of American society" (National Research Council, 1999a:13). The differences in opportunity structures that result from central-city/suburban differences in education, employment, income, and public service quality contribute to the unequal chances many city residents

TABLE 2-6 Average Per-Pupil Spending in Large Urban Districts, 1994-95

District	City	State	District Spending	State Spending	Difference in Spending
Districts Spending More than State Average					
Milwaukee City Public Schools	Milwaukee	WI	$6,922	$6,301	$621
Dade County School District	Miami	FL	5,734	5,220	514
Chicago Public Schools	Chicago	IL	6,064	5,553	511
Detroit Public Schools	Detroit	MI	6,953	6,465	488
Memphis City Schools	Memphis	TN	4,421	4,017	404
Los Angeles Unified School District	Los Angeles	CA	5,176	4,799	377
Dallas Independent School District	Dallas	TX	5,133	4,779	354
San Diego Unified School District	San Diego	CA	5,013	4,799	214
Districts Spending "Same" as State[a]					
Houston Independent School District	Houston	TX	4,785	4,779	6
Broward County Public Schools	Fort Lauderdale	FL	5,140	5,220	–80
Districts Spending Less than State Avreage					
Clark County Public Schools	Las Vegas	NV	4,584	4,730	–146
Baltimore City Public Schools	Baltimore	MD	5,915	6,427	–512
Duval County Public Schools	Jacksonville	FL	4,615	5,220	–605
New York City Public Schools	New York	NY	7,617	8,311	–694
The School District of Philadelphia	Philadelphia	PA	5,104	6,565	–1,461

[a]A difference of ± $100 is counted as "the same."

SOURCE: U.S. Department of Education, 1999a: Tables 94 and 168.

have to develop their inherent talents and capabilities. Alarmingly, these spatial variations in opportunity are especially exaggerated for blacks and Hispanics, who are especially likely to live in neighborhoods where opportunities are the most limited. In 1990, 17 percent of metropolitan-area blacks and 11 percent of Hispanics (compared with 1 percent of whites) lived in neighborhoods of concentrated poverty (census tracts with 40 percent or more of the households below the poverty level). While 34 percent of the black poor and 22 percent of the Hispanic poor in metropolitan areas lived in these high-poverty neighborhoods, only 18 percent of all poor people did so (Jargowsky, 1997).

Moreover, the problems of central cities and unequal opportunity are getting worse. A 1999 NRC report cites these disturbing trends (National Research Council, 1999a):

- In 1990 central-city median income was 77 percent of suburban median income, compared with 89 percent in 1960.
- In 1990, central-city poverty rates were 2.4 times those of suburbs, compared with 1.5 times in 1960.
- Between 1980 and 1990, per-capita income for whites in metropolitan areas rose by 19 percent, while for blacks it increased by only 13 percent.
- The number of high-poverty census tracts more than doubled between 1970 and 1990 and the number of people who live in them rose by 92 percent over that time. Blacks have been especially affected in negative ways by this development. Whereas 26 percent of the black poor in metropolitan areas lived in high-poverty census tracts in 1970, in 1990 34 percent did so. The comparable figures for the Hispanic poor were 24 percent in 1970 and 22 percent in 1990.

Conditions in cities and suburbs do not always diverge sharply. There is substantial variation in economic and social conditions across individual suburbs. There are inner-ring suburbs and/or industrial suburbs in many metropolitan areas whose residents face problems and barriers similar to those in central cities, although research on intrametropolitan differences almost always examines central-city versus suburban differences. It is possible that some suburban neighborhoods with low incomes and high poverty levels are even worse off than some central-city neighborhoods, because they share similar problems but may lack the commercial tax base of a central business district. One study found that central cities were actually more prosperous than their surrounding suburbs in nearly a third of metropolitan areas (Ellen, 1999). Central-city/suburban disparities clearly vary by region, with cities in the Northeast and the Midwest relatively worse off in comparison to their suburbs than cities in the South and the West (National Research Council, 1999a: Table 3-3). Cities in larger metropolitan areas are relatively worse off compared with their suburbs than cities in smaller areas (National Research Council, 1999a: Table 3-4). Strategies for change, therefore, cannot uniformly be applied to all cities, but must be adapted to local circumstances.

The diversity of conditions in both cities and suburbs no doubt helps explain why data on the financial condition of urban schools are not easy to discern. It is not immediately apparent that urban schools are funded at lower levels than other schools, although it is frequently assumed that they are. Despite the concentration of costly-to-educate children in urban areas, in 1991-92 (Table 2-5), average per-pupil revenues per urban/central-city student were virtually the same as for suburban/metropolitan students. When these revenue figures were adjusted (by imperfect measures) for differences in costs and student needs, per-pupil revenues in the urban/central-city areas were the same as those in rural areas and 3 percent lower than the suburban/metropolitan average.

Other data suggest that this small difference in the nationwide averages masks much larger differences that exist from state to state. *Education Week* (1998) calculated per-pupil 1993-94 spending levels for 73 urban districts and compared these averages with per-pupil averages for the state in which the city is located. Counting a difference of ± $100 as "the same," 39 of these 73 urban districts had higher per-pupil average expenditures than their states, 11 had the same, and 23 had lower. Of these 73 districts, 15 are also on the list of super-size districts enrolling more than 100,000 students in 1996 (see Table 2-4). (The 9 other super-size districts are suburban.) Looking at the latest year (1994-95) for which spending data are available for these 15 districts, per-pupil expenditures were higher than state averages in 8, the same in 2, and lower in 5 (Table 2-6).

Moreover, the picture of the resources available in urban districts compared with other jurisdictions depends heavily on the cost-adjustment factors that are used to account for differences in student needs and in geographical cost-of-living levels. The quality of comparative measures of spending depends on how fully these measures reflect underlying cost differences. As discussed in Chapters 4 and 7, there is room for significant improvement in the quality of the cost adjustments currently used to allocate and to report on educational revenues.

School Finance and the Interrelationship of Achievement and Student Background

The fact that student academic achievement is strongly linked with family background, which is in turn is affected by the social, economic, and political environment in which families live, reflects deep societal problems that go far beyond schooling. We reiterate our view that changes in school finance, or school policies more generally, are not likely to solve problems that go far beyond education. At the same time, such change both can and should do more to reduce the nexus between family background and student achievement. Finance reforms will need to focus not only on improving the capacity of schools to meet the needs of disadvantaged students but also on ensuring that such students are prepared to benefit from what schools have to offer—that is, on improving the capacity of the children to learn.

GOAL 3: RAISING REVENUES FAIRLY AND EFFICIENTLY

Raising revenue in a fair manner is important for its own sake, regardless of whether the funds are to be used for education or any other public service. The fact that taxes are compulsory does not give a democratic government license to tax people in an arbitrary or unfair way. Rather, the legitimacy of a democratic government requires that it tax people in a way that they perceive to be fair. In addition, the perceived fairness with which revenues are generated is important for education because it can affect the attainment of other educational goals. For example, if taxpayers thought a particular type of tax was so unfair that they refused to vote for higher taxes, the use of that tax would affect the amount of revenue that could be generated for education.

Efficiency with respect to revenue raising can take on several meanings. First, it may call for revenues to be raised with relatively low administrative costs. Second, following the economists' definition of efficiency, it may call for revenue to be raised in such a way as to minimize unintended behavioral responses by taxpayers who are trying to avoid the burden of the tax. Third, in the local government context, it may refer to how well the pattern of public spending and the taxes that support the spending across local jurisdictions corresponds to consumer preferences.

Two features of the way the United States raises revenue at the state and local level for education have direct implications for the fairness and efficiency of revenue raising. One is the heavy reliance on local school districts for raising revenue. Local revenue raising can promote efficiency in the third sense of supporting spending that is in line with consumer preferences. However, the large variation across districts in their capacity to raise revenue relative to the educational challenges they face requires some districts to impose much heavier tax burdens on their residents than other districts to provide a given quality of education services. Although some of the apparent resulting inequities may be offset in part by compensating differences in state aid to school districts or in local housing prices, undoubtedly some inequities remain. The other aspect is the heavy reliance of education funding on the local property tax, which many people believe imposes a regressive burden on taxpayers.

We have already described the pattern across states and over time in the division of financing responsibilities by level of government. In the following sections, we document the large role of the local property tax and describe the other components of the financing landscape: the efforts of state governments to use state aid to school districts to offset some of the variation in revenue-raising ability across local school districts and the role of the federal government. In

Chapter 8 we evaluate the validity of the concerns about the inequities and inefficiencies in the way the country currently finances K-12 education.

Role of the Property Tax

The extent to which local governments in general and school districts in particular rely on the property tax is reported by state in Table 2-7. As the first column shows, property taxes as a percentage of total local taxes in FY 1994-95 averaged nearly 75 percent. The share ranged from nearly 99 percent in New Hampshire, Rhode Island, and Vermont to about 36 percent in Alabama. It was 75 percent or greater for 29 states and less than 60 percent for only 7 states. The second column indicates the extent to which independent school districts (that is, those not a part of municipalities or counties) rely on the property tax. In the United States, property taxes accounted for more than 96 percent of the local taxes for school districts. Only 3 states (Kentucky, Louisiana, and Pennsylvania) have a share less than 90 percent.

Revenues at the state level come primarily from the personal income tax and the general sales tax (Table 2-8). Most states rely on a combination of these two

TABLE 2-7 Local Governments and School Districts' Reliance on the Property Tax

State	All Local Governments	School Districts
Alabama	36.26	100
Alaska[a]	80.31	NA
Arizona	72.77	100
Arkansas	64.93	100
California	69.37	99.27
Colorado	64.62	100
Connecticut[b]	98.86	NA
Delaware	82.24	100
Florida	80.49	100
Georgia	69.01	100
Hawaii[c]	81.06	NA
Idaho	95.23	100
Illinois	81.04	100
Indiana	89.59	99.82
Iowa	94.25	97.85
Kansas	81.99	100
Kentucky	50.19	64.90
Louisiana	38.92	40.80
Maine	98.26	100

TABLE 2-7 Continued

State	All Local Governments	School Districts
Maryland[b]	59.84	NA
Massachusetts[b]	97.23	NA
Michigan	88.93	99.48
Minnesota	95.47	100
Mississippi	92.14	99.19
Missouri	62.27	94.19
Montana	95.86	100
Nebraska	86.51	99.91
Nevada	61.29	99.48
New Hampshire	99.02	100
New Jersey	97.88	100
New Mexico	52.18	100
New York	61.53	98.21
North Carolina[b]	74.89	NA
North Dakota	89.44	99.56
Ohio	66.27	98.27
Oklahoma	54.55	99.70
Oregon	83.53	99.40
Pennsylvania	71.02	84.10
Rhode Island[b]	98.76	NA
South Carolina	89.23	99.69
South Dakota	80.44	96.84
Tennessee[b]	61.16	NA
Texas	77.10	92.24
Utah	74.57	100
Vermont	98.89	99.60
Virginia[b]	71.62	NA
Washington	58.14	99.84
West Virginia	82.02	100
Wisconsin	95.32	100
Wyoming	79.24	97.96
U.S.	74.18	96.30

NA = not applicable

[a]Alaska: Twenty school districts are dependent on the state, other school districts are dependent on boroughs.

[b]Connecticut, Maryland, Massachusetts, North Carolina, Rhode Island, Tennessee, Virginia: Most school districts in these states are dependent on a city, county, or township.

[c]Hawaii has one statewide school district.

SOURCE: Bureau of the Census, 1995a: http://www.census.gov/govs/school/95tables.pdf and Bureau of the Census, 1995b: http://www.census.gov/govs/www/esti95.html.

TABLE 2-8   State Income and Sales Tax Revenues, 1996

State	Individual Incomes Taxes Percentage of Total Own-Source General Revenues	General Sales Taxes Percentage of Total Own-Source General Revenues
Alabama	20.9	19.1
Alaska	0.0	0.0
Arizona	19.3	35.1
Arkansas	23.9	28.3
California	30.0	27.5
Colorado	33.9	19.7
Connecticut	27.2	25.4
Delaware	23.9	0.0
Florida	0.0	46.7
Georgia	32.8	29.6
Hawaii	24.1	34.5
Idaho	26.7	24.5
Illinois	26.4	23.1
Indiana	30.7	25.3
Iowa	26.5	24.3
Kansas	26.5	27.0
Kentucky	24.6	21.2
Louisiana	15.0	21.0
Maine	27.4	25.4
Maryland	32.4	18.6
Massachusetts	39.4	15.3
Michigan	24.1	27.0
Minnesota	32.9	23.1
Mississippi	15.6	38.5
Missouri	29.4	26.5
Montana	20.8	0.0
Nebraska	25.1	24.4
Nevada	0.0	47.0
New Hampshire	3.1	0.0
New Jersey	23.7	21.6
New Mexico	14.2	28.4
New York	40.0	16.0
North Carolina	34.5	20.8
North Dakota	10.2	19.0
Ohio	28.5	24.1
Oklahoma	25.4	20.3
Oregon	42.6	0.0
Pennsylvania	21.4	23.4
Rhode Island	26.0	20.8
South Carolina	25.6	27.1
South Dakota	0.0	32.2
Tennessee	1.5	45.4
Texas	0.0	36.6

TABLE 2-8   Continued

State	Individual Incomes Taxes Percentage of Total Own-Source General Revenues	General Sales Taxes Percentage of Total Own-Source General Revenues
Utah	28.0	28.7
Vermont	21.6	14.0
Virginia	32.8	15.2
Washington	0.0	46.5
West Virginia	20.1	21.3
Wisconsin	37.6	21.0
Wyoming	0.0	17.1
U.S.	25.4	24.5

SOURCE: Bureau of the Census, 1997: http://www.census/gov/govs/state/

revenue sources for about 50 percent of total own-source revenues and, according to Gold et al. (1995), for about two-thirds of the state revenue for primary and secondary education in 1992. The remainder of state revenue for education is from state corporation income taxes and various excise taxes. The mix varies across states: income taxes contribute more than a third of total state revenue in Massachusetts, New York, Oregon, and Wisconsin, and the sales tax contributes well over a third in Florida, Mississippi, Nevada, Tennessee, and Washington. Some states devote or "earmark" a portion of state revenue to the financing of education: 13 states earmark revenues from the sales tax, 7 from the personal income tax. Although several states have earmarked special revenue sources, such as proceeds from the lottery, for education, the revenues from these sources are typically quite small.

The preceding discussion seems to imply that the property tax is used exclusively by local governments and income and sales taxes exclusively by state governments. However, the correspondence between tax sources and level of government is by no means absolute. In addition to generating revenue from a local property tax, many local governments also generate revenue from income and sales taxes to finance education. In addition, some state governments rely on a statewide property tax for some of their revenue. The recent education finance reform in Michigan, for example, led to what is in effect a statewide property tax system. This overlap in revenue sources makes it essential to distinguish the governmental level at which the revenues are raised (e.g., state or local) as well as the specific taxes used (e.g., income, sales, or property). These distinctions have important implications for the fairness of a state's revenue structure as well as for its efficiency.

The Property Tax Under Attack

For the past few decades, the local property tax has been under attack. These attacks have taken two forms: (1) school finance cases that have declared many property-tax-based state systems as unconstitutional and (2) taxpayer revolts against the property tax. Plaintiffs in school finance cases have attacked the property tax because of its role in generating inequalities in spending across school districts. Because districts that are blessed with large per-pupil property tax bases can raise any given amount of revenue with lower tax rates than those with smaller tax bases, rich districts find it easier to raise revenue for education than do poor districts. Although it may appear that the property tax is the cause of any resulting differentials in spending across districts, we argue in Chapter 8 that the real culprit is not the property tax per se but rather the fact that any local revenue source is being used. Nonetheless, there is no doubt that the resulting disparities in spending across districts tend to give the local property tax a bad name.

Voters have reacted negatively to the property tax when property values rose rapidly and local governments failed to limit the resulting increases in tax bills. In 1978 California voters passed Proposition 13, a constitutional amendment that limited the local property tax rate to 1 percent and capped the growth of assessed values at 2 percent per year, except when parcels were sold. Massachusetts voters followed two years later with their own tax limitation measure, Proposition 2 1/2, which required municipalities to roll back their local property tax rates to 2 1/2 percent and limited the growth of property tax revenues in each jurisdiction to 2 1/2 percent per year.

While other states have avoided such broad based and restrictive measures, according to an Advisory Commission on Intergovernmental Relations (1995b) report, all but four states impose constraints on local governments' ability to raise revenue and/or to spend money. A total of 30 states limit local government tax rates and 27 states limit tax levies; 8 states limit expenditure growth, including spending on schools. Most states have implemented programs to relieve what they perceive as unfair burdens of the local property tax. The Advisory Commission on Intergovernmental Relations (1995a) reports that, as of 1994, 35 states have implemented circuit breaker programs that provide property tax relief to homeowners and (in some states) renters through a state income tax credit. These programs are generally targeted to individuals with low income or who are elderly. As of 1995, 37 states have responded to the political pressure of voters to reduce property tax burdens more generally through the provision of homestead exemptions that reduce property tax burdens for all homeowners. These various limitation and tax relief measures end up reducing the revenue that can be raised by local governments and school districts for education and other public services.

A central question for the committee is whether it is time to eliminate, or substantially reduce reliance on, the property tax as a major source of revenue for public schools.

State Aid to Local School Districts

State-raised revenue for education is typically distributed back to local school districts as state aid, either as basic support or as categorical grants. Basic support comes in three generic forms: flat grants, foundation programs, and guaranteed tax base programs (also called district power equalizing grants). Flat grants are the oldest and the simplest form of aid in that they provide a uniform amount of aid per unit (as measured, for example, by students or teachers). Although the purpose of the flat grant is to ensure some minimum level of education expenditure, historically the grant amounts have been so small that they have not served that function very well. Gold et al. (1995) identify only two states—Delaware and North Carolina—still using flat grants in 1993-94.

A much more common type of school aid is the foundation grant. Foundation aid is similar to flat grants in that it is designed to ensure some basic or foundation level of education spending. However, in practice it differs in two ways. First, the minimum or foundation level of spending is set at a much higher level—one that might represent, for example, the state's view of how much spending would be required for a district to provide an "adequate" level of education. Second, it typically requires that local districts contribute to the foundation spending level in proportion to their capacity to raise revenue for education. In practice this requirement usually means that the amount of state aid (per pupil) given to a district varies inversely with the size of the district's property tax base (per pupil), or by some broader measure of taxable capacity, such as a weighted average of the property tax base and the income of residents. To be more precise, the amount of state aid given to a district is the difference between the foundation spending level and the amount of local tax revenue that the district would generate from its local tax base by taxing itself at a required minimum tax rate. Such aid is lump sum aid, in that the amount of aid does not vary with the district's chosen level of spending. Districts would, however, typically be free to spend more than the foundation amount. As of 1994, 22 states had foundation programs that required local effort and 18 states had foundation programs that did not require local effort (Gold et al., 1995).

Guaranteed tax base or district power equalizing grants are matching grant programs. In the standard program, the state pays for a share of the expenditures in each district, and the share, or the matching rate, varies inversely with the size of the district's property tax base. The aim of a guaranteed tax base program is to make it possible for any district, whatever its tax base, to spend the same amount of money as a district with some target tax base at any chosen tax rate.[8] Each district would be free to tax itself at whatever rate it chose with the assurance that

---

[8]While this goal has superficial appeal, economists are quick to emphasize that it treats the size of the tax base as if it is exogenous, that is independent of the district's decision about how much to spend on education. In addition, it may not lead to the desired goal of wealth neutrality.

the combination of the revenue it generated locally at that rate and the amount of state aid it received would equal what the district with the target tax base could raise at that tax rate. The logic of such a program is that very wealthy districts—those with tax bases larger than the target base—would face negative matching rates and, instead of receiving aid, would have to pay money to the state. That is, the price to them of raising and spending an additional dollar on education would exceed one dollar. In practice, however, the guaranteed tax base formula is typically overridden so that all districts receive some small amount of state aid.

In contrast to aid for general support, categorical aid is given for specific expenditure categories, such as special education, transportation, buildings, and equipment. Categorical aid programs frequently do not incorporate capacity measures into the distribution formulas. However, state categorical aid for special education, as well as many of the federal categorical aid programs, are targeted toward districts with disproportionate numbers of needy students, where need is defined by learning disability, other physical disability, or poverty.

The Federal Role

The federal government has a relatively small direct role as well as a large indirect role in financing primary and secondary education. Direct programs of federal aid are designed to help achieve goals of greater equity and, more recently, higher student performance. In addition to the traditional federal emphasis on aid for disadvantaged students, new funds have been provided through the Goals 2000 program ($668 million in FY 1998) for grants to assist states with their programs to raise the educational achievement of all students (U.S. Department of Education, 1999a: Table 361). The small amount of these funds belies the larger role for the federal government envisioned in the Goals 2000 legislation. In that role, the federal government would use the funds appropriated for this purpose to induce the states to work toward national educational goals.

The federal government plays a much larger but indirect financing role through the deductibility of state and local income and property taxes from personal income subject to federal taxes. The deduction of state and local property taxes alone amounted to about $18 billion in 1999 (Office of Management and Budget, 1999). Because this tax break is in the form of deductions, the value to individuals rises with the income of the taxpayer and is dependent on the itemizing of deductions. The value to individuals also depends on state and local tax burdens, which vary across state and districts. Deductibility is a benefit to school districts in that it lowers the effective tax price to local taxpayers for education and therefore may make them more willing to spend on education. However, the distributional effects of providing assistance in this manner are worth noting. Greater benefits accrue to districts with larger proportions of taxpayers who itemize their deductions. Such districts are typically the ones with wealthy taxpayers who own their own homes. Few benefits accrue to large cities populated disproportionately by low-income renters.

Thus, the direct federal role has historically been very small and targeted to specific groups. Recently the federal government has tried to play a larger role through the adoption of funding mechanisms designed to influence how states and districts might go about improving the overall quality of education. A major question, addressed in Chapter 8, is whether it is time to expand the federal role—especially on the financing side.

STRATEGIES FOR MEETING THE GOALS

Policy makers can alter school finance systems in four generic ways as they attempt to drive the education system toward greater achievement and more efficiency. Which of these broad generic strategies are preferred depends on policy goals, judgments about the efficacy of various strategies to achieve those goals, and an understanding of the unintended side effects of various strategies.

During the final third of the twentieth century, education finance reformers emphasized a strategy of *reducing funding inequities and (more recently) inadequacies* among school districts. This reform strategy was consistent with their dominant objective at the time, which was to reduce the large fiscal disparities resulting from the tradition of local funding of education. Since significant disparities and inadequacies remain, this strategy will continue to be of interest, although its focus may need to change given the new interest in enhancing student achievement.

The generic strategy of reducing inequities and inadequacies in school finance also applies to the goal of raising revenues fairly. On the revenue side of the finance system, this strategy might be pursued via policies aimed at altering the level of government (e.g., local, state, or federal) at which revenues are raised or altering the types of tax (e.g., property, income, or sales tax) or other revenue sources that are used. However, any policy changes designed to enhance fairness in revenue raising will also need to be evaluated as well in terms of their effects on the efficiency with which revenues are raised and education is provided.

Meeting the new challenge of aligning school finance with the goals of enhancing achievement for all students and reducing the nexus between family background and student achievement will undoubtedly require increased attention in the years ahead to additional strategies for reforming school finance. One possible strategy is *investing more resources in developing capacity*. This refers not only to the capacity of the formal education system to provide services but also to the capacity of students to learn. Investing in capacity-building will facilitate the achievement of the goals only if the investment will generate greater future returns in the form of student achievement than will spending the money in other ways. As is the case with any investment policy, the resources to be invested might represent new funds or funds transferred from some other, presumably less effective, use.

A third generic strategy for school finance reform would emphasize *altering incentives to make performance count.* This strategy embraces changes in incentives that are designed to operate primarily within the existing system of governance. Changes in incentives that might result from major changes in governance and management structures, such as the introduction of a significantly greater role for schools or parents (or both) in finance decisions, are reserved for the fourth strategy. Strategy 3 emphasizes the development of accountability and funding systems that give teachers, schools, or students incentives to focus on student achievement.

A fourth generic strategy would focus on *empowering schools or parents or both to make decisions about the use of public funds.* This strategy embraces finance reforms that would promote major changes in governance and management by shifting the locus of decision making. It represents the most significant break with current school finance practice because it promises significant change in who gets to decide how education dollars are spent. Not surprisingly, then, it can be expected to arouse the most heated passions, with contentiousness related to how far particular policy options consistent with the strategy (school-site autonomy, for example, versus vouchers usable at both public and private schools) move decision making away from familiar patterns. It is likely, therefore, that even more than with the other strategies, the position individuals take on policy options consistent with strategy 4 will typically rest on more than the evidence about what the strategy might contribute to fairness and productivity. Views about the desirability of shifting decision making on the grounds that it will increase student achievement are balanced with additional considerations, such as how broken the current educational system is perceived to be, support for the tradition of public education, and attitudes toward the freedom for families to choose the children with whom their children will associate.

These four generic strategies reflect the broad choices available to policy makers as they debate specific policy options for reforming education finance programs. The four strategies do not encompass every specific policy that might be proposed for improving the finance system,[9] nor do policy options fit neatly and unambiguously within one or another strategy as defined here. There is also

---

[9]Nor do they directly address many reform strategies, such as changes in curriculum or the way it is taught, that are not primarily financial in nature but that people closely involved in the provision of education services might deem crucial to educational improvement. Likewise, they do not address changes in governance, such as the recent moves in some states to give direct control of selected big-city school districts to mayors. Mayoral control (being tried in Boston, Baltimore, Cleveland, and Chicago) clearly alters lines of accountability, but there is nothing inherent structurally in this governance chance that necessarily alters the distribution of financial resources.

an element of artificiality in the separation of the four strategies, in that policy makers do not and should not consider strategies and options in isolation. Finance policies ought to reflect the interrelatedness of the various facets of the finance system and the possibility (some would say likelihood) that it will take many complementary changes for reform to have its intended results. Nonetheless, the strategies are useful as a framework for organizing the discussion later in the report of major options for changing the school finance system.

To provide the foundation for the analysis of how these generic finance strategies might be harnessed to the goals for a good finance system, we turn now to a detailed discussion of the concepts of fairness and productivity as they have played out over time in the legislative, legal, policy and scholarly arenas.

Part II

Fairness and Productivity in School Finance

School finance policy was under intense scrutiny in the last third of the 20th century. Until comparatively recently, reformers concentrated on a strategy of reducing large disparities in available revenues and spending levels among school districts, which were the legacy of a school finance system originally built on local control. Using school finance policy to improve educational outcomes is a relatively new objective. Identifying policy options that will foster this objective hinges on having good information about how to use resources to improve the performance of schools and students. Researchers have increasingly focused their efforts on developing such knowledge. At present, however, the results are best viewed as tentative and contingent.

The recent history of efforts to understand and improve fairness and productivity, the subject of Part II, helps explain why existing finance policies took the shape they did and provides lessons that will be instructive in Part III in evaluating current proposals for reforming education finance.

3

Equity I—Spending on Schools

The United States is a country built on a perception of itself as a "land of opportunity" with "liberty and justice for all." Education has long been viewed as the major route to a good society and to improving the life chances of individual citizens. "Faith in the power of education . . . has helped to persuade citizens to create the most comprehensive system of public schooling in the world" (Tyack and Cuban, 1995:3).

Paradoxically, however, throughout the nation's history, Americans have tolerated great disparities in access to this pathway to opportunity. Until the last half of the 20th century, these disparities were often unacknowledged, hidden behind an aggregate picture of progress. This apparent march of progress, though, left many people behind. At mid-century (Tyack and Cuban, 1995:22): "A probe behind aggregated national statistics and the upbeat rhetoric of [school reformers] reveals major disparities in educational opportunities. These inequalities stemmed from differences in place of residence, family occupation and income, race, and gender, and from physical and mental handicaps. At mid-century American public education was not a seamless system of roughly similar common schools but instead a diverse and unequal set of institutions that reflected deeply embedded and social inequalities. Americans from all walks of life may have shared a common faith in individual and societal progress through education, but they hardly participated equally in its benefits."

As Tyack and Cuban indicate, manifestations of inequality were everywhere. In 1940 huge differences existed between rural and urban schools, magnified by large regional differences in educational funding. Both educational spending on and the educational attainment of rural children lagged behind their urban coun-

67

terparts. Two out of three blacks resided in rural areas, overwhelmingly in the South where regional poverty exacerbated racial discrimination. Among whites living in cities, whether or not students attended high school was strongly influenced by the income level of their families. Programs for children with disabilities and those with other special educational needs served fewer than 1 percent of all students in 1938. Compulsory attendance laws frequently excluded children with disabilities.

Inattention to inequality in education was about to change. The catalyst was the U.S. Supreme Court's decision in *Brown v. Board of Education*, 347 U.S. 483 (1954), declaring racial segregation in public schools illegal. The justices' declaration that "it is doubtful that any child may reasonably be expected to succeed in life if he is denied the opportunity of an education" became the springboard for a broad assault on differences in educational opportunity related to the socioeconomic, racial, and physical characteristics of students and their families. Much of the history of school reform in the latter half of this century, especially in the 1960s and 1970s, had as a central concern reducing educational disparities.

Many, though certainly not all, of these disparities related to money. Readily apparent and large differences in spending on education from district to district became one major target of change. Reformers sought new state and federal programs to provide additional funds for educating previously underserved or unserved groups. They also launched legal attacks on the underlying theory and structure of school finance. The existing system, which relied heavily on localities whose wealth and willingness to tax themselves varied greatly, appeared to make the quality of a child's education dependent on where he or she happened to live. Although, as we shall see, the relationship between spending on education and the quality of schooling has been the subject of much debate, reformers nevertheless argued that money provided the most "convincingly quantifiable" standard for judging the availability of education across districts. They further argued on grounds of fairness against postponing reform until the cost-quality debate could be settled. As Coons et al. (1970:30) put it: "if money is inadequate to improve education, the residents of poor districts should at least have an equal opportunity to be disappointed by its failure."

This chapter explores the pursuit of equity in school finance since mid-century, which until recently emphasized reducing spending disparities tied to the place of residence and increasing spending to meet special educational needs. The story is complicated to tell chronologically, because reforms aimed at revising the fundamental reliance of American schools on locally raised revenues (which have largely been pursued through the courts) have proceeded simultaneously with legislative and legal efforts to overcome specific education inequities through more piecemeal categorical-type programs. Examining the legal attack on traditional school finance mechanisms has the advantage of crystallizing a number of key finance and constitutional issues; so, after some comments on the meaning of equity, we take up that strategy first. We then describe a number of other developments in the past half-century related to the equity of educational spending.

Finally, and most importantly for the subsequent policy discussion in Part III, we assess what all this has accomplished in terms of reducing educational inequities as defined by spending disparities and in terms of equity issues as they are being reconceptualized today. What we will see is that much has been accomplished in terms of extending educational opportunities to all students, but that great disparities in education spending still remain. The biggest disparities, those among states, remain largely untouched by reforms that have focused on individual state finance systems. Inequalities in finance have proven stubbornly persistent, in large part because reducing or eliminating them requires steps that fly in the face of other values Americans hold dear, such as local control of schools and the freedom of parents to provide for their children.

Moreover, dissatisfaction has grown with school finance approaches that fail to address directly problems of growing public concern, notably the academic achievement levels of American students and the worsening conditions facing children who live in some central-city neighborhoods. The concept of equity motivating school finance reform today is shifting in emphasis from differences in the amount of money spent to the adequacy of the education that this money provides. The next chapter explores this newer approach to equity and the possibilities and challenges it poses for school finance.

THE MEANING OF EQUITY

Equity, a concept embodying notions of justice, impartiality, and fairness, is a widely shared value in American society. Yet equity lends itself to a variety of specific definitions reflecting the different goals that can be sought under the "equity" banner. Equity may, for example, involve equality (an equal distribution of something), but it need not (Monk, 1990; Putterman et al., 1998). An equitable distribution may actually involve substantial inequality, as for example when "extra" resources are provided to a group believed to have extraordinary needs. In this case, equity may be seen as providing unequal inputs in order to achieve equal outputs or outcomes.

Different definitions of equity mix and weigh central distinctions in differing ways. Researchers, legislators, lawyers and judges, and the public have used various mixes as they debate equity-based reforms, resulting in conflicting views about what constitutes fairness. Therefore, it is essential to clarify the definitional issues and to indicate how different equity definitions influence school finance discussions. Understanding the various meanings and goals that are associated with different definitions of equity can illuminate the accomplishments and shortcomings of prior attempts to make school finance more equitable and why this objective has proven so difficult to accomplish.

Berne and Stiefel (1984, 1999) have identified five key distinctions that can be drawn among equity definitions as they are applied to school finance systems:

1. Who is the focus of concern: school-age children, taxpayers, or both?
2. What is the unit of analysis: the nation, states, districts, schools, or students?
3. Which stage in the "production" of education is emphasized: inputs (dollars and/or real resources), processes, outputs, or outcomes?
4. Which groups are of special interest: students with low income, minority status, disabilities; low-income or low-wealth taxpayers?
5. How is the equity of the school finance system being evaluated: ex ante (judged by the equity of statutory design elements) or ex post (judged by the actual outcomes that result from behavioral changes of school districts as they respond to the design elements of a school finance system)?

The answers to these questions embodied in school finance systems have evolved as public debate has occurred over the nature of spending and outcome differences in education and as reformers attempted to find remedies for perceived inequities that could be successfully enacted through the political process.

School finance equity is not a new concern. Efforts to link methods of school finance to the fairness of the educational system can be traced back to the beginning of the 20th century and the work of Ellwood P. Cubberley (Guthrie et al., 1988:3). But school finance inequities came into sharp focus in the late 1960s, as education reformers began to realize that the promise of educational opportunity offered by the *Brown* decision was being thwarted by unequal per-pupil expenditures. Desegregation alone was insufficient to address the "inequalities in education [that] continue to be visited upon Negro children, especially in large cities," because of spending disparities (Wise, 1968:3). Interestingly, urban problems rather than rural poverty now loomed large, reflecting the mass migration of blacks to the cities following World War II. School finance inequities linked to race were now a national, and not primarily a southern, issue.

In the aftermath of *Brown*, reformers also became increasingly intolerant of the slow pace with which the executive and legislative branches of government moved to equalize opportunities. For the first time, courts became central players in school finance. In this area as in others, individuals and groups turned increasingly to the judicial system to obtain public benefits they were unable to gain in the political arena. Although legislative and executive branch officials generally determine how complex school finance issues are resolved, since about 1970 the framework for their policy making has increasingly been influenced by the rulings in court cases. Carr and Fuhrman (1999) explore the political reasons why school finance reformers have frequently found the courts more receptive to their arguments than the executive and legislative branches of government.

Our examination of equity in educational finance begins by tracing the development of school finance litigation carried out in its name. School finance reform was strongly influenced by the success in the courts of an approach to equity called "wealth neutrality," which concentrated attention on the spending disparities between school districts in a given state and in particular showed how they related to the variation in property tax bases (Minorini and Sugarman, 1999). It emphasized student equity, specifying that no relationship should exist between the education of children and the property wealth of the district in which they reside, while also embodying the concept that taxpayers should be taxed at equal rates to fund equal education (generally defined as equal spending) per child.[1] The wealth-neutrality approach has focused heavily on inputs to the educational system; both ex ante and ex post measures of it were developed.

PURSUING FINANCE EQUITY THROUGH THE COURTS

Efforts to reform school finance through the courts have had two distinguishing features. First, until recently, they focused mainly on attacking geographically based disparities in school spending that result from dependence on local wealth-based property taxes. Second, school finance litigation has taken place primarily in state courts under state law, a surprising venue given that federal courts and federal law have played the central role in lawsuits concerning other aspects of public education, such as school desegregation and student rights to free expression. The reasons reformers focused on wealth-based disparities in education spending and pursued their ends in state courts lie in two major events of the late 1960s and early 1970s that had immense influence on how equity in education finance was defined and pursued in the ensuing decades. The first was the publication of *Equality of Educational Opportunity* (Coleman et al., 1966). The second was the California Supreme Court's decision ruling against the state and its method of funding education in *Serrano v. Priest (Serrano I)*, 487 P.2d 1241 (Cal. 1971).

Equality of Educational Opportunity set off an academic and public debate that continues today by calling into question the relationship between resource equality and equality of educational outcomes with its finding that students'

---

[1]This concept of equity for taxpayers differs from the concept of taxpayer equity typically found in the public finance literature. From a public finance perspective, a system would be judged fair to taxpayers on the basis of either an ability to pay or a benefit principle, both of which are defined in Chapter 8. In general, neither the courts nor advocates nor researchers in school finance have focused on the public finance concepts of equity. If they had, the remedies proposed or legislated for taxpayers might well have been quite different, giving attention to patterns of public finance incidence, such as progressive, regressive, or proportional tax burden, that have not been much considered in the development of school finance formulas. See Chapter 8 for a further discussion of taxpayer equity issues from a public finance perspective.

family and other background characteristics were more important than school resources in determining student achievement. While its findings about the role of schools were then and remain controversial (and are increasingly being questioned by scholars evaluating new evidence with new analytical tools), uncertainty over the link between resource and outcome inequalities encouraged challengers of school finance systems to focus on the basic fairness of spending disparities (and thus on school inputs) rather than attempting to link spending levels to specific educational outcomes.

Serrano I was the first successful state court case related to state school finance equity. Based on wealth-neutrality arguments, state court judges in California overturned the state's existing system of school finance. Significantly, in the light of what would soon transpire in the U.S. Supreme Court, plaintiffs claimed that California's wealth-based system for raising educational revenues violated the equal protection clauses of both the U.S. Constitution and the California constitution. Dependence on local property taxes as a primary source of school funding, they argued, resulted in average per-pupil spending differences in the 1969-70 school year ranging from $407 to $2,586 in elementary school districts to $722 to $1,761 in high school districts (Franklin, 1987).

San Antonio Independent School District v. Rodriguez, 411 U.S. 1 (1973), made some of the same arguments as did *Serrano I* on behalf of a class of children throughout the state of Texas living in districts with low per-pupil property valuations. It differed, however, in that the case was brought in federal court and relied on the U.S. Constitution alone. Plaintiffs were successful in a lower court, and it appeared for a short time that the U.S. Constitution would indeed play a central role in shaping America's school finance system. However, *Rodriguez* was rejected on appeal by the U.S. Supreme Court, in part on the grounds that education was not a "fundamental interest" under the U.S. Constitution that warranted breaching long-standing patterns of federalism and involving the federal courts in state school finance issues.

While *Rodriguez* closed the door to school finance reform via the federal courts, *Serrano I* opened one in the state courts. Although the California Supreme Court emphasized the U.S. Constitution's Fourteenth Amendment in its ruling, a few additional words noted that the state constitution's equal protection clause also was applicable (*Serrano I*, 1971:1249, note 11). In its 1976 decision evaluating the sufficiency of the legislature's response to *Serrano I*, the state supreme court explicitly held that the federal equal protection analysis it had advanced in *Serrano I* was equally applicable to the California constitution's equal protection clause (see *Serrano v. Priest (Serrano II)*, 557 P.2d 929, Cal. 1976). *Serrano* thus paved the way for widespread legal challenges to school finance systems on the basis of the wealth-neutrality principle, while *Rodriguez* ensured that school finance litigation would flourish in state rather than federal courts and that state-by-state rather than national solutions to finance equity concerns would be pursued.

State constitutions provided grounds for school finance suits because most contain one or more provisions that either parallel the U.S. Constitution's equal protection clause or have been interpreted to afford similar protections (Williams, 1985). In addition, state constitutions, unlike their federal counterpart, contain a variety of so-called education clauses specifying education as a state function and requiring legislatures to provide a public school system that is described in various ways, often including "thorough and efficient" or "ample."[2]

Numerous lawsuits followed in *Serrano*'s wake. By 1998, legal cases had been brought against school finance systems in 43 states (Minorini and Sugarman, 1999). In 19 states, supreme courts found school funding systems unconstitutional. Litigation or the threat of litigation sometimes spurred changes in state financing systems even when there was no formal court order present. In nine states (in 1998) where plaintiffs lost their initial cases, further complaints were filed.

Plaintiffs who won in state supreme courts frequently found themselves back in court again and again, challenging the remedies crafted by state legislatures. Here, too, developments in California forecast what was in store in many states: repeated appeals to courts to overturn legislative responses to court orders. In *Serrano II*, the California court not only upheld its prior decision based exclusively on state rather than on federal constitutional grounds but also held that school finance legislation passed in response to *Serrano I* was insufficient. (It failed to meet the court's standard for equity, which required that differences in per-pupil spending, exclusive of categorical aids and programs for children with special educational needs, such as disabilities or limited proficiency in English, be no greater among most districts than $100 in 1971 dollars.) New Jersey, perhaps the most infamous example of repeated returns to court, went 25 years from the plaintiffs' first supreme court victory (*Robinson v. Cahill (Robinson I)*, 303 A.2d 273, N.J. 1973), to what appears to be the final settlement in the successor case (*Abbott v. Burke*, 710 A.2d 450, N.J. 1998), while in West Virginia legal challenges begun in 1979 were still subject to litigation in 1998.

Legal Theories in Support of Reform

The wealth-neutrality principle successfully argued in *Serrano I* was not the first legal theory put forward by scholars and legal activists hoping to attack school finance inequity in the courts. All early reformers focused their attention on the U.S. Constitution's Fourteenth Amendment provision that states not deny to individuals "equal protection of the law," but they developed differing notions

---

[2]State education clauses are collected in an appendix to Hubsch (1992). Some scholars (McUsic, 1991; Thro, 1993) have attempted to categorize state education clauses based on their wording so as to be able to predict results in school finance cases, but there appears to be little correlation between the language per se and the likelihood of success in a given suit (Underwood, 1995).

of what equal protection might require. In addition to wealth neutrality, proposals included ideas such as one scholar, one dollar; geographic uniformity; and unequal student need.

Wise (1968:4) linked school finance to the work of Coleman and others on equal educational opportunity by asking "whether the absence of equal educational opportunity within a state, as evidenced by unequal per-pupil expenditures, may constitute a denial by the state of the equal protection of its laws." His theoretical standard—that the quality of a child's education in the public schools of a state should not depend on where he or she happens to live—became a central argument in *Serrano*-type cases. Drawing on two important judicial developments in the 1960s (school desegregation and reapportionment cases), he argued that public education was a "fundamental interest" for equal protection purposes and that a standard of *one scholar, one dollar* (similar to the one man, one vote principle of the reapportionment cases) should apply to education spending.

Looking at the same unequal spending patterns, Horowitz (1966; Horowitz and Neitring, 1968) turned to a different area of the law from which he developed a similar principle of *geographic uniformity*. Horowitz argued that, like a state's law governing murder, school spending should not vary within a state based on geography alone. Unlike the one scholar, one dollar principle, however, which seemed to imply uniform per-pupil spending statewide, Horowitz's principle would permit district-to-district spending differences that might result, for example, from a legislative decision to spend more on children with disabilities or at-risk children, who might not reside in equal proportions in all districts.

Some legal aid lawyers who tackled the issue found both the Wise and Horowitz principles ill-suited to their purposes. They developed an alternative theory that focused primarily on *unequal student need*—and the resulting imperative, as they saw it, to spend more than average on the schooling of low-achieving children from low-income families, many of whom now lived in urban areas. The basic thrust of the legal aid lawyers' need-based constitutional claim was that rich and poor children have a right to have their educational needs "equally" met. This principle would not just allow but would in fact require unequal spending in the name of equity.

This need-based constitutional claim was actually the first to be litigated, but courts found it insufficient to justify a ruling against school finance systems, in part because it was then seen as judicially unmanageable. Federal district courts in Illinois (*McInnis v. Shapiro*, 1968) and Virginia (*Burrus v. Wilkerson*, 1969) rejected the claimants' theory on the grounds that they could not discern judicially manageable standards to gauge what students' needs were and whether they were being met. On appeal, the U.S. Supreme Court affirmed both lower court rulings without comment.[3]

---

[3]See *McInnis v. Shapiro*, 293 F. Supp. 327 (N.D. Il. 1968), *aff'd sub nom.*, *McInnis v. Ogilvie*, 349 U.S. 322 (1969); *Burrus v. Wilkerson*, 310 F. Supp. 572 (W.D. Va. 1969), *aff'd per curiam*, 397 U.S. 44 (1970).

At about the same time, Coons, Clune, and Sugarman (Coons et al., 1969, 1970) developed yet a fourth legal strategy for attacking school finance inequities, one which later came to be referred to as *fiscal or wealth neutrality*. They cast the key shortcoming of America's school finance system in a new way: the constitutional evil was that some school districts had little property wealth to tax in order to support their local schools, whereas other districts had lots of it. Although states offset some of the wealthier districts' advantage through a variety of state aid formulas designed to ensure all pupils some minimum level of spending, enormous wealth-based disparities in spending remained. Furthermore, less wealthy districts tended to impose on themselves higher tax rates per dollar of assessed value of property than did their wealthier counterparts. Yet despite the greater "effort" made through higher tax rates (and notwithstanding the state aid they received), property-poor districts had less money per pupil to spend. This wealth discrimination, argued the Coons team, was unconstitutional. They dubbed their core legal principle Proposition I: the quality of public education, measured most commonly by looking at dollar inputs, may not be a function of wealth other than the wealth of the state as a whole.

Proposition I, or wealth neutrality, appeared to offer several legal and political advantages over the other theories that might undergird school finance challenges: it could be readily measured and would be relatively easy for the courts to apply, unlike the need-based theory of the legal aid advocates; it left room for the state to choose among several finance options; and it allowed geographic-based differences in spending. For example, if two districts were equally wealthy, it would not be unconstitutional for one to choose to spend more than the other by taxing itself more. This held out hope for reducing the political battles over school finance, which for a long time had pitted less wealthy districts against wealthier ones as they contested for state funds.

To demonstrate how a new school finance scheme could meet their principle of fiscal neutrality and yet tolerate geographically different spending levels, the Coons team developed an ex ante measure of equity, which, they argued, would be achieved by state aid that was district power equalizing.[4] Such aid promotes equity in the ex ante sense that districts levying the same tax rate would have the same amount to spend, regardless of their property tax wealth.

Wealth neutrality was no panacea for all the school finance ills perceived by critics of the existing system. Some objected to district power equalizing, arguing that a child's education should not depend on the willingness of voters in the community to make a certain tax effort in support of education. Advocates for poor children living in big cities found wealth neutrality unattractive because, in their view, it did not sufficiently address the particular needs of urban residents.

---

[4]The measure can be mathematically equivalent to a percentage equalizing funding system, which had existed before in impure forms in New York, for example, but it was seen as new in the 1970s.

Low property wealth per pupil might be a good proxy for concentrations of family poverty in some districts, and, indeed, the low-wealth districts tended to be home to lower-income families. But this certainly was not the case in every district. In fact, many large cities were relatively wealthy, often containing some well-to-do families and valuable commercial property. As a result, despite having many poor residents, large cities often spent more on their students than the statewide average per pupil, although usually considerably less than was spent in nearby wealthy suburbs.[5]

Post-*Serrano* School Finance Litigation

Litigation has occupied a central place in efforts to reform school finance in the 30 years since *Serrano*. Plaintiffs and defendants have each had their share of victories and defeats, and the reasoning of courts in both instances is instructive about the possibilities and limitations of reform through appeal to constitutional guarantees. For 20 years after *Serrano*, traditional finance equity claims based more or less on the wealth-neutrality principle dominated the arguments made and evidence presented. Several notable exceptions occurred, however, with decisions in New Jersey, Washington, and West Virginia in the 1970s foreshadowing a new legal theory that would reemerge with renewed vigor in the 1990s. After a period of comparative quiet on the legal front in the 1980s, victories by plaintiffs in Texas, Montana, and Kentucky in one year (1989) marked the beginning of a new period of judicial activism. Moreover, the Kentucky Supreme Court, in ruling the entire state education system inadequate, gave reformers hope that courts might be prepared to address not only spending disparities but also the adequacy of the educational opportunities available to students.

Equal Protection and a Right to Education

Many of the state court decisions striking down school finance schemes following *Serrano* relied on equal protection clauses in state constitutions (Underwood, 1995). It became clear early that, despite similar wording, a state court might interpret its own constitution's equal protection clause differently from that of the U.S. Constitution. The state court might declare education to be

---

[5]It is noteworthy that none of the early school finance cases (nor most subsequent ones) was cast as a matter of racial discrimination. The decision to leave race out was partly based on the fact that, with the end of the system of separate black and white schools in the wake of *Brown v. Board of Education*, 347 U.S. 483 (1954), no formal structural discrimination existed against blacks in the funding of public schools, and it was partly a matter of uncertainty as to whether blacks as a class would be helped by successful school finance litigation. Advocates believed that black children living in low-spending districts would benefit, but many blacks were increasingly living in cities where the school finance problems were more complex than simply having a low property tax base and, as a result, spending less per pupil than elsewhere in the state.

a fundamental interest for purposes of state constitutional law, even if that proposition does not apply in federal constitutional litigation. A fundamental interest is a right that is explicitly or implicitly guaranteed under the applicable state or federal constitution. Rights that are fundamental are, when infringed, subject to a test of strict judicial scrutiny. Under that test, the state or federal law infringing upon that right must be justified by a compelling state interest. Alternatively, if the right infringed is not fundamental, courts may instead ask whether there is a "rational basis" for the unequal treatment.

Gradually, state courts have begun to rely in whole or in part on state constitutional provisions specific to education in deciding school finance cases. Some of those decisions use the state constitution's education clause to buttress the equal protection analysis, relying in part on the presence and content of the education clause to support treating education as a fundamental right (Enrich, 1995). Others, however, interpret the education clause independently—as itself requiring some degree of equity in educational funding or opportunity (Underwood, 1995; Enrich, 1995).

One state's education clause was singled out for attention in what was, after *Serrano*, the most notable early case won by plaintiffs, although the difference in legal argument had little practical significance. In 1973, the New Jersey Supreme Court found that the state's school funding system—which, like California's, resulted in property-poor districts spending half as much per pupil as wealthy districts—violated the state constitution. The court based its decision exclusively on the state's education clause, whose wording guaranteed to all students a "thorough and efficient system" of public education (*Robinson I*). Initially, however, the court seemed to treat the education clause as calling for the same kind of remedies—reductions in interdistrict spending disparities based on wealth—as *Serrano*-type cases. But in the late 1980s and 1990s, additional litigation in New Jersey would incorporate both the strict dollar equalization and the educational opportunity strands of the *Robinson*-era decisions. Then, the court would require that the state both equalize the spending in the poorest districts to that of the wealthiest districts and provide additional funding to the poorer districts to account for the extra educational needs of children from disadvantaged backgrounds (*Abbott v. Burke*, 643 A.2d 575, N.J. 1994).

New Jersey was not alone in presaging an eventual movement away from a narrow focus on wealth neutrality as the desired approach to school finance equity, even though wealth neutrality dominated the school finance literature and the scholarly and policy debates of the 1970s and 1980s. Court decisions in Washington (*Seattle v. State of Washington*, 585 P.2d 71, Wash. 1978) and West Virginia (*Pauley v. Kelly*, 255 S.E.2d 859, W. Va. 1979) also shifted thinking about equity away from the relative amounts of money available to spend on pupils (and how this related to where these pupils lived) and toward a concern for the level of resources necessary to enable students to have a fair opportunity to achieve desired educational outcomes.

In *Seattle*, the state supreme court interpreted the education clause of the Washington constitution to require that the state fund schools in a manner that allowed them to "equip our children for their role as citizens and as potential competitors in today's market as well as in the market place of ideas . . . to participate intelligently and effectively in our open political system . . . to exercise their First Amendment freedoms both as sources and receivers of information and . . . to be able to inquire, to study, to evaluate and to gain maturity and understanding" (*Seattle*, 1978:94)." Characterizing those outcomes as "broad guidelines," the court noted that "the effective teaching and opportunities for learning these essential skills . . . make up [the] minimum of education that is constitutionally required" (*Seattle*, 1978:95).

In 1979, the West Virginia Supreme Court took the notion of equal and adequate educational opportunities a step further (see *Pauley*). Like the Washington court, the West Virginia court identified a set of broad goals for a constitutionally valid education system: "[A] thorough and efficient system of schools . . . develops, as best the state of education expertise allows, the minds, bodies and social morality of its charges to prepare them for useful and happy occupations, recreation and citizenship, and does so economically" (*Pauley*, 1979:877). The state supreme court then went on to specify what such an education would accomplish in terms of student outcomes, ranging from literacy to social ethics. Following these guidelines, a lower trial court declared the system to be inequitable and inadequate and ordered the legislature to develop a comprehensive plan to bring the entire system into constitutional compliance (Franklin, 1987). The programmatic remedies sparked by the high court's decisions went beyond mere tinkering with the state school finance formula, and instead restructured the entire state education system; these remedies and their implementation were still being litigated in 1998.

Rejected Suits

Despite the notable success of school finance challenges in a few states in the 1970s, courts frequently rejected plaintiffs' efforts to overthrow finance systems. Cases won by the defenders of existing systems in the 1970s reflected judicial concerns that indicated the complexity of the issues involved and that would stymie efforts to reform school finance via lawsuit in the coming decades. Notable cases were argued in Idaho, Oregon, and Pennsylvania.

The Idaho Supreme Court in *Thompson v. Engelking*, 537 P.2d. 635 (Idaho 1975), expressed concern about judicial intrusion into matters traditionally reserved for the legislature. As the court noted, agreeing with the plaintiffs' contentions "would be an unwise and unwarranted entry into the controversial area of public school financing, whereby this court would convene as a 'super-legislature,' legislating in a turbulent field of social, economic and political policy" (*Thompson*, 1975:640). The court also expressed some doubt as to whether equal funding had a significant relationship to educational quality (*Thompson*, 1975:341-42).

The Oregon Supreme Court's 1976 decision in *Olsen v. State*, 554 P.2d 139 (Or. 1976), rejected a school finance challenge primarily on the ground that the state's asserted interest in promoting local control justified the disparities in funding produced by the finance system. Unlike the *Serrano* court, the Oregon court held that the fact that some districts in the state may have less local control over spending because they have access to fewer resources does not necessarily lead to a conclusion that the state equal protection clause has been violated. Among other things, the Oregon court feared that if disparities in local governments' ability to raise revenue for education led to an equal protection violation, that same logic might be used to attack disparities in resource availability for other government functions, such as police and fire protection.

In *Danson v. Casey*, 399 A.2d 360 (Pa. 1979), the court rejected a claim by the city school district of Philadelphia that the state's heavy reliance on locally generated revenues to fund schools, combined with the city school district's inability to raise such revenues, had led to a budget crisis in the school district requiring dramatic cutbacks in the educational programs offered to students. The plaintiffs contended that the finance system violated the Pennsylvania constitution's education clause, which required the state to provide for the "maintenance and support of a thorough and efficient system of public education to serve the needs of the Commonwealth" (Pa. Const. Article III, sec. 14). The court noted that Philadelphia spent more per pupil than a large proportion of the other school districts in the state and questioned the plaintiffs' alleged injury. The Pennsylvania court appeared to suggest that its "thorough and efficient" clause at most might ensure pupils some sort of minimum or basic level of educational opportunities. But the plaintiffs failed to allege that this basic level of educational opportunity had been denied.

Judicial concerns that resulted in the rejection of school finance cases in the 1970s dominated the legal landscape throughout most of the 1980s. From 1980 to 1988, two state high court decisions invalidated school finance systems, while eight upheld systems as constitutional.

When faced with state equal protection clause challenges, most courts took the view that education was not a fundamental right entitled to strict scrutiny under their state constitution (Underwood, 1995) and upheld existing finance systems and the local control they fostered. So too, in response to arguments based on education clauses, most courts during this period took a very narrow view of what those provisions required of the state legislatures (Underwood, 1995), refusing to mandate adoption of a particular school funding system or to disallow reliance on locally generated revenue as a source of funding for schools. In rejecting traditional equity claims, many of the decisions of the 1980s also expressed frustration that plaintiffs did not allege what they considered to be sufficient injury. Several criticized plaintiffs for failing to demonstrate that, merely by having less money spent on them, students in property-poor school districts were denied their constitutional rights. These decisions opened the door to future cases that moved away from an emphasis on wealth neutrality to allegations that the state was failing to afford districts sufficient resources to provide students with the basic, minimum, or adequate educational opportunity required by the state's education clause (Verstegen and Whitney, 1995; Enrich, 1995).

Renewed Legal Activism

Equity concerns and legal activism gained renewed prominence in 1989, when courts in Texas, Montana, and Kentucky declared their state systems of finance—and in the case of Kentucky, the entire state education system—to be inequitable and unconstitutional. In Texas, the court relied on a traditional finance equity rationale (*Edgewood v. Kirby*, 777 S.W.2d 391, Tex. 1989), embracing wealth-neutrality theory in the very state in which the U.S. Supreme Court had rejected it 16 years earlier. The plaintiffs' evidence focused on disparities in property wealth between the wealthiest and poorest communities in the state—reflecting a 700-to-1 ratio at the extreme—and the resulting disparities in per-pupil expenditures—ranging from $2,112 to $19,333 (*Edgewood*, 1989:392). Unlike *Serrano*, however, the new Texas decision relied not on the state constitution's equal protection requirements but rather on its education clause, which required that the state make "suitable" provision for an "efficient" system of free public schools allowing for a "general diffusion of knowledge."

The court deferred to the legislature to devise a constitutionally acceptable system. Solutions acceptable to the court were not easy to come by, however. Just as the New Jersey case returned to court several times during the 1970s, the Texas case appeared before the state supreme court repeatedly in the 1990s, with the court again and again having to judge the constitutionality of the legislature's revised school finance plans. Finally, in 1995, the court found that the legislature had devised a constitutionally "efficient" plan, and ended the long-standing litigation battle (*Edgewood*, 1995 WL 36074, 1995).

The legislative scheme that the court finally approved was quite innovative in its approach to achieving fiscal equity, combining a guaranteed base level of spending per pupil for each district in the state that taxes itself at a state determined minimum, a guaranteed yield system that provides each district with the opportunity to supplement the basic program at a level of its own choosing, and a controversial plan that involves a form of state recapture of part of the revenue generated by wealthy districts. The Texas legislation also included many nonfinance reforms. In this sense, Texas experience is similar to the earlier experiences in West Virginia and New Jersey, where school finance reform served as an opening wedge to other reforms focusing more directly on educational issues and not merely on questions about differences in interdistrict spending.

In Texas the inclusion of broader education reforms came about without court order; in Kentucky, by contrast, the overhaul of the state's entire educational system was explicitly mandated by the courts. This dramatic decision of the Kentucky Supreme Court riveted the attention of education reformers and is widely regarded as a turning point in efforts to find constitutional support for linking school finance to broader school reform. In *Rose v. Council for Better Education*, 790 S.W.2d 186 (Ky. 1989), the Kentucky court found that the education clause's "efficiency" language required that the state afford to all students equal access to adequate educational opportunities (Heise, 1995). While the court stopped short of ordering specific reforms, deferring to the legislative process (at least in the first instance), it did provide the legislature with broad guidelines about what would constitute an adequate education, the details of which can be found in Chapter 4.

Twenty years earlier, courts had rejected need-based claims in part because they did not know how to answer the question, "needed for what educational result?" In the *Rose* decision, the Kentucky court supplied its own answer and launched a new wave of school finance litigation based on an emerging definition of educational equity that emphasized the adequacy of educational opportunities afforded schoolchildren (Thro, 1990; Enrich, 1995; Heise, 1995; Underwood, 1995). We explore this development in detail in the next chapter.

The emergence of a new equity standard, however, has not ended concern about whether the older fairness standard based on wealth neutrality has been achieved. State court cases continue to be filed and decided on traditional equity grounds (e.g., *Brigham v. Vermont*, 692 A.2d 384, Vt. 1997). Federal policy makers continue to ask if and how federal funds could be used to reduce interdistrict funding disparities (e.g., U.S. General Accounting Office, 1997).

OTHER APPROACHES TO SPENDING EQUITY

Court challenges to state school finance systems have greatly influenced the shape of school finance reform since 1970 but by no means fully describe efforts to increase equity by improving funding for underserved groups. Even though the federal judiciary has not been a promising venue for directly addressing spending differences at the state and district levels, federal courts have spurred action on other fronts (notably desegregation and the education of children with disabilities). State programs have mirrored (and frequently presaged) federal categorical efforts. States have also undertaken more general and fundamental school finance reform even when not facing a court mandate to do so.

One result has been an explosion in so-called categorical aid addressed to specific educational needs, much of it (though not all) focusing on disadvantaged students. In fiscal year 1998 the U.S. Department of Education distributed $14.8 billion in categorical education aid.[6] At the state level, Gold et al. (1995:37)

---

[6]The federal government spends an additional substantial amount on child nutrition programs for K-12 education, which is administered through the U.S. Department of Agriculture. An estimate for 1998 was $8.8 billion (U.S. Department of Education, 1999: Table 361).

report that, in 1993-94, state categorical education programs included special education (all states), transportation (31 states), compensatory education (28 states), gifted and talented programs (40 states), bilingual education (30 states), prekindergarten programs (36 states), and capital outlay (30 states).

Federal Efforts to Improve Finance Equity

Federal efforts to encourage greater equity in education spending must be interpreted in the context of the unique role of the federal government in education in the United States. As reflected in the *Rodriguez* decision, education is not seen as a federal responsibility in this country, being viewed as one of the powers reserved to the states under the Tenth Amendment. Efforts to provide federal funds for elementary and secondary schools foundered for decades on this constitutional provision, on concerns about the separation of church and state (since private as well as public school aid was often at issue), and on uncertainty about what federal aid might mean for segregated school systems in the South. Before the 1960s, the only sizeable federal assistance to public schools came through "impact aid," a program enacted in 1950 to compensate school districts for revenues lost because of the presence of military bases or other federal activities that take place on tax-exempt properties.

Civil Rights and the War on Poverty

In addressing the segregation question, the *Brown* decision set the stage for aggressive efforts to improve educational opportunities for racial minorities. The federal government became the enforcer of the constitutional right to equal opportunities, beginning with the decision by President Eisenhower to use federal troops in 1957 to protect black students seeking to enroll in Little Rock's Central High School (Edelstein, 1977). In 1964 Congress passed the Civil Rights Act, further extending federal influence over school desegregation and access to equal education. Among other things, this act created the Office for Civil Rights, gave new powers to the attorney general to file school desegregation suits, imposed a process of compliance and review that could result in a cutoff of federal funds for schools that resisted desegregation, and provided technical assistance in desegregation and training services to local school districts and state education agencies. The act also called for a study of educational opportunity, which resulted in the report *Equality of Educational Opportunity* (Coleman et al., 1966). Eight years later, the federal government established the Emergency School Assistance Act to assist school systems in implementing programs not ordered by the courts to facilitate the desegregation process.

Desegregation and finance remedies often overlapped, as the *Milliken v. Bradley* litigation illustrated. In a case that became known as *Milliken I*, 433 U.S. 717 (1974), the U.S. Supreme Court overturned a lower court ruling ordering a metropolitan-area-wide desegregation plan in Detroit and its surrounding suburbs, on the grounds that the independent suburban school districts did not share the Detroit district's history of segregative activities. In response, the lower court then ordered (in *Milliken II*—402 F. Supp. 1096 (E.D. Mich.1975, *aff'd*, 433 U.S. 267, 1977)) an array of compensatory education programs, including remedial reading, teacher training, testing, and counseling, for children in Detroit public schools at a cost to the state of Michigan of $5.8 million (Heise, 1998).

The civil rights era also spawned Lyndon Johnson's war on poverty and enactment of the first general federal aid to education in the Elementary and Secondary Education Act (ESEA) of 1965. The logjam over providing federal aid to education was broken by crafting assistance aimed at providing compensatory services to low-achieving poor students, via Title I of the legislation. (Other parts of ESEA called for federal funding for innovative approaches to education, for the purchase of library books, for research, and for aid to state departments of education.) Title I, which by 1996 served about 6.5 million students in about 14,000 school districts (Sinclair and Gutman, 1996), provides extra educational services to children at risk of educational failure, with funding formulas linked to poverty levels within counties, school districts, and schools.

Agreeing to focus on disadvantaged students, however, did not mean that decisions about how to allocate federal funds would be easy. From the first time it considered Title I in 1965, Congress found itself embroiled in disputes over how funds should be distributed to states and districts. Early disagreements centered on whether proposed funding formulas would result in providing federal funds disproportionately to southern rural school districts (reflecting southern political strength in Congress) and insufficiently to areas of urban poverty in northern states. The question of how sharply to focus Title I funds on disadvantaged students in poor districts has been vigorously debated in virtually every Title I reauthorization. On one side, proponents of greater targeting have argued that Title I funds have been too widely dispersed, to the point that almost all districts receive some Title I aid. On the other hand, opponents of greater concentration have countered that poor children wherever situated ought to be served and that widely allocating funds ensures a broad base of public support for the program. In recent years, as Congress has considered the possibility of providing Title I funds to the states in a block grant, concerns have been expressed that state decisions about how to use Title I funds would result in less targeting on disadvantaged students than occurs under existing law, since states' own funds are less targeted than are federal funds.

"Equalizing" Spending

While the attention of federal policy makers has often been focused on the degree to which Title I funds are targeted to poor students, the question of interdistrict funding disparities and the possible federal role in diminishing these disparities has never been far from the surface. Unlike successful litigants in state courts, who sought wealth neutrality and not necessarily equal spending, federal policy makers talked of "equalizing" spending, although they have not always been clear about what this might mean. At various times since the passage of ESEA, Congress has considered (but failed to pass) legislation calling for the federal government to require school finance equalization or to provide federal funds to enable states to bring per-pupil spending up to some specified level. One comparatively recently example: in 1990, Representative Hawkins (D-Kentucky) introduced and held hearings on the Fair Chance Act (H.R. 3850), which would provide that after 1995 no state could receive federal funds from any program administered by the Department of Education to support its public schools unless the secretary of education certified that funding for public education in the state met standards for equalized spending as specified in the bill.

This and other far-reaching bills to make the federal government a major force in equalizing education spending have been unsuccessful, but Congress has passed more circumscribed measures to encourage states to achieve greater spending equity in their school finance systems. Title I requires that school districts provide services to Title I schools that are "at least comparable" to the services provided to non-Title I schools as a condition of receiving federal aid. "While the comparability requirement would appear to be highly relevant to. . . fiscal equity issues" (Taylor and Piche, 1991:50), the impact of this requirement is limited by the fact that it applies to districts only and leaves interdistrict disparities unaddressed. (When Title I was reauthorized in 1994, some civil rights and education groups argued that the comparability requirement should be extended to all schools within a state receiving federal aid, but they were unsuccessful in convincing Congress of the need for such a change.)

In 1974, Congress amended P.L. 81-874 on impact aid to foster state equalization efforts by permitting states with "equalized" school finance systems to treat federal impact aid funds paid to a district as part of local tax receipts in calculating state equalization payments. States claimed that without such permission their efforts to equalize would be hampered (Taylor and Piche, 1991:51).

This legislation had a direct effect on the development of quantitative measures of school finance equity (Alexander, 1982:209). The U.S. commissioner of education was charged with issuing regulations establishing operational tests for determining which state systems would qualify for special treatment under the impact aid law.

Two such measures resulted: an expenditure-disparity test and a wealth-neutrality test. The expenditure-disparity test has come to be called the federal range ratio and involves calculating the difference between the per-pupil revenues of the district at the 95th percentile and the per-pupil revenue of the district at the 5th percentile and then dividing this difference by the value for the 5th percentile. The commissioner of education decreed that to be considered equalized on this test, a state would have to demonstrate that its federal range ratio did not exceed 1.25 after adjusting for cost differentials recognized by the state. The wealth-neutrality test required that no less than 85 percent of state and local revenues for current expenditures be wealth neutral. To demonstrate that they had sufficiently equalized their systems, states would have to pass one of these two tests.

Using impact aid to create incentives for states to equalize education funding continues to draw congressional attention, although it is not clear that the incentives have much effect on state behavior. In 1988-89, only seven states applied and received certification as meeting one of the two standards—Alaska, Arizona, Kansas, Maine, Michigan, New Mexico, and Wisconsin, according to Taylor and Piche (1991:51). Taylor and Piche (1991:52) observed that it was possible to meet the wealth-neutrality test while having large interdistrict disparities: they cited Michigan's 2.3 federal range ratio as an example. In 1994 Congress removed the wealth-neutrality test, leaving only the disparity standard and reducing the permissible federal range ratio after FY 1998 to 1.2. In 1997, only three states (Alaska, New Mexico, and Kansas) applied and were certified as equalized for federal impact aid purposes, thus winning permission to take impact aid to districts into consideration when calculating state equalization payments.

Along with the impact aid incentive, Congress in 1974 also included a provision in the act reauthorizing elementary and secondary education programs that provided federal funds to states for technical assistance in revising their state finance laws. The amount of federal aid that became available was comparatively small ($13.5 million in 1977), but most states benefited from it (46 by 1977). They used the money for research (on issues such as taxation and local effort, a more equitable distribution of state aid, and alternatives for sources of state revenues); to review technical aspects of school finance formulas; and to support task forces and advisory committees, develop computer simulations, and launch or improve data collection. Six states—Arkansas, Missouri, New Jersey, Ohio, South Dakota, and Texas—reported that they enacted new legislation as a result of this funding or that they implemented new legislation with these funds or both (U.S. Department of Education, 1979).

In 1978 Congress authorized continuation of this equalization assistance and added a provision to have the federal government develop composite profiles of the states and conduct school finance studies, but the 1978 law was never funded. In 1994, the Goals 2000: Educate America Act (P.L. 103-227) included a section authorizing technical assistance for states to help them "in achieving a greater degree of equity in the distribution of financial resources for education among local educational agencies in the State" and calling on the secretary of education "to develop and disseminate models and materials useful to States in planning and implementing revisions of the school finance systems of such States" (section 313). The technical assistance provisions also were never funded, although this section provided some of the impetus behind the creation of our committee.

The continuing congressional interest in spurring greater spending equity and the continuing impasse over whether and how to do this were both in evidence later in 1994, when battles over funding allocation formulas for Title I were a major feature of that year's consideration of legislation reauthorizing federal elementary and secondary education programs. In the end, differences were resolved by creating two new formulas (to supplement the existing basic grant and concentration grant formulas) for allocating Title I funds to states, counties, and school districts. The original basic grant formula enacted in 1965 has governed the allocation of the vast majority of Title I funds since the program's beginning. Concentration grants were added in 1978 to target a small proportion of Title I dollars to school districts with higher numbers or proportions of poor students. The 1994 targeted grant formula called for allocating "new" money through a weighted-child formula that gave even greater weight to districts with such students. The education finance incentive program would have allocated new funds to states using factors that rewarded states for having higher levels of fiscal effort and within-state equalization. In subsequent years, however, Congress has not allowed Title I funding to flow through either the targeted grant or the education finance incentive grant formulas. Funding for concentration grants, however, has gradually grown from 4 percent in 1989 to nearly 15 percent of Title I funding for local education agencies.

Equity for Students with Special Educational Needs

As the above narrative indicates, the federal government's direct contribution to achieving spending equity has been on the margin, but Washington has had a much more significant impact since the 1960s in ensuring that educational services are available to all students, not only those from poor families but also students at risk because of disabilities or limited proficiency in English. As with desegregation, legislative activity was intertwined with litigation.

Traditionally, children with disabilities were often excluded from U.S. public schools on the grounds that they were uneducable. In a 1971 case (*Pennsylvania Association for Retarded Children v. Pennsylvania*, 334 F. Supp 1257, E.D. Pa. 1971) brought on behalf of retarded children, a federal district court agreed with evidence presented to it that all children are educable in some way, and that "uneducable" was an outdated and irrational concept (Roos, 1974:571). During the early 1970s, more than 30 federal court decisions made it clear that discrimination on the basis of disability was unconstitutional, although the Supreme Court did not rule on the issue. By 1973, 45 states had passed legislation that supported the education of students with disabilities (Guthrie, 1997:32-33).

In 1975, Congress enacted the Education for All Handicapped Children Act (P.L. 94-142, later renamed the Individuals with Disabilities Education Act). It requires states to provide a free, appropriate public education to all students with disabilities—called special education.

Litigation and legislation also intersect in the history of bilingual education. In 1973, in *Lau v. Nichols*, 414 U.S. 563 (1974), suit was brought on behalf of

Chinese-American students who were attending public high schools in San Francisco. The plaintiffs argued that they were being denied educational opportunities because they did not speak English. This denial, they claimed, violated their right to a meaningful public education (Sugarman and Widess, 1974:157). In 1974, the U.S. Supreme Court unanimously agreed, basing its holding on the 1964 Civil Rights Act, which specifically says: "No person in the United States shall, on the ground of race, color, or national origin, be excluded from participation, be denied, the benefits of, or be subjected to discrimination under any program or activity receiving Federal financial assistance" (42 U.S.C., section 2000d (1970)). Because regulations and guidelines issued by the Department of Health, Education, and Welfare were not being complied with, San Francisco schools were denying the plaintiffs educational benefits on the basis of race and national origin. The case was especially significant because it balanced the rights of students against possible judicial intrusion into local education policy making (Sugarman and Widess, 1974:157). Soon after *Lau* was filed, guidelines were published that ordered affirmative action steps to be taken by school districts to assist non-English-speaking students (Sugarman and Widess, 1974:169).

State Equity Efforts

Although we have given much attention to court-mandated school finance reforms, states have taken many actions in the past 30 or 40 years that were not directly the result of court orders. Often, this involved the creation of categorical programs to meet special student needs in response to the same conditions that inspired federal programs. Sometimes, states undertook (with or without the threat of litigation) more fundamental reform of their school finance systems. Some examples are illustrative.

Because the *Serrano* cases in some sense marked the beginning of school finance litigation (1971), it is notable that California had several categorical programs in place before 1971 that sought to direct funding to children with a variety of special education needs. These state-level categorical programs worked in addition to and in concert with federal categorical programs. The 1965 McAteer Act was responsible for state-level compensatory education funding. Furthermore, the federal Title I money was distributed, beginning in 1965, by a division within the state department of education that was established under the McAteer Act. Other pre-*Serrano* state efforts included: demonstration programs in reading and math (1969) that were targeted to disadvantaged students in grades 7-9; special teacher employment (1969) to reduce pupil-teacher ratios to 25-to-1 in areas of concentrated poverty; the Miller-Unruh Basic Reading Act (1965) to employ reading specialists on a priority basis to those schools with the greatest number of poor readers in grades 1-3; and the Educational Improvement Act (1969), which sought to ensure the cost-effectiveness of all compensatory education programs (Legislative Analyst, State of California, 1970:2).

Examples can be found in other states of legislation that sought to redress inequities in school funding as well, albeit at the margins. During a period of budget surplus in Texas in 1975, the legislature approved a package adding over $1 billion in new state aid and local funds to support the Foundation Schools Program. While this massive infusion of program aid was thought to fall short of achieving fiscal neutrality among Texas districts, it did move distribution in the direction of greater resource equalization (Johns, 1976:399). In 1975, Connecticut passed legislation that introduced for the first time some resource equalization into the school finance formula. Until that point, revenues in Connecticut were distributed purely on a flat grant basis. The program accounted only for about 4 percent of the funding formula, providing 144 of the state's 169 districts with a small equalization aid bonus (Johns, 1976:401). In the early 1970s in Oregon, the state did have a small equalization program (about 2 percent of the education budget) and a system called inter education districts (Baylis, 1997). These districts, usually organized as counties, were intended to equalize funding across school districts through redistribution. Baylis (1997:50) reports, however, that the inter education districts had little effect because voters rejected ballot measures that would have authorized new tax levies for redistribution.

Michigan exemplifies the situation of a state that decided to completely revamp its school finance system even though courts (in *Milliken* and in *East Jackson Public Schools v. State*, 348 N.W.2d 303, Mich. App. 1984) upheld the constitutionality of the existing system and ruled that education was not a fundamental interest under the state constitution. Opposition to property taxes was the catalyst for reform in this state, where such taxes accounted for an unusually high proportion of state and local revenues. Although voicing strong dislike of property taxes, voters rejected 12 statewide ballot proposals over a 20-year period designed to reduce property taxes as a source of school finance. In 1993, the legislature unexpectedly brought the debate to a boiling point by voting to eliminate the property tax as a source of local school finance. Practically overnight, the major source of school taxes had been eliminated with nothing to replace it. Faced with approving a new finance system or closing the public schools, voters approved a new system that centralized finance at the state level; reduced local property taxes and raised state taxes (notably the sales tax), with overall taxes becoming somewhat lower; and substantially raised per-pupil spending in the districts where it had previously been lowest (Courant and Loeb, 1997).

Finally, we should note here that states have been massively engaged in efforts to improve the quality of education and raise student achievement levels in response to the public concerns evidenced in *A Nation at Risk* (National Commission on Excellence in Education, 1983) and other critical assessments of the state of public schooling. While these efforts are intertwined with, and have implications for, education finance, they are not primarily issues of disparate spending. We discuss them in Chapter 5 along with improving school performance.

REFORM AND SPENDING INEQUITIES

In the 1970s, 28 states fundamentally changed their school finance structures, some under direct court order and most if not all of the rest influenced by the possibility that their existing systems could face constitutional challenge (Odden and Picus, 1992:247; Carr and Fuhrman, 1999:143). Virtually all state finance systems have been at least somewhat revised at some point over the past 30 years. State and federal attention has also been directed to the needs of students who were historically outside the educational mainstream.

What has been the effect of this intense period of reform? There have been some important advances on the equity front, but spending disparities still characterize U.S. education.

Perhaps the most significant accomplishment of the past 30 years is that it is now generally agreed that public schools have a responsibility to educate all children. It is no longer acceptable to exclude children with disabilities on the grounds that they are uneducable or to excuse low performance because students come from poor families or are non-English-speaking. There is certainly much more progress to be made in this area, but a threshold has been crossed.

In terms of education financing, the results are more mixed. Undoubtedly some state school finance systems are more equitable than they used to be. Looking at the nation as a whole, however, it is not clear that significant progress has been made in the last three decades in reducing spending disparities among states and districts. There has been great resistance to reforms aimed at reducing disparities, as the repeated resort to litigation indicates. Federal assistance has been far too small to overcome the inequities in spending that continue to result from state and local policies.

Impact of Finance Reforms

Efforts to evaluate changes in equity as a result of finance reform tend to focus on ex post measures of wealth neutrality, such as the educational revenues or expenditures of school districts and their association with district wealth. Since reformers often hoped that greater wealth neutrality would also reduce overall spending disparities in American education, researchers, legislators, and lawyers also frequently want to know the degree to which actual spending across districts is equal or unequal and how spending disparities have changed over time.

Early attempts to measure the effects of school finance reforms found that states made important progress in the 1970s in reducing the relationship between per-pupil spending and local property wealth per pupil, with states that had made school finance reforms showing more progress than others. Whether or not states had undergone reform, however, spending disparities among districts had not been reduced significantly, despite some comparatively minor improvements in reform states. (Several early studies are summarized in Odden, 1982.)

The economic downturn of the early 1980s and then the shifting of public attention from equity to quality concerns threw into question the extent to which even these early signs of progress were continued. Comparing data from 1985-86 to data from 1976-77, Schwartz and Moskowitz (1988) found that fiscal equity in terms of both horizontal equity (treating equally situated children equally) and fiscal neutrality had not changed significantly over that period. Somewhat later, Wyckoff (1992), comparing data from 1980 to 1987, found that while fiscal neutrality was stable, horizontal equity improved modestly.

Recent research seeks to gauge the overall impact of three decades of school finance reform efforts. Because of data limitations (i.e., the lack of comparable measures of property wealth among districts across states), multistate assessments of the impact of finance reform focus on the reductions in spending disparities across districts rather than attempting to measure changes in the wealth neutrality of spending.

The most comprehensive research on changes in spending disparities over time appears in a series of papers by Evans, Murray, and Schwab (Evans et al., 1997, 1999; Murray et al., 1998) investigating the impact of judicially mandated school finance reform. They examine the distribution of spending within states as well as the average level of spending across states, using data for the more than 10,000 unified elementary and secondary school districts at 5-year intervals over the 20-year period 1972-1992.[7] They also use econometric modeling to explore the effects of court-ordered finance changes.

Evans et al. (1999) found that disparities were reduced noticeably over that period in states in which courts mandated school finance reform. Using four different measures of inequality, they found that reform in the wake of a court decision reduces spending inequality within a state by 19 to 34 percent. Their findings are consistent with the results of case studies in individual states that have measured reductions in spending disparities after court-ordered reform (e.g., Joondeph, 1995, who examined Arkansas, California, Connecticut, Washington, and Wyoming and Adams, 1997, who examined Kentucky).

Evans et al. (1999) further found that court-ordered reform reduces inequality by raising spending at the bottom of the distribution while leaving spending at the top unchanged. As a result of court-ordered reform, spending rose by 11 percent in the poorest school districts, rose by 7 percent in the median district, and remained roughly constant in the wealthiest districts. Court-ordered finance reform led states to increase spending for education and leave spending in other areas unchanged, and thus by implication states funded the additional spending

---

[7]For comparability purposes, their study omitted districts that were not unified (i.e., districts that included only elementary or secondary grades), data from Montana and Vermont (which have few or no unified districts), and data from Hawaii (with its state-based system) and the District of Columbia (which is the sole system in its jurisdiction).

on education through higher taxes. As a consequence, in states where courts ordered reform, the state's share of total spending rose.

Evans et al. examined the impact of court-mandated reform on low-household-income districts to shed further light on progress toward one key objective of education finance reformers: to sever the link between the ability to pay for education (as measured in terms of wealth or income) and actual spending. For the most part, the literature has focused on the impact of court decisions on low-spending and high-spending districts. Because spending and income are only imperfectly correlated, more direct evidence of the effect of court action on districts in which household income is low is useful. Evans et al. found that, following court-mandated reform, total revenues rose significantly in the poorest districts, those in the lowest quartile of household income. All of the increased revenues came from state aid, and some of the state aid provided tax relief to poor districts (that is, these districts reduced their own spending somewhat, but by less than the amount of state aid they received). These results imply that court-mandated finance reform reduced the covariance between income and spending on education in a state. The method and findings are similar to the work of Card and Payne (1997), who also found that finance reform has weakened the link between income and spending.[8]

Evans et al. (1999) also looked at the impact of court-mandated reform on spending for black and white students. Because black students tend to live in low-household-income districts, court-ordered reform would be expected to redistribute resources toward black students. This is in fact what Evans et al. found for state aid; it increased by an estimated $664 per student (in 1992 dollars) following reform. However, since districts, especially low-household-income ones, substitute state aid for their own revenues to some extent, total pupil revenue for black students increased by $448 while per-pupil revenues for white students increased by $575.[9]

Court-mandated reform has therefore changed state school finance systems in the general direction that many reformers hoped for. Even without court orders, states have also sometimes moved in similar directions,[10] as we described previously, for example, in Michigan.

Although litigation and legislation have apparently generated more equitable state finance systems in some states, it is far from clear that the past three decades

---

[8]Given the importance of the wealth-neutrality objective in school finance litigation, it would be desirable to examine changes in the relationship between property tax wealth and spending. Unfortunately, comparable measures of taxable wealth do not exist on a nationwide basis, so researchers generally use resident income as an imperfect proxy.

[9]These estimates should be interpreted cautiously since the estimates of many parameters in the underlying equations were estimated imprecisely.

[10]We do not attempt to examine here how courts and legislatures may work together in changing the education finance system, thus confounding the issue of causation (see Fischel, 1998).

of reform efforts have reduced overall disparities in spending on elementary and secondary education in the nation as a whole. Again, the most comprehensive evidence comes from the Evans et al. studies, who found, as we shall see, that not much changed on average during the 1972-95 period. Before reporting these results, however, we should note that it is possible that analyses using more recent data may find more signs of improvement. In carrying out its own studies on funding gaps, the U.S. General Accounting Office (1997; 1998a; 1998b) also had to rely on the latest available data, which were from the 1991-92 school year. GAO contacted state officials to determine the extent to which states had changed their targeting efforts or state share of school funding between 1991-92 and 1995-96: 24 states reported targeting changes (presumably in the direction of more targeting on low-wealth districts), and 6 of these also reported making increases of 10 percent or more in their state share of education funding.

Between 1972 and 1992, however, Evans et al. (1999) found little improvement in most measures of spending equity, although overall spending per pupil grew significantly and the state shares of funding increased (Table 3-1). The first panel of Table 3-1 (which summarizes changes in expenditures adjusted for inflation by the national consumer price index but not for district-to-district differences in the cost of living or the population of students with special needs) shows the growth in real resources per student—an average rate of 2.1 percent per year during the 20-year period. Revenues from state sources rose very quickly during 1972-87 and, as a consequence, the states' share of total resources increased from 38.3 to 49.3 percent. Revenues from the states then grew slowly during 1987-92. Local funding increased throughout this period, including the last five years; in 1992, local governments contributed 47.0 percent of all of public education resources. The federal government played a small and shrinking role throughout 1972-92.

The second panel in Table 3-1 gives several measures of inequality in district spending at the national level.[11] All of the inequality measures in Table 3-1 follow a similar pattern. Spending at the 95th percentile was 2.72 times higher

---

[11]Each of the measures in Table 3-1 rises when inequality rises. The ratio of the 95th percentile in per-pupil spending to the 5th percentile in spending is a simple ranking that treats transfers to the top or bottom of the distribution the same; changes in spending in the rest of the distribution change the 95th to 5th ratio. The coefficient of variation is the standard deviation divided by the mean. This measure focuses on the extent of variation around average spending—both above and below the mean. The Gini coefficient measures the degree to which each cumulative percentage of pupils (e.g., 40 percent) receives an equal percentage of expenditures (e.g., 40 percent). Changes throughout the distribution of spending contribute to the values of the coefficient of variation and the Gini coefficient. The Theil index is similar to the Gini coefficient; however, it gives more weight to changes in the tails of the distribution. The Theil index is attractive in part because it is relatively easy to decompose it into disparity in spending between and within states. For more detailed descriptions of these and other measures, see Berne and Stiefel (1984).

TABLE 3-1 Summary of Current Education Expenditures, 1972-92

	1972	1977	1982	1987	1992
Funding per student ($1992)					
Local	1,923	1,881	1,799	2,163	2,621
State	1,394	1,708	1,903	2,451	2,587
Federal	325	346	297	315	368
Total	3,642	3,935	3,999	4,929	5,576
Measures of inequality					
95/5 ratio	2.72	2.37	2.22	2.53	2.40
Coefficient of variation	30.8	28.1	25.6	29.6	29.9
Gini coefficient (×100)	16.3	15.0	13.8	15.8	15.5
Theil Index (×1000)	43.7	37.1	31.0	40.7	40.5
Theil index decomposition					
Within states	13.7	14.4	14.0	12.6	13.4
Between states	30.0	22.8	17.0	28.2	27.1
National	43.7	37.2	31.0	40.7	40.5
Variance decomposition					
Within states	32.2	41.5	47.5	32.8	35.3
Between states	67.8	58.5	52.5	67.2	64.7
National	100.0	100.0	100.0	100.0	100.0

NOTES: Funding per student from the U.S. Department of Education, *1994 Digest of Education Statistics.* Education expenditure inequality measures are authors' calculations from the Bureau of the Census, *Census of Government School System Finance File (F-33),* various years. Calculations exclude school districts from Alaska, District of Columbia, Hawaii, Montana, and Vermont.

SOURCE: Evans et al., 1999.

than spending at the 5th percentile in 1972. This ratio then fell to 2.40 in 1992, suggesting a narrowing of the differences in spending across students. The Theil index fell during the 1970s and early 1980s, rose sharply between 1982 and 1987, and then remained roughly constant. Inequality according to all four measures was higher in 1992 than in 1982 and somewhat lower than in 1972.

The next two panels of Table 3-1 break spending inequality into two components: inequality due to differences in spending within states and inequality due to differences across states. Here the critical point emerges that between-state inequality is much larger than within-state inequality, with between-state inequality accounting for about two-thirds of the total. Table 3-1 also shows that more than 90 percent of the reduction in the Theil index during 1972-92 was due to a reduction in inequality between states; there was little change in inequality within states. This suggests that school finance reform focused at the state level is limited in its ability to equalize the education resources available to students, although it appears to have been important in staving off growing inequality. Evans et al. (1999) found that when they modeled what would have happened to inequality in the absence of court-mandated reform, within-state inequality would have risen sharply (instead of staying largely unchanged) between 1972 and 1992.

One interesting question is what difference it would make to the findings if spending levels were adjusted not simply by an overall inflation factor but for the differences in the costs of the resources across districts and over time. Evans et al. attempted to answer this question, although data limitations (i.e., cost indices that are not available before 1987) restricted their investigation of cost adjustments to the impact of adjustments on the level and the disparity in per-pupil resources at a point in time, 1992. They used three separate indices to adjust for differences in the cost of real education resources: the Barro (1992) index, Chambers' (1995) teachers' cost index, and McMahon and Chang's (1991) cost of living index.[12]

Table 3-2 shows unadjusted and adjusted estimates of revenue inequality and the decomposition of revenue inequality in a manner paralleling the treatment of expenditure inequality in Table 3-1. Adjusting for cost differences between metropolitan and nonmetropolitan school districts in 1992 results in a noticeable decline in inequality as measured in various ways. The amount of inequality due to differences in revenues between states continues to dominate inequality due to revenue differences within states, although the amount of variation accounted for by between-state inequality drops from 66 percent of total inequality to 53 to 60 percent.

---

[12]All three develop separate cost indices for urban and nonurban districts in each state; in some states, separate indices for the largest urban areas are also available. The Barro measure is an index of average teacher salaries that adjusts for teachers' education level and experience. Because a given district can influence teachers' wages by hiring only candidates with graduate degrees, this measure would overstate the adjustment necessary for purchasing power parity among districts. The teachers' cost index measure adjusts for regional variations in the cost of living and amenities. This measure removes the impact of within-state differences by adjusting for district-level characteristics that, unlike average teacher's educational attainment or tenure, are not subject to district control. Finally, the McMahon and Chang index is a geographic index that controls only for the differences in housing values, income, and population growth across districts; the McMahon and Chang index yields the smallest price adjustment. While these cost indices were developed specifically for adjusting education costs, it is not clear that they successfully capture the full difference in the costs of education across districts. Ideally, a cost index would account for the difference in wages that a central-city school district would have to offer in order to attract teachers with the same qualifications, ability, and training that wealthy suburban districts attract. We suspect that these indices do not capture those differences and that it is therefore likely that their use overstates the resources available to central-city students. Also, none of these indices incorporate differences in the variation in student needs; see Duncombe et al. (1996) for an important discussion of this issue. More is said about the cost of education issue in subsequent chapters.

TABLE 3-2 Summary of Resources Adjusted for Cost of Living Differences, 1992

		Cost of Living Adjustment		
				McMahon-
		Barro Cost	Chambers	Chang
Summary Measure	Unadjusted	Index	TCI	COL
Measures of Inequality				
95 to 5 ratio	2.47	2.07	2.08	2.19
Theil index	37.90	26.40	29.20	32.40
Coefficient of variation	30.10	24.40	25.70	27.10
Theil Index Decomposition				
Within states	12.90	12.20	12.20	12.90
Between states	25.00	14.20	17.00	19.50
National	37.90	26.40	29.20	32.40

TCI= Teachers' cost index; COL= cost-of-living index.

SOURCE: Evans et al., 1999.

In many ways, then, court-ordered school finance reform, where it was implemented, achieved its primary objective of fundamentally restructuring school finance and generating a more equitable distribution of resources than would have existed in the absence of such reform. The fact that virtually all states, whether under court order or not, have significantly altered their school finance formulas, usually in ways that make them more sensitive to district needs or relative wealth, is in no small measure due to the more active interest courts have taken in school finance in the last 30 years.

Nevertheless, the fact that new court cases continue to be filed, even on traditional equity grounds, and that disparities in interdistrict spending levels have far from disappeared, indicate that there are limits to how far school finance reforms are likely to go in reducing spending disparities, even when courts intervene.

Limitations on the Impact of Court-Ordered Reforms

The main lesson from the past 30 years is how persistent spending inequalities are in American education. There are a number of reasons why the long period of active reform has yielded only modest change.

First, Feldstein (1975) showed that the remedy that Coons et al. (1970) proposed to ensure wealth neutrality—district power equalizing or a guaranteed tax base—does not in theory sever the relationship between a community's expenditures per pupil and its wealth per pupil. School districts make decisions about spending per pupil based on their local tax price, income levels of residents, and other taste and socioeconomic factors. Feldstein demonstrated that district power equalizing does not correctly offset the effects of its tax price and other wealth-related factors, and therefore districts may not respond in ways that break the positive wealth-spending relationship. Research by Evans et al. (1997, 1999) and Card and Payne (1997) provides empirical support for Feldstein's analysis.

Odden's (1999) cross-sectional analysis does not speak to whether low-spending districts have lowered their tax rates in response to state aid, but it does indicate that districts may have low spending levels in part because they choose to tax themselves less than high spending districts. Odden looked at spending patterns in 1994-95 in three unidentified states that enacted different versions of school finance reform (two of which were full or partial district power equalizing programs) over the 1975-95 time period. He ranks districts in these states in deciles on the basis of revenues per pupil and shows that in all three states local property tax rates rose steadily as district wealth rose. Revenues per pupil thus rise with district wealth as well, despite the equalizing intention of state aid.[13] The U.S. General Accounting Office (1998b) studied four states that changed their finance systems between 1991-92 and 1995-96 and found that, in two of the four, state changes that moved in the direction of equalization were offset because poor districts reduced their local tax rates or wealthy districts raised theirs— or both.

The fact that district spending levels are still related to district wealth and tax levels reflects one of the philosophical conundrums of school finance reform. The wealth-neutrality standard adopted in *Serrano* and many other court decisions explicitly does *not* call for equal spending among districts, only that all districts are able to realize the same revenues from the same tax effort. Those who believe that unequal spending is unfair are therefore unlikely to be satisfied with the spending levels that meet the ex-ante wealth-neutrality standard. Those who value continued reliance on local control and discretion in making decisions about how much to spend on education will be more willing to tolerate continuing disparities in spending when they appear to reflect differences in local preferences for schooling versus other public goods (or tax relief).

Tensions over local control are part of the political context that frequently stymie or limit finance reform efforts, even when finance changes are mandated

---

[13]There is emerging evidence in some states that interdistrict school finance spending disparities may have decreased in the bottom half of the distribution but increased in the top half, while leaving the overall coefficient of variation about the same. In a multiple state study, Verstegen (1996) found that the McLoone index, which measures disparities within the lower half of districts ranked by spending level, has declined. The Verstegen index, a new measure of disparity for the top half, had actually increased.

by courts. Legislators and governors who must design and implement reforms find themselves contending with public opposition on a number of fronts (Carr and Fuhrman, 1999; Reed, 1997). Rather than equalize by reducing spending down to the level of low-spending districts, thereby forcing wealthier districts to reduce spending, policy makers may try to "level up." This effort to raise spending in low-spending districts often requires higher state taxes or redistribution of locally raised revenues from wealthier to less-wealthy districts, both of which are highly unpopular among those whose tax burdens would rise or who would see their tax dollars go to educate children in another jurisdiction. Some of this opposition is individual and personal; some stems from more general antitax and antigovernment sentiments. Demographics also play a role. Racial cleavages sometimes come into play, as voters see minorities (especially those dwelling in cities) as primary beneficiaries of reform. Poterba (1997) found that increases in the fraction of elderly residents in a jurisdiction is associated with a significant reduction in per-child spending, a result with ominous overtones in a society whose average age is rapidly increasing as the baby boom generation approaches retirement age.

The political climate affecting implementation of court-ordered school finance reforms at the state level manifests itself in different ways (Carr and Fuhrman, 1999). Sometimes, as in New Jersey and Texas, it results in a decades-long dance of litigation and legislation, with legislators and governors attempting a variety of remedies before finding ones acceptable to the court. Sometimes, as in Alabama, a strong antireform governor and strong antitax and antigovernment sentiments undercut efforts to build a consensus for educational reform, and virtually no change takes place. By contrast, Kentucky was able to marshal a strong coalition in favor of reform and revamped its educational system thoroughly and comparatively quickly after the 1989 court decision declaring the existing system unconstitutional.

For those whose objective for school finance reform goes beyond wealth neutrality to equality of funding for students no matter where they live, there is one final limitation to the impact of court reform that is perhaps the most significant of all. As noted earlier, two-thirds of disparities in per-pupil funding differences are attributable to between-state differences in spending rather than within-state differences. The proportion is still over half even when adjustments are made for the cost of education.

Federal aid to education at existing levels is limited in its ability to remedy these gaps. Federal funds help somewhat, because they are more highly targeted to poor students than are either state or local funds; in 1991-92 the majority of poor students lived in states that had significant funding gaps between poor and wealthy districts (U.S. General Accounting Office, 1998a). Because federal allocations are relatively small compared with state and local shares, however, the equalizing effect of federal funds does relatively little to reduce the overall funding differentials between low-poverty and high-poverty districts. At current federal spending levels, this would continue to be true no matter how highly targeted federal funds were. Jencks et al. (1972:25-6) pointed out over 25 years ago that local disparities in funding (which are wealth and poverty related) could be diminished if state or federal spending increased dramatically, even if this spending were not targeted at all but merely allocated on an equal per-pupil basis. More recently, the U.S. General Accounting Office (1998a) in its study of education funding in 1991-92 showed that targeting of state and federal funds helped but didn't completely close the funding gap between high-poverty and low-poverty districts.[14] The percentage of total funding from state and federal sources was more important, however, in reducing the gap than in how narrowly these funds were targeted on poor students. "For example, both California and Virginia had about the same combined state and federal targeting rates per poor student and the same average per pupil funding levels. However, California's much larger combined state and federal share reduced its funding gap to one that was smaller than Virginia's" (U.S. General Accounting Office, 1998a:5).

EQUITY AT THE DAWN OF THE NEW CENTURY

As the nation enters a new century, its success in addressing questions of fairness in its school finance systems is mixed. The nation awoke in the 1950s and 1960s to the problems of unequal educational opportunities and began to address them. Around 1970 it entered a notably vigorous era of debate and reform aimed specifically at breaking the link between the property wealth of school districts and the amount of resources they had available to spend on the education of schoolchildren. Many state finance systems were overhauled. Wealth neutrality almost certainly improved, although there is no good longitudinal measure to document this statement on a national basis. State and federal categorical programs directed resources to students with special education needs and to some extent compensated for funding inequities at the local level.

Overall, however, since the early 1970s, disparities in spending among districts do not appear to have changed much, although judicial intervention has ensured that they are smaller than they might otherwise have been. There are still large differences in the educational dollars spent on students depending on where they happen to live, particularly for students whose families are at the top and bottom in terms of income. Reducing spending disparities has proven difficult and contentious. The constitutional support for reform is quite variable across the states.

Many people continue to believe that basic fairness requires that educational

---

[14]In this study the poverty level of a school district was calculated on the basis of the district's number of poor students, as determined by the percentage of children living in households below the poverty level in 1989.

resources not be determined by where a student happens to live or that all students ought to receive the same amount of educational resources (with perhaps some adjustments for differing educational costs). Cases will continue to be litigated on these grounds, and legislation will continue to be offered in hopes of achieving these objectives.

Increasingly, though, it seems that finance reforms of the past, with their emphasis on the fiscal capacity of school districts, insufficiently address pressing equity questions of today, which include how to use the finance system to foster higher levels of learning for all students, regardless of background, and what to do about the desperate social, economic, and educational problems that plague some central-city schools.

A fundamental dissatisfaction with discussions about finance equity as they have been carried on over the past three decades has become apparent as the nation has become increasingly concerned about educational achievement levels. While equity as a concept can be applied to any stage in the education "production" process (inputs, processes, outputs, or outcomes), in practice finance reforms aimed at achieving wealth neutrality or equalizing spending have had a very strong input focus. Moreover, they have also been preoccupied with the *distribution* of inputs. This approach has seemed increasingly out of sync with educational reforms that are more and more concerned with the outputs and outcomes of the educational system and with setting and realizing absolute (rather than relative) standards of student achievement.

The interdistrict equity preoccupation of much school finance discussion in the last third of the 20th century is, moreover, less and less compatible with educational reform efforts that increasingly focus on the school (rather than the district) as the basic unit in the educational production process. It also has ignored considerations of *intra*district spending disparities, which in large urban school districts may be more problematic than interdistrict disparities in equalizing educational opportunities for students with the greatest educational handicaps.

Even the members of the legal profession who developed the strategy of wealth neutrality, which successfully made courts a central player in school finance reform, are finding themselves desirous of a new strategy for pursuing educational equity goals through the courts. Minorini and Sugarman (1999) suggest that the foregoing considerations partially explain this. In addition, they point to the changing landscape of school desegregation, which has reinforced the desirability of finding a new school finance legal theory. Since the *Brown* decision declared school segregation to be illegal in 1954, advocates for minority youth, frequently those in cities, have sought and received redress in federal courts for educational shortcomings that could be traced to de jure discrimination in the past. Courts ordered remedies that included busing and voluntary integration plans, but more and more involved improvements in the educational enterprise itself: in teacher quality, curriculum, facilities, and so forth. In the 1990s, however, it appeared that the litigation era reaching back to *Brown* was drawing to a close and that federal desegregation cases might soon no longer serve as a primary tool for trying to improve educational opportunities for inner-city poor and minority youth. Advocates began to think that school finance litigation might be a promising substitute (Tatel, 1992). For needy children attending high-cost, urban schools, however, school finance litigation would be far more attractive if the definition of equity on which it was based was broader than the conventional approach of wealth discrimination.

The new approach to equity that seeks to address many of these new equity concerns concentrates attention on the adequacy of education rather than on the distribution of education resources. The next chapter continues our investigation into educational equity by exploring the promises and pitfalls of expanding equity to encompass adequacy.

4

Equity II—The Adequacy of Education

Since 1989, when the Kentucky Supreme Court took the dramatic and unprecedented step of declaring the entire state system of elementary and secondary education unconstitutional for failing to provide all children an adequate education, the concept of "adequacy" has moved to center stage in discussions of fairness in school finance systems. The Kentucky decision highlighted an important lesson from the educational reforms of the 1960s, 1970s, and 1980s: improving the fiscal capacity of schools may be necessary, but certainly isn't sufficient, to achieve equality of educational opportunity. To some, the idea of adequacy offers a promise of overcoming problems that previous equity-oriented reforms failed to remedy, and to do so by linking school finance decisions explicitly and centrally to the quality of education provided to America's schoolchildren. To others, movement toward adequacy signals a discouraging retreat in the long battle for basic fairness by threatening to perpetuate an education system that tolerates large disparities in the educational resources provided to them. To almost everyone, it is a concept that is still emerging and evolving: there is as yet no consensus on its meaning and only limited understanding about how and what would be required to achieve it.

Nonetheless, a growing number of state court decisions suggests that adequacy is becoming the new equity standard to which state school aid plans should be held. States without such court mandates are also seeking new answers to the old question of what it costs to provide an "adequate" or "basic" or "core" education (Education Commission of the States, 1997). The blossoming of the standards-based school reform movement has caused some to suggest that basing school finance decisions on the educational needs of students, once ruled "judicially unmanageable" by several courts, may now be an achievable objective. These developments highlight the importance of exploring what is known about what is called the adequacy movement: how adequacy is defined, what court imperatives are driving it, how states are responding to it, and what conceptual and technical challenges will have to be overcome in implementing adequacy-based school finance systems. A key challenge (addressed more fully in the next chapter) is whether current knowledge about how to improve student achievement is strong enough to make it possible to design a school finance system that fosters this objective.

POSSIBLE MEANINGS OF ADEQUACY

Despite the absence of consensus on the definition of educational adequacy, a good sense of how it differs from other approaches to equity can be obtained by examining it in terms of the five key definitional distinctions mentioned in Chapter 3.

Adequacy is exclusively focused on schoolchildren and does not embrace taxpayers as objects of concern. Conceptually, the unit of analysis could be the individual child or the school, but in practice (especially as litigators have so far employed it in school finance cases), it has been applied to school districts. If education funding becomes more school-based than district-based in the future, as some reformers urge, the unit of analysis for adequacy would probably shift to the school level as well.

One of the major differences often cited between adequacy and other definitions of equity is the former's emphasis on outputs and outcomes. Attorneys have tended to make a distinction between equity and adequacy, defining equity as input focused and adequacy as output focused. As Berne and Stiefel (1999) point out, however, in principle it is entirely possible for inputs, outputs, and outcomes to be equitable or inequitable and for inputs, outputs, and outcomes to be adequate or inadequate.[1]

Adequacy does indeed place far more emphasis on outputs and outcomes than wealth neutrality or spending equalization; in fact, the latter approaches pay virtually no attention to the results of schooling. For definitional purposes, however, the key characteristic of adequacy seems to be less the input-output distinction and more its greater emphasis on absolute rather than relative stan-

---

[1]Berne and Stiefel cite the remedy applied in the settlement of *Abbott v. Burke*, 710 A.2d 450 (N.J. 1998), in New Jersey as an example of how the courts, through the concept of adequacy, may possibly join outputs, inputs, and processes. In New Jersey, the remedy has focused on resources, curricular offerings, and support services available to poor districts relative to wealthy ones. While the idea is to provide an adequate education for children in poor districts, the method for achieving this involves a focus on the details of programs, teacher quality, and technology.

dards. In the past, debates over equity focused on comparisons among children and districts and how well they fared relative to each other. Adequacy appears to demand the setting of absolute standards rather than defining equity in terms of the relative performance of school finance systems.

Adequacy may also result in different groups taking center stage as the focus of special interest. William Clune, a prominent legal scholar (and original member of the Coons team that developed the wealth-neutrality standard for school finance equity), illustrates in the development of his own thinking one direction that adequacy might take. From early descriptions of adequacy that included all children, his writing has evolved to define adequacy as a concept to be applied especially to urban, poor districts and to high-poverty students (Clune, 1995).

It is in determining how adequacy can be evaluated that there is perhaps the least consensus on defining the concept. Much of the remainder of this chapter assesses the various options being explored by courts and states as they attempt to apply an adequacy standard to school finance systems. In practice the distinction drawn here between older measurements of equity using distributional bases and adequacy as an absolute measure is frequently blurred when it comes to defining how the adequacy of a finance system should be evaluated, probably because concepts using absolute rather than relative standards are only now being developed. Some courts (e.g., *Harper v. Hunt* in Alabama[2]) have found the state finance system inadequate using comparisons with state and national input and output regulations and standards. Sometimes the ex post tests of adequacy are also comparative rather than absolute in nature, as when outcome measures such as test scores or graduation rates are compared with national statistics.

Developing absolute standards of adequacy (both ex ante and ex post) requires answers to two questions: Adequacy of what? How much is adequate? Strike (1988) has pointed out that the philosophical debate over distributive justice that has taken place over the 30 years since the publication of Rawls's *A Theory of Justice* (1971) provides some framing ideas for considering these questions.

In seeking an alternative to utilitarianism, which holds that just policies are those that produce the greatest good for the greatest number and defines "good" as happiness or utility, Rawls (1971) sought plural indices of social welfare rather than continuing to rely on happiness or utility. He developed the notion of "primary goods": things that a rational person wants whatever else that person wants, desirable because they are means to leading a wide range of different kinds of lives. He listed the primary goods as rights and liberties, powers and opportunities, income and wealth, and self-respect.

The Rawlsian theory of primary goods suggests a way of approaching an-

---

[2]Consolidated with *Alabama Coalition for Equity v. Hunt,* published as appendix to Opinion of Justices, 624 So.2d 107 (Ala. 1993).

swers to the "adequacy of what" question. Interpreted this way, adequacy might be viewed as requiring an allocation of educational resources sufficient to guarantee to every student a minimum set of those educational outcomes that are importantly connected to long term life prospects in our society.

In developing an alternative to Rawls's concept of distributive justice, Gutmann (1987) provided a possible approach to answering the "how much" adequacy question and thereby a means for overcoming equality of opportunity's second limitation, the absence of a principle for establishing levels of achievement or permissible differences in achievement. Unlike Rawls, whose definition of distributive justice featured distributive rules intended to provide an equal opportunity for everyone to pursue a self-chosen plan of life, Gutmann's definition gives greater attention to the value of a democratic society in which decisions are made deliberatively and collectively. Therefore she emphasizes a so-called democratic threshold principle for education, which claims that "inequalities in the distribution of education goods can be justified if, but only if, they do not deprive any child of the ability to participate effectively in the democratic process (which determines, among other things, the priority of education relative to other social goods)" (p. 136). The idea of a democratic threshold at least conceptually addresses the issue of achievement levels ignored by the equality of opportunity approach, and it provides in general terms an anchor for answering the question of "how much" adequacy.

Suggestive as Rawls's primary goods and Gutmann's democratic threshold principle are, however, they provide far from precise answers to the "adequacy of what" and "how much" questions. They point, though, to some of the issues that will arise in seeking greater precision.

To facilitate the discussion, we develop a shorthand whereby we view "adequacy of what?" as a question of *qualitative adequacy* and "how much" as a question of *quantitative adequacy*. To apply adequacy to school finance requires figuring out where to set the absolute level of this "bar" called adequacy: how *broad or narrow* should the bar be (qualitative adequacy) and how *high or low* should it be (quantitative adequacy)?

Qualitative adequacy involves decisions about what educational opportunities are most directly and powerfully related to the "primary goods" society wishes to distribute fairly among its citizens. These are usually issues of curriculum. Opportunities to become proficient in reading or math might be seen as central. Opportunities to participate in art or physical education might be viewed as more peripheral. The availability of swimming pools or carpeted classrooms might be regarded as unrelated to ultimate life chances. It is not hard to imagine, however, that people will disagree about where to draw the lines, both because they have differing values and because the relationship between opportunities and life chances may be different for different individuals in different circumstances.

Similarly, quantitative adequacy is likely to lend itself to differing interpretations of "how much" is enough. There might be an achievement level such that those who fall below it would be unlikely to be able to participate in the basic economic and political life of society. This suggests looking for a threshold level of some sort that defines how much input is needed to reach this level. Even if such a threshold level can be agreed upon, there will still be important questions to resolve. Threshold principles often apply to "all that are able," which involves not only judgments about the capacity of individuals but also about the resources society is willing to expend on teaching those with low capacity. Thus, there are choices to be made between setting the adequacy bar at a high level (and accepting that a larger number of students will not meet it) and a low level (which allows for fewer exceptions). On another front, deciding where to draw the line on quantitative adequacy must also take into account the possibility that there might be a law of diminishing returns, such that higher levels of educational resources result in ever-diminishing amounts of improvement in educational achievement or ultimate life chances.

Qualitative and quantitative adequacy thus raise numerous issues when considered independently; they also interact in ways that will pose additional challenges for the development of adequate school finance systems. For example, the interaction has interesting implications for the outcome of a state decision about whether or not to allow individual districts to provide more resources than called for by the state-determined "adequate" level. On one hand, let's say that a state school finance system embodies a broad definition of qualitative adequacy, incorporating most or all of the primary educational goods that will affect life chances significantly and/or that its quantitative adequacy level is sufficiently high that spending above the adequate level will not yield much in additional returns on the critical dimension of life chances. In this case, districts' freedom to spend whatever they want beyond the threshold may result in nice extras for students but will not compromise equality of opportunity. Such a "broad or high adequacy" policy is likely to be quite expensive and redistributive, however, and therefore politically unpopular with wealthier parents who would like to keep their resources in their local schools to benefit their own children. "Narrower or lower adequacy," on the other hand, erodes commitment to equality of opportunity by setting a floor under achievement that guarantees only participation in the basic institutions of society, not equal opportunity to enjoy all of society's primary goods.

Despite these difficulties, adequacy holds promise for overcoming two serious theoretical weaknesses with the more common concept of equality of opportunity. First, equality of opportunity—the idea that all children should have an equal chance to succeed and that education is one of the most efficient tools for ensuring this—is insufficiently attentive to *which* educational outcomes matter most in the sense of making an important contribution to the life prospects of individuals. Second, equal educational opportunity requires no particular level of achievement, nor does it forbid significant inequalities in achievement between high-achieving and low-achieving individuals so long as variations in achievement are not associated with "morally irrelevant" characteristics. (A morally relevant characteristic, in this view, might be individual student ability or effort, but not an accident of birth.) Adequacy might overcome these limitations in the equal opportunity definition of equity.

A final general observation about adequacy: while the concept is enjoying a newfound prominence, it actually is an idea with old roots in school finance theory and practice. Specifically, adequacy and traditional foundation aid programs have much in common. In recognizing this, we open the possibility that there are historical lessons from which to benefit in the current round of adequacy discussions. In particular, we should be alert to the possibility that adequacy (especially a low standard of quantitative adequacy) could reproduce the disequalizing consequences of traditional foundation plans.

Foundation plans began in the early part of the 20th century and efforts by school finance reformers to overcome problems with flat grants, the early form of state aid to school districts. Cubberley (1919a; 1919b) and Strayer and Haig (1923) elucidated and developed the idea of the foundation program. Foundation grants set a minimum level of spending per pupil below which a state does not permit a district's spending to fall. Each district is required to levy a property tax at a fixed rate; the state supplements the revenues from this levy up to the foundation level.

Foundation plans[3] implicitly define the foundation level as "adequate," but seldom were these levels determined by a systematic assessment of what was required to fund an adequate education. "Adequate" was determined through a political bargaining process, as legislators and governors negotiated on how much state revenue was available or could be generated through additional taxation. Sometimes states made gestures to the notion of adequate inputs by tying their foundation plans to their requirements for teacher certification or to maximum allowable class size levels or pupil-teacher ratios.

State foundation plans were frequently criticized by school finance experts (e.g., Odden and Picus, 1992:176-177) because of their disequalizing effect (they permitted districts that could afford to do so to spend above the foundation level) and because they incorporated no formal adjustment mechanisms to account for changes in educational costs (so over time the foundation level tended to fall below what districts needed to address basic needs). When these plans first came under legal challenge, it was their distributional equity, not their adequacy, that was at issue. Recently, however, the adequacy of foundation and other formulas for distributing education aid has also become a central concern.

---

[3]As of 1994, 40 states used a foundation grant program as the primary mechanism to distribute basic support (Gold et al., 1995).

THE SHIFT TOWARD ADEQUACY

While there were court decisions in the 1970s in New Jersey, Washington, and West Virginia that gave attention to the adequacy as well as the wealth neutrality of school finance systems, it was the Kentucky Supreme Court's decision in 1989 overthrowing the entire state education program that galvanized the shift toward adequacy in courthouses and statehouses. Between 1989 and mid-1998, courts in Alabama, Massachusetts, New Hampshire, New Jersey, New York, North Carolina, Ohio, Tennessee, and Wyoming also have ruled that their state constitutions' education clauses guarantee students an adequate level of educational opportunities that should allow them to achieve certain desired educational outcomes. In addition, claimants in Arizona won an adequacy case concerning capital costs of school construction; and adequacy-based lawsuits were pending in mid-1998 in Louisiana, Minnesota, Pennsylvania, and South Carolina.

Part of the reason that the 1970s decisions in New Jersey, Washington, and West Virginia did not spur more adequacy cases was that it was not evident at the time that the courts were doing anything significantly different than they did in traditional wealth-neutrality cases. Kentucky, however, clearly marked a sea change. In *Rose v. Council for Better Education,* 790 S.W.2d 186 (Ky. 1989), the state supreme court used "efficiency" language in the constitution's education clause[4] to declare the entire educational system inadequate and unconstitutional. The court established the objectives of an adequate education, proclaiming that it would provide students with the opportunity to develop at least the following seven capabilities:

- sufficient oral and written communication skills to enable students to function in a complex and rapidly changing civilization;
- sufficient knowledge of economic, social, and political systems to enable the student to make informed choices;
- sufficient understanding of governmental processes to enable the student to understand the issues that affect his or her community, state, and nation;
- sufficient self-knowledge and knowledge of his or her mental and physical wellness;
- sufficient grounding in the arts to enable each student to appreciate his or her cultural and historical heritage;
- sufficient training or preparation for advanced training in either academic or vocational fields so as to enable each child to choose and pursue life work intelligently; and

---

[4]The Kentucky ruling cited Section 183 of the state constitution, which calls on the state "to provide an efficient system of common schools throughout the Commonwealth."

- sufficient levels of academic or vocational skills to enable public school students to compete favorably with their counterparts in surrounding states, in academics, or in the job market.

The influence of the Kentucky case on other states was direct and apparent. Courts in Alabama, Massachusetts, and New Hampshire relied specifically on the Kentucky court's definition of an adequate education when providing guidance to their own state legislatures about crafting remedies for finance systems that had been declared inadequate.[5] Other state courts developed their own specifications about what constitutes educational adequacy. In 1993, the Tennessee Supreme Court found that the state constitution required the education system to provide districts with sufficient funds to permit attainment of certain broadly defined educational outcomes: "The General Assembly shall maintain and support a system of free public schools that provides at least the opportunity to acquire general knowledge, develop the powers of reasoning and judgment, and generally prepare students intellectually for a mature life" (*Tennessee Small School Systems v. McWherter*, 851 S.W.2d 139, Tenn. 1993). Similarly, in 1994, the Arizona Supreme Court ruled that the state's system for funding school facilities was unconstitutional because certain districts lacked the resources necessary to maintain adequate school buildings (*Roosevelt Elementary School District v. Bishop*, 877 P.2d 806, Ariz. 1994). That decision, while limited to capital funding, also suggested that similar claims of adequacy might apply to school districts' operating costs. In 1995, the highest court in New York used a civic rather than an economic rationale to undergird its finding that the state is constitutionally obligated to create and maintain an education system that provides children with "the basic literacy, calculation, and verbal skills necessary to enable [them] to eventually function productively as civic participants capable of voting and serving on a jury . . . [and] minimally adequate physical facilities and classrooms . . . to permit children to learn" (*Campaign for Fiscal Equity v. State of New York*, 86 N.Y.2d 307, N.Y. 1995).[6]

Courts that mandate adequacy do not always themselves define the objectives that an adequate education system should serve. In 1997, the Ohio Supreme Court ruled that by permitting dramatic deficiencies in facilities, materials and supplies, and class sizes in some of the poorer school districts, the state had violated its constitutional duty to provide students with a "thorough and efficient" education system (*DeRolph v. Ohio*, 79 Oh.St.3d 297, Oh. 1997). The court,

---

[5]See *Alabama Coalition for Equity v. Hunt*, published as appendix to Opinion of Justices, 624 So.2d 107 (Ala. 1993); *McDuffy v. Secretary of Education*, 615 N.E.2d 516 (Mass. 1993); and *Claremont School District v. Gregg*, 635 A.2d 1375 (N.H. 1997).

[6]The high court decision in New York established the criteria against which funding levels will be appraised in a case currently scheduled to be tried in a lower court in late 1999.

however, did not discuss what it would consider acceptable, leaving it to the state legislature to determine how to meet the constitutional requirement. In Wyoming, in a 1995 development in a court case that went back to 1980 (*Washakie v. Herschler*, 606 P.2d 310, Wyo. 1980), the supreme court ruled (*Campbell v. State*, 907 P.2d 1238, Wyo. 1995) that the legislature's response to its earlier decision had been deficient and ordered it to devise an acceptable remedy: "The legislature must first design the best educational system by identifying the 'proper' educational package each Wyoming student is entitled to have. . . . The cost of that educational package must then be determined and the legislature must then take the necessary action to fund that package. Because education is one of the state's most important functions, lack of financial resources will not be an acceptable reason for failure to provide the best education system. All other financial considerations must yield until education is funded."

Adequacy decisions in the courts do not always address the question of whether districts can provide education above the adequate level, but when they have, they have spoken with several voices. In Wyoming, local supplements are expressly forbidden. The Wyoming Supreme Court noted that "historical analysis reveals local control is not a constitutionally recognized interest and cannot be the basis for disparity in equal educational opportunity." The New Hampshire Supreme Court (*Claremont v. Governor of New Hampshire*, 703 A.2d 1353, N.H. 1997) and the North Carolina Supreme Court (*Leandro v. State of North Carolina*, No. 179PA96, 1997) both indicated that variations in spending resulting from local add-ons would be permissible so long as all districts are able to provide students with the constitutionally guaranteed minimum of opportunities. The finance system enacted in Kentucky in response to the 1989 ruling there allows local spending above the state-determined adequate level and so far has not faced legal challenge.

As happened in the wealth-neutrality litigation, not every state's high court has been receptive to adequacy arguments. In Illinois, where the state constitution's education clause explicitly requires the state to "provide for an efficient system of high quality public educational institutions and services," the supreme court rejected attempts by plaintiffs to evaluate whether the quality of education offered in many of their districts met that constitutional standard. According to the court, "questions relating to the quality of education are solely for the legislative branch to answer" (*Committee for Educational Rights v. Edgar*, 672 N.E.2d 1178, Ill. 1996). The high courts in Rhode Island and Florida relied on a similar rationale in rejecting adequacy-based claims. In Florida: "appellants have failed to demonstrate . . . an appropriate standard for determining 'adequacy' that would not present a substantial risk of judicial intrusion into the powers and responsibilities assigned to the legislature" (*Coalition for Adequacy v. Chiles*, 680 So.2d 400, Fla. 1996). In Rhode Island: "what constitutes an 'equal, adequate, and meaningful' [education] is 'not likely to be divined for all time even by the scholars who now so earnestly debate the issues'" (*City of Pawtucket v. Sundlun*, 662 A.2d 40, R.I. 1995).

Another possible dimension of an adequate education has been proposed in two Minnesota cases seeking, among other substantive education remedies, racial integration.[7] Advocates there have sought to have an adequate education defined in such a way as to include a racially integrated education. If this approach were to succeed, it would provide a way, through the state constitution's education clause, to remedy unintentionally created racial isolation, a situation that the federal constitution—through the equal protection clause—would not redress.

STATE RESPONSES TO THE ADEQUACY MOVEMENT

The adequacy movement is comparatively new; there is limited evidence to date on what is required to reform school finance systems on this basis. Early indications can be gleaned from a review of state responses so far.

The Kentucky example proved that moving to educational adequacy as the basis for reform may require legislative solutions going far beyond matters of school funding. The fact that Kentucky's legislature promptly enacted a comprehensive statewide education reform package in response to the court's decision is encouraging but, given particularly favorable political incentives in the state (Carr and Fuhrman, 1999), probably not reflective of how other states may respond to similarly far-reaching court mandates. The Kentucky Education Reform Act (KERA) recreated the state's entire elementary and secondary education system, encompassing finance, governance and program changes; increased school district revenue by 34 percent (19 percent adjusted for inflation) between 1990 and 1993; and reduced disparities in spending among districts and in the relationship between district wealth and spending (Adams, 1997). KERA also featured a strong accountability program based on a new assessment system and providing financial rewards for exceptional performance and significant sanctions for poor performance.

Legislative efforts to comply with adequacy rulings in states other than Kentucky have been noticeably more contentious. Chapter 3 introduced the long saga of school finance litigation in New Jersey, which had adequacy overtones from its early days and assumed a more explicit adequacy cast in the 1980s, when school finance reform advocates filed a new suit on behalf of the children in 29 of the state's poorest districts. The *Abbott v. Burke*, 575 A.2d 359 (N.J. 1990), decision decreed that the children in the 29 districts identified in the court case as special needs districts must have educational opportunities equal to those of

---

[7]See *Independent School District No. 625, St. Paul, Minnesota v. State of Minnesota*, No. 62-C2-009356 (Minn. 2nd Dist. Ct. filed Sept. 19, 1996) and *Minneapolis Branch of NAACP and Lee Xiong, et al., v. State of Minnesota*, No. MC 95-014800 (Minn. 4th Dist Ct. filed Sept. 19, 1995).

students in the wealthiest districts in the state; in a later ruling the court made clear that equal opportunity included access to all educational and extracurricular activities that were available in the wealthiest districts as well as funding for supplemental programs to address the special educational needs of urban districts. The politics of finding legislative remedies satisfactory to the court were complicated by the fact that the court created an educational entitlement only for children in the 29 poorest districts and did not address the finance systems' constitutionality in the remaining 450 districts. Opposition to increased aid to urban districts and to the tax increases necessary to fund this aid derailed initial legislative attempts to comply with the court's ruling. Nonurban legislators who voted for the initial legislative reform package almost all lost their seats in 1991 and opposition to the reform package played a significant role in the defeat of Governor James Florio in 1993 (Carr and Fuhrman, 1999). The case was only settled in 1998 when the state supreme court, after rejecting another legislative reform in 1997, finally approved a detailed and comprehensive reform package.

Experiences in other states have also highlighted the political difficulties that frequently follow adequacy rulings by courts. Despite the similarity of the judicial decisions in Alabama and Kentucky, the fate of the former has been quite different from the latter. Antitax groups mobilized against comprehensive reform in Alabama; the Alabama Education Association opposed the bill as well because of its accountability features. In 1994 the state elected a governor (Fob James) who explicitly opposed the court order and tried (unsuccessfully) to have it overturned. To date finance reform has not occurred in Alabama and plaintiffs are still seeking judicial remedies. In Wyoming, an initial legislative effort to define and impute costs to a "proper education" was quickly challenged in court by plaintiffs seeking yet more revenue for Wyoming schools. By 1998, though, the legislative and executive branches came together to pass a reform that they believe will hold up against judicial scrutiny, a reform that raised the state education budget by approximately 10 percent and elevated per-pupil revenue into the $7,000 range. Ohio's legislature voted a new funding plan designed to provide an adequate instructional system, but voters refused to approve the necessary tax increase. Arizona's legislative and executive branches made several efforts to revamp the state's system for funding capital facilities and costs after the state supreme court ruling in 1994; in 1998 the court for the fourth time declared the state's effort unsatisfactory and gave the legislature 60 days to develop an acceptable plan.

States that are not under court order to implement educational adequacy have also attempted to link their educational reform and school finance agendas by asking "What is a core education and what does it cost" (Education Commission of the States, 1997). Their experience as well as the experience of states under court mandates to orient their school finance systems toward educational adequacy indicates that there are a number of conceptual and technical challenges to overcome.

CONCEPTUAL AND TECHNICAL CHALLENGES

Deliberations in courthouses and statehouses suggest that a desire to implement adequacy may be outpacing current understanding of how to define and achieve it. In comparison to wealth neutrality and equal spending, equity defined as adequacy requires difficult value choices, as well as policy decisions in areas in which the available technical knowledge is weak. Implementing adequacy requires establishing anchors for identifying what is adequate; determining the costs of an adequate instructional delivery system; making adjustments for student, school, and geographic characteristics; adjusting for inflation from year to year; and developing an assessment system for measuring whether adequacy has been achieved.

Establishing Anchors: What Is Adequate?

We have already observed that adequacy requires both identifying desired educational outcomes and then making decisions about what kinds of educational experiences (qualitative adequacy) and how much achievement (quantitative adequacy) will be sufficient to meet the standard. We have also noted that sometimes courts provide the answer to at least the first of these dilemmas (e.g., in Kentucky), but often the question of outcomes and always the question of "adequacy of what" and "how much" are left to legislatures and governors to determine.

These are not easy questions to resolve through political processes. Value conflicts make it difficult for Americans to reach consensus about goals for education, or at least about which goals should receive priority. There are large uncertainties about which educational experiences are central to the achievement of specific goals. There are also large uncertainties about what levels of achievement are necessary for students to reach specific goals.

These are not insurmountable problems, and in fact headway is being made in addressing them. The Wyoming legislature, under a deadline from the court to define and cost out a "proper" educational package, developed a basket of education goods and services consisting of some 30 courses and kinds of knowledge designed to ensure that students acquired a common core of knowledge and a common core of skills. The basket served as the basis for subsequent efforts to identify and cost out the resources sufficient to achieve these objectives.

The standards-based reform movement (discussed further in Chapter 5) has inspired all states to undertake serious consideration of their educational objectives. Standards-based reform has encouraged states to deliberate on their own goals, to undertake the development of shared understandings about what students need to know and be able to do (i.e., to set content standards for education), and to develop systems to measure whether students do in fact master this content (performance standards). It is likely that standards-based reform reinforces the willingness of policy makers and judges to shift toward an adequacy standard for educational equity, by creating a receptive political climate and perhaps by providing judicially manageable standards that courts had a difficult time identifying in the past.

Nevertheless, the tortuous path to standards-based reform is also a cautionary tale about how long and difficult the process can be. As a recent National Research Council committee pointed out, it is not yet clear whether the guiding assumptions of standards-based reform are correct or that policies built on them will have their desired effect (National Research Council, 1997:33-46). The rhetoric that "all students can learn to high standards" leaves unresolved important philosophical and logistical issues, such as balancing high, uniform standards with students' unique educational needs and abilities. The extent to which consensus can be reached on curriculum and performance standards is unclear. Controversies over the specification of outcomes (e.g., in Pennsylvania), the content of curriculum frameworks and performance assessments (e.g., in California), and the content of voluntary subject-matter standards (e.g., the lopsided U.S. Senate vote condemning voluntary national standards in history) "suggest that consensus dissolves once the public moves beyond a general belief in the need for standards and assessments to questions about what those standards should be and how students should be taught and tested" (National Research Council, 1997:38). Moreover, major uncertainties remain about whether student performance can be measured validly and reliably and whether instruction consistent with the standards can be implemented in individual schools and classrooms.

The technical challenges in measuring student performance become increasingly important as the concept of adequacy shifts the focus of attention to the outcomes of education. A key issue is whether existing tests define and measure achievement in ways consistent with standards-based reform or other statements of desired educational outcomes. Large-scale, standardized tests[8] are tools for determining what students know and can do in specified domains. No large-scale assessment measures all aspects of student achievement. Moreover, many tests currently in use do not capture critical differences in students' levels of understanding, do not adequately reflect higher-order thinking skills called for by many new education standards, and do not reflect more comprehensive goals for student achievement that go beyond subject-matter knowledge to other valued skills and abilities. For example, a recent National Research Council (NRC)

---

[8]"Large-scale" tests are those administered to students from many schools. "Standardized" tests are similar tests given to many students under uniform conditions. This latter point is often misunderstood; it is common for people to assume that standardized tests must use a multiple-choice format. In fact, "even a written examination, one that is scored by teachers or other human judges and not by machine, is considered standardized if all students respond to the same (or nearly the same) questions and take the examination under similar conditions" (National Research Council, 1999b:29).

committee evaluating the National Assessment for Educational Progress (NAEP) pointed out a number of dimensions of achievement not sufficiently reflected in the current NAEP frameworks and assessments: problem representation, use of strategies, self-regulatory skills, explanation, interpretation, and individual contributions to group problem solving (National Research Council, 1999a:138). Assessment systems employing multiple measures of achievement (i.e., large-scale tests augmented with alternative assessments) may be necessary to capture the range of outcomes comprising an adequate education. The recent NRC evaluation of NAEP discusses one approach to a multiple-measure assessment system (National Research Council, 1999a), but at present it is the case that "policy and public expectations of testing generally exceed the technical capacity of the tests themselves" (National Research Council, 1999b:30).

Despite the difficulties, however, adequacy litigation and legislation are beginning to define ranges of achievement levels and exposure to knowledge and skills that can serve as ends toward which to orient a practical school finance distribution system. The next challenge facing policy makers is to determine the costs of an acceptable instructional system oriented toward these objectives.

Determining the Costs of an Adequate Instructional Delivery System

In a perfect world, the determination of the costs of providing educational adequacy would take into account differences among individual students that affect their educational needs. Policy makers, however, cannot easily design a resource allocation program for individuals. They must instead concentrate on building finance *systems*, ideally with an eye to providing districts, local schools, and even classroom teachers with resources and inducements to tailor instruction to the specific characteristics of students. These systems may on occasion prove blunt when measured against individual student needs; the methods currently available will probably appear primitive down the road when more research and better data allow existing approaches to be refined.

Varying approaches to designing an instructional delivery system differ in crucial ways, both in how they assign costs and how they make reference to educational outcomes. States with early "adequacy" rulings (e.g., Washington, West Virginia, and Kentucky) have continued to rely on traditional legislative processes, which depend on political bargaining to make allocation decisions about educational inputs and leave the links between outcomes and the costs of an adequate instructional delivery system largely unspecified.

More recently, policy analysts and researchers have begun to explore several approaches for calculating the costs of adequacy that link outcomes and instructional delivery more explicitly: (1) inference from outcomes by statistical analysis; (2) inference from outcomes by empirical observation; (3) professional judgment; and (4) a market-oriented approach based on the development of whole-school designs that school districts can "buy." (More detail about these methods can be found in Guthrie and Rothstein, 1999; Duncombe and Yinger 1999; and Odden and Busch, 1998.) The first and second of these approaches usually depend on states' having sophisticated student achievement testing systems that provide standardized statewide measures of student performance, with data linking this performance to student background characteristics. In states where such testing systems do not exist, then the third and fourth approaches, based on professional judgment or whole-school designs, seem at present to be the only alternatives, where "getting to adequate" necessitates building instructional resource models to which costs can subsequently be assigned.

Each of these alternatives results in an estimate of the cost of an adequate education for a presumed or hypothetical typical student. Conceptually the next step must then be to adjust this cost (or perhaps redefine the goal of adequate outcomes) for students in different socioeconomic circumstances and locations. The statistical analysis approach accomplishes this second step simultaneously with the step of identifying costs for the typical student. It is important for explanatory purposes, however, to keep the two steps separate, and we address cost adjustments explicitly in the following section. Separating the steps permits us to give appropriate attention to the cost adjustment issue and also to make clear that methods of cost determination may have different strengths and weaknesses, depending on whether they are being used to find average costs or to adjust costs for student and district differences.

Inference from Outcomes by Statistical Analysis

This approach represents the efforts of econometricians to apply the tools of statistical modeling to the determination of educational costs. The approach originated in efforts to determine how intergovernmental aid formulas should be adjusted to take into account public service costs beyond the control of local jurisdictions. Researchers tried to develop cost indices that would measure how much higher (or lower) the costs of providing a given level of services were in each district compared with a statewide average. Thus, initially, the studies focused exclusively on the differences in costs, with little attention paid either to the particular service level or what it would cost a typical district to provide that level. More recent studies have extended the approach, so that a specific service level (defined, for example, in terms of the percentage of students achieving various educational goals) can be specified and the cost of providing that service estimated for the district with average characteristics. Ladd and Yinger (1994) and Downes and Pogue (1994) made important theoretical contributions on which have been constructed cost models applied to education data from New York (Duncombe and Yinger, 1999) and Wisconsin (Reschovsky and Imazeki, 1998).

Rather than attempting to determine the costs of an adequate education as the sum of the costs of individual instructional components, statistical models take a "black-box" approach, choosing an acceptable level of pupil performance or proficiency and then using multiple regressional analysis to determine the dollar amount associated with it based on analysis of extensive data from individual districts. In many studies of this type, no attempt is made to control for the efficiency or inefficiency with which a district is operating. Implicitly such studies take as given the average amount of inefficiency across districts and assume that the efficiency with which a district operates is not correlated with other district characteristics that are included in the statistical model. In effect, inefficiency is assumed to be distributed randomly among school districts. Provided this assumption is reasonably valid, districts with above-average inefficiency are not rewarded when adequacy is defined or aid is distributed on the basis of results from this approach (as they would be, for example, if aid were distributed on the basis of actual expenditures). Nor, however, does this approach provide any incentive for the typical district to operate more efficiently.

The more sophisticated versions of this approach (Duncombe et al., 1996; Duncombe and Yinger 1997, 1999) enter a measure (albeit an imperfect one) of efficiency directly into the model and hence, to the extent that the model is correct, can adjust estimates of adequacy and/or state aid programs to provide incentives for districts to become more efficient.

These versions are more sophisticated in other ways as well. For example, Duncombe and Yinger used a statistical approach to determine the desired objectives of the education system as well as the costs of achieving it. Their approach determined which performance indicators are valued by voters, as indicated by their correlation with property values and school spending. The resulting "index of educational performance" for school districts in New York state includes the average share of students above the standard reference point on 3rd- and 6th-grade Pupil Evaluation Program tests for math and reading, the share of students who receive a more demanding Regents diploma (which requires passing a series of exams), and the high school graduation rate. While this approach results in a performance yardstick, Duncombe and Yinger note that it cannot determine the point on the yardstick that school districts should be expected to meet or that defines an adequate performance. The performance target must be based on the judgment of public officials, though once the target is set its costs can (at least in theory) be calculated via the statistical approach.

Because these indicators (test scores, graduation rates, and Regents diploma awards) may not accurately measure the totality of school outcomes that voters care about, Duncombe and Yinger also estimated models using "indirect" controls for school district performance. In such models, they define average performance as the level achieved by the district with average income, tax price, and voter characteristics, given its teachers' salaries and environmental factors. These (abstract) communities can then be used to observe how much per-pupil spending is necessary to achieve average educational outcomes, again while controlling for other cost or discretionary factors.

Reschovsky and Imazeki (1998) also utilized a statistical method to estimate the cost of adequacy in Wisconsin districts. They measure outcomes by 10th-grade test scores, controlled for 8th-grade scores of the same students. By this means, they attempt to isolate the "value-added" by school districts, reasoning that the 8th-grade score may reflect students' social capital and instruction in other locations as well as the effectiveness of instruction in the present district. "Adequate" outcomes were defined as the average 10th-grade value-added throughout the state; Reschovsky and Imazeki conclude that the cost of achieving this adequacy, before adjusting for student need and geographic differences, is $6,331 per pupil.

Applying sophisticated statistical models to the determination of adequate educational costs is in its infancy. In part because of its technical complexity, statistical modeling is unlikely to appeal to policy makers as the primary way of calculating the cost of an adequate education. Modeling holds great academic and theoretical interest and may suggest insights that would stimulate productive further research into the relationship between spending and student achievement, as when different modeling techniques lead to different cost estimates. However, in addition to complexity, statistical modeling has shortcomings that, given the present state of the art, limit its usefulness as a policy tool for determining the costs of providing an adequate education to the typical student.

The first of these relates to the limited number of outcome measures these models can incorporate without becoming impossibly complex mathematically. Duncombe et al. (1996) acknowledge this limitation, but assume that it may not be too serious since "outcomes often are highly correlated with each other." Whether or not this assumption is correct, it is also true that many of the desirable educational outcomes with which courts are concerned (e.g., in Kentucky) or legislatures (e.g., in Wyoming) are presently not measured and therefore cannot be quantified for use in such a statistical model.

Furthermore, even if it were possible to quantify all outcomes, such models could at best tell us what resource levels are generally associated with acceptable achievement (with inefficient practices removed, to the extent known), not what resource levels would be necessary, if used efficiently, for this achievement. To reach this level of analysis, the statistical controls would have to include alternative pedagogies and curricula, something beyond current sophistication. If the policy goal is for a legislature to adopt (or a court to mandate) the minimum level of resources necessary to achieve acceptable outcomes, this becomes a crucial distinction.

A more serious shortcoming of the statistical approach relates to its theoretical dependence on educational production function models. One of the longest-running debates in school finance concerns what is called the "production function" in education: whether it exists in any measurable way (Murnane and Nelson, 1984; Monk, 1990) and whether systematic relationships can be found between inputs and student achievement. Hundreds of studies have failed to yield agreement among scholars about the effects of resources on outcomes.

While the statistical models being described in this chapter are cost functions, not production functions, they can be derived directly from production functions and embody the same information. Continuing uncertainty about the underlying common relationships therefore raises significant doubts about the extent to which statistical models yield reliable information about the costs of an adequate education for the typical student.

Statistical methods for determining adequate educational costs appear to have a greater level of precision than the other methods discussed in this section, so it is important to keep in mind the assumptions and judgments behind them. Given restrictions on current ability to quantify desirable outcomes and the weaknesses in the production theory on which cost models are constructed, the apparent precision of statistical models may be misleading. While these methods may, especially as they are improved, provide important comparisons with methods of determining costs that are less elegant, they are not yet ripe for use as the primary means for policy makers and the public to discern or understand these costs. (They may at present be more useful in determining cost *adjustments*, once average costs have been identified—discussed in the next section.)

Inference from Outcomes by Empirical Observation

Another black-box approach involves establishing a level of acceptable pupil performance on an agreed-upon set of outcome measures, identifying school districts or schools that achieve the desired goals, and determining what these "successful" districts or schools spend. This level of resources is then deemed to be adequate. "The underlying assumption is that any district should be able to accomplish what some districts do accomplish, provided they have a similar amount of revenue and that amount is modified for individual districts to take into consideration cost pressures they face that are beyond their control" (Augenblick, 1997:4).

The empirical approach is described in detail in a 1995 investigation undertaken by Augenblick, Alexander, and Guthrie for the State of Ohio, and then revised in a report by Augenblick in 1997 (Augenblick et al., 1995; Augenblick, 1997). It initially involved constructing a representative pool of Ohio school districts, comprised of all Ohio districts save those that were characterized by high and low extremes of property wealth and per-pupil spending. Once such outliers had been removed, remaining districts were ranked by a composite of student performance measures in reading, mathematics, writing, and science. Districts whose average student performance was at the 70th percentile or higher on most measures were defined as providing a minimally adequate education.

Augenblick et al. next examined instructional arrangements of the districts that met the performance criteria. These districts' mixes of instructionally related components such as ratio of professionals to pupils, class sizes, school sizes, and course offerings were distilled and taken to be instrumentally exemplary for districts attempting to reach specified levels of achievement. These exemplary conditions and practices can be taken as a model instructional program, one empirically verified by student performance. It then becomes possible to assign costs to these empirically derived instructional components.

A problem with this approach is its suggestion that the identified instructional components and mixes are highly desirable. It can encourage state policy makers to fund specific instructional components and therefore restrict the discretion and initiative of local districts to organize resources and instructional delivery differently if they believe they can accomplish the same objectives more effectively. (This same criticism can also be leveled against the professional judgment approach described below.)

In response to this concern, Augenblick's 1997 report revised the earlier approach by eliminating any empirical observation of school inputs, only observing the average per-pupil spending level that was correlated with acceptable outcomes. In addition, and in response to other criticism, the more recent report abandons a norm-referenced outcome measure (the 70th percentile of the statewide district achievement distribution) and adopts a set of criterion-referenced measures (percentage of students passing minimum competency levels).

For his 1997 study, Augenblick identified 102 (out of 607) Ohio school districts whose students met 17 of 18 performance thresholds, or output criteria (outlier high and low property wealth and/or high and low spending districts were again eliminated from consideration). In addition to a dropout rate of 3 percent or less and an attendance rate of at least 93 percent, the remaining 16 criteria consist of specified passage rates such as 75 percent on the state's minimum proficiency tests. Once having identified a pool of districts that did not exhibit extremes of wealth or spending and in which students had met these state measured performance criteria, Augenblick constructed a weighted mean per-pupil revenue amount from among eligible district expenditure patterns.

The per-pupil dollar amount derived from this process was $3,930, based on 1996 Ohio spending levels (Augenblick, 1997). This became the Augenblick definition of "adequacy" for Ohio school districts, before adjustments for differences in cost pressures beyond district control. He adjusts for these cost pressures using a regression model that assumes that districts spend about what they need to spend to respond to the pressures they face. The model determines the cost-pressure adjustments by regressing district per-pupil expenditures on various cost pressures (e.g., the proportion of special education students in the district).

A similar empirical observation approach was used by the Illinois Commission on Education Funding in 1996 to estimate the cost of the foundation of an adequate education. The commission calculated a foundation level of adequacy (i.e., $4,225 per pupil in 1995-96) and then recommended that the foundation level be adjusted for regional cost-of-living differences and for student poverty rates. Despite the governor's endorsement, the commission's report was not adopted by the state legislature.[9]

A seeming virtue of the Ohio and Illinois approaches is their transparency. Compared with statistical analysis, the assumptions appear clear and comparatively easy for policy makers and the public to understand. This seeming transparency, however, may be an illusion. In the case of the Augenblick approach, for example, the amount of funding determined to be adequate depends on the order in which the model's various steps are carried out and on how many of the steps are included and how (e.g., the adequate amount changes depending on whether or not the data are weighted by district size and depending on how extreme districts in terms of wealth and income are handled). Moreover, the approach controls poorly for differences in the socioeconomic background of the students. Because the ranking of how well districts do on the performance measures is undoubtedly correlated with student backgrounds, the approach of taking average costs in districts meeting the standards is a biased estimate of what costs would be in a typical district. This problem would be reduced if the calculated cost were viewed as a minimum and then carefully adjusted for the costs of more difficult to educate students. But the assumption behind the adjustments for cost pressures—that all districts currently adjust fully for the pressures beyond their control—seems questionable and possibly unfair to the districts facing the highest pressures.

Another limitation of the empirical observation approach, as of the statistical models discussed above, is that the minimum proficiency tests measure only certain cognitive outcomes, not the full range of cognitive, value, and behavioral outcomes that courts and legislatures have used to identify an adequate education. As noted above, it may be that further study will determine that all outcomes are positively related, i.e., a district most of whose students pass proficiency tests in reading, mathematics, writing, and citizenship is also likely to be a district that adequately develops student interests in the creative arts or a district most of whose students have adequate social ethics to interact constructively with others in society. However, with no available research on these relationships, it would be premature to jump to such conclusions.

Professional Judgment

A third strategy for determining what an adequate education looks like is to rely on professional judgment to construct an ideal-type delivery system, without

---

[9]Augenblick et al. (1997) also report that a related empirical approach has now been adopted by Mississippi, which has identified 30 successful schools in which test scores are satisfactory and concluded that the costs of operating these schools is "reasonable." This cost of education in these 30 schools is being defined as the cost of adequacy, with adjustments made to this necessary cost for districts with varying costs of living, student poverty rates, etc. As of this writing, however, the Mississippi method has not been described in the published education finance literature.

either statistical or empirical inference from actual measured outcomes. The components of such a system can then be identified and costs assigned to them. While, at first glance, such an approach may seem unscientific, the approximations inherent in professional judgment may be no less precise than those embedded, though more hidden, in statistical or empirical methods. It is possible that professional judgment, if carefully exercised, may be better able to adjust for the vast multitude of factors involved than is a statistical or empirical approach.

A school finance system in which the state funded, or guaranteed funding, for a defined set of resources in each district (including class sizes, teacher salary levels, a specific number of administrators and clerical staff, etc.) was once common, particularly in southern states (Augenblick and Myers, 1994). It is no longer widely used, however, and this system predated a concern to link these resource models to a notion of "adequacy." The notion of input adequacy, however, was implicit in these systems. Once adequacy became an explicit concern, a professional judgment approach was developed by Jay Chambers and Thomas Parrish in proposals they made for funding adequate education systems in Illinois in 1992 and in Alaska two years later (Chambers and Parrish, 1994). Because they recognized that no precise technology exists for linking resources to outcomes in education, they declined to term their goal "adequate," using the term "appropriate" instead. Calling their method the resource cost model (RCM), Chambers and Parrish convened committees of teachers, administrators, and public officials to deliberate and determine what resources were necessary to deliver an appropriate education. They toured facilities across the states and met with local educators and policy makers. In Illinois, for example, they concluded that teacher staffing resources should be provided so that a regular grade 1-3 class should have 22 pupils; that a speech therapist should have a caseload of 62 pupils; and that school buildings insulated to a proper standard should have resources to purchase energy to maintain a year-round building temperature of 70 degrees.

The charge of these committees was not entirely to specify the resources of an appropriate education, because they were also told they must "keep a balance between the resources they would like to see specified for each educational program and what they believed to be affordable" (Chambers and Parrish, 1994:53) given the states' fiscal and political realities. Operating under these guidelines, the process resulted in a recommendation for an appropriate funding level that was 2 percent greater than present total funding in Illinois, and 16 percent greater than present total funding in Alaska. However, the Chambers-Parrish specifications of appropriateness, developed through this process, would have required substantial redistribution of resources from district to district within these states.

Having specified an appropriate level of resources by this consultative process, employing professional judgment, Chambers and Parrish utilized a statistical analysis to estimate the costs and the within-state cost differences of providing these resources. The result, however, was that "policymakers [in both states] tended to find the overall system somewhat incomprehensible and complex"

(Chambers and Parrish, 1994:72). The RCM was not therefore ultimately adopted as a basis for policy in these states.

More recently, a consulting group led by James W. Guthrie utilized a professional judgment approach relying on both consultation with local experts (as did Chambers and Parrish) and reliance on research and whole-school design models (see next section) to calculate an adequate level of resources to be distributed to Wyoming school districts (Guthrie et al., 1997). The Wyoming approach differed from the earlier work of Chambers and Parrish in four important respects.

First, Guthrie et al. had been retained by the state legislature to design a system to fulfill a mandate of the Wyoming Supreme Court in *Campbell v. Wyoming*, 907 P.2d 1238 (Wyo. 1995). The court prohibited the legislature from considering the total cost of a new education funding system, requiring that the "best" (i.e., adequate) system be funded regardless of cost: "lack of financial resources will not be an acceptable reason for failure to provide the best education system." Therefore, unlike the Alaska and Illinois experts for the RCM, the Wyoming professional expert groups were not asked to balance adequacy against total costs in making their recommendations.

Second, in defining adequacy, Guthrie et al. consulted with professional expert groups in Wyoming and nationally but did not rely exclusively on the opinions of practitioners. Rather, these opinions were used to inform the consultants' views, based on national research and prior experience, regarding the resource elements necessary to produce adequate outcomes.

Third, learning from the Illinois and Alaska experiences, Guthrie et al. did not use a complex statistical method (regression models) to calculate resource costs or cost adjustments, believing that they would be unlikely to be able to explain how these calculations were made in a manner that would be understood and accepted by policy makers, educators, and citizens. Rather, less sophisticated but more easily understandable methods, still based on economic theory, were employed.

Fourth, because the Wyoming legislature was ordered by the court to come forth with recommendations for adequacy on very short notice, Guthrie et al. calculated the costs only of the main elements of an adequate education, using less precise methods to estimate other costs. (For example, the cost of utilities was calculated by taking the average cost of Wyoming districts in the prior year, with no attempt to specify resources necessary to reach a target temperature for classrooms when controlled for building insulation standards.)

In this case, the professional judgment approach was used not only because of concerns about poorly specified outcome measures in education generally, but because the state of Wyoming did not utilize a standardized achievement test like that in Ohio, Illinois, Mississippi, or Texas, even for narrowly defined academic outcomes, and so even poorly specified outcome data were not available. In many states without adequate assessments, the professional judgment and whole-school design methods may be the only alternatives available, without resorting to the sorts of indirect voter preference models suggested by Duncombe and Yinger.

Like inference from empirical observation, the professional judgment approach opens the possibility of centralizing a great deal of instructional decision making at the state level, if state policy makers use the approach not only to determine the amount of resources to make available to each district but also to fund individual components. This possibility has been of concern in Wyoming, as it was in Ohio. In Wyoming, state officials are seeking to avoid the danger of implementing adequacy in an overly prescriptive way by viewing state resources as a block grant that districts are free to use as they see fit to construct an adequate educational program.

The professional judgment approach can, as noted, be used when concerns about poorly specified outcome measures in education and/or the unavailability of outcome measures preclude inferences about adequacy from either statistical models or empirical observation. It is imprecise, but it has the virtue that its imprecision is transparent. It also involves experts explicitly weighing the best available knowledge about instructional components and their connection to desired educational outcomes, instead of taking the black-box approach to these issues, as do the approaches discussed above.

The method may be vulnerable to criticism because of a different black-box issue. Each of the individuals on the expert panels constitutes a black box of one. It is impossible to be sure of the basis of their professional judgment or to guarantee that each person is free of the kind of conflict of interest that would lead them to make judgments based on their own circumstances or the consequences for their arriving at particular "adequate" revenue levels. Moreover, the professional judgment approach may not turn out to be reliable; panels may arrive at different conclusions while using similar information. This did not happen initially in Wyoming, where two panels operating six months apart did arrive at similar judgments, but larger samples will be needed before the issue of reliability can be satisfactorily assessed.

Inference from Whole-School Designs

It may now or soon be possible to specify adequate resource levels based on a distillation of national empirical research about effective schools and judgments of professional researchers regarding effective practices. Such specifications might be based on "whole-school designs," off-the-shelf school blueprints intended for adoption in their entirety by schools (Odden, 1997; Odden and Busch, 1998). The New American Schools organization has adopted seven of these designs for promotion to schools, including Atlas Communities, based primarily on the School Development Program (SDP) developed by James Comer; the Audrey Cohen College System developed at the college of that name in New York City; Co-NECT, a school design developed by a Cambridge (Massachusetts) consulting firm; the Expeditionary Learning program affiliated with Outward Bound; the Modern Red Schoolhouse, designed by the Hudson Institute; the National Alliance for Restructuring Education, which cooperates with schools (e.g., in Kentucky) to restructure their resources to meet higher academic standards; and Roots and Wings/Success for All, developed by Robert Slavin's team at Johns Hopkins University. Other well known designs include the Edison Project, the E.D. Hirsch Core Knowledge Curriculum, the Accelerated Schools model developed by Henry Levin at Stanford, Theodore Sizer's Coalition of Essential Schools, and the CMCD program (Consistency Management and Cooperative Discipline) now being disseminated in Texas, Chicago, and Norfolk, Virginia (Fashola and Slavin, 1998; Glennan, 1998; Northwest Regional Educational Laboratory, 1998; Stringfield et al., 1996).

Whole-school designs are constructed to elevate student achievement. They are also intended by their designers to be salable to local school districts. They can be "purchased" to be implemented. Usually the design teams insist that they be engaged to oversee the training necessary for a school district staff team to implement the design. Because, however, these design teams realize fully that the marketability of their models depends importantly on having a satisfactory price, they are sensitive to costs.

None of the above-listed designs can yet be said to be firmly established by research, in the sense that the achievement of students in schools following these models has been proven superior in replicated controlled empirical or experimental studies. However, many education policy makers are impressed with anecdotal evidence concerning the success of some or all of these programs, with some limited empirical data that tends to confirm it. These designs will become more formidable if research continues to accumulate regarding their effectiveness. The resources specified by each of these designs (with the exception of the National Alliance for Restructuring Education, which does not promote a single design as such, but tailors its recommendations to individual affiliated schools) could be priced, and the sum might be considered the cost, at the school level, of an adequate education. One complicating factor, though, may be that this approach does not yield a very precise definition of the cost of adequacy. One recent estimate of 1996-97 first-year costs of implementing New American Schools designs ranged from $82,600 to $354,000 per school of 500 students above the core costs of a principal and regular classroom teachers, or $165 to $708 per pupil (Odden and Busch, 1998). Moreover, cost estimates may turn out to be quite sensitive to local circumstances.

Making Adjustments for Student, School, and Geographic Characteristics

It has long been recognized that school districts face differences in input prices and differences in the educational needs of their students, both of which affect the cost of providing educational services. Traditional approaches to school finance equity (such as wealth neutrality and equal spending) could in theory accommodate adjustments to take account of these differences, but in reality these cost differences have been tackled in unsystematic and sporadic ways. The shift toward adequacy, however, makes the issue of adjusting costs unavoidable. It is unfair to hold a high-cost district or school to the same standard of adequacy in its educational program as a lower-cost district or school unless the district or school is given enough resources to compensate it for the higher costs that are outside its control. Indeed, if policy makers fail to take these cost differences into account as they revise their formulas for distributing education aid, they may leave high-cost districts serving disadvantaged students worse off than they were before.

While at least one approach to cost adjustment accounts simultaneously for geographic and student differences (see the discussion of Duncombe and Yinger's work below), it is useful, at least initially, to discuss these different adjustments separately to emphasize the need to take both kinds of cost issues into account. Doing so helps illuminate an important fact. There has been quite a bit of analytical work done on geographic adjustments, and the conceptual issues have been relatively thoroughly explored. Yet school finance distribution formulas seldom explicitly incorporate geographic adjustments. (It is possible that adjustments are being made implicitly, in the sense that weights and other features are added that drive dollars to areas that are perceived to have higher input prices.) In contrast, the knowledge base about the differential costs of educating children with differing needs (such as those from non-English-speaking or economically disadvantaged backgrounds) is comparatively weak. Despite this weak conceptual basis, many school finance programs attempt to account for these differential costs, either by adjusting the per-pupil weights in allocation formulas to account for the presence of special-needs students or via separate categorical programs aimed at these students.

School finance experts have historically approached the problem of adjusting input costs from place to place by focusing on personnel costs, since personnel represent 80 percent of local school budgets (Peternick et al., 1998). Three examples of personnel-based indices developed to assess resources and costs are Barro's (1992) average-teacher-salary (ATS) index, McMahon and Chang's (1991) cost of living index, and Chambers' (1995) teacher cost index (TCI). (See footnote 12, Chapter 3 for an explanation of these indices.) The TCI is the most sophisticated of these approaches for examining national differences in teacher salaries and distinguishing the "cost" of education from actual education expenditures (which are influenced by district decisions about the level or mix of resources to use as well as by conditions outside district control). It is of more theoretical than practical use at this stage, however, as it is still considered developmental and its complex regression methodology and national adjustment factors are difficult for state policy makers to explain and defend, especially in the absence of adoption and certification by an authoritative official body (Rothstein and Smith, 1997). Instead, the handful of states which currently take account of differences in the cost of education from place to place do so by using state wage indices (Ohio), consumer price indices (Colorado, Florida, Wyoming), or regression analysis using state rather than national data (Texas). The advantages and disadvantages of the various methods (which are described in Mishel and Rothstein, 1997, and Rothstein and Smith, 1997) illustrate that there is no precise or correct method of making the proper adjustment for geographic differences, but that each method brings the state using it closer to a fairer distribution of education resources than would exist in the absence of the adjustments. Moreover, Mishel and Rothstein (1997) suggest that further advances in developing usable education cost indices might come from more research into the numerous geographic cost indices that have been developed for noneducation programs and exploration into the regional patterns that might become evident across methodologies.

Compared to input-price differences, states and the federal government have been more likely to recognize differences in the costs of educating students who are at risk educationally for a variety of reasons. This is accomplished either through special funding programs or by adjusting the allocation formulas in general aid programs to take account of the presence of at-risk students. For the purposes of this discussion of calculating the costs of adequacy, it is the cost adjustments in the general aid formulas that are of most interest.

In 1993-94, 36 states used some form of weighting procedure to adjust basic education support for the additional educational services needed by specific student populations (Gold et al., 1995). (Not all these adjustments necessarily reflected at-risk populations; some states used weights based on differences in grade levels and educational programs.) There appears to be little consistency among states in how these adjustment factors are established. Gold et al. (1995:36) report, for example, that the weights for students in special education programs "appear to vary from being close to arbitrary to being very directly related to actual costs."

Researchers conducting cross-state spending or revenue comparisons (e.g., Parrish et al., 1995, 1998) frequently adjust per-pupil numbers for student needs by using weights of 2.3 for special education students and 1.2 for poor children and children with limited proficiency in English. As Parrish et al. (1995) point out, however, these cost factors are very imprecise due to a lack of relevant data.

The 2.3 factor for special education comes from a study (Moore et al., 1988) using data from a nationally representative sample of 60 school districts in school year 1985-86 and represents the average cost of serving a special education student as a multiplier of the cost of serving a regular education student. This single number, besides perhaps being unreflective of current practice, masks considerable variation in the costs of providing services to students whose disabilities differ substantially in severity and in the intensity of services required.

The 1.2 weight often assigned to children in poverty is based on the average federal Title I allocation for a school year. Levin (1989) derived the 1.2 weight based on average revenues and Title I (then called Chapter 1) allocation per student for 1987. While this indicator may be the best currently available for determining a weighting for students in poverty and is easily understood, it results from federal budget decisions about what to spend on Title I, not on a calculation of the costs of educating poor children and of compensating for prior deprivation that may affect their educational performance. It makes no allowance for the possibility that the additional costs of educating poor children may be higher on a per-pupil basis when there are large concentrations of poor children in a school than when the proportion of poor children is lower. Orland (1990), for example, suggests that attending school with other students from poverty backgrounds is more detrimental for a poor child than being poor but attending school with middle-income students. There is something about the impact of a concentration of low-income students that is itself detrimental. It may be simply that the social capital of one's classmates, or the lack of it, affects learning. Moreover, the 1.2 ratio also understates even the amount of additional money made available for compensatory services to poor students in 1987, since it did not take account of state compensatory programs. The 1.2 weight typically assigned to limited-English-proficient children is merely an extension of the poverty adjustment. Parrish et al. explain the selection of this weight by citing the absence of reliable and representative data on the costs of services to these students and on the logical conclusion that such students are unlikely to cost less to educate than poor students.

Assigning weights to at-risk students, of course, assumes that such students can be identified; but even this is problematic. Poor children, for example, are frequently identified by their eligibility for the free or reduced price lunch program, but this is an imprecise indicator at best. Participation rates vary widely, even among schools that may be socioeconomically similar. Older children are often reluctant to be included in the program and their schools do not push the issue; participation rates in elementary school also relate to how aggressively school administrators and teachers promote it. Counting the number of children with disabilities is complicated because each state can use its own operational definitions for classifying such children, and districts can and do use different criteria for determining whether a child with a disability is counted in the special education or regular education population.

Econometricians, as noted above, have recently made important theoretical and empirical strides in developing statistical models to adjust for the cost of public services beyond a local government's control and have applied these models to education (Duncombe and Yinger, 1999; Reschovsky and Imazeki, 1998). These models contain adjustments for both input-price differences and for the presence of special-needs students.

The most sophisticated application of this approach is found in the work of

Duncombe and Yinger (1999). Using data from 631 school districts in New York, they estimated the average effects on district spending of the following "cost factors," that is, characteristics of each district that are outside the immediate control of school officials that affect the costs of educating students: input prices, district size, percentage of children in poverty, percentage of female-headed households, percentage of students with severe disabilities, and the percent of students with limited English proficiency. This work is more sophisticated than other efforts to develop cost estimates in that the authors use a creative (but somewhat controversial) method to control for the relative efficiency or inefficiency of each district and in that they explicitly account for the fact that educational outcomes, spending on education, and production are all simultaneously determined.

Emerging from their analyses are estimates of cost indices for each district. A district's cost index is 100 if it has average values of all the cost factors, exceeds 100 to the extent the district faces a harsher than average environment for educating students (as measured by its cost factors), and is less than 100 to the extent that the district faces a less harsh environment for educating students. For example, based on their most complete model, the authors estimate that the cost indices for the state's upstate large cities (which include Buffalo, Rochester, and Syracuse) average 189. This figure implies that the cost of providing an adequate education in those districts would exceed the cost of adequacy for the average district by 89 percent. In contrast, costs in 47 small upstate cities are estimated to exceed the average by only 9 percent, while those in upstate suburbs fall short of the average by about 9 percent. The most striking cost indices are for Yonkers (with a cost index of 192) and New York City, with a cost index of 397. (All figures are in Duncombe and Yinger, 1999: Table 8-2, column 2). Taken literally, the New York City estimate would imply that the city would need almost four times as much revenue per pupil as the typical district to educate its students to an adequate level. However the estimates for New York City are quite dependent on the particular specification of the equation and range from 112 to 397. These very large differences underscore the challenges of specifying the model correctly.

This econometric approach to estimating cost differentials highlights the important observation that education costs may well vary quite dramatically across districts depending on the characteristics of the district. As Duncombe and Yinger document, their estimated cost indices exhibit much greater variation across districts than those based on the weighted pupils method currently used by New York State, which weights secondary, disabled, and other-at-risk students more heavily than the typical student, or those based on average teacher salaries. The implication is that relative to the district with average cost factors, the state is currently providing inadequate assistance to some districts (those with high cost indices) and is giving relatively too much state assistance to other districts (those with low cost indices).

Although not yet sufficiently developed to be translated into actual state determinations of funding adequacy, this type of research is extremely important in that it highlights the potentially large variation in cost differences across districts. It is not yet ready to be used by policy makers because a number of technical issues deserve further attention (such as the best way to account for inefficiency), the results vary with the specification of the equation (as evidenced by the variation in results for New York City), insufficient attention has been paid to some important issues (such as ensuring that the teacher salary measures used in the analysis are outside the control of schools so they are not confounded with teacher quality, and accounting for how the cost indices would be likely to vary depending on the desired level of educational outcomes), and the lack of transparency of the approach to policy makers. This last limitation should not be viewed as diminishing the potential usefulness of this approach. As this approach is perfected further, the cost indices it generates can be used as a standard against which more straightforward and easy-to-understand measures can be compared. The ultimate goal would be to develop simple measures that appropriately capture the cost variations that emerge from a conceptually and statistically sound model.

Adjusting for Scale Economies

School finance distribution formulas in approximately 15 states, ranging in enrollment size, income and ethnic diversity, and economic complexity from California, New York, and Florida to Utah and Wyoming, contain a size adjustment factor (Gold et al., 1995). Some states adjust for large size. They accord large districts added per-pupil revenue, presumably justified because there are diseconomies in operating unusually large organizations. Other states adjust for unusual small size, districts, schools, or both.

In some instances, small schools or districts are accorded added revenues on a sliding or weighted scale commensurate with enrollment levels. In other instances, states provide added funds to ensure that selected core curriculum offerings are affordable, even when enrollment levels are too small to generate the necessary funding under other formula provisions. Other states have adopted a per-pupil multiplier by which revenues are increased for students enrolled in small schools (Odden and Picus, 1992).

No two states have adopted a distribution scheme that contains a similar formula component or approach specifying additional revenues a school or district should receive because of enrollment size. The general understanding that per-unit operating costs are known to increase with small or large enrollments (diseconomies of scale) does not translate to policy agreement on specific levels of added costs. This is true both for school and district diseconomy adjustments.

Research on scale economies has been impeded by a general lack of school level spending data. School districts assert that they spend more per pupil in quite small schools. They assuredly do. However, seldom can they report specifically how much more such schools spend and in which accounting categories. Until more accurate spending data are available over a broader sphere of districts, it is unlikely that a technical base for scale adjustments can be constructed.

School administrators, having been informed that scale economies exist for schools, have often opted to construct large schools. Some city school districts have constructed elementary and secondary schools accommodating literally thousands of students. Whatever, if any, economic advantages such large size may confer, it is far less clear that there are commensurate educational advantages. Indeed, given the prospect of estrangement and anomic behavior among students in unusually large schools, administrators might do well to reexamine their preferences for large scale.

Existing research regarding scale economies suffers from another deficiency. Researchers have adopted overly simple models that, even when school-level spending data are employed, do not take student achievement sufficiently into account. There is evidence (Barker and Gump, 1972; Haller et al., 1990; King, 1994; Lee and Smith, 1997) to suggest that small school settings are educationally advantageous to the students enrolled in them. There are reported benefits such as greater student academic engagement and commitment to meeting instructors' expectations. Also, there appears often to be a productive linking of community to school in smaller settings. If research were conducted properly, policy makers would have a better sense of the balance of advantages and disadvantages between school and district size and student performance.

The solution to scale diseconomies that was most widespread in the middle of the 20th century was to offer financial inducements for districts to close small schools and for states to consolidate small school districts. However, in light of the shortage of evidence that elimination of small operating units in fact has saved money and may have diluted favorable learning settings and communitarian engagement, states have been reducing consolidation pressures.

Recent slowing of state efforts to eliminate small units has not, though, resulted in research about the funding levels needed for them to operate productively. The absence of appropriate data on which to construct a firm research base has led to each state constructing idiosyncratic revenue distribution arrangements. These arrangements are far more of a political than a technical construct.

One of the vexing situations facing state policy makers is to distinguish between a community's preference for small schools and the necessity of having small schools. Presumably, population sparsity and rural remoteness can trigger the need for a "necessary" small school. Here, it is generally acknowledged, the state has an obligation to allocate added revenues to ensure that students are fairly treated. However, if a community merely chooses to have a small school in order to take advantage of the sense of engagement that such an institution may offer, is the state still obligated to pay the added costs? State policy makers generally answer this question in the negative. However, specifying statutorily what is to separate a necessary from a preferred small school may prove difficult. Among the adjustments are distance. A necessary small school can be defined as one in which a student must travel a specified distance, say more than two miles, in order to attend. States have also attempted to impose a criterion for distance between schools. If schools are located within a specified radius of one another, then it is thought that this is a sign of a preferred, not a necessary, circumstance.

Adjusting for Inflation

After the challenges of determining what an adequate education costs in any given year are met, another task remains: adjusting for inflation each year so appropriations tied to adequacy keep up with changes in the costs of education. Failure to adjust for inflation was one key reason why state foundation grants, a common finance mechanism earlier in the century, over time fell badly below the amounts districts needed to meet basic educational needs.

Disagreements among analysts about how to take account of inflation make it hard to draw conclusions about how the production efficiency of schools has changed over time. The same conceptual dilemmas will face analysts seeking to adjust adequacy levels for inflation. On one hand, school inflation will generally be more rapid than consumer price or gross national product inflation. The latter are heavily influenced by improvements in manufacturing productivity that cannot be matched by schools that rely heavily on labor and where opportunities for technological improvements are comparatively limited. Therefore using consumer price or gross national product indices to adjust for inflation in education will underestimate the real increase in education costs. On the other hand, efforts to develop price indices specifically for education have been few (the major example being an index developed by Halstead [1983; Research Associates of Washington, 1993] that extends back to 1975) and are controversial. In particular, treatment of teacher salaries in education-specific indices has been questioned. The Halstead index is based on actual salary changes and therefore does not reflect the fact that teacher pay reflects district choices about whether to pay teachers more or less than comparable workers, choices that are presumed to affect teacher quality (Rothstein and Mishel, 1997). Efforts to develop inflation adjustments that can be used in specific states to update adequacy levels are in their infancy. An early example for Wyoming is described in Guthrie and Rothstein (1999); the authors also note that how best to account for inflation in any given state may depend on specific characteristics of that state, such as the competitiveness of its teacher labor market.

PROMISES AND PITFALLS

The shift toward adequacy as the equity standard to be sought is appealing because it offers the promise of reorienting debates over school finance toward fundamental issues of education reform.

Adequacy focuses school finance discussions squarely on issues of education and student achievement. It thus brings education finance into the central policy dialogue about education, which is concerned with improving school and student performance. More than other equity concepts, adequacy is therefore directly rather than just indirectly related to goals 1 and 2, which have to do with student achievement. Adequacy suggests, but does not guarantee, that educational policy will increasingly be driven by a concern for spending resources in instructionally effective ways, which speaks to goal 1.

Adequacy implies that discussion of the level of educational resources to be made available should include explicit consideration of what the public and policy makers want the educational system to accomplish and what kinds of educational opportunities students must be given to meet these objectives. This orientation stands in contrast to much past and current decision making about education finance, which often is dominated by political bargaining over how to distribute available funds.

Adequacy promises to be especially important for addressing the second of the three goals: reducing the nexus between student background characteristics and student achievement. It requires, rather than just permits, attention to cost adjustments, a topic addressed further in Chapter 7. It also may lead to more focus on urban areas, where education is generally thought to be least adequate. Court cases and policy debates over the adequacy of school funding in cities should help resolve the question of whether money is the key problem in urban schools and focus attention on all the factors affecting the productivity of these schools.

While attracted by the appeal of these promises, the committee notes that there are major unresolved questions that must be addressed if school finance is to be held to an adequacy standard. By raising these questions, we do not intend to prejudge the ultimate usefulness of the adequacy concept; earlier concepts of equity were also daunting in their infancy, but over time much progress was made in defining and measuring them. What we do intend to point out is that adequacy as an equity concept still requires much development and must be used with an awareness of this fact. As courts and policy makers seek to apply an adequacy standard and as researchers attempt to improve understanding of adequacy, they must keep in mind the importance of addressing the following kinds of issues.

• The meaning of adequacy is still unclear. Major questions remain open: is it a wide, high standard or a narrow, low standard? Does it focus attention and resources primarily on the disadvantaged or does it contribute to improving achievement for all students? These are not technical questions for which scientific answers can be provided; they will require difficult political judgments that may be subject to the same kinds of public resistance that have faced finance reformers in the past.

• What will it mean to extend the concept of adequacy as an equity standard to federal, school, and student-level policies, not just to the district level, where most court decisions to date have focused? How can the concept be applied to school finance decisions that might arise under different institutional arrangements for public funding of education, e.g., to a system that embraces charter schools or vouchers or both as well as traditional public schools?

• If states permit district add-ons to the state-determined "adequate" spending level (as some court decisions already explicitly allow, while others do not), is this not likely to result in spending disparities that continue to put children from poor families or children living in poor communities at a relative disadvantage in terms of the educational opportunities they are offered? If add-ons are allowed, might not this reduce the support of people in wealthy communities for having the state set a high level of adequate spending?

• What happens to the definition of an adequate education when it collides in the political arena with demands to "adequately" fund a host of other worthy objectives, such as better health care, a cleaner environment, well-maintained roads and bridges, safer streets, and so on? Even when a state court (as in Wyoming) finds grounds in the state constitution for giving education pride of place before all other public services, is it really possible to resolve basic resource allocation decisions about education in some rational and technical fashion rather than in the political arena? In this sense, is adequacy really something new under the sun or mainly a new and perhaps misleading label for the customary and unavoidable process of political bargaining?

• How will courts or legislators determine if funding is adequate? It would clearly be a mistake to require that all students attain a certain level of achievement, since by that criterion any school that did not reach that goal would be entitled to additional funding no matter how inefficient it might be. The intent instead should be to ensure that schools have the resources that they would need to achieve the desired outcome, assuming that they produced education reasonably efficiently. The challenge arises in figuring out what that amount is.

This last point emphasizes the fundamental problem with adequacy as a new standard for school finance—namely, that it requires better knowledge than currently exists about how to determine what an adequate education costs. In fact, the state of the knowledge base is such that we are far from being able to provide empirically sound answers to the key questions of "adequacy for what" and "how much is adequate." This fundamental problem becomes clearer as we take up the issue of educational productivity in the next chapter.

5

Improving the Productivity of Schools

The 1980s and 1990s saw public attention shift from the paramount concern for educational equity that characterized the late 1960s and 1970s to a growing concern for how well schools are performing and how effectively the nation's huge education budget is being spent. Skepticism about the quality of schools was reinforced by a series of critical reports from blue-ribbon committees and commissions—15 of them in the single year of 1983 when *A Nation at Risk* came out (Guthrie et al., 1988:151). Questions about whether the public was getting value for money from its education spending were reinforced by a highly visible debate among scholars about whether money matters in determining the quality of education provided to the nation's schoolchildren. These developments pushed the question of the productivity of education to the forefront of the education policy agenda and highlighted the importance of learning how to spend education dollars wisely.

Sorting out what is known about educational productivity is crucial for its own sake, but also because of its implications for achieving educational equity. How readily this concept can be translated into practical school finance systems depends on how well financial resources are used to produce the desired educational outcomes. Likewise, the fate of efforts to align school finance systems with efforts to accomplish key education goals—raising achievement levels for all students and breaking the nexus between student background characteristics and student performance—hinges on the ability to make finance decisions that lead to improved productivity of schools.

While interest in obtaining education as inexpensively as possible has long been a concern of those who finance schools, it took a back seat following World

War II to the need to expand the school system quickly to cope with rapidly rising enrollments stemming from the baby boom. Scholars and reformers returned to the issue of how best to use education dollars with new vigor in the years after publication of the Coleman report (Coleman et al., 1966), with its finding that resource differences apparently had little effect on the outcomes of schooling. To the traditional efforts of psychologists and educational psychologists to understand learning and how to enhance it were added new efforts by economists and others interested in understanding how the resources purchased by schools were linked to educational outcomes (Monk, 1990:312).

Much has been learned from the investigations of these researchers. The issue of educational productivity remains a complex one, however. For a number of reasons, the concept itself is elusive and difficult to measure. There is as yet no generally accepted theory to guide finance reform efforts; rather there are multiple theories, each of which is incomplete. The various theories do not generate consistent strategies for action. In addition, empirical studies seeking to determine the best ways to direct resources to improve school performance have often not produced consistent findings. This is not surprising, given the conceptual difficulties and data limitations.

All of this is not to argue that there is no useful theory or evidence about promising avenues to pursue to increase educational productivity: there is a great deal. Shortcomings in current scientific methods for studying educational productivity, however, mean that much of existing knowledge is best viewed as tentative and contingent. The chief implication of this fact for school finance is that good policy will reflect both the best knowledge available to date *and* the need to continue experimenting and evolving as new knowledge becomes available.

DEFINING AND MEASURING PRODUCTIVITY

"Educational productivity" is a term with a variety of possible meanings.

When Americans say that they want their schools to perform better, they are saying that they want their schools to be more "productive." This usage of the term corresponds to the dictionary definition of productivity as the ability of an entity to produce abundantly or to yield favorable or useful results.

Productivity also has a narrower definition, however, one drawn primarily from economics. The economic perspective on productivity emphasizes the relationship between outputs and inputs of a firm or organization or economic sector. At its most familiar, perhaps, productivity is a measure of output per unit of labor. Statistics on productivity measured in this way are routinely gathered, especially for private-sector firms, and widely reported. They have also been the subject of much public discussion over the past 30 years, especially because private-sector productivity growth in the United States had suffered a slowdown beginning in 1973 and lasting until the 1990s, reversing the economic conditions that had prevailed and undergirded American prosperity since World War II.

In education, productivity is often taken to mean using the inputs and processes of schooling in ways that increase desired outcomes. The most common measures of outcomes have been students' academic achievement while they are in school (often measured by scores on standardized tests) and student performance upon entering the labor market (generally measured by wages) (Burtless, 1996:3).

This comparatively narrow view of the desired outputs of education, and therefore of the meaning of productivity in education, does not take into account the variety of goals that Americans typically hold for their schools. Improvements in character, citizenship, and physical and mental health are just some of the nonacademic outcomes that schools have been expected to foster. Moreover, schools (like churches, for example) are often valued for the quality of the experience itself. For example, many people would argue that an important aspect of school performance is the kind of environment children experience during their many years of enforced school attendance. In other words, the *process* of schooling may be a valued aspect of school performance in and of itself, distinguishable from the value placed on the outcomes of education.

The variety of goals Americans hold for their schools is a key reason why educational productivity is hard to define and measure. To make operational the concept of productivity first requires the specification of which educational outcomes are of primary interest. While applying the concept of productivity in education is often frustratingly hard, it is worth observing that contrary to popular wisdom, productivity is also a complex topic in business. The committee found that the difficulties in grappling with the concept echoed those of an earlier National Research Council panel, which was established to think about how improved organizational linkages might contribute to productivity growth in American business. That panel found itself similarly torn over the appropriate concept and definition of productivity to use. It noted (National Research Council, 1994:8):

> Perhaps the panel is not alone in being unable to arrive at a consensus. In a review of the literature on productivity, Pritchard (1991) found that the term *productivity* was used to encompass constructs as diverse as efficiency, output, motivation, individual performance, organizational effectiveness, production profitability, cost-effectiveness, competitiveness, and work quality . . . .
>
> Panel members held one or the other of two positions regarding the concept of productivity. Some wanted to define productivity as the ratio of outputs to inputs, in line with the original definition of the term by labor economists. They believe that this is the only definition that is unique to the concept. Others argued that this definition is too restrictive. They believe that productivity must encompass concepts such as quality and effectiveness to be meaningful.

That panel resolved its dilemma by adopting a systems model of organizational performance and recognizing productivity as but one of seven interrelated and interdependent criteria of organizational performance. For that panel, the seven criteria were effectiveness, efficiency, quality, productivity, quality of work life, innovation, and profitability (or, for cost-center organization systems, budgetability—Sink and Smith, 1994:134-7). In this view, productivity provides just one part of the performance picture, and the different criteria of performance in addition to productivity might each require several different measures.

In the committee's judgment, it is essential to recognize that the question of improving school performance similarly requires consideration of a variety of criteria in addition to the input-output ratio orientation of the economic definition of productivity. Likewise, the multiplicity of process and outcome objectives of education must be reflected in any evaluation of whether American schools are accomplishing what the nation demands of them.

For the purposes of this report, nevertheless, we deliberately adopt a narrower focus for productivity analysis, one in keeping with our charge: What do we know about how to improve school performance in terms of improving the academic achievement of students? Academic achievement is widely (although perhaps not universally) recognized as a key objective of education. It is the most frequently measured outcome. It is generally viewed as a springboard to the "good life," defined not only as economic opportunity via participation in the labor market but also as opportunity actively to engage in and benefit from the social, cultural, and political aspects of society.

Settling on academic achievement as the focus of interest in school performance, however, reduces but by no means eliminates the difficulties in defining and measuring educational productivity. Several additional problems deserve mention.

First, as discussed in Chapter 4, there are serious disagreements over how well existing measures capture the most significant aspects of academic achievement.

Second, weighing outcomes is a problem even if one narrows the discussion to something as seemingly simple as academic achievement measured by test scores in various subject areas or as graduation from high school. This situation differs from the private sector, where outcomes can be weighted by prices. For example, consider a firm that produces cars and trucks. Total output can be measured as the sum of the cars and trucks with each weighted by their price. The prices are appropriate weights because they reflect both the consumers' valuation of the two types of products and the relative costs of producing the two products. With respect to education, the appropriate weights for the various outcomes is not obvious and, because different people or groups of people are likely to have different values, is ultimately a political issue.

Resources—that is, the inputs used in the education process—are also multidimensional. However, because resources are purchased through the private market, it is not unreasonable to add them together using their prices as the weights. One major complication arises to the extent that different levels of resources are used for different students. For example, if some of the teachers in a school are used to teach special education students and those students are in smaller classes than regular students, it would be inappropriate to treat the average number of teachers per student (based on all students) as the resource level for educating regular students. This issue is especially salient to the extent that special education or other students are not tested under a state's regular system for assessing student performance. That is, when some groups of students are excluded from the state's measure of student performance, the resource costs of educating them should not be included in the measure of inputs.

A further complication arises because a child's family background and certain characteristics of the community in which he or she lives (for example, the incidence of poverty) contribute significantly to his or her educational success. By highlighting these types of factors, the 1966 Coleman report (Coleman et al., 1966) and recent work by Miller (1995) and Steinberg (1996) suggest that educational outcomes are not produced by schools alone.

Actually, the situation is even more complicated because human interactions and motivations are at the heart of the educational process and these interactions and motivations are constantly in flux and are difficult to observe (Murnane and Nelson, 1984:368-9). Good teachers continuously adjust their "production techniques" to the particular situation of their classroom and the individual students in it. Students, who are the presumed objects of the educational process, are also subjects: active, thinking, feeling, inconsistent human beings whose attitudes and moods and values and varying degrees of willingness to commit themselves to academic pursuits influence productivity mightily. And many of them, in addition, do not think of themselves foremost as students. They are young people trying to work out their needs and longings and insecurities and identities in this vast arena called the school because that is where society tells them they have to go, whether or not they take the formal learning part seriously. Moreover, the way in which these students engage or decline to engage with their studies in the school, and the values they acquire and the behavior they exhibit, are shaped as much (or more) by the peer culture and the youth media environment as by school inputs.

For all of these reasons, defining and measuring the productivity of American schools is far from an easy task. Over the years many have expressed skepticism about how accurately or fully production relationships in education can ever be captured (e.g., Levin, 1974; Guthrie, 1976; Murnane and Nelson, 1984; Monk, 1990; Hanushek, 1997b). This caveat must be kept in mind in reviewing the research on improving the educational performance of schools and the academic achievement of their students.

UNDERSTANDING EDUCATIONAL PRODUCTIVITY

Scholars from a number of disciplines have conducted studies aimed at understanding how educational resources are linked to the academic achievement of schoolchildren, resulting in what Monk (1990:315) has characterized as a "large and unwieldy body of research." The growing breadth of academic perspectives being brought to bear on educational productivity is a good sign for the ultimate prospects of understanding the complex relationships involved. The downside of all of this activity, however, is the difficulty of trying to ascertain what is known about educational productivity and sorting out the diverse and sometimes conflicting messages emerging from studies that ask different questions, draw on different theoretical models, utilize different research approaches (in methods of both selecting study subjects and collecting evidence), and weigh evidence differently.

Standards of evidence are particularly problematic when multiple research traditions are involved. Studies carried out utilizing quantitative research methods and random samples of schools or students may be easier to evaluate because "the canon of positivist, *quantitative* research is well established" and "there is a relatively high degree of agreement about what constitutes a good quantitative research design" (Kroesen et al., 1998:2). Yet such studies often suffer from serious limitations in the details they can capture about the important determinants of outcomes in an activity like education. Qualitative research methods (interviews, observations, ethnographies) can incorporate information about how schools work that extends far beyond the statistics gathered in surveys or administrative records and that probes not only which but how resources make a difference in learning. However, the methods used for choosing who will be studied in these qualitative ways sometimes lead to serious questions about the generalizability of the results. Moreover, the "canon for qualitative research is less clear" and, according to one thoughtful guide to the literature, the profound philosophical differences among those who use these methods may mean "there may never be agreement on the 'standard' or 'good' ways of using qualitative research" (Kroesen et al., 1998:2).

We deal with these difficulties by making transparent the different research approaches underlying the findings and by pointing out the strengths and shortcomings of the incomplete theories and imperfect methods and data that characterize virtually all educational productivity studies.

The large and unwieldy research base seems to provide at least three alternative lenses for viewing the important relationship between educational resources and academic achievement. The first two, input-output studies and studies of effective educational practices, while differing significantly in method, both "rest on the notion that there is an imitable 'technology' of education, in that it is presumed that if one system or school or class can do something within certain effects, so can others" (Murnane and Nelson, 1984:356). Researchers in these two traditions focus on finding the resources or the educational practices that are associated with good performance and can enhance school effectiveness. They approach this task in dramatically different ways, however, with input-output researchers treating schools as a black box and focusing on identifying the statistical relationships between resources and achievement, while students of effective practice concentrating on specifying the exact nature of what goes on inside the classroom and the school that seems to matter for student performance. The third lens offers an institutional perspective on schools and educational productivity, suggesting that the environments in which schools function exercise a crucial influence on the educational choices schools make (or have thrust upon them). Like the first lens, the third lens is not specifically concerned with *how* schools use resources to improve effectiveness; instead, lens 3 focuses on creating conditions that will encourage school personnel to use their resources well.

We adopted these lenses as a heuristic device, not intending to suggest that research neatly falls into these categories. The lenses have proven helpful to us, however, in sifting a large amount of evidence and in understanding why the messages from research about educational productivity are so difficult to bring into sharp relief.

Lens 1: Input-Output Studies

Input-output studies (also known as studies of the education production function) have fueled the fires of debate over whether money matters in education since the Coleman report of the mid-1960s produced its surprising and counterintuitive finding that school resources (at least those it measured) did not have much effect on the academic achievement of students.

The Coleman report became the progenitor of literally hundreds of additional studies, not only because of the controversial nature of its conclusions, but also because it represented one of the most massive and complex social science efforts that had been mounted up to that time. It involved a huge data collection effort (the Equality of Educational Opportunity Survey) that gathered information on 570,000 students and 60,000 teachers from a sample of 4,000 schools across the country. It entailed special testing of students in five grades on their verbal, reading, and mathematics comprehension. Students also filled out extensive surveys regarding their family background and other education-related factors (such as the amount of time they spent on homework, their classroom experiences, and their classmates). Teachers provided information on their educational backgrounds, professional activities, working conditions, and attitudes about school. In addition, extensive information on school facilities was also collected. Coleman and his colleagues utilized the most sophisticated statistical techniques available to look at the effects of school resources on student achievement while taking account of differences in the background characteristics of students and other likely influences on educational outcomes.

The Coleman report finding that drew the most attention and controversy and that has been studied and debated ever since was:

> Taking all these results together, one implication stands out above all: that schools bring little influence to bear on a child's achievement that is independent of his background and general social context; and that this very lack of an

independent effect means that the inequalities imposed on children by their home, neighborhood, and peer environment are carried along to become the inequalities with which they confront adult life at the end of school. For equality of educational opportunity through the schools must imply a strong effect of schools that is independent of the child's immediate social environment, and that strong independent effect is not present in American schools (Coleman et al., 1966:325).

The research techniques and theoretical underpinnings on which the Coleman team and subsequent analysts have built draw on a production function framework first developed in economics to describe the relationship between the output of a firm and the inputs used in the production process. This framework assumes "that a systematic process governs the transformation of inputs into outcomes" (Monk, 1990:342). It translates this relationship into a mathematical function that can be applied to data based on the actual experiences of firms. The results express the amount of additional output that can be obtained from additional quantities of input.

Education researchers in the input-output study tradition typically (though not always) apply statistical multiple regression techniques to survey data on schools to measure the education production function. They attempt to isolate the effects of educational inputs that can be manipulated (typically those that can be purchased or otherwise directly shaped by policy) while controlling for influences not readily controllable by educational authorities. The quasi-experimental research design draws on the natural variation in school resources and other practices found in schools and school systems, rather than trying to manipulate these variations deliberately via true experimental research, such as that frequently conducted in the medical sciences. Only a handful of education experiments have been conducted, in which random assignment of subjects to treatment groups allows for direct measurement of treatment effects (thereby avoiding the potential for biased or misleading findings that can result from the need in quasi-experiments to control for important nonschool differences among subjects via statistical techniques). The most significant of the education experiments for this discussion of productivity involves a Tennessee study of the effects of class size on student achievement in the early grades, discussed below.

In the 30-plus years since the Coleman report was published, literally hundreds of input-output studies have been conducted seeking to confirm or deny the Coleman findings and extend the research to include additional possible explanatory variables and apply new or different research techniques.

Hanushek (1986, 1996, 1997a) undertook influential summaries of 377 educational production function studies, which led him to conclude that "there is no strong or consistent relationship between variations in school resources and student performance" (Hanushek, 1997a:141). Hanushek focused on what the input-output studies revealed about the impact of inputs frequently assumed to matter to educational achievement and therefore frequently studied: teacher-pupil ratio, teacher education, teacher experience, teacher salary, per-pupil expenditure, administrative inputs, and school facilities. He conducted his summary using a synthesis method known as "vote counting." This method essentially involves examining the regression coefficients for the same resource from different studies; categorizing each result according to whether it indicated a positive or negative or zero effect on academic achievement; and tabulating the results to summarize the overall conclusion about the effect of the resource based on all the studies that examined it.

Hanushek's summaries have probably had an impact second only to the original Coleman report itself in persuading people that money (or school) doesn't matter in efforts to improve education. Therefore, it is important to emphasize his point that he cannot find *systematic relationships* between variations in school resources and student performance. This is quite different from saying that schools and their attributes never matter. As Hanushek has expressed his view in recent work: "This finding of a lack of any general resource relationship is, however, very different from finding that schools have no differential impact. A number of subsequent studies [i.e., subsequent to the Coleman report] document rather conclusively that schools have significantly different effects on student achievement, even if the good schools are not necessarily those rich in traditionally measured inputs" (Hanushek, 1997b:302).

One possible objection to Hanushek's literature review is that the variables he examined did not involve the full array of school-related input measures that might possibly influence student achievement. Monk (1990) reviewed studies focusing on an additional set of school inputs suggested by educational production theory: learning technologies, the uses of time, public versus private organization of schools, and the size of districts and schools. Like Hanushek, he found no conclusive evidence in the literature that these resources systematically contribute to higher student achievement.

For a quarter of a century after Coleman, the dominant view of scholars in the input-output tradition was skepticism about the possibility of finding reliable relationships that could guide policy makers in their decisions about how to allocate resources and organize schools in ways that would lead to improved student academic outcomes. Comparatively recently, the prevailing view that school inputs cannot be unambiguously linked to student achievement has begun to be challenged, although a new consensus about the nature of the input-output relationship has not yet emerged.

A major challenge to Hanushek's work has come on methodological grounds. Hedges, Laine, and Greenwald (1994a) argued that Hanushek's vote-counting method for synthesizing studies results in a bias against finding positive effects of resources on student outcomes. They point, for example, to the fact that while vote counting can be used to summarize the direction and significance of the effects of resource variables on outcomes, it cannot determine the magnitude of any statistical effect.

Hedges et al. therefore applied a statistical technique called "meta-analysis" to the same studies that Hanushek examined. Meta-analysis is designed to combine statistical significance values from different studies that test the same hypothesis, thus testing the combined statistical significance of the relationship between school inputs and educational outcomes across studies (rather than counting each study separately). Hedges et al. concluded from their summary that the relationship between resources and student achievement is significant and generally large.

The debate among the synthesizers over what the literature says about whether money and schools matter has not yet been won by either side. Ongoing exchanges continue between Hanushek and the Hedges team; see, for example, Hanushek (1994) and Hedges et al. (1994b). Serious shortcomings in many studies of school productivity give both sides ammunition to question the conclusions drawn by the other about the meaning and significance of the results.[1] A recent Brookings Institution effort to answer the question "Does money matter?" (Burtless, 1996) reflected the range of scientific disagreement on the influence of school spending without resolving the differences that have emerged from over 30 years of research on the subject.

Meanwhile, scholars continue to undertake new studies using improved datasets and statistical approaches designed to overcome methodological criticisms of prior input-output research. Many of these studies are reporting positive findings about the relationship between school resources and student academic performance. Our sense is that the deep skepticism of the first 25 years after the Coleman report has given way in the academic community to a more cautious optimism that some regularities in the relationship may be identifiable through input-output research. Nevertheless, caution remains the operative word, since positive findings that schools make a difference (assuming that they hold up in repeated studies) may not easily translate into specific policies for improving the connection between resource use and results.

This dilemma can be seen in considering the implications of recent research suggesting that factors relating to teachers (especially teacher quality and class size) are significant in explaining differences in student academic achievement. A much-cited study by Ferguson (1991) dealt with one major criticism of

---

[1]Ferguson and Ladd (1996:265) point out that neither the Hanushek nor the Hedges et al. literature surveys attempted to distinguish between methodologically sound versus weak studies. Studies using the production function approach to studying educational productivity have frequently been criticized on one or more methodological grounds. Misspecification of production function models (i.e., omitting important variables, using inadequate proxies for variables that cannot be directly measured, or using cross-sectional data when longitudinal analysis might be more relevant) and the use of aggregated data (i.e., data on school districts) rather than disaggregated data (i.e., data on schools or students) are some of the reasons why the findings of input-output studies have been questioned.

input-output studies (the limited number of explanatory variables they typically include) by drawing on a large and unusually complete set of data assembled by school districts for the state of Texas. The dataset included comparatively rich information on teachers (such as their scores on a statewide recertification exam as well as their experience, education, and salary levels), average school characteristics (such as school size), as well as district characteristics such as total enrollment and pupil-teacher ratios, measures of school spending by major category, the size of the district's property tax base per student, and characteristics of surrounding districts as well as of each district and its students itself.

Ferguson found in Texas that the quality of schooling explained between a quarter and a third of the variation among Texas school districts in students' scores on statewide reading exams and that most of this effect was due to a single measure of teacher quality: teachers' performance on the recertification exam. Teaching experience and educational level also mattered, as did class size.[2] Reducing class size appeared to be very important in the primary grades. Ferguson and Ladd (1996) followed up his Texas work with an analysis of data for Alabama, making some methodological improvements (e.g., measuring class size directly rather than rely on a proxy measure and disaggregating data not just to the district but also to the student level). The analysis largely confirmed the earlier Texas findings and provided "strong support for the hypothesis that measurable school inputs affect student learning. . . . The primary unresolved issue is the level of the class size threshold below which further reductions would lead to no additional systematic gains in student learning" (Ferguson and Ladd, 1996:288).

An issue that arises in production studies in education is the direction of causality. It has long been recognized in production function research that biased estimates of coefficients can arise if there is two-way causality (see Berndt, 1991:457, for a brief discussion and references to the literature). Production function studies in education presume that the direction of causality is from inputs to achievement. This is eminently plausible. However, it is also quite plausible that causality also runs in the opposite direction. For example, the work of Hanushek et al. (1999) suggests that teachers prefer certain types of students over others. If more able teachers seek out schools with higher-achieving students, then a classic case of simultaneous equation bias is present. Likewise, if districts spend more for education when achievement is higher, then again reverse causality may be present. The neglect of potential simultaneous equations

---

[2]Ferguson, along with most researchers, was forced by data limitations to estimate class size by measuring pupil-teacher ratios. As he and Ladd point out in a subsequent study (Ferguson and Ladd, 1996:272), pupil-teacher ratios are an imperfect proxy for class size. Since reducing class size is an expensive policy option, it is useful to know as accurately as possible if smaller class sizes matter; therefore research measuring class size directly, as Ferguson and Ladd and the Tennessee class size experiment do, is an important advance.

bias in much education research is arguably an important reason for inconsistent findings across different studies. The difficulty of sorting out causality in quasi-experimental studies helps explain why truly experimental studies, though few in education, are often quite influential. The most significant example is a major class size experiment launched in 1985 in Tennessee.

Project STAR (summarized in Finn, 1998) ran from 1985 to 1989 in 79 elementary schools in Tennessee. Entering kindergarten students were randomly assigned to one of three class types: small (enrollment of 13-17), regular (enrollment of 22-26), or regular with a full-time teaching aid in addition to the regular teacher. Classes remained the same type for 4 years, through 3rd grade, while a new teacher was assigned at random to each class each year. About 7,500 pupils in more than 300 classrooms participated. After the original STAR project ended, Tennessee authorized a follow-up study (the lasting benefits study) to see how long the original benefits of small classes would persist.

Differences in the three class types were highly statistically significant, thanks to achievement gains in the small classes and not in the regular classes with aides. The benefits of small classes were found to be greater for minority students (most of whom were black) and for students attending inner-city schools. After kindergarten, the effects on reading and mathematics achievement were typically twice as large for blacks as for whites (Nye et al., 1993) and even larger for blacks in inner cities (Krueger, 1997). The effects were robust even after sensitivity analysis examined several limitations in the study design and implementation (Krueger, 1997), although researchers have questioned the extent to which meaningful gains occurred after the first year of enrollment in a small class (Hanushek, 1998).

Because of the experimental nature of the class-size study (and, no doubt, because its results correspond to the belief of many parents and teachers that smaller classes are better than larger ones), the Tennessee results have spurred efforts around the country to reduce class sizes, especially in the early grades. While not necessarily disputing the Tennessee findings, however, scholars have questioned whether reducing class sizes is the more effective use of resources.

Hanushek et al. (1998), for example, have drawn on the Texas database mentioned earlier, now augmented by longitudinal data on academic test scores for several cohorts of students at different grade levels, to examine whether there are significant differences among schools in their ability to raise academic achievement, what characteristics of schools seem to account for any differences in impact, and whether any such differences are systematically related to school resources or to measurable aspects of schools and teachers. While they found that schools vary greatly in the impact they have on student achievement and that the differences centered on the differential impact of teachers, they also found that differences among teachers are not readily measured by simple characteristics of the teachers and classrooms. In other words, the study provides strong support for the idea that teacher quality matters but indicates that the limited set of teacher attributes usually captured in input-output studies (those that directly affect school costs, like how much experience a teacher has or whether he or she has a master's degree) do not explain much of the variation in teacher quality. Class size had some impact on children from low-income families (especially younger children), but the effect of class size was swamped, according to the authors, by differences in teacher quality. The authors thus implicitly question the current weight being given in policy circles to class size reduction. They also point out a series of questions about class sizes that are highly relevant for policy purposes but about which there is as yet little or no knowledge.[3]

Using a comprehensive, longitudinal database and statistical mixed-model methodology developed to support the Tennessee Value-Added Assessment System, Sanders and his colleagues also found that teacher effects were the dominant factors affecting student achievement gains. Their results indicated that classroom context variables (including class size) were comparatively unimportant (Sanders and Rivers, 1996; Wright et al., 1997).

The input-output lens continues to generate provocative insights into educational productivity, and improved data and research methods may result in fewer conflicting findings in the future than in the past. Monk (1992), in his update on educational productivity research, cautions against assuming too quickly that new optimistic findings will be sustained upon further examination. Past history explains part of his caution, but so does the continuing fact of

> serious conceptual inadequacies in the underlying productivity model. Despite these studies' growing econometric sophistication, they remain fundamentally primitive black-box formulations where analysts have made little progress toward modeling what makes education distinct from other types of . . . production function techniques. In particular, scant attention has been paid to the nested nature of educational production wherein schools themselves produce inputs that are subsequently (or even simultaneously) used in the production of final outcomes. Neither has much progress been made toward modeling dynamic aspects of educational productivity. Instructional realities are not static and do not reproduce themselves in simple ways. The failure to model the changeable nature of education production processes is a serious limitation on this line of research (Monk, 1992:309-10).

---

[3]"The analysis of class size policies must address a series of fundamental issues: are the estimates of effect sizes relevant over the entire range of class sizes? What is the monetary value on achievement gains? And, what are the costs of class size reductions, particularly if we consider the average salaries required to reduce class size without reducing average teacher quality? Finally, the analysis would have to consider the alternative uses of the resources. Current spending on preschool, after school and summer programs is quite low particularly for lower income children, and to be efficacious it must be the case that the gains from resources devoted to class size exceed the benefits of using such resources in other ways" (Hanushek et al., 1998:33, footnote 27).

Research that examines school performance through the lens of effective practice, by contrast, does attempt to get into the black box and offers additional perspectives on how resources and student academic performance might relate.

Lens 2: Studies of Effective Educational Practice

While input-output studies largely trace their parentage to the 1966 Coleman report, scholars in schools of education and in fields such as psychology, sociology, and anthropology have been seeking to identify and understand the factors influencing school performance since the turn of the century.

Research in the effective practice tradition, unlike the economic research described above, is not guided explicitly by the idea of a production function in education, although much of it, too, appears to have been a search for a "technology" of education that could be identified and replicated. The search for this technology has been carried out in part through statistical studies, but more commonly via other methods such as case studies and program evaluations. These more qualitative approaches have enabled researchers to examine aspects of schools not readily captured in large-scale surveys or in administrative record-keeping systems, but at the price of raising serious questions about the reliability of the results and their generalizability to schools other than those specifically studied. Monk illustrates the difference in describing a subset of effective practice research, called effective school studies, of the 1970s and 1980s, but his point applies to the larger research tradition as well: "Instead of focusing on inputs and attributes, the alternative strategy is to focus first on outcomes. In particular, the idea is to identify a school believed to be unusually successful according to some criteria. Once identified, the school becomes the subject of intensive study, often making use of observation and interview data. The goal is to understand why and how the school attains its success. The underlying hope is that through the accumulation of such studies of successful . . . schools, insights can be gained into how to improve education offered elsewhere" (Monk, 1990:413).

Such an approach raises concerns among statisticians because it is likely to generate upward-biased estimates of the explanatory variables. In addition, by focusing on successful schools alone, researchers are unable to determine which factors are responsible for the superior measured outcomes rather than simply being correlated with them, and they are unable to determine which factors are of secondary importance. While the effective practice approach yields the benefit of intensive observation of a small sample, it has traditionally foregone the larger sample benefits of the less fine-grained production function approach.

Increasingly, though, scholars are drawing on insights from qualitative studies as well as developments in statistics (such as hierarchical linear modeling, which can help disentangle individual from organizational or group effects) to search for evidence of stable relationships using quantitative research designs that can address selection bias and other methodological concerns.[4]

Many studies of effective practice concentrate on teaching techniques, curricula, and organizational design, hoping to identify effective approaches that can be transferred to other educational settings. Unlike the input-output studies, which stemmed explicitly from a desire to explain the influences on academic performance, studies of effective practice frequently refer to measures other than or in addition to academic achievement. In fact, specific links to improvements in academic achievement have often been assumed or implied rather than explicit.

Thus, another important difference between input-output studies and traditional studies of effective practice is in the questions and evidence they consider. Smith et al. (1996) point out that in most of the former, "there is no measure of whether the teachers and schools in the surveys were focusing their instruction on bringing all students to achieve to high standards. There are not even any measures of the curriculum coverage or the depth to which material was taught. There are no adequate measures of teachers' quality, their knowledge of curriculum, or their ability to engage students. There are no measures of the degree to which schools have the autonomy and responsibility they need to design effective strategies or of the degree to which the overall district and state systems support the efforts of the schools . . . The school survey data used by most researchers generally do not include these measures. Very little of what has been found to influence achievement by psychologists, sociologists, and political scientists who actually get into and study classrooms and the educational system is ever evaluated as an 'input' in surveys" (Smith et al., 1996:21-2).

Researchers seeking to identify effective practice also reach outside education for evidence about improving performance in other kinds of organizations that might be applied to schools. Odden and Busch (1998:26-7) list a series of strategies used by organizations seeking significant improvements in performance: "set clear performance goals at the top, flatten the organizational structure, decentralize power and authority to work teams, involve employees in making key decisions about how to organize and conduct their work, invest heavily in capacity development, and hold teams accountable for results."[5]

---

[4]For examples of the latter, see Cohen and Hill (1998), on whether teacher development specifically linked to standards-based reform improved student achievement in California; Lee and Smith's 1997 analysis of what high school size works best and for whom, using hierarchical linear modeling and data from the National Educational Longitudinal Study; and Bryk and Driscoll's 1988 use of the High School and Beyond longitudinal study to explore issues related to schools as learning communities.

[5]The key literature they cite as the sources for these strategies includes Barzelay (1992); Katzenbach and Smith (1993); Lawler (1986, 1992, 1996); Mohrman (1994); and Mohrman et al. (1994).

While the research base of studies in the effective practice tradition is so large that it defies a short summary, Smith et al. (1996:15-18) identified eight key ideas growing out of the past 25 years of research on educational effectiveness that have been important in influencing current thinking about education reform:

- All students can learn to far higher levels than we ever imagined in the past.
- What a student is taught matters.
- The quality of teaching matters.
- Teachers are more likely to teach well things that they understand well and that they have been taught to teach.
- Schools, and the teaching and learning that occur in them, are more likely to change when the staff of the school has ownership and some control over the nature of the change.
- Teachers and the public do not have a common conception of what is meant by high and internationally competitive academic standards.
- Individual school reform has a long, complex, and unhappy history in the United States.
- The education system often does little to support change or to sustain schools that appear to be effective.

Unlike the findings from input-output studies, which have tended to be inconclusive about how to change schools to improve performance, research on effective educational practice has been used to develop logically coherent and research-based designs for improving education.

A central theme in current reform efforts is that improvement requires changing what happens in classrooms between teachers and students. Most previous attempts to reform education have not really had much effect on teaching and learning (Elmore and McLaughlin, 1988; Tyack and Cuban, 1995). School reforms thus appear to be a constant in American education, but the intensity and visibility of reform efforts tends to come in cycles, the latest of which was spurred by the raft of critical reports that emerged in the early 1980s.

Some scholars (e.g., Smith and O'Day, 1991) argued that the first wave of school reform in response to *A Nation at Risk* (National Commission on Excellence in Education, 1983) and other criticisms of public schooling failed to produce meaningful gains in learning because it followed a conventional, top-down, "more of the same" strategy to educational change: expanding and improving educational inputs (longer school day, increased graduation requirements, better teachers) and ensuring competency in basic skills (graduation tests, lock-step curricula, promotional criteria). It "did little to change the content of instruction, to directly involve teachers in the reform process, or to alter the reigning notions of teaching and learning" (pp. 233-234).

A second wave of reform that began building in the late 1980s addressed these shortcomings by calling for fundamental rethinking and restructuring of the process of schooling. Second-wave thinking was distinguished by the argument that schools, as the basic unit of productivity in education, ought to be the unit of improvement. "Upgrading classroom life is best done on a school-by-school basis. Teachers assist each other. Principals help create the setting and secure additional help. The action and rewards for in-service education and school improvement shift from where they have been traditionally—with the superintendent's office and districtwide activities—to the principal's office and the school as the key unit. Research increasingly supports such a process" (Goodlad, 1984:129).

The focus on improving practice at the individual school overcame objections that traditional reform strategies ignored (1) the idiosyncratic and context-dependent nature of education production due to the human relationships involving teachers and students that determine the effectiveness of teaching methods (Murnane and Nelson, 1984; Elmore and McLaughlin, 1988) and (2) the historical evidence from a century of public school reform that schools change reforms as much as reforms change schools (Tyack and Cuban, 1995).

School-based reform strategies focus on both classroom instructional programs and on school (and to a much lesser extent, district) restructuring. Smith and O'Day (1991:234) reported that the second wave of reform produced in short order an "avalanche of ideas, strategies, and structures." Evidence of this avalanche can be found in a recent report (Northwest Regional Educational Laboratory, 1998), prepared to help implement the Comprehensive School Reform Demonstration (CSRD) program enacted by Congress in 1997. CSRD provides financial incentives for schools, particularly Title I schools, to implement school reform programs based on reliable research and effective practice and including an emphasis on basic academics and parental involvement. The Northwest Regional Education Laboratory made an initial listing of 26 whole-school reform models and 18 skill- and content-based reform models for schools to consider in developing proposals for CSRD funding, while emphasizing that the list was not comprehensive and was not meant to limit the array of reform ideas being considered by schools, districts, and states.

School-based change efforts typically emphasize capacity building (especially the professional development of teachers) and decentralized decision making (including parental and community involvement). Despite these general similarities, reform models differ widely when it comes to specific practices in such areas as instructional strategies, types and uses of assessment, and features of school organization (e.g., school-based management) and climate. Wang et al. (1997) reviewed 12 widely implemented reform programs (both whole-school and skill and content); they identified 54 prevalent program practices in these programs of which they characterized 25 as being "firmly grounded in research on what influences student learning."

One of the most potentially significant developments of the second-wave awareness of the importance of the individual school and the inefficacy of many earlier, piecemeal reforms has been the development of designs for change that call for restructuring the whole school, not just individual elements of it. Whole-school designs (the best known of which were listed in Chapter 4) provide schools with frameworks for restructuring virtually all aspects of the school, including curriculum, classroom organization, assessment, the allocation of decision-making authority over resources, and more. Frequently they use skill- and content-based models of reform in various curricular areas as building blocks in the comprehensive reform design.

Interest in implementing whole-school designs overlaps with other school-based reform proposals to alter educational management systems at the school and district level. The target of change here is the traditional centralized district management strategy, in which the central office has made all key decisions for the schools in its district: when and where to build schools and how large to make them, what the curriculum program would be (including selection of textbooks and instructional materials), how schools would be staffed (how many teachers, how many specialized personnel), what kind and how much professional development would be provided, and so forth.

One restructuring proposal to free schools from the constraints of traditional district control has been school-based management (SBM). SBM is not a new reform strategy: it emerged initially in the 1960s in response most particularly to the desire of inner-city residents to have more influence (community control) over their schools (Murphy and Beck, 1995; Tyack, 1993; Wohlstetter and Odden, 1992). Management changes that devolved some authority to the local level could be found in many large U.S. cities in the 1970s and 1980s, including New York, Chicago, Washington, DC, and Dade County, Florida. As concerns about educational productivity increasingly took center stage, SBM gained new adherents who drew lessons for schools from new organization patterns emerging in U.S. industries (Odden and Busch, 1998). Trying to overcome a long productivity slump, the latter were attempting to increase their competitive advantage in world markets by transforming themselves into high-performance workplaces that rejected the 20th century mass production factory model of organization for a new model emphasizing flexible decentralization, participative management, and greatly increased attention to development of the firm's human resources (U.S. Office of Technology Assessment, 1990:115).

SBM has been practiced in many ways, but various approaches are built on one key premise: "that the school site becomes the central locus of control in decision making. The rationale behind SBM is that those who are closest to the primary business of schools will make the best-informed decisions. . . . The term 'school-based management' has many variations—school-site management, school-site autonomy, shared decision making, shared governance, school improvement program (or project or process), school-based budgeting, and administrative decentralization" (Summers and Johnson, 1996:76-77).

Three main models of SBM have emerged (Bimber, 1993; Wohlstetter and Odden, 1992). The first model places *principals* in control, with this individual serving as a chief executive with broad-reaching powers over budget, staffing, and program design. There may be some kind of school-site council, but it tends to serve in an advisory rather than decision making capacity. The second model focuses on *administrative decentralization*, delegating decision making to teachers and giving them broad discretion over the professional judgments needed each day as they encounter students in classroom learning situations. School-site councils under this model tend to give the greatest representation to teachers and other school-site educators. The third model is characterized by a shift of power from educators to *community-based control.* Most visibly exemplified in the 1988 Chicago school reforms, this approach shifts power from the school board and professional educators to parent and community representatives by giving them majority representation on school-site councils with significant control over budgets, personnel, management, and program design.

Evaluation of SBM has been hampered by the multiplicity of objectives and practices that have been pursued, by the fact that real devolution of decision making to the school level has been far less than the rhetoric around SBM would imply, and by the failure of most of the research on SBM (as revealed in a literature review by Summers and Johnson, 1996) even to address the question of effects on student achievement. Assessments based largely on SBM as it was implemented in the 1970s and 1980s suggested that it seldom had the positive benefits predicted for it, either in terms of improving student achievement or changing the behavior of schools and school participants (Malen et al., 1990; Murphy and Beck, 1995; Newmann and Wehlage, 1995; Summers and Johnson, 1996; Wohlstetter and Odden, 1992). More recent research (Odden and Busch, 1998; see Chapter 6) suggests that older strategies of SBM lacked the necessary organizational conditions for it to lead to improved student achievement.

While much restructuring has focused on the school level, there have also been efforts to reform district operations, to reorient them toward improvements in teaching and learning while retaining a significant measure of central control. One prominent example is Community School District #2 in New York City, which has based a comprehensive and sustained district-wide reform agenda on a strategy of instructional improvement through professional development. While more and more budget and administrative responsibility has been lodged at the school level, largely in the hands of principals, central control has remained strong in areas key to the success of the strategy, such as personnel decisions, the hiring of professional development consultants with expertise consistent with the strategy, decisions about which instructional areas will receive priority attention, and policies and practices that keep school-site decisions focused on district-wide priorities (Elmore, 1997a).

Changes in school and district practice, based to a greater or lesser extent on the research base developed using the lens of effective practice, have clearly had an impact on American schools. What is much less clear at this point is whether these changes are making a difference in the academic performance of students. This is not to be critical, but rather to acknowledge two important facts about the status of knowledge on the effects of recent reforms. First, evidence of effectiveness will be complicated to find for some of the same reasons that bedevil input-output research: methods of analysis are contested; it is difficult to isolate the effects of particular changes because numerous things tend to change at the same time; and context may matter importantly in how reforms play out in different places, complicating the explanation of effects and limiting generalizability.

Moreover, new approaches to practice such as whole-school restructuring have not yet been fully implemented, yet alone independently evaluated. Implementing whole-school designs such as New American Schools and the Edison Project has proven more time-consuming and complex than designers originally anticipated (Bodilly, 1998; Chubb, 1998; Glennan, 1998). RAND looked at the progress of 40 schools in the first two years (1995-97) of the scale-up phase of New American Schools and found "significant variation among the schools in the levels of implementation obtained, which ranged from no implementation through the stages of planning, piloting, implementing, and fulfilling" (Bodilly, 1998:xiv). Nearly 45 percent were not yet clearly implementing the core elements of a design across the school. The Edison Project, which began its research and development phase in 1991, only began operating schools in 1995 and had only 25 in operation in 1998 (Chubb, 1998).

Reviews of what is known about school and curriculum designs are beginning to appear (Fashola and·Slavin, 1997; Kentucky Department of Education, n.d; Northwest Regional Education Laboratory, 1998; Slavin and Fashola, 1998; American Institutes for Research, 1999), but at this point most of the currently popular designs lack evidence about the research base of the program, effects on student achievement, effective implementation, and replicability. Designs have achieved popularity in spite rather than because of strong evidence of effectiveness and replicability. "Typically they have been advanced by supporters because the model is associated with a well-known educator or theorist, because they have worked well in pilot sites, because they are based on a plausible theory of school reform, or some combination of these factors" (Consortium for Policy Research in Education, 1998:2).

Finally, theories about the science of learning are evolving. Research developments in the cognitive sciences are challenging prior understandings how humans learn and suggest that ideas about effective educational practice may undergo substantial revision as scholars and practitioners learn how to bring the insights of research into the classroom (National Research Council, 1999).

Lens 3: The Institutional Perspective

While school-based reform efforts and changes in district practices aimed at building school capacity show promise of improving school performance, it remains an open question whether they will be implemented or sustained in any comprehensive way. Skepticism about the potential of school-by-school change stems both from the magnitude of the task and from evidence that the institutional environment within which schools operate is too fragmented and oriented toward short-term results to support meaningful improvement throughout the system. Opinion is divided on whether systemic reform can be accomplished by deliberate policy action within the current institutional framework or whether parents and students should be allowed to opt out of the public school system as it is currently structured because there is something inherent in that structure that "systematically creates and nurtures the kinds of schools that no one really wants" (Chubb and Moe, 1990:25).

Those who argue that improvements in educational productivity require close attention to institutional influences do not disagree with the second-wave reformers about the importance of focusing on teaching and learning at the school level and giving individual schools the autonomy to adopt effective practices and adapt them to their local contexts. Rather, they argue that these ideas by themselves are insufficient, because they ignore the key question: not "what works?" but how the desirable characteristics of schools can be developed and nurtured. In this view, central features of the way American schools are governed, especially the dispersion of control over educational policy among many actors and the political pluralism of a constitutional system that encourages "conflict as an antidote to the concentration of power" (Elmore, 1997b:41), inhibit the emergence of effective organizations. In other words, what Chubb and Moe call the "institutions of direct democratic control" undermine school autonomy, fail to support successful schools, and put insufficient pressure on schools whose performance in unsatisfactory (Chubb and Moe, 1990; Smith and O'Day, 1991; Elmore, 1997b; Brandl, 1998). Viewing schools in terms of the environment in which they operate gives yet another perspective on the productivity problem in education and its solution.

Smith and O'Day (1991:237) graphically describe "the fragmented, complex, multi-layered educational policy system," which they identify as a "fundamental barrier to developing and sustaining successful schools in the USA":

> This system consists of overlapping and often conflicting formal and informal policy components on the one hand and, on the other, of a myriad of contending pressures for immediate results that serve only to further disperse and drain the already fragmented energies of dedicated and well meaning school personnel. On the formal policy side, school personnel are daily confronted with mandates, guidelines, incentives, sanctions, and programs constructed by a half-dozen different federal congressional committees, at least that many federal departments and independent agencies, and the federal courts; state school administrators, legislative committees, boards, commissions and courts; regional or county offices in most states; district level administrators and school boards in 14,000 school districts (with multiple boards and administrative structures in large systems); and local school building administrators, teachers and committees of interested parents. Every level and many different agencies within levels at-

tempt to influence the curriculum and curricular materials, teacher in-service and pre-service professional development, assessment, student policies such as attendance and promotion, and the special services that schools provide to handicapped, limited English-proficient and low-achieving students.

The complexity of this institutional environment has been building for a century, but the pace of change intensified after World War II and especially after the mid-1960s (Kirst, 1995).

Since the "common school" of the nineteenth century, in which local control was paramount, more and more layers have been added to the organization of the public schools. Many of these layers were added during the Progressive Era of the late 19th and early 20th centuries, in which reformers argued that schools should reflect the highly bureaucratized nature of business organizations if they were to be efficient (Tyack, 1993). The new institutional form in education was designed to rid education of problems stemming from the existence of large lay boards and the active involvement of politicians. The new "modern" system strove to centralize control, standardize practice, put control in the hands of professionals, and run the system by scientific principles. Community values were to be represented by elites on locally elected boards, but managing the schools was left to professional administrators.

By the 1960s, this system was under attack by groups whose interests the new system did not serve well. Teachers were dissatisfied at being treated like low-level functionaries in a bureaucratic system (Tyack, 1974), and minority groups protested their relegation to low academic tracks in a system that then credentialed and certified their low standing (Berg, 1970; Weeres and Kerchner, 1996; Tyack, 1974, 1993). The system responded with a place at the table for teachers, recognition of disenfranchised groups, and a governance system run by bargaining and interest group pressures, rather than by central enlightenment (Kirst et al., 1980). Responsiveness to demands, often in the form of new specialized bureaucratic units and new programs, became the basis of accountability. Researchers used the term "fragmented centralization" to characterize the altered system (Meyer, 1991). Fragmentation was exacerbated by the growing involvement of state and federal officials in funding education as well as in handing down programmatic and accountability mandates (Kirst, 1995).

Observers disagree on whether reforms powerful enough to overcome the shortcomings of direct democratic control can be instituted within the current system of publicly controlled schools or whether control must be taken out of the hands of bureaucrats and political partisans via the creation of an education marketplace. This debate reflects the cardinal economic choice societies face when deciding how to allocate scarce goods and services: whether to use the market or government as the predominant regulator (Wolf, 1993:1). With regard to the public schools, the argument is currently one between those who believe in the possibilities of reforming the bureaucratic, professional model of public schooling that emerged at the beginning of the 20th century and those who believe that this model is bankrupt.

Those who would address the problem within the framework of the existing school system "compare the existing public school system to a business firm that has been poorly managed and needs to rationalize and integrate its parts. Its advocates say there is nothing inherently wrong with a public education system that is controlled by policy-making boards and administered by a traditional bureaucracy; today's problems can be solved by re-engineering the system so that its parts are correctly aligned" (Hill et al., 1997:105).

Smith and O'Day (1991) noted that school-by-school reform engaged primarily those who already had a history of reform experience and interest, not necessarily those whose practices were most in need of change. They also pointed out the changes in content and pedagogy being called for by second-wave reformers implied rethinking the knowledge and skills that children are expected to learn and the nature of the teaching and learning process itself. They judged that "[s]uch a reorientation is not likely to happen on a widespread school-by-school basis among educators who have themselves been schooled in a philosophy and settings that embody fact-based conceptions of knowledge, hierarchical approaches to skill development, and a near total reliance on teacher-initiated and teacher-directed instruction." They called for "a coherent *systemic* strategy that can combine the energy and professional involvement of the second wave reforms with a new and challenging state structure to generalize the reforms to all schools within the state" (p. 234).

This systemic strategy operates alongside the second wave of school reform; it emphasizes state (and to a lesser degree federal) actions to complement school and district restructuring by creating a more coherent environment within which successful schools can thrive and by creating external pressure for change when it does not emerge spontaneously. The linchpin in the system is the development of content standards expressing shared understandings about what students need to know and be able to do, with which other elements of the educational system (school curricula, assessments, teacher education and professional development, and accountability) can be aligned.[6] With content standards and performance

---

[6]We emphasize the use of content standards as the linchpin to which other parts of the educational process will be aligned because this is the systemic reform strategy that currently drives policy at the federal level and in the majority of states. Hill et al. (1997:105) point out that an early and influential proponent of the concept of systemic reform was David Hornbeck, who "formulated a strategy for statewide governance reform in Kentucky, based on the concept of a rationally linked system of statewide goals, performance standards, examinations, and rewards and penalties for students and schools." Hornbeck's blueprint guided the complete overhaul of Kentucky's education system that grew out of the court rulings (referenced earlier in this report) that declared the system inadequate. Hornbeck's focal point for alignment was state goals, rather than the curricular standards more commonly used in systemic reform, but his overall arguments for and approach to systemic reform were the same as those of the standards-based reformers.

standards (i.e., examples and definitions of what proficiency in the content standards would look like) together defining what students should know and how well they should be expected to perform, authority for determining how these goals should be met can be decentralized down to the district or (preferably, in the eyes of many) the school level, in keeping with the tradition of local control of education and consistent with both economic and "good practice" research, which suggests that those closest to the "production site" are in the best position to make efficient and effective decisions about meeting the needs of students in specific classrooms and schools.

The standards-based systemic strategy has dominated state education reform efforts for a decade and has become remarkably pervasive. Model subject-matter standards have been developed by organizations of experts in a number of academic fields (e.g., the pioneering mathematics standards issued by the National Council of Teachers of Mathematics and science standards developed by the National Academy of Sciences, drawing on materials and ideas developed by the American Association for the Advancement of Science and the National Science Foundation). A 1998 survey (American Federation of Teachers, 1998) revealed that every state except Iowa has set or is in the process of setting common academic standards for students: 47 states have or are planning to have assessments aligned with learning standards; 24 have or will have high school exit exams based on the standards; and 20 have or are developing incentives to motivate students to achieve a higher standard than that required of all students (American Federation of Teachers, 1998). There is evidence that systemic reform may be beginning to pay off. For example, a study of the two states (North Carolina and Texas) that have made positive gains on the greatest number of indicators being tracked by the National Education Goals Panel confirmed that the gains were both significant and sustained. Moreover, the study concluded that the most plausible explanation for relatively large gains in both states on NAEP tests could be found in the policy environment: "an aligned system of standards, curriculum, and assessments; holding schools accountable for improvement for all students; and critical support from business in developing, implementing, and sustaining these changes over time" (Grissmer and Flanagan, 1998:i).

Despite this progress, states and districts have found that systemic reform presents many challenges. For example, although many states developed coherent education policies around standards, few have removed the previous policies that conflict with the new direction of reform. In addition, political pressures have caused some to change strategies during a short time. Other states have found it difficult to achieve consensus around standards for student achievement (Massell, 1994; Massell and Fuhrman, 1994; Cohen, 1995). Differing views of reform among local staffs and other priorities have made change at the local level difficult as well (Cohen, 1996; Hertert, 1994; Massell et al., 1997; Spillane et al., 1995). Finally, it is worth noting that some of the challenges arise because not everyone accepts the premises of standards-based reform. For example, some people may believe that the control over knowledge involved in national or statewide standards is inconsistent with personal liberty or pluralism. As an earlier National Research Council report noted, "though standards-based reform was conceived as a way to compensate for the fragmented system that governs education in the United States, the institutional arrangements it espouses still reflect that fragmentation. All three levels of government are involved, with the federal government essentially serving as a 'bully pulpit,' exhorting states and localities to move in a new direction, states choosing to play roles that range from strict regulator of local behavior to cheerleader for reform, and local communities responding to federal and state initiatives while still trying to maintain their own agendas" (National Research Council, 1997:31).

Skeptics about the possibilities of improving educational performance within the existing institutional environment question how significantly institutional arrangements can be changed so long as direct democratic control of schools exists. They argue that real school improvement cannot happen under anything like the current arrangements (e.g., Chubb and Moe, 1990; Hill et al., 1997). Drawing on organizational theory, in particular the "new institutionalism" (March and Olsen, 1989), they maintain that the educational choices of actors in the system are shaped by the institutional context in which they move. "Different institutions constrain and aggregate individual choices in very different ways, and this, in the end, is why different kinds of organizations emerge, prosper, or fail within them." In this view, "familiar arrangements for direct democratic control do indeed impose a distinctive structure on the educational choices of all the various participants—and . . . this structure tends to promote organizational characteristics that are ill-suited to the effective performance of American public schools" (Chubb and Moe, 1990:21).

One way in which the institutions of direct democratic control influence the organizational structure of schools is by distributing authority broadly. Chubb and Moe (1990:35) argue that "under a system of democratic control, the public schools are governed by an enormous, far-flung constituency in which the interests of parents and students carry no special status or weight." This distribution of authority is problematic for Chubb and Moe (while it might not be for others) because they seem to assume that the preferences of parents and students *should* have greater standing in deciding what schools should be like.

Even if one accepts in principle the idea that authority over education *ought* to be widely dispersed in a democratic society, there are still grounds to be concerned that existing arrangements for exercising that authority may interfere with the development of effective school practices and the ability of professionals to adapt these practices to local circumstances. The problem arises from the particular institutional arrangements through which the United States has chosen to bring into balance the variety of interests and values contending for influence over public education. There are three fundamental approaches to mediation and control: bureaucracy, markets, and "clans" or self-governing communities of interest and value (Ouchi, 1980). Bureaucracy, which is appropriate when the quality of performance is not transparent and when potential conflicts of interest are present, has been the preferred method for managing superior-subordinate relationships in light of stakeholder interests and values. And, as noted earlier, the organization of school systems has become increasingly bureaucratic over the years as interest and values have become more complex and as more and more layers of control have been added.

While bureaucracy can be a force to promote fairness and quality, it also can interfere with the efforts to improve educational productivity in a number of ways. Bureaucratization can whittle away discretion and autonomy at the school level (Chubb and Moe, 1990; Hill et al., 1997; Brandl, 1998). Policy makers increasingly act to reduce the discretion permitted at the school level. They do this (1) to reduce compliance problems that can result from school personnel who may or may not be inclined to act in accordance with policies determined at higher levels of the system; (2) to reduce the possibilities of other actors in this system of multiple authorities using the existence of discretion left in local hands to impose their own (possibly competing) interests; and (3) to insulate their decisions from change by future policy makers. Bureaucrats have incentives to expand their budgets, programmatic authority, and administrative controls; and so their increasing presence, too, serves to reduce the discretion and autonomy left to school personnel. Teachers unionize to gain influence in an environment increasingly characterized by powerful, organized interests outside the school; collective bargaining results in detailed contracts that further formalize public education and reduce or eliminate managerial discretion.

Bureaucratization can also draw administrators away from duties concerned with instruction. As the environment within which schools operate becomes more complex, key aspects of education become institutionalized. Administrators become increasingly involved in complying with the decisions made at higher levels about teachers, students, and curriculum and spend less time providing instructional leadership (Meyer and Rowan, 1978; Rowan, 1981).

Bureaucratization can constrain teachers in their efforts to teach as well (Chubb and Moe, 1990:58-59). Regulations "produce bureaucratic rather than professorial controls over the content and structure of the work . . . [These] controls [are] aimed at standardizing procedures rather than building knowledge that can be applied differently, depending on the given needs of the child." While teaching requires a great deal of flexibility and creativity, such controls often "place teachers in the unprofessional position of having to treat diverse students uniformly" (Darling-Hammond and Cobb, 1996:20). Thus, bureaucratization encourages depersonalized and standardized instruction and keeps pedagogical strategies simple and routine as possible (Darling-Hammond, 1996).

Bureaucratization can also lead to a lack of accountability for education outcomes. Because educational bureaucracy is not closely related to the work of instruction, schools may not exercise meaningful control over their instructional activities or outputs, despite shifts toward "accountability." Meyer and Rowan (1978:80) suggest two reasons for this. First, "close supervision of instructional activity can uncover inconsistencies and create more uncertainty than unenforced demands for conformity to bureaucratic rules." Second, centralized governmental and professional controls in education are weak and schools depend heavily on local funding and support. Thus, Meyer and Rowan argue that administrators may actually avoid developing formal controls over instruction so that inconsistencies between local practices and instructional rules are not uncovered. The lack of accountability coupled with the heavy hand of bureaucracy over the formal aspects of education may help explain why the weight of tradition operates so powerfully. "Over long periods of time schools have remained similar in their core operation, so much so that these regularities have imprinted themselves on students, educators, and the public as the essential features of a 'real school'" (Tyack and Cuban, 1995:7).

Finally, bureaucratization can deny schools and school systems free resources to invest in school improvement. "Competition for resources has created an overconstrained system in which every dollar is allocated to teacher salaries or to existing programs. New funds, e.g., from tax levy increases, are spoken for before they arrive, usually to fund deferred maintenance or roll back increases in average class size. Even the supposedly flexible categories of funds, such as staff development, are committed in advance to separate categorical programs or to programs selected by central office administrators" (Hill et al., 1997:29).

How important the institutional environment is as a barrier to educational productivity depends on the extent to which bureaucracy and direct democratic control affect school systems as the foregoing arguments suggest they do. Chubb and Moe (1990:64) argue that environments that are relatively homogeneous and problem-free are likely to be the least bureaucratic, while urban environments ("teeming with diverse, conflicting interests of political salience" and home to deeply troubled schools) are more likely than suburbs or rural areas to suffer from the negative consequences of bureaucratic controls and political pluralism. These are, of course, the places where productivity problems are the worst and where the need for exceptionally effective schools is therefore the greatest.

Alternative institutional arrangements for providing public education are often grouped under the broad label of (1) "choice," giving parents more control over which schools their children will attend, including traditional public schools or more recently charter schools, which are freed from much public regulation or (2) "privatization," referring either to the use of public funds at private schools, particularly through vouchers, or to greater involvement of private or nonprofit firms in the provision of education (through contracts from school districts, for example). These alternative institutional arrangements and what is known about their effects on educational achievement are discussed in detail in Chapters 6 and 7. Although choice and privatization options have been growing, they are not unique to the current period of reform. Families, especially relatively well-off families, have been able to exercise school choice by choosing where to live. Within-district and cross-district choice plans (including magnet school options) were a common remedy selected by or imposed by courts on school districts as they struggled in the latter half of the 20th century to accomplish desegregation goals, but the existence of special public schools for students with particular academic or vocational talents and interests (like the Bronx High School of Science and the Aviation High School in New York) goes back much further.

Here, we simply note several distinguishing features of the current debate over choice and privatization options: the attention being paid to their potential for raising student achievement as well as for serving other educational purposes valued by Americans; the growing willingness of states and districts to try new institutional arrangements for providing publicly funded education; and the intensity of the controversy over the desirability of making these comparatively radical shifts in familiar patterns of educational governance.

USING FINANCE-RELATED STRATEGIES TO IMPROVE SCHOOL PERFORMANCE

A quarter of a century ago, a book entitled *Indeterminacy in Education* reviewed social science research generated in the first decade after the Coleman report and came to the conclusion that "educational policymaking is now in a state of indeterminacy. No satisfactory criteria exist by which to make important decisions regarding [among other things] school finance" (McDermott, 1976:1).

We are not yet certain about how to make schools better or how to deploy resources effectively. The hope that productivity studies might provide ready answers to public officials about how much money to allocate, under what circumstances, to whom to obtain specified academic outcomes is as yet impossible to fulfill. Still, our assessment of the last several decades of research and policy development on educational productivity makes us more optimistic than our mid-1970s predecessors about the prospects for making informed school finance choices.

The past 25 years worth of insights have generated a host of ideas about how to use school finance to improve school performance. Input-output research has heightened interest in policies affecting key variables that appear linked to student achievement, such as teacher quality and class size. The renewed involvement of economists in educational productivity studies has brought a long-absent economic perspective to school finance and has drawn attention to the lack of performance incentives and financial accountability measures in traditional school finance systems. Studies of effective practice have spawned a vigorous effort to make school reform actually affect what happens between teachers and students in classrooms, raising interesting questions about how school finance reforms, such as school-based management and teacher development, can influence the processes of teaching and learning. The focus on classrooms has also raised awareness of the need to ensure that students come to school ready and able to learn. The institutional perspective on school performance has highlighted fundamental disagreements about the way Americans have conceived of their public schools for the better part of a century and a half, by calling into question the traditional reliance on government both to fund and to supply public education and by raising the possibility of giving greater attention to market options for supply (such as public or private school choice for parents and contracting-out to private providers for services).

These advances in the understanding of educational productivity will be further enhanced as researchers work on developing more accurate and comprehensive outcome measures and as policy makers systematically try and evaluate instructional and policy options.

No matter how much progress is made in understanding productivity through improved research and practice, there is an important sense in which education continues to be and probably always will be indeterminate. In the foreword to the 1976 volume on indeterminancy in education, Arthur Wise noted that indeterminacy was used in several senses in the book: as lack of a consensus on the aims of education as well as a state of being "not fixed," "not clear," "not established," or "not settled" (McDermott, 1976:x). He also noted, however, that in mathematics "an equation is said to be 'indeterminate' when it can be satisfied by more than one value for each unknown" and he asked "Is the search to reduce technical indeterminacy in education a search for equations which can be satisfied by only one value for each unknown?"

We suggest that indeterminacy will always characterize educational production because of the impossibility (and undesirability) of standardizing the characteristics and behavior of the key factors of production in the education productivity equation: teachers and students. In other words, the search for answers to improving school performance and student achievement will never yield just one value—that is, solutions that will work for all schools and students in all times and places.

In the face of this indeterminacy, there are no simple answers about how to use school finance to make schools better. Instead, we seek to identify major strategies for change and to synthesize and evaluate the evidence on how well and under what conditions such strategies might contribute to meeting our goals for an education finance system. We will return to this task in Part III.

Part III

Strategies for Meeting the Goals

Education finance is only one part of a total system of education. Many of the concerns about the financing of education reflect large issues regarding the overall education system. Hence, proposals for changing the finance system can be presented in at least two ways: (1) as a menu of options for driving the education system in desirable directions or (2) as intertwined components necessary to achieve a given vision of overall education reform. Despite the conceptual appeal and logic of starting with a vision of overall reform and designing a finance system consistent with that vision, we structure the discussion of finance reform in line with the first approach; that is, as the options available for driving the education system in the directions embodied in our three goals: (1) promoting high achievement for all students in a cost-effective way, (2) reducing the nexus between family background and student achievement and, (3) raising revenue in a fair and efficient manner.

The reason for proceeding in this way is the absence of a single consensus vision of how the education system as a whole should be changed. Although many observers agree that the education system requires change, people disagree on the best way to change it. These disagreements have various and overlapping roots: people view school performance through different lenses; they hold different values, which influence their views of desirable methods of change; and they can reasonably draw different conclusions from patchy and conflicting empirical evidence about the effectiveness of specific reforms.

The following chapters examine the major policy options relevant to each goal. The options are arranged within the framework of the four generic strategies for altering finance systems introduced at the end of Chapter 2:

- Reduce funding inequities and inadequacies.
- Invest in capacity.
- Change incentives to make performance count.
- Empower schools or parents to make decisions about public funds.

Although we examine policy options separately by strategy, in many cases the strategies will be most effective if they are combined in a coherent way. In general, the case for combining strategies is most compelling when policy makers are trying to work within the existing system of school governance. Some proponents of major change in the governance system (e.g., through vouchers allowing parents to choose public or private schools) see little reason to combine finance strategies. To them, the introduction of more choice and competition among schools will provide whatever incentives are necessary to induce schools to make the types of investments needed to improve student learning.

The importance of making major changes in the governance system takes on special urgency in the context of goal 2, because many decades of attention to the educational problems facing at-risk children and urban schools in the framework of the existing educational system have so far resulted in improvements that are marginal at best. The seriatim discussion of individual policy options for goals 1 and 2 arranged by finance strategy may mask an important overall question, which we as a committee wish to highlight specifically, although we are not of one mind about how to answer it.

The question is whether it is more important to focus on finance changes that leave the structure of American education basically intact (as the first three strategies assume) or to explore options that would constitute a strong break with past practices (as policies emphasizing school and parent control over education dollars might do). Many reforms are occurring in schools and districts serving high proportions of at-risk students. It is still unclear, though, whether the current round of reforms will be more successful than previous ones. At the same time, how effective new structures would be is not yet knowable either, since many are largely untried. Thus policy makers face fundamental choices for which we cannot provide scientific solutions. These choices will rest on individual conclusions about the prospects for meaningful change within the current educational structure and on values in addition to those of enhancing fairness and productivity.

6

Achieving Goal 1: Promoting Higher Achievement in a Cost-Efficient Way

Promoting higher achievement for all students in a cost-efficient way poses fundamental challenges for the education system and will require significant changes in education finance. Among the finance options to be explored in this chapter are placing greater emphasis on the concept of educational adequacy; investing in the capacity of the system, particularly through improved professional development of teachers; changing incentives for teachers and other key participants to focus more on student achievement through new salary structures and accountability systems; and significant restructuring to give more authority over spending to schools and to parents. No single strategy or policy option is a panacea, all involve trade-offs of various types, and some of the strategies or individual options are likely to be most effective if combined with other strategies or policy options. Instead of laying out a blueprint for specific change, our aim in this chapter is to provide policy makers with information that will allow them to weigh the benefits and costs of each policy option.

REDUCING FUNDING INEQUITIES AND INADEQUACIES

As applied in school finance court cases for the past 30 years, equity concerns typically apply to the distribution of funding across districts. Equity defined in this way—but extended to the patterns of funding across schools and across states—continues to be an important concern that we address further in connection with goal 3, raising revenues fairly and efficiently. However, a continued focus on this definition of equity is not likely to promote the goal of raising student achievement across the board.

More promising is the new legal focus on adequacy. Because the move from equity to adequacy shifts attention away from the distribution of funding levels across districts to the adequacy of funding for desired outcomes, the strategy of trying to ensure that school funding is adequate is potentially crucial to the goal of increasing achievement for all students. In the absence of adequate funding, it will be difficult for states, districts, or schools to generate high and ambitious levels of student achievement for all students.

Policy makers, however, face the vexing problem of determining how much money would be required for true adequacy. This difficulty arises in part because there is so little firm knowledge about how school spending or inputs translate into school outputs given the current nature of teaching and learning. We know even less about what would be required to reach more ambitious achievement standards or what would be required if education were delivered in a more efficient manner.

Will a push through the legal system to increase the adequacy of funding help to achieve the goal of higher achievement for all students? Given that the outcome is uncertain, the best we can do is to identify some of the issues that will affect it. One issue is whether the courts are likely to be more amenable to adequacy than to equity complaints. Notably, as discussed in Chapter 4, not every high court has been receptive to an adequacy argument. For example, high courts in Illinois, Rhode Island, and Florida all rejected adequacy-based claims on the grounds that it is the responsibility of the legislature, not the courts, to decide on the quality of education. Thus, the main uncertainty here is the willingness of the courts either to specify what educational adequacy entails or to require that state legislatures specify those desired outcomes. Without a relatively explicit statement of desired educational outcomes, the court will not be able to determine whether a state is providing adequate funding for education.

A second issue is how state legislatures are likely to respond to adequacy judgments from the courts. State politics played a large role in how states responded to court decisions related to financing equity. On the surface, an adequacy approach (with its focus on the level of outcomes) may be more broadly appealing than the redistributive remedies that typically emerge from cases based on equity considerations. Such an approach may be easier to sell to a public that wants more accountability from government (Carr and Fuhrman, 1999). In practice, however, adequacy, too, is likely to call for politically controversial redistributive remedies, in that additional funds are most likely to have to be directed to those districts with the lowest-performing students. Moreover, lack of knowledge about the educational production function—and disagreement about whether it even makes sense to talk about such a function—adds a huge element of ambiguity and uncertainty to the concept of adequate funding, one that could well provide a basis for legislative stalling and inaction.

As documented in Chapter 3, court cases (those focusing on equity or adequacy claims or both) appear to have raised school spending in the low-spending districts without at the same time lowering it in the high-spending districts (Evans et al., 1999). Evidence from a few of those states suggests as well, however, that the additional revenue received by the recipient jurisdictions has been devoted primarily to the same activities as schools undertook before and hence may not have done much to increase student achievement (Goertz and Natriello, 1999). This evidence provides support for the committee's view that changes in funding alone are not likely to be sufficient to increase student achievement.

Regardless of the success of adequacy as a legal strategy, it is the committee's view that adequacy of funding has a central role to play in any education reform strategy designed to increase student achievement. In particular, discussions of educational funding should include explicit considerations of what the public and policy makers want the educational system to accomplish and what kinds of educational opportunities must be provided to meet those objectives. However, the committee also concludes that the provision of adequate funding by itself will do little to foster significant improvements in overall student achievement. Thus, while improving the adequacy of funding may be a necessary part of any education reform effort—and is likely to be especially crucial for districts or schools serving disproportionate numbers of disadvantaged students—it is only part of an overall program for increasing student achievement in a cost-efficient way.

INVESTING IN CAPACITY

To many education reformers, especially those committed to standards-driven systemic reform, a central element of any finance reform program is investing in capacity. Such investments are necessary to ensure that the system can deliver the quality of product required to enable students to achieve to high levels. Thus, this strategy calls for strategic investments that will yield high rates of return in the form of student achievement. These might include investments in school inputs, such as the capacity of teachers, the quantity of teachers (to reduce class size), technology and school buildings, and investment in the capacity of students to learn, such as preschool programs and family support services. Developing the capacity of students to learn can be extremely important in some cases but, because the returns are likely to be greatest for students from disadvantaged backgrounds, we defer the discussion of that type of investment to the next chapter. In addition, we defer to that chapter investment strategies that focus (1) on reducing class size (because there is some evidence that the benefits of that strategy are greatest for low-performing students) and (2) on technology and facilities, because current policies for financing these investments appear to generate even greater inequities across districts than is the case for operational spending. In this chapter, we examine whether new approaches to paying for teachers and teacher development could align investments in teacher capacity more closely to the goal of improving overall student achievement.

Overview of Issues Related to Teacher Capacity

The capacity of a teacher to be successful depends of a variety of factors, including his or her knowledge of the subject matter, of how students learn, and of methods for teaching. These types of knowledge are needed for a teacher to succeed in promoting student learning by, for example, selecting good teaching materials, making wise instructional decisions, and assessing student progress. Moving toward the goal of higher levels of achievement for all students will require two other types of teacher capacity as well. One is the ability and the skills to teach the kinds of knowledge and skills demanded by 21st century jobs and citizenship, and the other is the skills to teach highly diverse groups of students, with increasing proportions whose language and culture differ from their own, as well as increasing numbers of students with disabilities and other students with special educational needs. New developments in the science of learning, for example, are increasing awareness of how important it is for teachers to pay careful attention to the prior knowledge, as well as the skills, attitudes, and beliefs, that learners bring to school. Prior knowledge not only consists of the individual learning that students bring to the classroom but also knowledge that they acquire from their social roles, such as those connected with race, class, gender, and cultural and ethnic affiliations. Teachers must be helped to develop teaching practices that start from the structure of a child's prior learning and are sensitive to the cultural and language practices of students and the effect of those practices on classroom learning (National Research Council, 1999b).

The committee is persuaded by the evidence reviewed in Chapter 5, including recent work by Hanushek et al. (1998) using Texas data and Wright et al. (1997) using Tennessee data, that teacher quality matters for student achievement. At the same time, we note that research has not been able to systematically link teacher quality to traditional teacher measures, such as experience or holding a master's degree. These measures are of particular interest for finance, since they are the ones that are linked to teacher pay and hence affect the cost of providing education. Ferguson (1991) and Ferguson and Ladd (1996) show that a different measure—but still an imperfect one—of teacher quality, namely teacher test scores, does emerge as an important determinant of student achievement in both Texas and Alabama.

Other studies document the importance of teacher preparation. For example, Goldhaber and Brewer (1997) report positive effects on student math and science achievement of subject-specific training programs and, using a matched comparison design, Hawk et al. (1985) show similar results for mathematics achievement. Darling-Hammond's (1990) review of the literature provides support for the importance of teacher preparation and certification.

To summarize, there is little doubt that the quality of teachers matters. The challenge is to develop the best policies to enhance it. Perhaps the most frequently discussed policy change involves altering teacher education and induction practices, which in the first instance is not a finance option but has finance implications for teacher training institutions, would-be teachers, and school districts. Two other policy options, raising teacher salaries and expanding professional development, fit more closely with the concept of financial investments intended to build teacher capacity. We examine these three options, with more attention to the latter two, in the following sections.

The challenge of enhancing teacher quality must be addressed in context. One aspect of the context is the rising demand for new teachers. The Department of Education estimates that the nation's schools will need to hire about 2.2 million new teachers during the next decade, a figure that reflects both a continuation of the growth in student bodies that started in the mid-1980s and a growing number of teacher retirements (U.S. Department of Education, 1998a). The fear is that this rising demand will put pressure on schools to lower their standards and to hire unqualified individuals. Given that about one-half to two-thirds of the new teachers hired will be first-time teachers, the rising demand also implies that attention needs to be paid to the quality of the training new teachers receive and the quality of professional support as they start their careers. Failure to provide that support could exacerbate the current situation, in which 22 percent of new teachers leave the profession during the first three years (U.S. Department of Education, 1998a).

Another contextual aspect is the great variation across areas and in the quality and preparation of teachers and in the outlook for teacher shortages. For example, while 28 percent of high school mathematics teachers nationally lack as much as a minor degree in the subject, state levels range from a low of 9 percent for Missouri to over 45 percent for Alaska, Washington, and California (NCES data reported in Darling-Hammond, 1997: Appendix B, Table 3). Differences also emerge between central cities and other areas. For example, 21 percent of the public school teachers who teach science in grades 7-12 in central cities report no degree (major or minor) in their main teaching area, more than twice the 9 percent in other areas (Lewis et al., 1999: Table 5).

In a 1997 report prepared for the National Commission on Teaching and America's Future, Darling-Hammond emphasized that shortages of well-prepared teachers are largely a problem of distribution rather than numbers. Demand for teachers is particularly great in the South and the West, and in port cities on both coasts, whereas slow-growing states have teacher surpluses. Wealthy districts with high salaries and desirable working conditions rarely experience shortages in any field, whereas districts and schools with large numbers of low-income and minority students are much more likely to face difficulty recruiting qualified teachers and to hire unqualified teachers or to use substitute teachers to fill positions (Darling-Hammond, 1997). A recent story in *Education Week* provides further evidence that many regions have surplus teachers in some areas and shortages in others (Bradley, 1999).

Teacher Education Programs and Licensing Standards

Building teacher capacity by improving the education of new teachers responds to long-standing observations about the shortcomings of teacher education in the United States and to new standards in some disciplines, such as those developed by the National Council of Teachers of Mathematics, that clarify what teachers need to know and be able to do to promote all students' learning. The impetus to change licensing standards comes also from international comparisons—from U.S. students' poor showing on the Third International Mathematics and Science Study (TIMSS), coupled with evidence that other nations invest much more intensively in developing new teachers (Paine and Ma, 1993). Finally, it reflects concerns about the importance of assuring that the large number of new teachers who will be needed during the next decade are adequately prepared to teach.

Research is emerging that clarifies shortcomings in existing teacher education programs and provides guidelines for improvement (Darling-Hammond, 1997; National Research Council, 1999b). Standards for teacher training programs are now emerging. However, quality control is quite limited, research on teacher learning is still relatively new and limited, and teacher education programs vary widely in how well their graduates are prepared to teach. National strategies to promote improvements in the quality of teaching include standard-setting for teacher education programs, for teacher licensing, and for teaching excellence. These include national professional standards for teacher education programs developed by the National Council for Accreditation of Teacher Education (NCATE), standards that are being developed by the Interstate New Assessment and Support Consortium (INTASC), and national standards for advanced certification developed by the National Board for Professional Teaching Standards (NBPTS). Such standard-setting initiatives are intended to provide frameworks within which state and local systems can develop quality controls that upgrade the preparation and support of teachers.

As a committee on education finance, we were not able to thoroughly evaluate a strategy for enhancing teacher quality through the use of stricter accreditation requirements and higher requirements for teacher certification. However, we have two comments to make about this strategy. First, despite its apparent logic, some observers have questioned parts of it, such as the desirability of having education programs accredited by NCATE. Ballou and Podgursky (1998, 1999) provide evidence showing that teachers emerging from accredited programs are no more qualified than teachers emerging from other programs. These two researchers are also concerned that requiring accreditation may eliminate programs that currently provide teachers to districts that serve disproportionate numbers of disadvantaged students.[1] Second, raising entry barriers to teaching (through, for example, extending the amount of time it takes to get certified or through limiting the number of ways that one may enter the teaching profession) could be undesirable to the extent that it disproportionately discourages the most able students—those who have the greatest alternative opportunities—from making the investment to enter the teaching profession.

Improving teacher preparation and developing professional standards for teachers are fully consistent with the goal of raising achievement for all students. Whether teacher quality will best be enhanced through teacher licensure exams, holding teaching colleges and universities more responsible for the preparation of the teachers they prepare, or other mechanisms is beyond the scope of this committee. We simply urge that policies aimed at improving teacher preparation and certification be evaluated at least in part for their impacts on overall student achievement.

Teacher Salaries

Several arguments are frequently offered for raising teacher salaries, including the fair treatment of existing teachers, the need to keep teacher salaries in line with the salaries of other college graduates so as to attract qualified people into the teaching profession, and as a way to increase teacher quality. Of most interest to us here is the extent to which raising teacher salaries across the board is a good way to raise the quality of teachers.

Before we turn to that issue, however, we briefly look at the trends in teacher salaries relative to those in other occupations. Table 6-1, using data based on the decennial censuses of population for the period 1940-1990 (reported in Hanushek and Rivkin, 1996), shows percentages of male college graduates earning less than the average male teacher and similar percentages for women. The lower the percentage, the less attractive is teaching as a profession. The table shows a decline in the attractiveness of teaching as a profession for men from 1940 to 1970, with a partial turnaround since then. For women, the drop is more precipitous and has no recent turnaround. As of 1990, only 36.5 percent of college-educated men were in jobs that paid less than that of the average male teacher, and 45.3 percent of college-educated women were in jobs that paid less than that of the average female teacher.

A refinement of the analysis that isolates the patterns for 20- to 29-year-olds indicates that the relative position of teacher salaries for young female teachers

---

[1]Information from Pennsylvania underscores these concerns. In that state, the districts with the highest proportions of NCATE-certified teachers have the lowest proportions of students going on to postsecondary education (Strauss, 1998:152). Although this observation provides no information on causal links, it is consistent with the two concerns raised by Ballou and Podgurksy and calls out for more investigation of the reasons for the observed pattern.

TABLE 6-1   Position of the Average Teacher in the Nonteacher Earning
Distribution, 1940-1990

Year	Percentage of Male College Graduates Earning Less than the Average Male Teacher	Percentage of Female College Graduates Earning Less than the Average Female Teacher
1940	52.5	68.7
1950	36.2	55.0
1960	28.7	52.7
1970	25.7	47.1
1980	31.0	50.1
1990	36.5	45.3

SOURCE: Hanushek and Rivkin, 1996. Data obtained from the U.S. Decennial Census of Population, Public Use Microdata, 1940-90.

(the women who have the most lucrative opportunities outside teaching) is approaching that for men. On the basis of that convergence, Hanushek and Rivkin (1996:29) conclude that schools will not be able to count on a continual supply of high-quality female teachers in the future and that the rising opportunity costs for women will put upward pressure on school budgets given that women made up 68 percent of all teachers in 1990. Overall, these trends based on average salaries suggest that teaching is becoming less financially attractive for college graduates compared with other occupations. While the average salaries mask what has been happening to the structure of salaries, a more detailed analysis of salary trends by teacher experience or education level is not likely to change this basic conclusion.

But will higher salaries increase teacher quality? One reason they may not emerges from empirical observations from New York, Michigan, and other states that salary increases are often disproportionately directed toward the more experienced, senior teachers, an outcome that results from the contract bargaining between local teachers' unions and school district officials (Lankford and Wyckoff, 1997; Monk and Jacobson, 1985; Murnane et al., 1987). The backloading of salary increases onto veteran teachers means that salaries for entering teachers are kept relatively low. The low salaries for entering and inexperienced teachers may well interfere with the ability of the system to attract high-quality new teachers into the profession, and those how enter may well leave before they are eligible for the higher salaries available to more experienced teachers. Thus, the salary bargaining process in which veteran teachers exert a lot of power means that money devoted to increases in teacher salaries is not being used as effectively as it could be toward the goal of increasing the capacity and quality of teachers.

A 1997 book by Ballou and Podgursky using national data provides further support for the view that rises in teacher salaries may not increase teacher quality. In particular, they convincingly document that increases in salaries during the 1980s did not increase the quality of the new teachers attracted to the profession. They explain this finding in part by the possibility that, despite the higher salaries, highly qualified college students may have been discouraged from making the investment in teaching by the decline in openings for teachers that occurred as veteran teachers responded to the salary increase by staying in the profession longer. Thus implicitly these researchers draw attention to the importance of the structure of salary increases.

Two aspects of the Ballou and Podgursky study could limit its applicability to the potential efficacy of future increases in teacher salaries. First, it is a national study that abstracts from the tremendous variation across the country in the market conditions for teachers. Indeed, a recent study by Loeb and Page (1998), based on a state-level panel dataset, supports the view that teacher salaries can affect the quality of schooling and student outcomes. Using school dropout rates as their primary measure of student outcomes and hence of school quality, the authors conclude that, holding all else equal, raising teachers' salaries by 10 percent would reduce dropout rates by 3-6 percent. Their careful attention to the specification of their equations and in particular their focus on changes rather than on levels makes the analysis convincing and worthy of attention. Their rough calculations suggest that the cost of raising teacher salaries by 10 percent would slightly exceed the benefits as measured by the present value of the increases in individuals' future salaries associated with their higher educational attainment. However, the authors note that their measure of the benefits of an increase in teacher salaries probably underestimates the true benefits, since it is based on a single measure of student outcomes. They note further that if salary increases were better targeted, they are likely to be more cost-effective than the across-the-board increases they examined.

Second, the Ballou and Podgursky study applies to a period of declining enrollments and a general teacher surplus, a market context that the authors used to help explain their findings. In a market with excess supply, an across-the-board increase in teacher salaries provides an incentive for the existing stock of teachers to remain in the profession longer than they otherwise would, which in turn limits the number of new openings. Given the outlook for a tighter market for teachers in the future, and a very tight market in such fields as mathematics and science and in some areas of the country, salary increases could potentially be more successful in attracting higher-quality teachers in the future than they were in the 1980s. Nonetheless, this different market context does not negate the conclusion that when or if they are planning to raise teacher salaries, policy makers trying to increase the quality of teachers entering the profession will need to pay more attention to the structure of salaries and in particular to the level of entering salaries than has been the case in the past. In addition, they may want to change the current salary structure in ways that would increase the incentives for existing teachers to become more productive, a topic discussed further in the section on strategies to change incentives.

Developing the Capacity of Practicing Teachers

National survey data show that the country is doing a poor job of improving the capacity of practicing teachers. While about half of all teachers had some professional development during 1993-94, only 15 percent spent nine or more hours in any area of professional development (Darling-Hammond, 1997:34-35, and Appendix B, Table 5). Traditionally, most professional development for teachers has consisted of brief district-sponsored workshops, which can be useful for training in specific skills but are of little value for learning subject matter in any depth or learning how to assess student learning in the context of teaching. These long-standing shortcomings are increasingly problematic, given the new roles for teachers suggested by findings from research on learning and in light of the fact that teachers will need more knowledge and radically different skills than they generally now have if education reform efforts are to succeed (National Research Council, 1999b).

While there is still a lot to learn about professional development, some types appear to be far superior to others. Bureaucratic forms of professional development fail to support teacher learning. By contrast, effective programs are characterized by teachers' active involvement in planning and doing professional development, sufficient time and support for making significant improvements in practice, and an on-site professional community as a context for teacher learning and for nurturing commitment to serving all students. (For field-based research on processes of teacher learning and teacher community see, for example, cases reported in Cohen et al., 1993; Lord, 1994; Schifter and Fosnot, 1993; Talbert and McLaughlin, 1994).

Research conducted in the context of state systemic reform adds to this knowledge base and to principles for effective professional development. A 10-year study of California mathematics education reform included a 1993 survey of teachers that allowed the researchers to test a variety of hypotheses about the links between, first, the type and form of professional development and changes in classroom practices and, second, those practices and student achievement (Cohen and Hill, 1998). The first set of linkages are more convincing than the second set, because the survey data had to be aggregated to the school level for the achievement part of the analysis and the survey sampled only four or fewer teachers at each school. The study shows that professional development works best—in the sense of changing teacher practices—when it is closely related to the new curriculum. Also, time spent on professional development matters for its success. Although this analysis was cross-sectional, and thus controlled for neither teachers' nor students' prior performance, the findings are consistent with related research on student achievement in California and with the field-based research in the project. A study by Wiley and Yoon (1995) of student performance on the California mathematics assessment also found that teachers' extended opportunities to learn about the mathematics curriculum and instructions were associated with higher student achievement.

A survey by Kennedy (1998) of eight studies that examine the relationship between in-service training and student achievement provides additional insight about the types of in-service professional development programs that are likely to be most effective. The most effective programs, she concludes, are those that concentrate on teachers' knowledge of the subject, on the curriculum, and how students learn the subject. As she notes, the promise of this approach, combined with her conclusion that programs that focus on teacher behaviors are not effective in raising student achievement, suggests that more extensive research on content-based approaches would be desirable.

Further suggestive evidence that investment in teacher development can increase student achievement comes from cross-state comparisons. Darling-Hammond (1997:11-14) reports that states investing heavily in a teacher capacity-building strategy over the past decade—North Carolina, Connecticut, and Kentucky in particular—had outstanding 1990-96 gains in students' mathematics scores for grades 4 and 8 on the National Assessment of Educational Progress (NAEP). North Carolina, for example, introduced a whole set of programs designed to increase teacher quality, including boosting minimum salaries, requiring schools of education to be accredited, investing in improvements in teacher education curriculum, launching a beginning teacher mentoring program, and introducing incentives for teachers to become board certified. Nevertheless, it is not possible to say definitively how much of the achievement gains should be attributed to investments in teacher capacity, since such investments generally did not occur in isolation. In North Carolina, for example, a whole set of strategies was introduced, including a sophisticated school-based accountability system (Grissmer and Flanagan, 1998).

The main lesson to emerge from the research on professional development is that there appear to be positive returns from some types of professional development but not from others. Noteworthy as well is that the professional development that appears to be most successful in the studies cited here is that embedded in a comprehensive program for educational improvement, such as standards-based systemic reform. Thus, general professional development would seem to be a much less productive investment than a professional development program that is closely tied to other components of an overall reform effort. Importantly, however, even the studies that show positive effects of professional development programs are limited, in that they do not compare the returns of professional development programs in the form of student achievement with the costs of such programs.

Final Reflections on Investment Policies to Develop Teacher Capacity

Not included in this set of policies aimed at developing teacher capacity is a potentially important one—the restructuring of teacher salaries to change the incentives for practicing teachers, which is included below in the section on altering incentives to make performance count. In one sense, the distinction we have made here between financial investments in capacity and altering incentives is a bit misleading. It is designed to distinguish policies that require significant resources (either new resources or resources transferred from other purposes), such as raising teacher salaries and investing in professional development, from those that use the financial system to change the incentives facing teachers. In fact, as should be clear from the discussion of the investment policies in this section, the distinction between capacity building and incentive programs is fuzzy and in many cases the strategies will be most effective if they are used together.

CHANGING INCENTIVES TO MAKE PERFORMANCE COUNT

The main policy options for changing incentives within the existing system include changing the incentives of teachers, primarily through changes in the structure of their salaries, and changing the incentives for schools, using school-based accountability and incentive programs.

Incentives for Teachers

Teachers are typically subject to a single salary schedule that gives higher pay to teachers with more experience and with advanced degrees, regardless of whether the advanced degree is related to what they teach. While such a structure could in principle generate salaries that vary approximately with the effectiveness of teachers, many researchers (e.g., Hanushek, 1986, 1997) have argued that the resulting pattern of salaries bears almost no relationship to the effectiveness of teachers and, consequently, that the current salary schedule provides few or no incentives for teachers to become more effective. This argument is bolstered by many empirical studies that find little or no systematic relationship between the experience or education of teachers and the performance of their students. While some researchers (e.g., Ferguson and Ladd, 1996) have found evidence that the relationship may be somewhat stronger than earlier studies suggest, none disputes the basic claim that the structure of the salary schedule provides little incentive for teachers to become more effective. This statement does not imply that teachers have no incentives to become more effective, only that the salary schedule itself does not provide those incentives.

Merit Pay and Career Ladders

Many school districts over the years have experimented with various programs of merit pay for effective teachers or career ladders that identify effective teachers and provide them with leadership opportunities in such areas as curriculum and professional development. For a variety of reasons, merit pay programs typically have not survived for very long and those that have survived seem to be in the wealthier districts and have evolved from a true merit pay plan, in which teachers are rewarded for better work, to ones in which teachers are rewarded for taking on more tasks (see Murnane and Cohen, 1986). Although career ladder programs have shown somewhat more positive results, states typically have not maintained funding for them in a consistent manner over time (Odden and Kelley, 1997:34).

Several concerns have been raised with regard to merit pay (see Educational Research Service, 1978; Hatry et al., 1994; Jacobson, 1987; Johnson, 1986; Murnane and Cohen, 1986). For a variety of reasons, teachers do not like them. In part, this reflects the difficulty that principals have had in developing appropriate criteria for measuring the effectiveness of teachers that correspond to professional standards of good practice. There is also a widely expressed concern that merit pay for individual teachers may lead to competitive behavior among teachers and other school personnel. Those who raise this concern see it as counter to the view that teachers should be working cooperatively to improve the learning environment within a school. Cohn (1996) notes that similar issues arise in other contexts and, in response to such concerns, incentive pay plans in business often include a group incentive component. Other concerns are that districts and states often fail to provide stable funding for such programs. That instability both weakens their incentives and sends a signal that they are not core elements of a state or district program.

A study by Hatry et al. (1994) of 18 merit pay and career ladder programs showed that most of the districts were unsuccessful in creating lasting and effective programs. Though there were some positive effects in some districts in the form of reduced teacher turnover and absenteeism, most of the programs suffered from low teacher morale, high costs, and administrative burdens. A study by the National Research Council (NRC) on the potential of merit pay for improving performance of federal government employees (National Research Council, 1991) found little direct evidence on which to answer this question conclusively and concluded that positive effects might be found but could be attenuated by some of the same factors that have caused concern in education. While individual merit pay may have as-yet untapped potential, the difficulties encountered by school districts that have tried it have led to a shift in emphasis among education policy makers and researchers to group, or school-based, incentives.

Linking Pay to Knowledge and Skills

As an alternative both to the single salary schedule and to merit pay or career ladder programs that provide pay or other benefits in return for performance, teacher salaries could be linked to the skills and knowledge that research suggests are needed for teachers to be effective. Odden and Kelley (1997) argue that this approach, which in the context of professionals is often referred to as competency pay, has been successful in the private sector and would be particularly appropriate for an education system focused on raising student achievement. The goal of such an approach is to "provide incentives for teachers to develop their knowledge, skills, and competencies in new and more effective forms of pedagogy, deeper and more conceptual subject matter knowledge needed to teach consistently with the ways children learn advanced cognitive expertise, and the leadership and management skills needed to engage in effective school-site management and decision making" (Odden and Kelley, 1997:51).

A competency-based salary structure could be implemented in various ways. One possibility is to introduce into the existing system of teacher licensure and certification teacher bonuses that are tied to teacher knowledge and skills. An alternative is to restructure the whole system of licensure and tenure so that movement through the various steps is contingent on the teacher reaching higher levels of professional knowledge (see Odden, 1996:248). Such a structure would differ in significant ways both from the current approach to pay and from a merit pay system. It would differ from the current system in that advancement and pay would no longer be based on simple quantitative measures such as years of experience or advanced degrees. It would differ from merit pay programs in that the "best" teachers would no longer be singled out and rewarded with additional pay. Instead, a competency-based salary structure would reward teachers for developing skills that are identified as important, such skills being assessed relative to predetermined, clear-cut standards. Rather than creating competition among teachers, it signals the types of competencies the school or district wants its faculty to acquire (Odden and Kelley, 1997:81-82).

Restructuring salaries in this way is appealing because it would align salaries more closely with the goal of raising student achievement. However, a number of issues remain and would need to be studied. The key questions include: How can we ensure that the knowledge and skills are the ones that are highly correlated with how effectively teachers increase student learning? Would such a package of skills vary with the types of students that teachers are serving? How could one avoid the danger that such skill packages may become uniform and hence inappropriate for teachers in some schools? Is there a danger that teachers will simply get the additional training in order to increase their salary without transferring the new skills to the classroom? Is there any concrete evidence that such an approach would lead to more effective teaching in the classroom? As the elements of knowledge and skills salary structures are introduced, research should be mounted to answer these questions. More widespread implementation should depend on what those answers are, even though the logic of the proposed change seems compelling.

Other Financial Incentives

Given the variation across parts of the country and across areas within states in the size and seriousness of teacher shortages, a variety of other financial incentives designed to facilitate the move from areas of teacher surplus to areas of teacher shortage are worth examining. Such incentives might include, for example, bonuses for new teachers and scholarships for teacher candidates in areas of shortage. Some states are currently experimenting with such programs. For example, Massachusetts recently offered $20,000 signing bonuses to outstanding teachers throughout the country and expects to process 600 applications for 50 positions (Bradley, 1999:10). More significant from a structural perspective is the desirability of states' reexamining their rules with respect to such issues as the portability of pensions and teacher licenses. Current limitations on portability and the transferability of licenses hinder the movement of teachers from suburban areas to urban areas as well as across states. Given that society as a whole has become increasingly mobile, eliminating some of these impediments to teacher mobility appears to have potential as a means of keeping good teachers in the profession and employing them in areas where they will be most productive.

Incentives for Schools

Many states are now experimenting with school-based accountability and incentive systems designed to focus the attention of schools on increasing student achievement. Such programs, for example, in North Carolina, South Carolina, Texas, and Kentucky, are typically systems administered from the top down, in that they operate within the traditional public school system and are typically imposed on schools from above. A fully developed system would start with a curriculum and clear content standards describing what the state or district wants children to know and be able to do. As part of that step, policy makers would need to develop a consensus on which subjects are most important and will be the focus of the accountability system. The next step is to locate or to develop assessment tools that generate reliable and valid measures of how well students have mastered the curriculum. Those measures of student performance would then serve as the basis for measuring how effectively schools increase the learning of their students. How best to measure the performance of schools is a thorny issue, and one to which we return below. The state or district would then provide a system of rewards and positive incentives for schools to increase student performance and would develop a set of sanctions or intervention strategies for low-performing schools. As is emphasized below, productive intervention strategies for low-performing schools are a crucial component of a well-designed account-ability system. In their absence, a school-based accountability system may become simply a system for assigning blame rather than a system for improving student performance.

Such systems are fully consistent with the goal of altering incentives to make performance count, given their focus on student outcomes rather than on the inputs that typically were the focus of state accountability systems in the past. A second characteristic is that they focus attention on the school as the improvement unit rather than on the school district, on the teachers, or on the students. The focus on the school is designed to encourage all school personnel to work cooperatively toward a common, well-specified goal. Provided schools are given more management authority than in the past, the schools then would be in a position to rearrange the use of resources toward the goal of higher achievement.

One possible disadvantage of the focus on schools as the unit of accountability is the free rider problem: bonuses are typically given to all teachers (and possibly support staff as well) in an effective school regardless of their contribution. A further, potentially more serious problem with the focus on schools is that good teachers in low-performing schools may prefer to leave such schools in favor of schools where their chances of earning a financial bonus are higher.

Use of Tests for High-Stakes Accountability

Central to all the school-based accountability and incentive systems is the measurement of student performance, as typically measured by test scores. In Chapter 4, we commented on the current status of assessment. We turn here to the uses of tests for high-stakes accountability.

Because student test scores are so highly correlated with student background characteristics, it is essential that school-based accountability systems focus on gains in, rather than levels of, student performance. Otherwise the indicators of success would measure the background of the students rather than the contribution of the schools to student learning. Thus, measuring a school's value-added is at the heart of any sophisticated accountability system. Koretz (1996), Meyer (1996), Clotfelter and Ladd (1996), and Ladd and Walsh (1998) describe the technical challenges involved in using assessments for educational accountability and in developing value-added indicators of school performance. In addition to the technical challenges are considerations related to costs. As Meyer and others note, value-added indicator systems may be costly if they involve frequent testing and comprehensive data systems containing information on student test scores and student, family, and community characteristics. In short, they may require a major commitment on the part of school districts and states. Potentially, however, computer-adaptive tests could provide the requisite data without suffering from these shortcomings (Klein and Hamilton, 1999). The NRC Committee on Title I Testing and Assessment (National Research Council, 1999c) examined a variety of issues involved in using assessments for accountability, including the thorny question of how to determine how much improvement it is reasonable to expect schools to achieve in a given period and how such expectations can be determined.

High-stakes testing can have negative as well as positive effects on classroom practice. Teachers may focus on the content to be covered on the test to the exclusion of other relevant material or spend inordinate amounts of time administering worksheets and drilling students on basic facts in preparation for multiple-choice tests (Smith, 1991; Koretz, 1996; Linn and Herman, 1997). Teachers also may coach students on test items. Such coaching appears to explain why Kentucky, a leading state in using tests for school accountability and education reform, found that large score gains on its state assessment were not reflected in gains on NAEP or on college admission tests. Moreover, gains were far higher on items that had been administered the previous year (Hambleton et al., 1995; Koretz and Barron, 1998). Avoiding these negative effects requires that policy makers desiring to use test scores for high-stakes purposes be aware of such potential misuses and ensure that testing programs build in the necessary features to minimize distortions in both classroom practice and test results.

Another danger in high-stakes testing is that tests may be misused. Tests are created with specific uses in mind. Experts agree that the validity, reliability, and fairness of a test can only be assessed in the context of how the scores on that test are used. Policy makers, practitioners, and the press, however, are prone to use test scores to meet a variety of needs, many of which may not have been anticipated by test developers.

North Carolina, which developed tests specifically for its new school-based accountability program, provides an example. Faced with the pressure from that program, several school districts are now trying to shift the pressure for performance down to the student level. Some school districts, for example, are now requiring that students who do poorly on the state test go to summer school and, if they continue to fail the test, to be held back. The controversial issue here is whether the state test, which uses matrix sampling and was developed for the purpose of school-wide accountability, is valid for the purpose of individual accountability.

The NRC Committee on Appropriate Test Use concluded that existing mechanisms for enforcing appropriate test use (mainly professional norms and legal action through administrative enforcement or litigation) are inadequate and suggested consideration of possible new methods, practices, and safeguards (National Research Council, 1999a). The committee did not recommend a particular strategy or combination of strategies, but it noted that promoting proper test use will require multiple strategies.

Recognition, Rewards, and Sanctions

Rewards for effective schools can take the form of public recognition or cash bonus for effective schools or teachers and staffs within the schools. While views about the importance of the financial awards differ, two concerns about them arise. One is that if they are large, they may encourage teachers and others to go to inappropriate lengths to win awards, including, for example, outright cheating, examples of which have been found in both Kentucky and Dallas. Other less nefarious changes in behavior may ultimately have even greater consequences. For example, to the detriment of low-performing schools, the existence of financial bonuses provide good teachers at those schools new financial incentives to transfer to a school where they are more likely to win an award.

If financial rewards are part of the program, the experience from several states suggests that they be funded by a reliable funding source. If the funding is subject to an annual appropriation, teachers may be skeptical about whether it will continue to be available (see the example of Kentucky in Elmore et al., 1996). The history of funding of such programs in other states does not bode well for teachers' confidence that funds will be forthcoming in the future. For example, both Indiana and Texas included funding in their programs in the early 1990s but both have now eliminated funding for teacher bonuses.

Potentially even more significant than the positive recognition and financial awards for effective schools is how the state or district treats the poorly performing schools. Accountability programs typically include both intervention strategies and sanctions for such schools. The experience from the various states suggests that state policy makers have more work to do in determining the best approach for dealing with the low-performing schools that are identified by the accountability systems. Sanctions will work only to the extent that fear of being sanctioned forces schools to improve their performance before they are sanctioned. The application of sanctions after the fact is problematic in that it may hurt the students as much, or more than, the personnel being sanctioned. Technical and financial assistance may be able to improve school performance in some cases, but it is unlikely to be helpful in all.

Will Such Incentive Programs Increase Student Achievement?

There is no simple answer to this question, although three types of research shed some light on the issue. First is evidence from the experience with similar incentives from the private sector, which shows that programs should not be viewed as a substitute for good management, which includes ensuring that teachers have the capacity to perform their jobs and providing a positive work environment. In addition, empirical evidence from the private sector is neither solid enough to conclude that financial incentives generate large increases in productivity nor detailed enough to provide much guidance for the design of incentive programs in the education sector (Kohn, 1993; Nalbantian and Schotter, 1997).

A second source of evidence is studies of two specific accountability programs. To our knowledge, these are the only systematic studies of the effect of the programs on achievement. The first study examines the Dallas accountability program (Ladd, 1999), and the other examines the five-year experience of Charlotte, North Carolina, with its Benchmark Goals Program (Smith and Mickelson, forthcoming). The Dallas study examines the impact of that program on student performance on the Texas Assessment of Academic Skills (TAAS), a test that is linked to the state's curriculum and that serves as the basis for the statewide accountability system but is only one of two tests used in the Dallas system. The study design involves comparing the paths of student outcomes in Dallas schools to those in five other big Texas cities during the period that included the year before the Dallas program was implemented (1991) and the following four years (1992-95). This study finds evidence of gains in student achievement for whites and Hispanics but not for black students. Other positive effects included greater declines in the dropout rates and greater gains in attendance rates in Dallas than in the other big Texas cities. The study of Charlotte's program is less encouraging, in that it finds few or no gains from the incentive system (Smith and Mickelson, forthcoming).

One possible explanation for this mixed evidence of gains in achievement is that neither the Dallas nor the Charlotte program was embedded in an overall program of education reform. The need to embed such accountability programs in larger overall reform programs that include, for example, the development of professional capacity emerges as an important lesson from the experience with such programs to date. Evidence for this conclusion comes from the work of researchers under the auspices of the Consortium on Policy Research in Education (CPRE) designed to examine various theories of teacher motivation (Heneman, 1997; Kelley, 1997). They found that teachers within a school were more motivated to exert effort when the school met a variety of enabling conditions, including having a curriculum aligned with the state assessments, adequate revenues, strong districts and principal leadership, and adequate professional development for all teachers in the school. Further suggestive evidence for this conclusion emerges from the rapid gains in North Carolina test scores that were mentioned earlier. The combination of that state's accountability system and professional development strategy appears to be having a positive impact on student achievement.

EMPOWERING SCHOOLS OR PARENTS OR BOTH TO MAKE DECISIONS ABOUT THE USE OF PUBLIC FUNDS

The fourth generic finance strategy is to give more power to schools to spend as they wish or to parents who can use it to pay for the school of choice for their child. Thus, compared with traditional funding mechanisms, this strategy provides for a lot more choice and flexibility, both on the part of the schools and on the part of parents and their children. Such a strategy can be implemented through policies that alter the existing public school system in mostly incremental ways (for example, by giving public schools control over finance and other decisions) or through policies that effect major changes in the overall governance system (e.g., by permitting charter schools to operate outside the traditional regulatory system or giving vouchers to parents to use at either public or private schools). The more spending authority is given to the schools, the freer they are to make their own trade-offs between the quality and quantity of teachers, between the number of teachers and other staff, and between personnel and other inputs such as computers and library books. The best example of this approach in the United States is illustrated by the funding of charter schools. Once such schools are granted a charter, they are funded on the basis of the number of pupils they serve and are free to use those funds to achieve the purposes set forth in the charter. Because of the flexibility given to charter schools, the programs they offer inevitably would differ one from another in significant ways. For that and other reasons, the freedom for parents to choose whether to send their child to a particular school would be a logical component of this type of funding arrangement.

By giving existing schools more flexibility in the use of funds or encouraging the establishment of charter schools, policy makers hope to promote innovations that will improve the quality of education. The incentive to provide a high-quality education comes from the fact that, if schools do not do so, they will lose students and will lose the funding associated with those students. A variation of this approach, but one that is consistent with the concept of introducing more flexibility into the provision of education, is to have schools or school districts contract with the private sector to provide educational services. Supporters of more contracting hope to harness the profit motive of the private sector to make the provision of education more efficient. Significantly, the expansion of the charter school movement has increased interest in the use of private firms, either as firms hired by the developers of charter schools or, in the states where it is allowed, as the developers of new charter schools.

When funds are, in effect, given to parents, the parents have more say about which school their child attends. As noted in Chapter 5, funds can be given to parents in various ways, including tax credits for tuition or other educational expenses or in the form of vouchers for education that can be used in any school, whether it be public or private. Many arguments can and have been made for giving parents more choice over the schools their children attend. One of these is to encourage schools, both existing schools and new schools, to be more responsive to parental demands than they currently are, which would improve the quality of education to the extent that parents are looking for quality. Another is the view that when parents are free to choose the schools their children attend, each school may become a more coherent community with a shared mission and shared set of values than is the case when children are assigned to schools. The hope is that this shared sense of community would make each school a more effective organization and hence able to provide higher-quality education. As Brandl (1998) notes, these two mechanisms of competition and community through which parental choice might improve schools need not be in conflict and would complement each other in a well-designed system.

Much has been written on these strategies for improving schools. In a book of this type, we obviously cannot do justice to all the literature. Our more limited intent in the following sections is to rely primarily on empirical studies to determine how likely it is that strategies of this type will increase student achievement or, alternatively, will generate any given level of achievement in a more cost efficient manner. We start with the school-oriented strategies of site-based management, charter schools, and contracting with private firms. We then turn to various policies that enhance parental choice.

Effects of School-Oriented Strategies on Student Achievement and Efficiency

Although we begin this section with school-based management (SBM), it is worth noting that most so-called SBM programs in the United States to date have included only limited financial autonomy. Hence, we have little direct U.S. evidence on the effects of giving schools more financial autonomy. Nonetheless, the findings from the literature are suggestive. Charter schools, in contrast, provide a better example of meaningful devolution of financial authority to the school level, but as the evidence on the effectiveness of charter schools is still quite limited and the jury is still out on their effectiveness in promoting high achievement and encouraging innovation. Moreover, limitations on capital funding for such schools have put them at a disadvantage. Finally, the limited experience with contracting between school districts and private firms provides more insight into the nature of contracting problems than it does about any potential of that strategy.

School- or Site-Based Management

Studies that have examined the decentralization of authority to schools have raised questions about the logic of the theory (Hannaway, 1993, 1996; Wohlstetter and Odden, 1992). One expectation, for example, is that school personnel and parents, as opposed to administrators in the central office, will focus more directly on teaching and learning. Studies show, however, that the participation of school-level participants, in particular parents and teachers, is weak (e.g., Malen and Ogawa, 1988; Easton and Storey, 1994; Hess, 1993) and that decisions do not seem to focus more heavily on teaching and learning concerns (e.g., Hess, 1993; Weiss and Cambone, 1994).

Consistent with this finding, a review of 18 studies by Summers and Johnson (1996) found not only little effect on student achievement but also little effect on the expected behavior of schools and school participants. Few of the studies even attempted to estimate impacts on achievement (suggesting that higher student achievement may not have been the goal) and those that did estimate impacts on achievement found no statistically significant impacts, although some found that school-based management programs had a positive, but small, impact on student attendance.

The most dramatic U.S. experiment with decentralization of authority to the school level is the 1988 Chicago reform that set up 550 local school councils in which parents had a statutory majority and which had the authority "to hire and fire the school principal, determine the school's educational priorities, and approve the spending of discretionary funds, eventually amounting to half a million dollars or more" (Shipps et al., 1998:1). The effects on student achievement were mixed at best. Some schools appeared to have improved student performance; others remained unchanged; and some performed worse (Bryk et al., 1998). About half the schools did not seem even to take advantage of the freedom and resources offered under the law to try to change their schools (Sebring et al., 1996). Some people have interpreted the fact that in 1995 Chicago increased central control in a striking way as an indication of the instability of decentralization reform efforts, which calls into question whether this form of school governance can exist in the turbulent and politically charged environment of big U.S. cities. However, others have interpreted the change as the logical extension of a decentralization strategy that is designed to increase student achievement (see Hess, 1999).

Odden and Busch (1998), drawing on an extensive body of recent research studies, conclude that newer strategies of SBM point to a series of organizational conditions that must exist at the school level for SBM to lead to improved student achievement. In their view, there are nine key steps that must characterize SBM: center change on student learning and a rigorous instructional program; involve all teachers in decision making; allow schools to recruit and select staff; invest in training and professional development; create a professional school culture; create a comprehensive school-based information system; provide rewards and sanctions; select principals who can facilitate and manage change; and give schools control over their budget.

Charter Schools

Charter schools represent a more complete form of decentralization than school-based management, in that schools are exempted from much district and state regulation in exchange for the accountability that comes from the possibility that their charter will be revoked or of other sanctions imposed by the state. Charter schools are a relatively recent phenomenon, and few systematic studies about them are available. While no information is available yet on their contribution to student achievement, some information is available on whom they serve, limitations related to accountability, their effect on public schools, and the problems they face in obtaining funding.

Contrary to opponents' predictions, the early experience with charter schools does not support the view that they disproportionately serve white and economically advantaged students (U.S. Department of Education, 1998b; Vanourek et al., 1997). The second-year report of a national study of charter schools showed that, while in 1996-97 they enrolled a smaller proportion of students with disabilities than other public schools in their state, their racial composition, the proportion of low-income students, and the proportion of students with limited English proficiency were similar to statewide averages. Moreover, when the analysis was extended to the district level, it showed that about 60 percent of charter schools were not racially distinct from their districts and another third enrolled a distinctly higher percentage of minority students than the district. Racial/ethnic enrollment patterns differ, however, across states with charter schools, with some states (California, Colorado, and Arizona) having a somewhat higher average percentage of white students in charter schools than in all public schools, whereas others (Massachusetts, Michigan, Minnesota, Texas, and Wisconsin) had lower average percentages of white students in charter schools (U.S. Department of Education, 1998b).

With respect to accountability, Wohlstetter and Griffin (1998:14-15) found that in practice "the myth of greater accountability for charter schools far exceeded the reality." Although the 17 schools in their study reported that they appreciated the value of a sound accountability system, not one had such a system in place and the schools derided the use of externally imposed standardized tests because they would not assess accurately what the school was trying to accomplish. Similarly, a study of charter schools in ten California districts (UCLA Charter School Study, 1998) reported that, in most instances, charter schools were not yet being held accountable for enhancing the academic achievement of their students; they were more likely to be held fiscally accountable.

One of the rationales for charter schools is that they will promote greater effectiveness and efficiency in regular public schools. In the only study of this issue of which we are aware, Rofes (1998) conducted case studies of 25 randomly selected school districts in which charter schools were operating. Although more work on this issue would be desirable, his findings are suggestive. Based on interview data, he concluded that about one-quarter of the school districts responded to charters in an energetic way and had significantly altered their educational programs. In one district, for example, the formation of a local charter served as a catalyst for improving the district's middle school. Other responses included opening schools organized around a specific theme, setting up pilot schools, creating add-on programs such as an after-school program or an all-day kindergarten, and offering more diverse activities or curricular resources. Another quarter of the respondents responded more moderately by making significant efforts to aggressively market their schools to the public or by becoming more receptive to community input.

From the perspective of school finance, the most striking aspect is the financial disadvantage under which many charter schools operate. In many states, charter schools receive as operating expenses just the state share of operating revenues, not the combined state and local revenue that is available to the public schools. Even more burdensome is the lack of capital and start-up funds. A large percentage of charter schools, particularly those for which the charter was granted by nondistrict entities or those that are start-up schools, have no access to local district funds levied for capital improvements and do not have access to the capital market. As a result, most charter schools, are forced to use a portion of their operating funds or to seek funds from private sources to secure, furnish, and maintain facilities (Bierlein and Fulton, 1996). Furthermore, except in two states (Arizona and New Mexico), charter schools receive no extra state support for planning or implementation.

Without minimizing the conceptual difficulties of determining a charter school's fair share of funding, the committee simply notes that charter schools in most states have not been put on the level playing field with the public schools that would allow them to compete effectively. At the same time, we note that fair treatment with respect to the financing of capital facilities could increase overall costs of providing education unless existing school facilities are turned over to the charter schools or are sold or rented out.

The jury is still out on charter schools. Early interest and enthusiasm for them has probably been far greater than most policy makers expected, but the difficulty of establishing these schools is probably also far greater. Moreover, no information is yet available on their impacts on student achievement.

Contracting with Private Firms

Contracting with private firms would appear to have some important advantages over the alternative of enabling groups to set up charter schools. Unlike the charter schools for which start-up capital is a serious problem, private firms have access to capital that allows them to expand and make investments. In addition, because firms could run multiple schools, they are able to operate like a "virtual" school district and can ensure that the schools they run have sufficient capacity to operate effectively. In addition, they have strong incentives to provide quality control to preserve the firm's reputation. Third, contracting gives the school district more control over the types of schools being provided without its being involved in the running of the schools. However, the well-publicized experiences of Baltimore and Hartford with the private firm of Education Alternatives Inc. (EAI) did not give contracting a good name.

Part of the problem in Baltimore was that the school district negotiated a bad contract with EAI that required the district to pay more to EAI to run nine elementary schools than it would have cost to run the schools themselves. This outcome occurred because the district agreed to pay the average per-pupil cost of running all schools in the district rather than the average cost of running the cheaper elementary schools (Walsh, 1995; Brown and Hunter, 1996). Despite its additional funds, EAI was unable to produce any positive effects on student achievement. Although EAI initially released test score results that showed improvements in the schools it managed, these scores were later discredited when the Baltimore school district released district scores that showed student performance in the EAI schools was lagging. A University of Maryland study also shows that EAI schools in Baltimore produced no real difference in student performance or in the impact of technology on learning (Molnar, 1996). For this reason, as well as concerns by the district about some of EAI's practices, such as moving students out of special education classes and the use of college interns as teachers' aides, Baltimore terminated its contract with EAI in 1995 (Molnar, 1996). The experience of Hartford was a bit different, in that EAI was hired to perform back office management functions in that city rather than to operate the schools, but that contract too was cancelled in early 1996.

The Edison Project has had the longest history in operating contract schools, but data on its effects is limited and the number of schools still relatively small. Thanks in part to the growth of charter schools, however, the firm is now growing. The school year 1997-98 marked the third year of Edison's operation and at that time, the company had 25 public school partnerships serving nearly 13,000 students. For 1998-99, the number of schools was expected to increase to 75. The only data available on student test scores are reported by Edison itself (although they are compiled by independent researchers). Comparisons of changes in test scores between Edison's student and a control group indicated some positive effects overall (Edison Project, 1997). At least one school showed striking gains, but in others there were small declines. No public information is available on the other private firms, including the Sylvan Learning Systems, that have emerged in this market.

In sum, solid information on the effects of these initial trials with private firms is limited. Moreover, little is known about how such firms will behave over time as their need to show profits increases and, indeed, it is not yet clear whether the firms will be able to provide a high-quality product and still make a profit. The one bright light for the Edison Project and other private firms is that the expansion of state charter school legislation has opened up a new opportunity to run schools as charter schools, which could give these firms a chance to grow enough to benefit from economies of scale.

Conclusions About School-Oriented Policies

On the basis of the evidence, we cannot be assured that any of these approaches will by itself fulfill the goal of higher achievement in a cost-efficient manner. However, we note that the newness of the charter school movement makes it difficult to evaluate. Charter schools may well fulfill their proponents' predictions about exerting productive impacts on the rest of the public school system sometime in the future, and indeed preliminary evidence of these impacts is positive in some areas.

In fact, in the committee's view, some of these options are likely to be quite promising for the goal of increasing achievement, especially if they are included as part of a larger education reform strategy that encompasses, for example, clear outcomes-based accountability standards. Additional flexibility at the school level may be crucial as a way to achieve greater achievement, given the absence of a clear and identifiable production function for education that applies to all students. However, that flexibility will be productive in increasing achievement only to the extent that higher achievement is the goal, that schools are somehow held accountable for achievement, and that teachers have the capacity to teach effectively and students the capacity to learn.

Effects of Greater Parental Choice on Student Achievement and Efficiency

Many parents already exercise school choice, through their choice of where to live or by electing to enroll their children in private schools. One problem with the first form of choice is that by bundling the choice of school with the residential choice decision, any tendencies toward residential segregation by income or race will be exacerbated. Another disadvantage to either form of choice is that not all families can exercise it equally. Rather, wealthier families have more options than poorer families as they can more easily move to another location, or alternatively they could send their children to private schools. Moreover, low-income families in big-city school districts have even fewer choices than others, since even if they move to another location within the city they still receive education services from the same district. We return in Chapter 7 to the implications of the constrained choice available to low-income families in large urban areas.

Various strategies have been proposed, and implemented, to expand parental choice and to break the connection between residential location and choice of schools. Historically, the goal of many strategies that provide for more choice within a district, such as for example magnet schools and controlled choice programs, had more to do with reducing racial segregation than with increasing student achievement or making schools more efficient. Newer forms of parental choice include open enrollment schemes that allow children to choose schools in other districts, charter schools, and vouchers that can be used in any public or private school.

Of interest here is what we know about the effects of parental choice either on student achievement or on the productive efficiency of the education system. Economists have been particularly interested in the issue of efficiency, so we begin with some theoretical predictions about choice that emerge from the economics literature before turning to the empirical evidence. Our attention here to the predictions from economic theory are not intended to discount other mechanisms, such as the contribution of parental choice to the development of schools as organizations with shared values, which also could lead to greater productivity. Instead, we include the economic predictions here because of the insight they provide about different forms of choice programs. The point is that choice programs differ in their potential to increase the efficiency of the education system. Moreover, the impacts of the various choice programs are likely to vary by type of district.

Economic Predictions About Different Forms of Choice

Economic theory suggests that schools or districts will operate inefficiently unless they are disciplined by competitive market pressures. Given this perspective, not all forms of parental choice are likely to be equally effective in promoting production efficiency. For example, choice programs within districts may provide pressure for individual schools to become more effective as they attempt to retain students, but provide no pressure for the district administration itself to become more efficient. Choice programs between districts could provide some of that pressure, as districts would be in danger of losing some of their students to other districts. However, in an interdistrict choice program, some economists worry that an important link between education quality and housing values will be weakened. According to this argument, residents in a district have an incentive to care about the quality of education provided by the district to maintain housing values in the district. With an interdistrict choice program, students have access to the district's school without residing in the district, which breaks the link between the quality of neighborhood schools and house values, and thereby the monitoring function could be weakened. These two offsetting incentives could conceivably lead to a reduction of school quality in a district.

Charter schools are, in principle, quite different from other forms of public school choice because of the potential for entry and exit. Unlike other forms of choice, charter schools have the potential to undercut the monopoly power accorded to a public school in a typical public system in the United States. A charter school might enter and supplant an ineffective public school. Similarly, a charter school is not endowed with the monopoly rights to a geographic area in the way that public schools typically are. So, in principle, the force of entry brings charter schools closer to the textbook competitive norm than other forms of open enrollment. Similarly, voucher-like arrangements have the potential to encourage entry of schools that would potentially supplant ineffective public schools. The significant point here is that many economists believe that parental choice is likely to lead to the greatest gains in productive efficiency when there is the potential for a supply-side response in the form of the entry of new schools or the closing down of existing schools.

Types and Quality of Empirical Evidence

Empirical evidence on the effects of parental choice on achievement and productive efficiency comes in various forms, some of which are more reliable than others. Because there has been a large amount of choice within the education system for a long period of time, there are a huge number of studies of the effects of choice. Not all of these studies, however, shed light on the question in which we are interested: Would the introduction of significantly more parental choice into the education system increase achievement or the productivity of the system? Moreover, some of the studies are far better than others, either because of the study design or because of the quality of the data.

The evidence, which is far from perfect, provides some limited support for the view that parental choice can lead to better educational outcomes. This evidence comes from a number of sources. Rouse (1997) and Greene et al. (1997) found that students in the Milwaukee voucher program showed achievement gains, especially in mathematics. Evidence from some of the privately funded programs has also begun to emerge: Peterson et al. (1998), for example, found that New York students who received vouchers from a private foundation scored higher on standardized tests. This study is noteworthy because it is the first one to be based on a true experimental design. Because the program was oversubscribed, those who were awarded a voucher were selected at random. Thus the evaluation is based entirely on the comparisons between those who were selected and those who were not selected for a voucher.[2] In addition, there is some evidence that Catholic schools are more effective than public schools. Evans and Schwab (1995), for example, find that Catholic school students are more likely to finish high school and go on to college.

But while this evidence is suggestive, it would be very difficult to argue that it constitutes an ironclad case in favor of more parental choice. In many cases, researchers looking at the same problem have come to very different conclusions. Witte et al. (1995), for example, conclude that the Milwaukee experience offers no evidence that private schools have been more effective. Neal (1997) and

---

[2]Issues still arise about how to handle the applicants who were awarded a voucher but did not use it, especially given that the researchers had a lower success rate in testing those students than in testing the students who used the voucher.

Figlio and Stone (1997) conclude that while urban minority students often realize significant benefits from a Catholic school education, Catholic schools are no more effective than public schools for other types of students.

The problem here in part is the ability of researchers to control fully for unmeasured differences among students and families. To be sure, the recent studies of Catholic school students have made great strides compared with earlier studies in controlling for the selection bias that arises because the students who choose differ from those who do not. Nonetheless, Catholic school students and students who use vouchers to attend private schools in Milwaukee differ from other children in at least one fundamental way that is difficult to control for using standard statistical procedures: someone was willing and able to take the necessary steps to take them out of the public schools. Research (e.g., Wells and Crain, 1997) has shown that parent-child relationships are very different in families that exercised their option to participate in a school-choice plan. Choosers (in all income groups) are more actively involved in their children's educations and more actively direct their children in important decisions. It is possible to mistakenly attribute the success of children whose parents choose private school for them to the school rather than to differences in parenting. Similar problems will arise if private schools are able to successfully screen potential students or expel students as a result of poor behavior and poor academic performance. (This problem, however, does not apply to the New York City privately funded voucher program described above.) Hence, evidence from the statistical studies is at best suggestive.

Of interest is not only the effect of choice on the achievement of the choosers but also its effect, through the competition for students, on the traditional public schools. In addition to one interview study on this issue related to charter schools already cited (Rofes, 1998), more general research on this question is provided by Caroline Hoxby, who makes use of the variation across school districts in the amount of competition they face naturally from public schools in other districts or from private schools to draw inferences about the effects of a voucher program on overall student achievement. Hoxby (forthcoming) concludes that districts with less concentration of enrollment (more competition) have higher test scores and that competition makes a bigger difference in districts with less educated adults (where less than 20 percent of the adults have a bachelor's degree) and in districts in states with more local control. Because this study focuses on the form of choice that is most common in the United States, choice among public school districts, the evidentiary base is large. Moreover, the study is ambitious in that it uses data from a number of large U.S. databases and explicitly addresses the potential problem of reverse causation.

In two other studies, Hoxby (1995, 1996) measures the effect of competition from private schools and concludes again that such competition increases the achievement of students in the public schools. If Hoxby's results are correct, they are potentially very important. However, technical criticisms have been raised in connection with her papers on private schools as well as some questions of interpretation (Kane, 1996). In addition, in contrast to the Hoxby findings, a new study by Sander (forthcoming) that examines the effects of private schools on the achievement of public school students in Illinois finds no direct effects. Like Hoxby, Sander uses Catholic religion as a means of identifying the private school effect, and in particular, of addressing the statistical problem of simultaneity that arises because in areas with poor public schools more students are likely to opt out of the public school system in favor of private schools. Given these conflicting findings, the question of the effect of competition on public schools must be considered unsettled at this point.

In sum, the U.S. research on parental choice, including choice that extends to private schools, is limited largely by the absence of experience on a large scale with voucher programs or with broad-based choice programs that break the link between residential location and school choice. Much remains to be learned about the potential for choice to increase student achievement. The most urgent context for that additional learning appears to be in urban areas, with their large concentrations of disadvantaged students.

It is worth noting, however, that other countries have had more experience with parental choice programs that break the link between place of residence and schooling, including some public funding of private schools, than has the United States. The experience from Europe with those programs provides reasonably clear evidence of the potential for an undesirable side effect of some choice programs, namely that schools may become more socially stratified (Vandenberghe, 1996, for Belgium; Ambler, 1994 for France; and Karsten, 1994, for The Netherlands). The mechanism by which competition might increase stratification is intimately tied with how parents choose schools. For example, to the extent that parents' perceptions about the quality of a school depend in part on the socioeconomic characteristics of the students in the school, parents will tend to transfer their children into districts or schools with higher average incomes (Fossey, 1994; Armor and Peiser, 1997; Fowler, 1995; 1996). In Scotland, which includes state-subsidized private schools and public school open enrollments, most parents appear to choose schools based on the social status of the student body (Glenn, 1990). Similarly, Echols and Willms (1995) find that Scottish parents who choose are more educated, have a higher occupational status, and tend to select schools with high average test scores and socioeconomic status.

School choice programs will not necessarily increase social stratification. Indeed, there are many examples in the United States (such as the experience with magnet schools and with some of the new voucher programs that are restricted to low-income parents) that do just the reverse. Such an effect can be avoided by careful attention to the design of a choice program, an issue to which we return in Chapter 9.

CONCLUSIONS

Although this review of knowledge provides no silver bullet strategy for raising student achievement, it provides a variety of promising policy directions for designing an improved financing system, one that will harness school finance more closely to the goal of increasing achievement for all students. Provided the existing system of school governance is maintained essentially in its current form, the committee's main conclusions are that capacity building and incentive strategies must be designed with careful attention to their effects on student achievement and that they will need to be combined in thoughtful ways if they are to promote the goal of higher achievement for all students in a cost-effective way. For example, a policy of investing in the capacity of existing teachers is likely to be more effective if it is combined with a change in incentives that make performance count than if it is implemented by itself. Similarly, the success of a program designed to hold schools accountable may depend on the extent to which teachers have access to the skills they need to improve the performance of their students. That still leaves open for policy makers, however, the significant choice of whether to try to promote higher achievement and greater productivity of the education system primarily within the context of the existing system or to opt for major changes in the system of school governance.

7

Achieving Goal 2:
Breaking the Nexus

Completely severing the link between the background characteristics of students and student achievement will require much more than changes to schools and the school finance system. By themselves, schools cannot be expected to overcome the serious social, economic, and political inequities that contribute to large disparities in the academic achievement of children from different racial, ethnic, and economic backgrounds. At the same time, in the committee's judgment, schools, and the system of which they are a part, can and must do more to reduce the link between family and student traits and student achievement.

To that end, this chapter explores options for aligning finance policies with this goal. Finance policies with particular relevance for goal 2 include cost-adjusting school funding formulas and addressing inequities in access to facilities and technology funding; investing in children's capacity to learn via early childhood interventions and links between education and other community services; investing in schools' capacity to educate via reforms to enhance teacher quality, reduce class size, or adopt whole-school redesigns; altering incentives by rethinking the use of categorical programs such as Title I and special education; and giving schools or parents—or both—more control over how education dollars are spent.

REDUCING FUNDING INEQUITIES AND INADEQUACIES

If money did not matter, the large disparities in school funding across districts and states that have been so persistent over time might not matter very much. However, not only is the committee convinced that money can matter, but we also are convinced that it can and should be made to matter more. Indeed, that is the intent of many of the finance reform strategies discussed in Chapter 6. The problem is that the more successful those strategies are, the more likely it is that the effects of funding disparities will be magnified to the detriment of the children in the underfunded schools. Given that many of the children in those schools are likely to be from disadvantaged backgrounds, the goal of reducing the nexus between family background and student achievement will require even greater attention than in the past to reducing those funding disparities and inadequacies. We reiterate the point we made at the outset: basic fairness compels attention to continuing inequities in American education.

Why has it been so hard to reduce these inequities? The answer lies more in the political tensions resulting from values in conflict than in lack of technical knowledge. Technical problems certainly exist; for example, measures don't yet exist that capture fully the differences among states in state tax wealth and effort, thus complicating efforts to design a fair way for the federal government to assist struggling states. The technical problems, however, are amenable to at least proximate solutions. The political challenges are more vexing. In most states, it has been politically difficult to redistribute resources from wealthy to poor districts, and only with pressure from the courts have states reduced some of the historical inequities. Federal aid constitutes so small a proportion of education funding that it is limited in its ability to overcome disparities within and among states.

While we have no easy solutions to the political challenge, we have no doubt that districts or schools serving disproportionate numbers of disadvantaged students will need more funding than other schools if they are to have a chance of raising their students' performance to acceptable levels. To that end, education finance programs will need to be adjusted to reflect the additional demands that educationally at-risk students place on schools. Hence, policy makers will need to include need-based cost adjustments in school finance formulas. In addition, policy makers should be concerned about disparities in educational facilities and technology funding, which are subject to different finance policies than are current operating expenditures and have not received the same scrutiny on fairness grounds as have the latter.

Adding Need-Based Cost Adjustments to School Funding Formulas

Need-based cost adjustments are important because schools or districts with large concentrations of difficult-to-educate students face many more challenges than other schools. Because their students come to school less ready to learn than students in higher-income suburbs, successful schools will need to provide more individual attention to their students and may need to offer smaller classes. In addition, such schools will have to pay more to hire teachers to induce them to teach in relatively harsh environments and, if they are unable to do that, to provide more professional development to raise the skills of the teachers they are able to hire. Finally, they typically have to spend more to maintain a safe environment for their students.

In discussing funding adequacy, we emphasized that the amount of per-pupil funding that would be adequate for a typical district (or school) within a state would need to be adjusted for the differences across districts in the input prices they face and in the educational needs of their students if funding adequacy is to be ensured for all districts. Failure to make such adjustments works to the disadvantage of students in large cities, where the costs of inputs are typically high and where there are large concentrations of at-risk students.

We also pointed out that the art of calculating cost indices that accurately reflect the additional costs of educating at-risk students raises a lot of thorny issues that have not been fully resolved. A large part of the problem is that there is not a good understanding of the relationship between the inputs used in the education process and the outcomes produced. That is, the production function for education is not well defined in that researchers often cannot find systematic and stable relationships between inputs and outputs given current levels of outputs and current ways of delivering services. The challenge for analysts is complicated further in considering that production relationship (and its impact on costs) in a new environment in which outcome standards are more ambitious than in the past and schools are under pressure to become more efficient in generating those outcomes.

Yet despite the technical difficulties in estimating indices of how costs differ across districts because of the mix of students they serve, the committee strongly urges states to make the effort to develop reasonable indices and to use them in calculating state aid. (This could be done either by adjusting general aid formulas using these indices or by ensuring that the total state aid going to districts, schools, or students via general and categorical aid reflects cost differences.) This will require in part the development of better information on the cost of educating at-risk children. Some of our suggestions for the improvement of data collection activities of the National Center for Education Statistics, particularly about modifying finance data collection to better reflect the costs of programs and services, are important components in the development of improved cost indices (see Appendix A). States and districts should also take advantage of the improved statistics on children and families in poverty that will become available on an annual basis when the Census Bureau's American Community Survey is implemented in 2003.

Failure to take cost differences into account is detrimental to the districts and schools with large concentrations of disadvantaged students and can reinforce rather than reduce the nexus between family background and student achievement. At the same time, the committee is well aware that any additional funding for such districts and schools will not by itself ensure higher student achievement.

While such funding adjustments may be a necessary step toward goal 2 of breaking the nexus, it is clearly not sufficient.

Financing Facilities and Technology

School facilities and technology are financed differently than general operating expenditures of public schools. States play a smaller role and while the federal government provides some support for technology, it provides little support for building and renovation. Since it is state and federal funding that tends to mitigate funding inequities resulting from differences in local wealth, the differences in financing patterns suggest that access to funds for facilities and technology tends to be more unequal across school districts than is funding for current operating costs.

Facilities

In 1995, the General Accounting Office (GAO) conducted the first comprehensive survey of school facilities in 30 years, examining the condition of 10,000 schools in more than 5,000 school districts. The study found that one-third of schools had at least one building in need of extensive repair or replacement; two-thirds had at least one inadequate building feature; and nearly three-fifths had at least one unsatisfactory environmental condition. GAO estimated that it would cost over $112 billion over three years to upgrade facilities nationwide to a good overall condition and to meet federal laws on accessibility and the removal of hazardous substances (U.S. General Accounting Office, 1995c). Moreover, a second GAO report found that school facilities are not up to the current demands being placed on them: three-fourths do not have a system or building infrastructure for modern technology; 40 percent cannot meet functional requirements for laboratory sciences; more than half do not have flexible instructional space; two-thirds do not have adequate space for such services as before- or after-school care or child care (U.S. General Accounting Office, 1995b).

State investments in educational facilities are currently growing, thanks to the booming economy; in 1998 states devoted a record $15 billion to school construction (Keller, 1999). Nevertheless, this level of investment is far below what GAO suggested is needed.

GAO also found that school conditions varied from state to state and that schools in central cities and schools enrolling more than 50.5 percent minorities or more than 70 percent students in poverty were disproportionately likely to suffer from deficiencies (U.S. General Accounting Office, 1996). An earlier study (Parrish et al., 1995) found that urban districts enrolling high percentages of poor students in 1989-90 spent more of their budgets on core instruction than on capital outlays, compared to less disadvantaged districts. Yet these are areas where construction costs may actually be higher, because of cost-of-living differences. Honeyman (1990) also reported that districts with low taxing ability demonstrated the greatest level of deferred maintenance. Ladd (1998) found that districts in poor fiscal condition devote a smaller share of education spending to capital outlays than districts in better fiscal condition. About 10 percent of the $300 billion spent on public elementary and secondary schools annually is directed for capital expenses, primarily in connection with facilities construction, renovation, and extensive maintenance.

Facility construction and repair are undertaken through mechanisms and systems quite distinct from those used to support recurrent education expenses. Local revenue bonds have historically been the major source of support. State involvement has grown since the 1940s, when only 13 states subsidized the funding of educational facilities: now 40 states provide some funds for capital outlay (construction or major renovation) and at least 13 states have comprehensive facilities programs (U.S. General Accounting Office, 1995d). (A comprehensive program provides funding and technical assistance, conducts compliance reviews, maintains current information on the condition of school buildings statewide, and has more than one full-time staff member.)

School facilities appear to be an understudied aspect of school finance. Facilities finance systems have not been subject to the same equal protection scrutiny over the past 30 years as have systems for funding recurring education expenses. (This is beginning to change: e.g., the Arizona adequacy court case was a case specifically about facilities, and a few other court cases have also addressed facilities disparities.)

Neither has school facilities finance received much attention from either efficiency or productivity perspectives. The connection between the quality of school facilities and student achievement has been difficult to demonstrate (Monk, 1990; Duke, 1998, suggests it has not been much studied), but it has been suggested that the quality of school facilities is important in that they serve to attract teachers and families differentially to particular school districts where conditions are better and worse (Murnane, 1981). Another point worthy of greater research attention is the efficient deployment of school facilities and the capital they represent. In private-sector accounting, these assets would be under heavy pressure to produce outcomes. In public-sector accounting, these facility assets are assumed to be necessary and worthy of maintenance. However, little consideration is given to how these substantial costs can contribute more favorably either to student achievement or to lowered schooling costs.

Greater attention needs to be paid to facilities and to the relative ability of districts to fund necessary building and maintenance. States without programs to assist districts in equalizing the cost of facilities construction and renovation should consider establishing them.

Financing Technology

Technology, if it is used appropriately, has great potential to help students and teachers develop the competencies needed for the 21st century (National Research Council, 1999). Technology financing, however, is more piecemeal and idiosyncratic than other school financing (Pelavin Research Institute and American Institutes of Research, 1997). This is especially problematic given conclusions like that of the Panel on Educational Technology of the President's Committee of Advisors on Science and Technology (1997) that the nation needs to increase its technology-related expenditures from roughly 1.3 to at least 5 percent of all public K-12 educational spending. Both the panel and Pelavin Research Institute/American Institutes of Research, which examined technology-related issues in depth, point out that initial acquisition costs represent a minority of technology expenses. In addition to financing acquisition, schools must be concerned with making increased provision for technology in their regular operating budgets to cover, among other things, the costs of training teachers to make effective use of technology.

The Pelavin/AIR report (1997:39) points out that "[l]ow-income school districts are likely to face the greatest funding challenge, not only because their sources of funding may be limited but also because the cost of deploying technology in their schools may be high for various reasons, including having more older buildings and greater security problems." While states and local areas devote about equal resources to current (operating) expenditures, local governments contributed twice as much as state governments to expenditures on educational technology in fiscal year 1994: 40 percent compared with 20 percent; the federal government contributed 25 percent. The Pelavin/AIR report (1997:43) noted that the "piecemeal approach to funding technology prevalent in most schools cannot sustain widespread, substantial use of technology throughout the nation's schools." The "exceptional methods" used to date to fund many technology investments are not likely to be replicable in many schools. The Pelavin/AIR report assesses a variety of ways to fund initial technology-related costs and annual operating costs and emphasizes that state and federal governments have an important equity role to play in funding technology, as they do in other areas. It also highlights the need for schools and districts to treat technology separately in their budgets; technology is unlike any other budgeted expenditure (being a hybrid of traditional categories like labor and capital and recurring material expense). Giving it its own line item or budget category will help in projecting and planning for future needs and makes it less likely that districts and schools will ignore the post-acquisition expenditures that will be necessary if technology is to fulfill its promise in enhancing student learning.

Technology financing is one example of how attention to the capacity of the educational system to make good use of money interacts with issues of overall funding levels and disparities. We turn in the next section to a broader discussion of capacity investments that may need to accompany sufficient funding in an overall effort to break the nexus between student background and academic achievement.

INVESTING IN CAPACITY

Research on improving the education of disadvantaged students emphasizes the importance of increasing the duration and the intensity of student exposure and instruction (Bloom, 1964; Slavin et al., 1989), as well as addressing the out-of-school conditions that limit children's readiness to learn. The following sections assess several promising investment policies for addressing one or more of these elements. The first set of policies involves investments beyond traditional K-12 education: early childhood programs and programs that link education and other children's services. The second set focuses on finance policies for K-12 schools that might lead to more intense educational experiences for at-risk youth.

Investing in the Capacity of Children to Learn

A strong consensus has emerged among policy makers, practitioners, and researchers about the importance of increasing investments in the capacity of at-risk children to learn, by focusing on the school-readiness of very young children and by linking education to other social services so that the broad range of educational, social, and physical needs that affect learning are addressed. Numerous ongoing programs providing early childhood intervention and school-community linkage provide evidence of the promise and problems of such policies, suggesting that there is still much to learn about how to make these investments most effectively.

Early Childhood Interventions

A major question for school finance is whether the nation is underinvesting in preprimary school education and child care and whether greater investment would contribute to minimizing later gaps in academic performance between advantaged and disadvantaged students. Of particular relevance for achieving goal 2 is the possibility of increasing the nation's investment in early childhood programs explicitly concerned with compensating for social-environmental disadvantages or developmental disabilities that are correlated with such later problems as low motivation and academic underachievement.

Available evidence supports the idea that early intervention programs targeted at disadvantaged children, especially high-quality programs with intense and comprehensive services, can have a number of positive benefits. The evidence is strong enough to warrant continued attention to expanding these programs. Much remains to be learned, however, about how to preserve the gains that disadvantaged children make in early childhood programs, which now tend to fade over time. The absence of quality follow-through and the tendency for other children to catch up mitigate the early initial advantages that preschool programs can afford (Natriello et al., 1990; Zigler and Muenchow, 1992). The lasting effects from these programs seem likely to depend in part on increasing the effectiveness of K-12 schooling. As Ferguson (1998:365) points out, the ideal of universal access to preschool might ironically lead to greater achievement gaps (he referred to black-white test score gaps) if disadvantaged students later attend less effective elementary and secondary schools than their preschool counterparts from more advantaged backgrounds.

Enrollment of children ages 3-5 in preprimary programs has grown rapidly over the past 30 years, from 27 to 65 percent of the population between 1965 and 1997 (U.S. Department of Education, 1999a: Table 46).[1] In 1997, 39 percent of 3-year-olds, 66 percent of 4-year olds, and 88 percent of 5-year-olds were enrolled in such programs. Private school programs dominated public school programs for 3- and 4-year-olds, while a large majority of 5-year-olds enrolled in school were enrolled in public kindergartens.

Despite the growth in preprimary schooling, it appears that by comparison to many other economically advanced nations, the United States invests less in its youngest children. Enrollment rates of 3- and 4-year-olds in early childhood and primary education are relatively low in the United States (Organisation for Economic Co-operation and Development, 1996). Enrollment of 3- and 4-year-olds in this country is also related to household income, with noticeably higher rates among families earning over $50,000 (U.S. Department of Education, 1999c:96). It has been estimated that average annual public spending in the United States on children from birth to age 5 is only about a quarter of average annual public spending on children from age 6 to 18, a difference due primarily to expenditures on elementary and secondary schools (Karoly et al., 1998:108).

Three recent articles review the literature on early childhood interventions aimed at at-risk children and emphasizing early childhood development (Barnett, 1995; Karoly et al., 1998; Reynolds et al., 1997);[2] the three reviews reach very similar conclusions. Model or demonstration programs were generally of higher quality (as measured by such factors as higher-quality staff, closer staff supervision by experts, lower child-staff ratios, and smaller group size) than large-scale

---

[1]Data collection procedures changed in 1994; data for that year and later are not necessarily comparable to earlier years.

[2]Early intervention programs with other foci, such as public health programs providing prenatal care, immunizations, and nutritional supplements and welfare and other safety-net programs, while an important part of a comprehensive early childhood policy, are not included in the literature reviews examined by the committee.

public programs, including Head Start.[3] Services varied considerably (and are not always well documented in the literature, especially for the large-scale programs). The focus was generally on children age 2-5, although age of entry and length of participation differed from program to program. Services ranged from classroom services to home visits to parental support and development activities and health and nutrition assistance. Model programs had "much higher levels of funding per child" (Barnett, 1995:28) than did the large-scale programs. Virtually all of the programs targeted minority or low-income children.

The research reviews all emphasize shortcomings in the research and evaluation designs that raise cautions about relying too heavily on any particular study. Research on early childhood programs varies widely on elements as how comparison groups were formed, sample sizes, program attrition, and how effects were measured. Despite their shortcomings, however, when evaluated together they lead reviewers to a consistent set of conclusions about what is known and unknown about early childhood intervention programs.

Early childhood programs *can* benefit participating children and their families along a number of dimensions: "The hundreds of studies of demonstration and large-scale programs that now exist provide very strong evidence that most programs of relatively good quality have meaningful short-term effects on cognitive ability, early school achievement, and social adjustment. There is also increasing evidence that interventions can produce middle-to-longer-run effects on school achievement, special education placement, grade retention, disruptive behavior and delinquency, and high school graduation. Debate about the nature of the very long term effects continues, however. The cognitive and social benefits for children are in addition to the physical health, nutrition, and family benefits associated with program participation" (Reynolds et al., 1997:6).

The debate about long-term effects stems in part from the fact that evidence about them comes mostly from model rather than large-scale programs. Given the advantages that model programs have over large-scale programs in quality and cost, the implications that can be drawn from them about the likely effects of large-scale programs *as they are currently structured* are "inadequate to inform public policy" (Reynolds et al., 1997:10), although the model program whose graduates have been followed up for the longest time suggests that the payoffs from early and high-quality intervention programs *might be* very substantial (Barnett, 1995; Karoly et al., 1998).

Fulfilling the promise of early intervention programs depends on making greater investments in efforts to answer key policy questions where evidence is

---

[3]Model or demonstration programs were specifically developed by researchers to study the effects of particular program designs; many have been implemented at just one site. Large-scale programs include the federally funded Head Start program and other state or local programs (some funded with federal Title I funding).

currently weak or nonexistent. In particular, analysts agree that there is still much to learn about optimal program designs and about whether programs have higher payoffs when targeted at children and families deemed to be at greatest risk. Within the overall at-risk population, little is known about how best to identify children who would benefit most and how program effectiveness varies across programs with different attributes. Better information to guide policy makers on these key issues could come from investing in more demonstration programs designed to address the impacts of different program designs, from making the most of evaluations already under way by funding further follow-ups and expanding the set of benefits measured, and from making sure that careful evaluation is a component of any large-scale public program implemented on the basis of existing knowledge.

Given the current state of knowledge, it is impossible to give a definitive answer to the question of how much more the nation should invest in early childhood intervention programs in hopes of breaking the nexus between student background characteristics and academic achievement. Clearly such programs have the potential for making a big difference in children's lives, but just as clearly the cost of such programs may be very high. (Barnett, 1995:46, estimates that serving all poor children under age 5 in quality part-day or full-day programs could cost $25 to $30 billion; adding subsidies to nonpoor families could raise this amount much higher.) The committee suggests that as policy makers consider the expansion and improvement of early childhood intervention programs, the following points should be kept in mind.

First, quality counts. The research evidence indicates that positive effects come from high-quality programs, which are comparatively costly. Existing large-scale public programs like Head Start typically cost less and have lower-paid and less-qualified staff than the most effective model programs. Policy makers may thus need to address the trade-off between serving larger numbers of children in programs of lower quality or focusing available resources on providing high-quality services to a smaller group. Another trade-off may face policy makers in states striving to reduce class size in the early grades of elementary schools at the same time they are expanding early childhood programs. Both strategies increase the demand for well-trained personnel, who may not be in sufficient supply (at least in the short run) to provide qualified individuals for both preschool and school programs simultaneously.

A corollary to this point is that in situations of limited resources policy makers should consider focusing services on children from disadvantaged backgrounds if it is impossible to guarantee services to all children. While the research evidence on how to target early childhood programs among at-risk children of different ages and with different needs is inconclusive, analysts agree that early intervention services provided to the disadvantaged have greater payoffs than services provided to children whose home environments do not place them at educational risk.

Second, given the evidence of short-term and possibly significant long-term benefits from high-quality early childhood interventions, states and local areas that do not now provide early intervention programs for at-risk children should consider expanding their efforts. A recent survey (Mitchell et al., 1998) found that 39 states fund at least one kind of prekindergarten program, but 11 invest no funds in either prekindergarten programs or Head Start. (The survey does not consider local funding, nor does it count federal investments in Head Start or other programs.) State investments vary widely, from $1 million to over $200 million annually; and the number of children served in state-funded prekindergarten programs ranges from a few hundred per state to over 40,000. Programs differ significantly in the ages served, educational offerings and staff qualifications, quality control mechanisms, and provisions for planning and evaluation. While we cannot neatly quantify the need, this variability suggests that some states should give greater attention to developing high-quality early intervention programs for at-risk students as one facet of their overall approach to developing the capacity of all children to learn.

Linking Education and Other Community Services

In recent years it has become increasingly evident to policy makers and practitioners that improving educational opportunities for at-risk children requires not just reforming schools but also addressing the health, social, financial, and political inequities of their families and communities. An impressive array of programs have been initiated (see, for example, Blank and Steinbach, 1998) attempting to link and coordinate the many services—including, among others, education, foster care, protection from abuse and neglect, health care, housing, employment, and nutrition—that federal, state, and local governments provide to disadvantaged children and adults. In many cases, supporters have found the challenges in linking services larger than they expected; positive program effects have thus come more slowly than they hoped. Nevertheless, it is notable that, despite the difficulties, sponsors continue to believe that a comprehensive approach to reform is crucial in serving at-risk children and families. Some important lessons have already been learned about the need for stable, permanent, and sufficient funding accompanied by fewer categorical strings.

Two fundamental principles undergird the growing number of programs aimed at coordinating services: (1) children with multiple needs require comprehensive and coordinated service strategies and (2) local communities represent an indispensable asset for effecting linking programs and resources across agencies and public and private institutions (Hayes et al., 1995). These principles are applicable to all at-risk children wherever they live, but they have special power in high-poverty urban neighborhoods and in distressed rural areas (Stern, 1994), where the need is especially acute to rebuild community-wide opportunity structures as well as to improve schools.

Foundations and local public and private agencies have supported coordination efforts, and federal and state governments have also encouraged cross-agency cooperation (Kritek, 1996; Orland and Foley, 1996; Woods, 1996). Congress has passed at least 12 laws since 1991 encouraging the development of more coordinated services for children. Title XI of the Improving America's School Act of 1994, for example, funds programs designed to encourage local education agencies, schools, or consortia of schools to undertake coordinated services projects. State efforts mirror the federal concern: for example, the 1991 Kentucky Education Reform Act, passed in response to a court decision invalidating the state's school system, required the formation of Family Resource and Youth Support Centers. Initially designed as school-based centers for linking services, they have since been disconnected from schools in order to establish expanded channels of communication between parents, school officials, and other social service providers.

Community-based service coordination efforts closely aligned with schools are a subset of a broader set of comprehensive community initiatives that seek to replace "piecemeal categorical approaches with 'comprehensive' efforts that cross sectoral and programmatic boundaries and attempt to build on the interconnections among economic, social, and physical needs and opportunities" (Aspen Institute, 1997:7). They also incorporate many of the burgeoning array of community-based programs aimed at improving the lives of children, youth, and families, including after-school programming aimed at ensuring appropriate after-school supervision for children and youth, reducing juvenile crime, and promoting student learning. School-linked initiatives "are set apart from the wider universe of community initiatives by a strong connection to the schools, a shared commitment to improved academic outcomes for students, and growing interest in eventually contributing to improvement in the overall quality of teaching and learning" (Blank and Steinbach, 1998:69). A new organization, the Emerging Coalition for Community Schools, is bringing together leaders in the areas of education, youth development, family support, and community development with government officials and representatives of foundations and the private sector to support the further development of community schools.

What have we learned so far about the potential for youth and community initiatives to make a positive difference in the lives of at-risk children and their families? Analysts reviewing the available evidence (e.g., Blank and Steinbach, 1998; Melaville, 1998) indicate that preliminary evidence is encouraging, although it also indicates that these initiatives face huge obstacles. They also caution that long-term evaluations are just beginning and that, as Melaville puts it (1998:7), what is known is "not nearly enough to support the rapid development of new initiatives and to ensure that knowledge and practice in this field are captured, made widely available, and expanded." A similar conclusion emerges from a recent publication on after-school programs issued by the federal attorney general and the secretary of education. This report identifies a number of innovative or promising after-school program activities, but also emphasizes the "critical need to fund and conduct more extensive, rigorous evaluations of after-school activities and their impact on the safety, social development, and academic achievement of children" (U.S. Department of Education and U.S. Department of Justice, 1998:6).[4] Enhanced efforts to understand what works and how to replicate successful programs are crucial to make good use of the funds increasingly being made available for after-school efforts, including $40 million appropriated by Congress in 1997 for awards to rural and inner-city schools through the 21st Century Community Learning Program, which the Charles Stewart Mott Foundation has joined in supporting.

The promises of and problems facing efforts to expand coordinated and community-based services are well captured in evaluations of one of the major undertakings to date: the New Futures initiative of the Annie E. Casey Foundation. The foundation launched New Futures in 1988 as a five-year effort to prepare disadvantaged urban youth for successful lives as adults. It gave each of five mid-sized American cities[5] between $7.5 and $12.5 million over the five-year period to restructure how they planned, financed, and delivered educational, health, and other services to at-risk youth. The goals for each city were to improve student achievement, reduce adolescent pregnancy and school dropout rates, and increase the number of youth who go on to a job or college after high school. The program was independently evaluated by an outside group (Center for the Study of Social Policy, 1995), and the foundation issued its own assessment of its experience with the program (Annie E. Casey Foundation, 1995).

Results of New Futures were at best mixed. The foundation's self-assessment was sober in tone, its continuing faith in comprehensive system reform initiatives tempered by experience that demonstrated that such change is extremely difficult, takes time, and won't work in every community. Some communities lack the interest, leadership, or management capacity needed to sustain long-term change processes. In many low-income communities, service-system and institutional change initiatives by themselves were insufficient to transform educational, social, and health outcomes. In these locations, initiatives involving

---

[4]This report also warns that evaluating after-school programs will be challenging and that existing evaluations share the shortcomings of much education related research. Citing a study by Fashola (1998), the report notes that "few evaluations of after-school programs use comparison groups in their study designs. As a result, many studies are compromised by self-selection bias, meaning that students who choose to attend after-school programs may differ from those who do not. Students may be more motivated since participation is generally voluntary, or in programs that target students with difficulties in school, the participating students may begin the program with comparatively low achievement. Another challenge in evaluating after-school programs is the difficulty of isolating measures that can be attributed specifically to the impact of an after-school program" (1998:57).

[5]Pittsburgh, Pennsylvania; Bridgeport, Connecticut; Savannah, Georgia; Little Rock, Arkansas; and Dayton, Ohio.

social capital and economic development that target the whole community appear to be necessary precursors for change.

The outside evaluators found that none of the cities participating in New Futures made any progress in reducing annual school dropout rates, in reducing teenage pregnancy and parenthood rates, or in increasing the number of high school seniors who by April or May of their senior year had been accepted for college or had a full time job lined up. While substantial test score gaps remained between black and white students, there were measurable gains in reducing the numbers of low-achieving students on reading tests. The proportion of sexually active teens declined, and the reported use of birth control devices among sexually active teens increased.

While not fulfilling the original goals, these were hopeful signs, and the evaluators also determined that the New Futures cities built some of the interim steps that may in the longer term lead to improved outcomes for at-risk children. For the most part they were unable to define comprehensive action plans that cut across multiple agencies and compel interagency cooperation. In every city, though, collaboratives (1) raised awareness of the problems of at-risk youth; (2) started a new dialogue among leaders and community representatives who had not previously sat down together; (3) developed rich school-based information systems; (4) created a new body of knowledge around collaboration and local governance; (5) demonstrated how to build substantive relationships between the public and private sectors by combining money and leadership; and (6) launched new ongoing community-based decision-making structures for addressing youth problems beyond the initial five-year period. The independent evaluators noted that "these accomplishments can be viewed as precursors to any sustained numerical outcome improvements" (Center for the Study of Social Policy, 1995:xi).

These findings about New Futures mirror other conclusions about community and youth initiatives. The difficulties should not be underestimated. More evidence of this fact comes from the experience of the Pew Charitable Trusts, which decided in 1992 to undertake an 11-year, $56 million effort to work with five states to overhaul their social, education, and health services for children through creating family centers near schools to provide social, psychological, and medical services to children. Two years later, and after spending $5 million, Pew announced that it was abandoning the Children's Initiative because it no longer felt that the program's goals were feasible within the time and resources anticipated (Sommerfeld, 1994).

Despite the challenges, sponsors continue to believe that comprehensive reform initiatives remain, in the words of the Casey Foundation "the only plausible way to address the multiple needs of at-risk children and families. We remain convinced that fundamental changes in the systems serving children and families are absolutely essential to creating more effective interventions, supports, and frontline practices capable of producing measurable better outcomes for disadvantaged kids" (Annie E. Casey Foundation, 1995:vii).

Two finance issues are intimately intertwined with the future of these programs. The first has to do with overall resources. Reviews of school-community initiatives (e.g., Blank and Steinbach, 1998; Melaville, 1998) stress the importance of stable, permanent, and sufficient funding to sustaining these efforts. In addition, the way in which funds are made available matters. Most importantly, the categorical system, though which most federal and state funds flow to specific agencies within communities, reinforces rather than helps break down regulatory and cultural barriers to cross-agency cooperation and the development of optimum service strategies that serve community rather than agency needs (Blank and Steinbach, 1998; Orland et al., 1995). Higher and more reliable funding flowing through less categorical channels therefore appears to be a necessary if not sufficient condition for enabling communities to advance in efforts to address the multiple needs of disadvantaged children and families in a comprehensive way.

Investments in the Capacity of Schools to Educate

That more investment is needed in the capacity of schools to educate concentrations of disadvantaged students would seem to be obvious given the poor academic performance of many of those students. The challenge, however, is to determine which types of investments are likely to be the most productive and how to structure such investments to make them effective. We do not have good answers to this challenge. From the discussion of productivity in Chapters 5 and 6, it should be clear that the quality of teachers is likely to be a key component, that reduced class size might help under certain conditions, and that whole-school restructuring may have significant potential. We discuss each of these potential investments in turn.

Enhancing Teacher Quality or Reducing Class Size

Despite the fact that it is often difficult to specify precisely the characteristics of high-quality teachers, research increasingly substantiates the fact that some teachers are more successful than others in fostering student learning. While scholars continue to disagree about the effects of particular teacher characteristics such as education level and experience on student achievement, several studies using large databases and sophisticated statistical methodologies (Ferguson, 1998; Ehrenberg and Brewer, 1994) have found that measures of teacher cognitive skills (such as certification test scores and the quality of the undergraduate institution the teacher attended) do appear to matter for student achievement. Furthermore, the research of Ferguson (1991) and Kain and Singleton (1996) in Texas and Ferguson and Ladd (1996) in Alabama documents that schools that serve concentrations of disadvantaged students typically are less successful than others in attracting teachers with strong cognitive skills, so such students are likely to be at a significant disadvantage relative to other students.

A recent ongoing study based on an unusually rich Texas database, containing micro panel data on more than 1.8 million children in five student cohorts attending more than 4,500 elementary schools, provides compelling new evidence of the challenge such schools face with respect to teachers. Kain and Singleton (1996) document that teachers employed in schools with high fractions of disadvantaged minority students have lower ability (as measured by verbal and written test scores on a state teachers' exam), fewer years of education, less experience, and more students in their classes than do teachers in schools with larger percentages of higher-income and white students.

Ferguson's Texas study also points out that the effect of teacher quality is cumulative. Among Texas districts in which students performed poorly in the early years of elementary school, those districts employing teachers with unusually high test scores saw student performance levels in mathematics converging by 11th grade with the levels of districts whose students initially performed well. The scores of children whose teachers had low test scores also converged over the course of their education, but at a much lower level.

While Ferguson's findings are plausible, the issue of causality arises here, as it does in much other research on education. Perhaps there were distinctive characteristics of the districts that were able to retain teachers with high test scores (for example, unusually gifted school administrators or parents with a particularly high degree of commitment to educational quality). Those same factors may have also been responsible for the better performance of students in those districts. Thus, while Ferguson's results are plausible, there is a need for further research that addresses the causality issue.

So how does one promote greater investment in teacher quality in schools serving disadvantaged students? Clearly some special efforts will be needed. Any general policy, such as increasing teacher salaries across the board, may well exacerbate the problems of schools serving disadvantaged students, as the wealthier school districts are in a better position than the poor ones to pay the higher salaries. Moreover, other policies such as tough teacher testing could well decrease the supply of teachers available to teach in the schools with the harshest teaching environments, although Ferguson (1998) found in Alabama that testing new teachers narrowed the gap in basic skills between incoming black and white teachers, to the advantage of black students who are more often matched with black teachers. Ultimately, there seems to be no escaping the fact that schools with harsh environments will have to pay significantly higher salaries than other schools to attract their share of high-quality teachers, or will have to spend more money on professional development to upgrade the skills of the teachers they are able to attract and retain.

Improving the quality of teachers is one option for increasing the intensity of instruction offered to at-risk students; another is reducing class size. While these two approaches could well be complementary, policy makers may face budgetary trade-offs in considering how far both can be simultaneously implemented. The question was raised in Chapter 5 concerning whether class size reduction, especially across-the-board reduction, is the more effective use of resources, given the greater impact of improved teacher quality. Reducing class sizes is expensive. A reduction from 25 to 15 students per class would require a 66 percent increase in the number of teachers. There are new capital costs as well, since the number of classrooms must be increased. The California class size initiative for kindergarten through third grade costs over $1.5 billion annually (CSR Research Consortium, 1999).

Nevertheless, reducing class size is often an attractive option for policy makers focusing on improving education for at-risk students. It is something they can legislate and implement relatively quickly, while methods of improving teacher quality are more indirect and uncertain. Evidence from the Tennessee STAR study and other research investigations on class size (summarized in Chapter 5) consistently shows that smaller class sizes result in larger achievement gains for poor, minority, and urban children than for other students. (This evidence stems from research on class size reductions in the early grades, where the most current and best studies have focused.) The key questions, we repeat, are likely to be ones of trade-offs: Are qualified teachers available for the additional classrooms, so that teacher quality will not be affected? Does a school or district have reason to conclude that other investments (to improve teacher quality or to provide one-on-one tutors or longer school days or years or summer school) align more closely with their overall programs for augmenting the intensity and duration of instruction provided to disadvantaged students?

The danger of imposing particular solutions on all schools and the importance of seeing school reform (at least within the current institutional structure) as requiring many interconnected strategies for change are illustrated by the results of a natural experiment that took place in Austin, Texas, beginning in 1989. As part of the settlement in a school desegregation court case, each of 15 elementary schools serving large numbers of disadvantaged students were given $300,000, above normal school spending each year for five years (Murnane and Levy, 1996). All 15 of the schools reduced class size. Only two of them, however, showed improvement in student academic achievement. These were the only two schools that accompanied the class size reductions with a host of other changes: placing children with special needs in regular classes; adopting for all students the reading and mathematics curriculum normally provided only to gifted children; bringing health services to the schools; and investing heavily in getting parents involved in their children's schooling, including having them participate in school governance, budgeting, and hiring. With educators around the country exploring a great variety of approaches to school reform in an effort to improve student learning, it is almost certainly the case that a particular policy change like class size reduction might sometimes enhance these efforts and sometimes come at the expense of other approaches that better complement local reform initiatives.

Whole-School Reform Models

Chapter 5 described the growing interest in so-called whole-school redesign, a reform approach that explicitly addresses the need to change many aspects of schools simultaneously to bring about meaningful improvement. Whole-school restructuring has focused heavily on schools educating large numbers of disadvantaged students, where prior piecemeal reforms have generally failed to raise academic achievement from levels that begin distressingly low. While it is too early to have much evidence about whether whole-school restructuring will live up to its promise or about which whole-school designs will prove to be lastingly effective, the logic behind this approach to building school capacity is compelling. An important question, therefore, is what level of investment will be required to implement it.

Keltner (1998) examined actual first-year implementation costs at 58 schools using one of six of the New American Schools designs. He examined the resources for teacher time, personnel, design services, and materials and conferences that each school devoted to comprehensive reform. He found that schools committed on average $162,000 each to implement their chosen whole-school design in academic year 1996-97, which probably understates current resource requirements.[6] Not all of this represented additional cost; about 38 percent or $62,000 came from reallocating existing resources and the remainder from sources outside a school's normal operating budget ($53,000 from Title I; $30,000 from district budgets; $11,000 from outside grants; and $6,000 from volunteer sources). Resource needs differed widely across schools depending on which design they choose, with designs ranging in cost from $100,000 to $300,000.

Keltner concluded that the Comprehensive School Reform Demonstration (CSRD) program, enacted by Congress in 1997 and described below in the section on Title I, would provide enough additional money to Title I schools (over and above their regular Title I allocations) to allow most of them to implement comprehensive reform. The program will not be sufficient to enable schools that do not receive regular Title I funds to adopt many whole-school designs. Districts or outside grants will have to provide the necessary funds, which may not be available in poorer districts. Odden and Busch (1998) also point out that resource allocation to implement whole-school designs may be restricted by local, state, or federal rules that may require waivers, changes in collective bargaining contracts, or regulatory reform.

---

[6] In 1996-97 design teams were still in the process of figuring out the true costs of providing team consulting services to schools and were in effect subsidizing schools by not charging full costs. Keltner estimates that current average first-year implementation costs would be more like $180,000.

CHANGING INCENTIVES TO MAKE PERFORMANCE COUNT

Most federal and some state aid for elementary and secondary education is categorical in nature and is designed to provide specialized services to certain groups of students. Most K-12 aid allocated through the U.S. Department of Education flows from two such categorical programs: (1) Title I is aimed at low-achieving students living in areas with high concentrations of poverty and (2) assistance for students with disabilities (special education) is authorized by the Individuals with Disabilities Education Act. (Other, much smaller categorical programs recognize the educational needs of migrant and gifted children and children with limited proficiency in English.)

Questions have arisen about the extent to which the incentives deliberately or inadvertently created by categorical programs serve educationally desirable purposes and whether and to what extent it continues to be appropriate to treat children with special needs separately in an educational system increasingly oriented toward fostering higher levels of learning for all students. Our findings suggest that educational effectiveness has been compromised in the past by making sharp distinctions between students with special needs and other students and that current efforts to move toward more integrated school programs should be reinforced.

How categorical programs influence the way schools approach the educational task of serving at-risk children is a complicated issue, which differs somewhat from program to program. We cannot explore the issue in all its complexity here. We do want to comment, however, on current directions in Title I, because it is the nation's largest categorical education program. We also made a committee decision to devote particular attention during our study to special education for children with disabilities, a decision that is reflected in the extended discussion below. Special education warrants comparatively intensive review, in our view, because it is built on a policy framework of open-ended, mandated, individual student entitlements that is quite distinct from general school finance and important in its impacts on the budgets of many school districts.

Title I

The targeting of Title I funds (i.e., how highly they should be concentrated on the highest-poverty districts and schools) and the instructional effectiveness of Title I funds have been perennial challenges (Orland and Stullich, 1997). In 1993-94, 92 percent of all school districts, 62 percent of all public schools, and 45 percent of all low-poverty schools (less than 20 percent poor) received Title I funds, while 19 percent of the highest-poverty schools (at least 75 percent poor) did not receive any Title I funds (U.S. Department of Education, 1996).

Chapter 3 described the 1994 debates over Title I funding formulas designed to increase the targeting of funds to poorer schools. While new funding formulas for grants to local education agencies were never implemented, the 1994 legislation changed within-district allocation provisions, and Congress has increased the proportion of Title I funds being allocated through concentration grants, both changes designed to direct a greater share of funds of higher-poverty districts and schools. The recently released assessment of Title I since the 1994 reauthorization (U.S. Department of Education, 1999b) indicates that targeting has increased somewhat at the school (but not district) level, but that funds continue to be distributed widely. The percentage of districts receiving Title I funds (over 90 percent) is virtually unchanged since reauthorization. The percentage of funds going to the districts with highest and lowest poverty is also about the same. The highest-poverty *schools* are now more likely to receive Title I funds; 95 percent of such schools now participate in the program. The percentage of low-poverty schools (currently defined as schools with 35 percent poor) receiving Title I funds has dropped to 36 percent, and these schools receive only 18 percent of Title I funds. Overall, 58 percent of public schools receive Title I monies.

At the same time, evaluations of Title I going back to the early 1970s and as recent as 1997 question the instructional effectiveness of the program (Elmore and McLaughlin, 1988; Orland and Stullich, 1997; Puma et al., 1997). Orland and Stullich (1997:15) note that "this consistent finding across national Title I assessments is especially significant because policymakers have made escalating attempts over the last two decades to amend Title I policy and administration in an effort to secure greater local attention to issues of instructional quality and effectiveness."

Title I has been characterized by a complaint common to categorical programs: that regulations governing financial accountability foster a compliance mentality, resulting in process considerations taking precedence over instructional concerns. Such regulations have grown out of legislative provisions intended to ensure that Title I funds were used only to supplement, not supplant, funds that would otherwise be made available from state and local sources for Title I-eligible children and were used for these and not other children.

Perhaps the most serious charge that has been leveled by critics against Title I from an instructional perspective is its fragmenting impact on school organization and practice. While not required to use "pull-out" services (removing Title I students from regular classrooms for part of each day), schools found this the easiest way to be sure they did not run afoul of procedural compliance requirements. While the shortcomings of pull-out services (particularly when they are disconnected from regular classroom instruction) were identified as long ago as the early 1980s (for example, see Peterson, 1983), such services persist. In 1991-92, 74 percent of Title I schools still used them (Millsap et al., 1993). The newest Title I evaluation (U.S. Department of Education, 1999b) indicates that 68 percent continue to employ the pull-out model, although many also use in-class forms of assistance as well.

The detrimental instructional consequences of Title I's legal and administrative framework have been widely recognized and increasingly addressed in both regulations and periodic legislative reauthorizations. The last reauthorization, in 1994, made a number of changes in response to the limited impact of earlier reforms. A larger percentage of schools was made eligible to use Title I funds in school-wide programs, Title I evaluation was linked to the regular local instructional program and academic standards that apply to non-Title I students, and new requirements were added to the use of local Title I funds for high-quality professional development. In 1997 Congress gave an additional boost to school-wide programs by enacting the Comprehensive School Reform Demonstration (CSRD) program, often referred to as Obey-Porter after its sponsors. The program makes $145 million available to states to assist up to 3,000 schools implementing comprehensive research-based designs with grants of $50,000 or more that are renewable for up to two years. The program allocates $120 million of this money to Title I schools.

Whether these changes will lead to greater instructional effectiveness is an open question. Orland and Stullich point out, however, that current financing arrangements continue to create significant barriers to the implementation of instructionally desirable reforms at the local level: "Funding practices in Title I restrict the adaption of "leading-edge" program design reforms in two important ways: (a) the generally low level of program funds in relation to local needs, and (b) the continued requirement to comply with basic fiscal accountability provisions. Put simply, a context of limited funds thinly spread for a carefully-designated target population is at serious odds with program design features expected to improve program effectiveness" (Orland and Stullich, 1997:17).

Preliminary evaluation of the effects of the 1994 reforms give some hope that previous shortcomings of Title I are being addressed: the recently released National Assessment of Title I (U.S. Department of Education, 1999b) describes a number of ways in which Title I is now working in sync with standards-driven reform. Nevertheless, it is too early to say whether the new law will have significantly greater impact on the achievement of at-risk children than earlier versions have had, for at least two reasons. First, Congress called for phasing in the 1994 reforms over a number of years, so it is as yet too early to say what their ultimate effects will be. Second, the independent review panel established to oversee the congressionally mandated assessment of the post-1994 Title I has stated that "financial support for evaluation at the federal level has been inadequate" (U.S. Department of Education, 1999b:n.p.). Congress in 1994 mandated two major studies of Title I effectiveness (a National Assessment of Title I and an Omnibus Longitudinal Evaluation of School Change and Performance) but failed to appropriate sufficient funds to include all the study topics and features mandated by the law. The national assessment, for example, had to rely primarily on other sources rather than its own surveys of policy implementation and student achievement. The longitudinal study (unlike prior Title I studies) has had to limit its coverage to 71 elementary schools in 18 moderate- to high-poverty school districts in 7 states. Evaluation funds for Title I have averaged only $5 million annually since reauthorization, 0.1 percent of Title I appropriations (Independent Review Panel on the Evaluation of Federal Education Legislation, 1999).

In the committee's view, the failure to devote sufficient resources for meaningful evaluation is unfortunate. Without reliable information on the effectiveness of the educational services being delivered to children targeted by Title I, it is impossible to say whether the federal government gets the largest possible bang for its buck by relying so heavily on the Title I format. On fairness grounds, however, we do want to emphasize the significance of Title I in reducing spending disparities. While not as highly targeted on areas with high concentrations of poor students as many evaluations have recommended (Commission on Chapter 1, 1992; Rotberg and Harvey, 1993; U.S. General Accounting Office, 1994; Independent Review Panel on the Evaluation of Federal Education Legislation, 1999), Title I allocations are still more highly targeted than most state education aid. Thus, as GAO recently concluded: "In this context, any proposal to consolidate federal education funding into grants that give more discretion to states would need to consider that the targeting of those federal funds might become more like that of the state funds. That is, the federal funds—and the combination of federal and state funds—might become less targeted to poor students" (U.S. General Accounting Office, 1998:22).

Special Education

As Chapter 2 noted, the costs associated with federal requirements that all children with disabilities be provided with a "free and appropriate education" have been rising rapidly and have become a major financial concern in many school districts. Special education for children with disabilities is now one of the largest programs in public schools, with estimated costs in 1995-96 between $32 and $36 billion.[7] Unlike other categorical education programs, the size of which is constrained by the size of budget appropriations, special education is an entitlement program, guaranteeing the provision of "appropriate" and individually determined services to eligible students regardless of cost. These provisions, along

---

[7]Exact current expenditures for special education are unknown because of data limitations that are described in this section. The estimate of $32 billion (Parrish and Chambers, 1996) in 1995-96 is based on a projection of $265 billion in current expenditures for K-12 public education for that year (Gerald and Hussar, 1995) and a 12 percent allocation to special education programs (Moore et al., 1988). The higher estimate of $36 billion, used by the U.S. Department of Education, is achieved by multiplying average per-pupil expenditure for all students ($5,640) by the number of students with disabilities on December 1, 1995 (5,619,000), and then multiplying this sum by the "special education to regular education marginal cost ratio" (1.14) obtained from a study by Kakalik et al. (1981) (U.S. Department of Education, 1997).

with the guarantee of procedural safeguards protecting the rights of children with disabilities and their families, are contained in P.L. 94-142, now known as the Individuals with Disabilities Education Act (IDEA), which was first passed in 1975.[8]

Although federal law creates the legal framework undergirding special education entitlements, state and local governments are responsible for most (an estimated 93 percent) of the costs (U.S. Department of Education, 1997). IDEA authorizes the federal government to pay 40 percent of the excess costs associated with educating children with disabilities; federal appropriations, however, have never exceeded 12.5 percent of excess costs and now cover only about 7 percent of estimated excess costs (National Research Council, 1997). Educational opportunities provided to students with disabilities vary from place to place, thanks to heavy reliance on state and local funding coupled with the responsibility given to state and local officials for determining (within the federal framework) the basic eligibility of students for special education, types and intensity of services to be provided, and the settings in which the services will be delivered. At the same time, legislative action and judicial opinions have resulted in special education services being viewed as a right by many advocates and families who receive the services. This rights framework affects how special education is funded.

Population Growth and Encroachment

The size of the student population eligible to receive special education services has grown steadily (from 3.7 to 5.9 million students in the 20 years since passage of P.L. 94-142 in 1975), and the scope and costs of services have also increased (e.g., costs grew 50 percent more rapidly for special education students than for students without disabilities in New York State between 1980 and 1993— Lankford and Wyckoff, 1996). The growth in the numbers of special education students has occurred largely among students with so-called mild or moderate

---

[8]The civil rights of Americans with disabilities of all ages are also protected under two other pieces of federal legislation: Section 504 of the Vocational Rehabilitation Act of 1973 (P.L. 93-112) and the 1990 Americans with Disabilities Act (ADA) (P.L. 101-336). Section 504 applies to a broader range of institutions and individuals than does IDEA and requires that comparable educational benefits be provided to individuals with and without disabilities in the interest of nondiscrimination and equality of opportunity. It also requires the provision of reasonable accommodations of individuals with disabilities who are otherwise qualified to participate in an educational program or activity. ADA builds on these principles and includes a national mandate to provide reasonable accommodations in areas such as private-sector employment, all public services and public accommodations, transportation, and telecommunications. The primary impact of ADA has been to require a more comprehensive effort within the schools to prepare students for greater participation in community settings rather than relying on specialized facilities designed primarily for people with disabilities (National Research Council, 1997). As a result, Section 504 and ADA have become the main vehicles for litigation in special education during the past few years (Martin et al., 1996).

disabilities rather than severe ones. Four-fifths or more of students who are labeled as disabled are considered to have mild disabilities.[9]

Rising concerns about meeting mandated special education costs, especially in already stressed urban school districts, and press reports about escalating expenditures (Shapiro et al., 1993; Dillon, 1994; *Wall Street Journal*, 1993) have given rise to widespread allegations that special education entitlements are encroaching on funding for so-called regular education. In some resource-strapped school districts, the use of the special education designation has been seen as an opportunity to obtain additional resources and has led to concerns about over-identification of special education students.

A key problem in all analyses of special education is the absence of comprehensive, current data on costs, making it impossible to support or refute contentions about the alleged uncontrollable nature of special education expenditures on a national basis. The most recent large-scale collection of data on state special education expenditures occurred during the 1985-86 school year (Moore et al., 1988) and still provides the basis for most program estimates. The federal government stopped routine administrative collection of data of special education expenditures after the 1987-88 school year because it was generally recognized that the state data reports were not reliable or useful. An effort by the Center for Special Education Finance to obtain more recent data for 1994-95 uncovered the fact that fully half of the states in the survey did not know the statewide cost of their special education programs. Only 24 states were able to report special education expenditure data at the federal, state, and local levels; and only 13 indicated that they could do so with a high degree of confidence (Wolman and Parrish, 1996). Two studies limited to a small number of districts (Rothstein and Miles, 1995) or a single state (Lankford and Wyckoff, 1996) document special education costs rising faster than average costs for students without disabilities.

Such findings do not definitively address issues of encroachment, however, since that concept assumes (1) that special and regular education are discrete activities instead of complements; (2) that education is a zero-sum game in which funds for expanding educational opportunities for students with disabilities have

---

[9]IDEA recognizes 13 categories of disability. The degree of an individual's disability can range from mild to severe within a category. (For descriptions of mild, moderate, and severe disabilities, see National Research Council, 1997:75-77.) The largest categories of disability (specific learning disability and speech or language impairment) account for almost three-fourths of all school-age children with disabilities and are almost always mild. The level of disabilities in the categories of mental retardation and serious emotional disturbance (nearly 20 percent of disabled children) can range from mild to severe, but at least half of these students function at the mild level (National Research Council, 1997). Given the large numbers of children with disabilities in these four categories (over 90 percent: see National Research Council, 1997:87), it is worth noting that most of the children with moderate and severe disabilities will be in these categories, even though most of the children in the four categories are only mildly disabled.

come instead of rather than in addition to money society was prepared to spend on students without disabilities; and (3) that services for students with disabilities since IDEA are completely new, instead of partially replacing educational services that were provided without being labeled "special education" in the years before IDEA.

Addressing Student Needs

Instead of focusing on encroachment, we think it is more useful to consider whether the entitlement and categorical approach to educating children with disabilities best serves their learning needs.

Before 1975, students with disabilities were frequently excluded from public schools altogether. In the early 1970s, school districts in only 17 states were serving half of their known population of children with disabilities, and 26 states were serving less than a third of this group (Martin et al., 1996). IDEA ensured that public education would embrace all children, including those with disabilities, by creating a policy framework emphasizing individual rights and procedural requirements (National Research Council, 1997).

Special education has thus been dominated by an orientation toward supplemental services developed outside the mainstream of general education, which creates separate student populations based on specified eligibility requirements, encourages specialized assessment and diagnostic services to determine type of disability and functional status, creates legal protections for children who become part of the special education population, and subsidizes and monitors the additional costs of intensive and supportive interventions for children who are eligible for services. Proponents of this orientation argue that a categorical program designed for the specific population of students with disabilities is essential to improve their education and social development, especially since their educational needs may surpass what is or can be offered in general education classrooms (Fuchs and Fuchs, 1995; Council for Learning Disabilities, 1993; National Joint Committee on Learning Disabilities, 1993; Renick and Harter, 1989; Coleman, 1983). It is the memory of this history of exclusion and unmet needs that proponents refer to when they see threats to special education today.

We suggest, however, that the goal of raising achievement for *all* students requires the explicit and full participation of students with disabilities in school, district, and state accountability systems and consideration of their needs in all policies and practices involving curriculum, instruction, and finance. As with other populations with special needs, it is vital that educators view these students as part of their core responsibility and not just the responsibility of a specially designated subset of education professionals. IDEA calls for children with disabilities to be educated "to the maximum extent possible" with children who are not disabled and in regular educational environments whenever possible, and in fact the proportion of time children with disabilities spend in regular classrooms has been growing. There is still a separatist orientation about much of special education, however, despite concerns that special education placements have been educational dead ends for many students and that many special educators are ill informed about educational improvement efforts affecting general education (such as standards-based reform). The challenge is to address the special needs of students with disabilities while simultaneously improving educational outcomes for them.

Some students, especially those with the most severe disabling conditions, will always require some amount of specialized programs and services, as provided by the existing approach to special education. Nevertheless, the facts that over 70 percent of all students with disabilities now spend at least 40 percent of their day in a regular classroom and 45 percent attend regular classes for at least 80 percent of the day (U.S. Department of Education, 1998) suggest that a second scenario, with less of an emphasis on classification and categorization, may be feasible for many. This scenario involves a more comprehensive and integrated approach to providing resources and services for a broad spectrum of children, including those with mild to moderate learning disabilities as well as other children who require additional assistance in acquiring academic skills (such as children with limited English proficiency or vocabulary skills, children who experience excessive absences from school, or children from areas of concentrated poverty) who have not been classified within the special education system. Distinguishing between severe and other disabilities is useful in thinking through funding options. At the same time, the goal of an integrated services approach for students whose disabilities are not severe, with a unifying system of policies and procedures and a common set of measures and outcomes, is to move away from the fragmented and differentiated policy frameworks that have traditionally guided general education, special education, and other categorical programs.

Integrated Approach

In a more integrated educational system, the presumption would be that each child has a right to be included in the general classroom unless justification can be made to place him or her in a separate instructional setting because of special learning needs. Aides and specialists would be more firmly integrated into the general classroom program than they are now. The process of developing individual education plans would be retained only for those students whose disability requires that they spend more than half their day outside the general classroom. Based on the current population of students being served in special education, we estimate that about 20 percent of such students would require high-intensity services and supports that could not be provided within the classroom or the general school system without serious disruption.

Moving to a less categorical approach to educating children with disabilities could overcome a number of criticisms of past special education practices. State formulas that tie funding to the number or characteristics of students identified as requiring, and who receive, special education services or to the costs incurred by local districts in serving these students are thought to encourage the overclassification of children as disabled, to be inflexible in terms of where children with disabilities can be served, and to encourage more restrictive and costly placements (i.e., in settings apart from regular classrooms) (Parrish, 1995; Verstegen et al., 1997). Incentives for separate treatment of children with disabilities may also reduce tolerance within the general education system for diversity and flexibility in learning styles and mitigate against strengthening remedial services within general education. The availability of a separate special education system to which children with learning or behavioral problems can be referred gives regular classroom teachers an excuse for handing off responsibility for such youngsters to others.

Concerns about the desirability of separate placements, especially for the very large majority of students whose disabilities are considered mild, are exacerbated by the fact that the criteria for classification are more ambiguous than the criteria for severe disabilities. The latter, especially those that involve physical or sensory impairments, are generally clear and universally shared. By contrast, there is mixed research on the extent to which students with mild forms of disability can be distinguished reliably from other students variously called "low-achieving" and "educationally disadvantaged" (Lyon, 1996; Kavale et al., 1994; National Research Council, 1997).[10] Variability among educational agencies in interpreting and implementing federal guidelines within the context of their own traditions and resources means that some children who qualify for special education services in one school would not qualify elsewhere, creating discrepancies that raise concerns about fairness.

Questions about the separate treatment of students with mild disabilities are further bolstered by findings that the content and forms of remedial supports and services that are now commonly provided to children with mild disabilities do not differ significantly in form or content from those that are offered to other children who have learning difficulties or who are slow to achieve academic progress (National Research Council, 1997). A common curriculum is often involved in meeting the needs of a broad array of students with learning problems, but the degree and intensity of service may need to differ according to the specific needs of the individual child. In the area of reading, for example, another National

---

[10]Again, we point out that not all children with moderate or severe disabilities are in the categories associated with clear physical or sensory disabilities. Although most children with learning disabilities, speech or language impairments, mental retardation, and serious emotional disturbance have mild disabilities, the size of these categories means that the minority of students in these categories with more disabling conditions still outnumber the students who are autistic, blind, deaf or hearing impaired, or who suffer from multiple disabilities, orthopedic impairment, other health impairment, traumatic brain injury, and visual impairment.

Research Council committee has recently concluded that "children who are having difficulty learning to read do not, as a rule, require qualitatively different instruction from children who are 'getting it.' Instead, they more often need application of the same principles by someone who can apply them expertly to individual children who are having difficulty for one reason or another" (National Research Council, 1998:327).

Finally, like Title I, special education has been accused of emphasizing compliance over performance. Legal requirements relating to the rights of students with disabilities have resulted in a unique educational approach that begins with the child as the point of reference. The child must be evaluated *before* school personnel can begin special programming, the evaluation must involve all areas related to the suspected disability, and reevaluation must take place at least every three years. If the evaluation determines that the child has a disability under federal guidelines, the child is entitled to special services without regard to cost. No specific legal criteria exist to determine what educational programs or services constitute an appropriate education; instead, general standards have emerged from court cases and federal legislation and rest on three broad principles.[11] The specific program and services to be made available to each child are determined by school and specialized personnel and codified in an individualized education program (IEP). Federal law provides procedural safeguards for parents, including requirements for notice about proposed actions that affect the placement of their child in the school system, the right to attend meetings concerning the child's placement or IEP, the right to appeal decisions to an impartial hearing officer, and the right to be reimbursed for legal fees that result from parental challenges to school system decisions.

The absence of professional standards of practice, the reliance on IEPs, and the extensive procedural safeguards provided to parents have negative as well as positive effects. In particular, critics deplore the emphasis on inputs or services rather than outputs or achievements, the fostering of adversarial relationships between parents and school officials, and the encouragement of a defensive approach to special education within the schools.

Our suggestion to move in the direction of integrating special education more fully into the regular education system is not an original idea and in fact is consistent with a number of reforms already taking place around the nation. It is also consistent with funding changes that rely more on census-based approaches for determining how much federal or state aid flows to the local level for educat-

---

[11]The three principles are: (1) the educational program should be related to the child's learning capacity; (2) the program should be designed for the child's unique needs and not merely what is offered to others; and (3) the program should be reasonably calculated to confer educational benefit (Martin et al., 1996).

ing students with mild and moderate disabilities. Census-based funding assumes that some percentage of the district or school population has disabilities and provides funding on that basis rather than on actual counts; interest in such funding has developed as part of a broader reconsideration of federal and state funding in light of three goals: (1) to maximize flexibility in service delivery; (2) to be "identification neutral"—that is, the number of students identified as eligible for special education is not the only, or primary, basis for generating state special education aid, and students do not have to be labeled "disabled" in order to receive services; and (3) to be needs-generated, so that funding for special education is based on service needs rather than on the type of educational placement or disabling condition (Parrish, 1997).

The 1997 reauthorization of IDEA took a first step toward embracing census-based funding; once the appropriation for part B of IDEA exceeds $4.9 billion, distribution of the additional dollars will not depend on the number of students with disabilities identified and served but will shift to a census basis. Under census-based funding, a state's share of new IDEA money will depend on its total school-age population (weighted 85 percent) and its total school-age population in poverty (weighted 15 percent). The new IDEA also allows more flexibility in the use of special education funds (including allowing benefits to accrue "incidentally" to non-special education students as long as the IEPs are being fulfilled), strengthens provisions to ensure that state funding formulas do not encourage segregated placements, calls for IEPs to relate programming to achievement in the general education curriculum and calls on states to include children with disabilities in statewide assessments and alternative assessments, puts limits on the attorney's fees that parents of special education students can collect, and encourages the use of mediation rather than formal due process hearings to resolve disputes between parents and schools over IEPs.

At least six states (California, Massachusetts, Montana, North Dakota, Pennsylvania, and Vermont) have also adopted some form of census-based funding for their own state special education funds, and several also use some form of poverty adjustment or add "mainstream weights" to pay for the support services that special education students need when served in a general education classroom. Some states (e.g., Florida) are also piloting efforts to relate state aid to student learning characteristics and service needs, rather than placement or disability.

For students with mild and moderate disabilities, we are encouraged by the development of new approaches to special education finance like census-based funding that reinforce the move to accommodate students with disabilities as fully as possible within general education. Moving away from classification and categorization, however, requires that attention be paid to professional development (to prepare teachers to handle students with a diverse array of learning needs in the same classroom), to flexibility for schools in using special education funds, to accountability mechanisms, and to mechanisms for funding students with severe disabilities (those who would continue to have IEPs) and for helping schools and districts meet the unusually high costs of these students or of exceptional concentrations of students with mild disabilities. The advantages of a more integrated approach notwithstanding, we acknowledge that the categorical treatment of students with disabilities has served as an important safeguard that their needs would be met. Neglect of these children by public schools is a recent and vivid enough memory for advocates to engender understandable suspicion of anything that undermines the individual educational entitlements these children have won. The existing program, which serves a diverse but identifiable population, is therefore unlikely to be replaced with a set of general services designed for a more complex and diffuse group of students unless careful attention is paid to both capacity and accountability issues.

Capacity and Accountability Issues

First, an integrated services approach requires that both personnel and facilities have the capacity to meet the needs of a diverse group of learners. Including students with disabilities in regular education requires extensive professional preparation at several levels: preservice teacher education for both general and special education personnel, in-service education within school systems, and ongoing technical assistance and support to ensure effectiveness of programming. IDEA recognized that the nation's schools were not prepared to provide an appropriate education to all students with disabilities and included requirements for states and local school districts to provide programs for personnel development (Turnbull, 1993). Funding to ensure adequate preparation for all educational personnel in school systems, however, has never been realized.

During the first decade of special education law, efforts focused on building a sufficient cadre of special education personnel to meet identified student needs. It is only in the last decade that the preparation of general educators to meet the needs of students with disabilities has begun to be emphasized. At the same time, many special education faculty have had only limited exposure to new curricular reforms and standards-based approaches; they will need development opportunities to prepare them to work in the general classroom and to help integrate their efforts into whole-school reform programs. States and school districts will also have to step up to new fiscal challenges in preparing their school buildings to accommodate the needs of diverse learners (U.S. General Accounting Office, 1995a).

Integrated services will also be encouraged by continuing efforts to increase flexibility in the use of categorical federal and state aid and to grant states waivers from federal requirements when appropriate. Steps in the direction of flexibility are evident in most recent federal legislation, including the 1994 reauthorization of Title I, the Goals 2000 law, and the 1997 IDEA amendments. Permitting flexibility raises fears that spending on populations previously targeted by categorical programs might be lost, however, so it will be important that greater flexibility is accompanied by efforts to ensure that the needs of students with disabilities continue to be addressed in more integrated settings.

Accountability for the education of children with disabilities in integrated settings would be enhanced by both including these students in ongoing large-scale assessments as well as developing standards of practice. A 1997 report (National Research Council, 1997) extensively reviewed the issues involved in incorporating students with disabilities into standards-based curriculum and assessment reforms. At present, there are no generally recognized standards, linked to desired outcomes, providing benchmarks for determining what constitutes an appropriate education for students with various kinds of disabilities. The diversity of the characteristics of students with disabilities poses challenges to the development of professional standards, as does the fact that traditional categories of disability do not have a demonstrable relationship to specific outcomes or to prognoses (Epps and Tindal, 1987; Kavale, 1990; Kavale and Glass, 1982). Nevertheless, progress is being made. Efforts have begun to establish diagnostic constructs based on a child's placement along a number of continuous dimensions of disability, rather than an either-or dichotomy (National Research Council, 1997). At the same time, others (e.g., Reschly, 1996) are working on a service-based approach to identify outcomes that could be associated with certain levels of service investment for broad clusters of students with disabilities.

New approaches at the state and federal level to special education finance like census-based funding and less reliance on individual entitlement and classification pose potential risks to localities. Some of these risks will be magnified if school finance becomes more school- or pupil-based (rather than district-based) in the future. One risk is that local districts or schools may have unusual concentrations of students with disabilities, a fact that census-based funding would fail to address. We suggest that states that move to census-based funding ought to allow appeals when there is evidence of unusual concentrations of students with disabilities. A second risk is the financial drain that students with severe disabilities can pose for schools or small districts. These students with disabilities are, as we have noted, the easiest to identify. We suggest that states consider establishing risk pools to pay the "excess costs" of such students.

A major question about special education finance is whether the federal government should in the future pick up a greater share of the unfunded mandate it has created for states and local districts. Not only is the federal share currently very low, but IDEA imposes a large regulatory overlay especially on districts and schools. At the same time, new approaches to special education at the state level pose both possibilities and challenges for federal officials. When states move to fund their special education responsibilities through census-based funding rather than individually identifying all students with disabilities, they lose out on federal aid under current arrangements. It is not clear that continued reliance on individual categorization is necessary at the federal level, though we recognize this is a complicated question with many arguments on both sides (as described in Parrish and Chambers, 1996). If states adopt the suggestion to establish risk pools for covering the excess costs of educating students with severe disabilities, a new funding option for the federal government might be to fund these pools, in effect making it a national responsibility to meet the special programs and services such students require.

Reforming special education to emphasize a more integrated services approach for most students with disabilities will not necessarily be cheaper than the current categorical system. It does, however, hold out promise for improving the quality of education offered to students with disabilities and enabling them to reach their full potential by incorporating these children as fully as possible into the primary school mission of improving learning for all students.

EMPOWERING SCHOOLS OR PARENTS OR BOTH TO MAKE DECISIONS ABOUT THE USE OF PUBLIC FUNDS

Definitive evidence is not available about the effects of major changes in who has the power to determine how education dollars are spent. Such changes are highly controversial because they threaten existing authority relationships. In the face of uncertainty and controversy, the arguments for change are strongest in places where school performance under current governance arrangements has been hardest to improve. This suggests that urban areas with large concentrations of disadvantaged students are the most compelling targets for such reforms, especially reforms that give parents more choice over the schools their children attend.

There are several reasons why choice options may be both more feasible and effective in promoting educational fairness and productivity in urban areas than elsewhere.

First, the population is more concentrated. Therefore transportation cost issues loom less large than in less densely populated areas.

Second, urban dwellers currently have less school choice than other Americans. Many urban residents are black, and the residential segregation of blacks is still strong. This is true within school districts as well as across district lines. The effects on school segregation are illustrated by data from Chicago, where 37 of 63 high schools have more than 99 percent black enrollment, although only 63 percent of district students are black (*Chicago Magazine*, 1995). Also, in a neighborhood school system, the price of housing can ration access to neighborhoods with better schools (Black, 1998; Epple and Romano, 1996). This creates a link between income and education quality because higher-income households can more readily pay a premium for housing in neighborhoods with better schools. The structure of metropolitan areas in the United States (large central cities surrounded by suburbs) tends to result in a disproportionate number of low-income households concentrated in a large multischool district.

Third, urban districts, more so than suburban or rural districts, resemble monopoly providers and so may suffer most from the inefficiencies that accompany monopoly supply. Again, Chicago provides an example: the city of Chicago has 63 high schools in one school district. Roughly 77 districts surrounding Chicago have a total of 95 high schools (*Chicago Magazine*, 1995).

In addition, the features of small neighborhood school systems that may be desirable from the perspective of school performance—households that are predominantly owner-occupants, where both parents and homeowners without children have incentives to care about school quality (Hoxby, 1996)—are less pronounced in large-central city districts. In central cities, the majority of households are renters rather than owner-occupants; residents without children in school do not have the financial stake in the quality of neighborhood schools that owner-occupants do. The owners of rental housing have less political influence relative to owner-occupants, because the former are fewer in number and often reside elsewhere. This is likely to be exacerbated in large districts by the relatively greater difficulty that residents encounter in affecting district-level policy. Hence one would expect neighborhood school organization to be less effective in large city systems with predominantly renter-occupants than in small suburban districts with predominantly owner-occupants.

Finally, urban residents arguably have benefited least from prior school reforms: urban schools still produce the lowest academic achievement and suffer from high dropout rates. Research suggests that recent studies comparing Catholic school performance to public school performance show more positive effects for urban minority students than for others, though as also noted the problem of selection bias (while not as bad as in earlier research) still makes it difficult to draw firm conclusions about public-private school differences.

Both theory and experience suggest that different forms of choice would affect urban education in different ways.

Breaking up large city systems into small districts comparable in size to suburban districts (that is, mimicking neighborhood schools) would likely be a step in the right direction from an incentive standpoint, and this is one way to increase school choice. However, the incentives with renter-occupants would probably not be as strong as with owner-occupants. In addition, the tax base per student in such newly created small districts would necessarily vary a great deal, and some form of equalization would be essential for such restructuring to have desired outcomes.

Interdistrict and intradistrict choice options have limitations in urban settings. Parents in districts with good schools pay a housing price premium to reside in these districts and are unlikely to be receptive to enrolling students from poorer-performing districts. In fact, where interdistrict choice is now permitted, not much actually occurs. Intradistrict choice may be more viable, but still parents who have located in neighborhoods with good schools may resist student enrollments from outside the neighborhood. Districts can enforce open enrollment, but if there are significant differences in school quality, this is likely to lead wealthier households to leave for the suburbs or to enroll their children in private school. Moreover, intradistict choice is not an effective mechanism for improving performance when problems exist at the district level.

Charter schools have incentives to attract and admit students; their survival depends on it. They also have incentives to serve students well in order to retain them. They are likely to introduce more competitive forces than traditional forms of public school choice because they can potentially supplant poor-performing schools. They may also be effective in disciplining inefficient management if the district does not have too much control over their operation. However, to the extent that charter schools remain an intradistrict mechanism, subject to the authority of existing district management, there may be limits to the extent to which they can bring about change where change is needed most.

Vouchers that enable students to use public funds to attend private schools may offer city residents the most effective enrollment vehicle for improving educational quality by rewarding schools that perform well and punishing schools that do not. Such rewards and punishments are key features of well-functioning private markets. Because private schools face this disciplining mechanism, voucher-supported private schools are likely to have the strongest impact in improving school performance. This is particularly the case if the program is funded at the state level, so that the voucher schools are not tied to a particular school district either in oversight or resources. Hence, on a priori grounds, such schools might be expected to be the most likely to succeed in increasing productivity and effectiveness of the educational system.

Despite these theoretical arguments in favor of vouchers, they are and have been one of the most controversial ideas in American education. They raise (if parochial schools are included) church-state issues that, while perhaps not as powerful politically as they once were, still arouse strong emotions, to say nothing of possible federal and state constitutional barriers.

The legality of religious-school vouchers is unclear, and advocacy groups on both sides of the issue are hoping to bring a case before the U.S. Supreme Court that would result in a definitive ruling. Meanwhile, courts in several states have rendered conflicting opinions. For example, the state supreme courts in Wisconsin and Ohio ruled that programs in Milwaukee and Cleveland that permit vouchers to be used at religious schools are legal under both federal and state constitutions (*Jackson v. Benson*, 710 N.E.2d 276, Wis. 1998, *Simmons-Harris v. Goff*, 710 N.E.2d 276, Ohio, 1999).[12] In Maine, the state supreme judicial court

---

[12]The Ohio Supreme Court at the same time struck down the Cleveland voucher program on technical grounds unrelated to the constitutional church-state issue. The Ohio legislature subsequently (June 1999) reinstated the Cleveland program in a manner that avoids the technical problem with the old law. However, at the beginning of the 1999 school year, a federal district judge issued an injunction halting the Cleveland voucher program on the grounds that it probably violates consti-

and the federal appeals court ruled that "tuitioning" programs (wherein towns without public high schools reimburse parents for sending their children to public or secular private schools in other communities) may not include religious schools. The courts based their rulings on both federal and state constitutional arguments (*Bagely v. Raymond School Department*, 728 A.2d 127, Me 1999, *Strout v. Albanese*, 1999 U.S. App. LEXIS 10932, 1st Cir. May 27, 1999). The Vermont Supreme Court relied solely on the state constitution in making a similar ruling on that state's tuitioning program (*Chittenden Town School District v. Vermont Department of Education*, No. 97-275, 1999 Vt. LEXIS 98, Sup. Ct. filed June 11, 1999). Related cases raise church-state issues in other (nonvoucher) contexts—e.g., state-authorized education tax credits that include religious schools in Arizona and Minnesota and cases related to technology and other kinds of aid in a number of states. When federal constitutional issues are invoked, grounds exist for appeals to the U.S. Supreme Court. Any of a number of current cases could ultimately provide the occasion for the court to settle the question of what public aid may or may not be used at religious schools. Perhaps Florida's new statewide school voucher law, the first statewide law in the country, will be the test case lawyers have been seeking. One day after the law was signed on June 21, 1999, the first lawsuit challenging it was filed.[13]

Legal issues apart, many opponents see private school vouchers as a threat to traditional American support for public schools. Some urban educators argue that they would remove much-needed funds from public education just as urban districts are engaging strenuously in efforts to improve their academic performance. Opponents fear that they would exacerbate the stratification of population by income, race, or other student characteristics, potentially making matters worse rather than better with respect to achieving goal 2. Experience with parental choice programs overseas lends some credence to concerns about increased stratification, although of course urban American schools are already stratified to a significant degree.

There is some theoretical research that addresses these concerns. For example, Epple and Romano (1998, 1999) find that flat-rate voucher systems tend to promote more stratification by ability than public neighborhood schools systems but less stratification by income. As Chapter 6 noted, there is very little

---

tutional mandates for the separation of church and state. As this volume goes to press, the federal judge partially reversed the injunction and decided to allow Cleveland children who were enrolled in the voucher program last year to continue attending private school for the first semester of this school year, while the full case is argued. In the meantime, no new students are being given vouchers.

[13]In Florida, each public school has just been graded for the first time by the state on an A-to-F basis. The state will offer vouchers to students attending schools that receive Fs two times in four years. In fall 1999, only pupils in two elementary schools in Pensacola will be eligible for the vouchers, on the basis of previous poor ratings received by these schools.

empirical evidence with which to evaluate the theoretical claims made both for and against vouchers, and the evidence that does exist is often hotly contested. While limited data are available that can be used to test predictions about voucher programs directly, theoretical predictions can be tested by analysis of data for existing public and private schools. Epple et al. (1998) test the aforementioned predictions about stratification made by Epple and Romano and find that all predictions regarding stratification within and across the public and private school sectors are supported by the data.[14]

The foregoing suggests that charter schools and vouchers, rather than interdistrict and intradistrict choice programs, are the choice options most worthy of further exploration as vehicles for improving poor-performing city schools. Charter schools are in effect a naturally occurring experiment, although one that is not being as fully and systematically evaluated as it might be. Also, the fact that charter schools have unequal access to capital funding means that they do not face a level playing field with traditional public schools.

Existing voucher programs are so small that they are not ever likely to yield the kind of answers about the effects of vouchers and the most effective voucher designs that would be necessary to allay the concerns of those who question vouchers, not on legal grounds, but on the grounds of their unproven impacts on school performance and stratification. This raises the question of whether it is time for a large-scale experimental demonstration project with school vouchers. The committee wrestled long with this issue and discusses it further in Chapter 9.

---

[14]This analysis uses a unique dataset (prepared by David Figlio and Joe Stone) that was generated from the National Education Longitudinal Survey, the Schools and Staffing Surveys, and data collected by Dun and Bradstreet.

8

Achieving Goal 3:
Raising Revenue Fairly and Efficiently

Most of the policy discussion related to the fairness of school financing systems focuses, as it should, on the pattern and level of educational spending or outcomes. However, another aspect of equity should not be ignored: How fair is the distribution of the burden of the taxes or fees used to generate revenue for schools? Some aspects of this revenue perspective on equity are obviously intertwined with the spending and outcome issues embodied in the concepts of school finance equity and adequacy discussed in Chapters 3 and 4. However, many other aspects are not. Moreover, the basic principles typically used to evaluate the fairness of revenue sources differ from the standard equity principles underlying the school finance literature.

In addition to equity, other aspects of the revenue system are also important, such as how much it costs the government to administer the system, how stable the revenue sources are over the business cycle, and how extensively the tax system distorts taxpayers' decisions in undesirable ways. Policy makers who are striving to achieve the goal of raising revenues in a fair and efficient manner need to pay attention to all of these issues. In addition, they need to consider any trade-offs or complementarities with the other two goals of a good financing system: increasing achievement for all students and reducing the nexus between achievement and family background.

Two main aspects of revenue raising should be distinguished—the particular revenue source that is used (i.e., property, income, or sales taxes) and the level of government (i.e., school district, state, or federal government) that is responsible for raising revenue. Table 8-1 displays the main options for the United States.

In this chapter we argue that the local property tax remains the best way to

TABLE 8-1 Tax Options for the United States

Type of Tax	District	State	Federal
Property	X	possible	
Sales		X	
Income		X	X

raise *local* revenue for education. That is, *provided a decision is made to lodge significant responsibility for raising revenue at the local level, the local property tax is preferred to other local taxes for that purpose.* That analytical conclusion is depicted in Table 8-1 by the designation of property taxes as the single revenue source for local school districts. While local sales and income taxes are potentially feasible and are currently used in some states, the property tax is the preferred option.

At the state level, the relevant major revenue sources are state income and sales taxes, with 41 states using income taxes and 45 using sales taxes. States traditionally have not made much use of state-level property taxes to finance education. However, several states have recently shifted toward statewide property taxes or their equivalent, and other states could do so as well. Hence, along with state income and sales taxes, we identify statewide property taxes as a larger potential source of revenue for education than in the past.

Although the federal government now provides only about 7 percent of the revenue for K-12 education, in principle it could do a lot more. In the absence of major tax reform at the federal level (in the form, for example, of a shift away from the federal income tax to a value-added tax or other form of consumption taxation), the relevant revenue source for education at the federal level is the federal income tax.

After evaluating the property tax in some detail, this chapter addresses four questions about the revenue system. The first question is whether the mix of local taxes should be altered by reducing reliance on the property tax and increasing reliance on other local taxes or a modified version of the property tax. The second is what state revenue source would be best if heavier reliance were to be placed on state revenue sources. The third is whether it would make sense to shift away from local revenue raising in favor of much greater reliance on state revenues. And the fourth is whether it would be desirable to increase significantly the federal role in revenue raising for K-12 education.

EVALUATION OF THE PROPERTY TAX

Evaluating the local property tax as a source of funding for local schools is significantly more complicated than evaluating a state or national tax because of the close relationship between the revenues collected and the amount of spending in each school district. This close relationship suggests to some people that the property tax should be evaluated as a benefit tax—that is, as a tax that is specifically paid for the services provided by a community, rather than in more standard ability-to-pay terms, which examine the distribution of the tax burden separately from what the funds are used for. When looked at as a benefit tax, the local property tax appears to perform better on efficiency grounds and, according to some people, also better on equity grounds than when it is looked at through the lens of the more traditional tax literature. In the following sections we refer to both perspectives.

Efficiency

Most taxes induce some inefficiency by encouraging taxpayers to alter their behavior in ways that would reduce their tax liability. In the case of the property tax, the standard concern is that households will respond to the tax by investing less in housing or that firms will respond by investing less in property subject to the property tax or by shifting their investments to areas with low property tax rates (Mieszkowski and Zodrow, 1989).

In contrast to this emphasis on the inefficiencies of the tax, the benefit-tax approach emphasizes that the local property tax may generate efficient decisions, especially with respect to the level of education services. Particularly in large suburban areas where households can choose among many small, relatively homogeneous school districts, households gain access to the education services provided by a district in return for paying its local property tax. Presumably, people will have a tendency to sort themselves among districts in line with their preferences for education, so that those with stronger preferences for education will end up in districts with more education and higher property taxes than those with weaker preferences. In effect, the property taxes act more like prices that consumers willingly pay for education than compulsory taxes. This analogy is particularly apt, according to the advocates of this perspective, when local zoning regulations ensure that residents in each school district end up in houses that are similarly valued, so that they pay similar property taxes for their uniform public education (see Hamilton, 1975; Fischel, 1992; Hoxby, 1996b).

This view, which is generally consistent with the well-known strand of public finance literature initiated by Charles Tiebout in 1956, draws attention to the efficiency benefits that accrue from local provision and financing of public goods. Significantly, however, the benefit-tax approach would apply to any local tax, not just to the local property tax. That is, the efficiency claims for the property tax relate more to the governmental level at which revenues are raised than to the desirability of the property tax or any other specific local tax. For this reason, we defer to later in the chapter a fuller discussion of the potential trade-offs between efficiency and equity that might arise with a shift to a larger state role in education finance.

Furthermore, the benefit-tax argument applies most directly to small, relatively homogeneous suburban districts only when local zoning enforces housing uniformity within districts, and it is not particularly pertinent to central city or rural districts. In light of these limitations, it seems reasonable to treat the property tax like other taxes and to recognize that it will induce some distortions in behavior. Because all taxes induce distortions, the relevant question from this more traditional perspective then becomes how the distortions associated with the property tax compare with those associated with other potential local taxes, such as the income or the sales tax.

Fairness

There is little doubt that many taxpayers view the local property tax as unfair. In 1978, for example, voters in California shocked the nation by supporting Proposition 13, a statewide initiative to reduce drastically the level and rate of growth of local property taxes. Massachusetts voters followed with their own stringent tax limitation measure two years later. While the motivation for these and other measures to limit property taxes are obviously mixed and complex, voters appear to have been motivated in part by their perception that the local property tax was unfair.[1] Acting on concerns of this type, legislators in many other states did not wait for statewide referenda to reduce property taxes, but instead jumped on the anti-property-tax bandwagon and introduced policies designed to provide property tax relief to all or to specific groups of taxpayers.

Further evidence of continuing taxpayer dissatisfaction regarding the property tax emerges from annual surveys administered between 1972 and 1994 by the U.S. Advisory Commission on Intergovernmental Relations. During that period, between 25 and over 30 percent of the respondents consistently rated the property tax as the least fair tax (compared with federal and state income taxes and the state sales tax) and typically much less fair than the main alternatives to property taxes for financing education, state income and sales taxes.

Taxpayers have lots of reasons for believing the property tax is unfair. Many of these relate to the way the tax is administered (e.g., see Netzer and Berne, 1995, for examples specific to New York State). Compared with other taxes such as income and sales taxes, the property tax is more difficult to administer fairly because it requires that property be assessed. Ideally, the assessed value of a property should reflect its market value. However, where there are few market transactions, the value of the property must be approximated by one of several imperfect methods. It is not surprising that the assessment of property is subject

---

[1]These and other factors are explored by Citrin (1979) in California, Gramlich and Rubinfeld (1982) in Michigan, and Ladd and Wilson (1982) in Massachusetts.

to error and to political influence in some states and, consequently, frequently departs from market value.

Another complicating factor is that any given parcel of property is likely to be subject to taxation by several local authorities, such as a county government, a municipality, a school district and perhaps several special-purpose districts. Such complexity may well confuse local taxpayers and make them view the overall burden as unfair. Finally, the fact that property taxes are typically levied only once or twice a year makes them more visible than income taxes, which are largely collected through withholding, or sales taxes, which are collected in small amounts at the cash register.

Other reasons for concern about the fairness of the property tax arise in particular circumstances. In California in the late 1970s, for example, part of the concern arose from the rapidly rising housing values and the three-year assessment cycle, which combined to produce huge increases in property valuations and tax burdens in a single year, increases that bore no relationship to the taxpayer's ability to pay as measured by current income. In Massachusetts, the high levels of property tax burdens made the tax difficult for some taxpayers to accept.

Beyond some of these taxpayer concerns, many of which are clearly valid and reflect underlying problems with how the tax is administered, experts in public finance also have much to say about the fairness of the property tax based on the two basic principles of tax equity. However, as the committee discovered, not all economists agree.

Those economists who emphasize that the local property tax is like a benefit tax would typically defend it on fairness grounds by appealing to the benefit principle of tax equity. According to this principle, a tax is fair if the burden of the tax is distributed among taxpayers in line with the benefits they receive from the services funded by the tax. However, in the committee's view the benefit principle is not very applicable in this context, largely because it is based on an unacceptable ethical foundation. Because the demand for education is highly correlated with parental income and education, this approach to equity would accept as fair differences in education levels across jurisdictions that correspond to differences in preferences and family ability to pay for education. Although such a pattern increases the efficiency with which education is provided (in the sense that those who have greater willingness to pay for education get more) compared with a uniform state-wide level, the committee sees no reason to assert that such an outcome is fair, especially given the acknowledged significance of education to a child's life chances.

An additional complication arises in using the benefit principle to evaluate the equity of property taxes because of the phenomenon of tax capitalization. For example, if two school districts provide similar education services but one does so at a lower tax rate (perhaps because of the presence of a power plant in the district), homeowners are likely to have bid up housing prices in the low-tax district enough so that new homeowners would receive no net financial benefit from living in the district with the lower tax rate. Thus what may appear as an inequity—the fact that households in one community pay a lower tax rate than those in the other for the same services—turns out not to be an inequity if one takes into consideration the fact that the households paying the lower tax rate pay more for their housing.[2]

More useful and appropriate for evaluating the equity of the property tax, in the view of the committee, is the ability-to-pay principle. From this perspective, the key question is: How regressive is the property tax?

It turns out that there is no simple answer to this question. The incidence of the property tax has, in fact, been one of the most controversial topics in the field of local public finance. The controversy centers around the so-called old view and the new view of the incidence of the tax. Those who apply the old view argue that the tax is regressive on the grounds that landlords and business firms are able to shift much of the burden of their real estate taxes onto renters and consumers in the form of higher prices. The new view, in contrast, emphasizes that the property tax is a tax on wealth, so that the ultimate burden of the tax is distributed in line with earnings from wealth. Since those earnings rise disproportionately with household income, the tax burden, according to this view, could be progressive— that is, the tax would place a heavier burden on higher-income households than on lower-income ones. Fortunately, as noted by McLure (1977), the two views can be reconciled by interpreting the old view as one component of the new view. In particular the old view is most applicable to differences in property tax rates across jurisdictions.

This reconciliation leads to the general consensus that what makes the property tax regressive is the differences in tax rates across jurisdictions. Regressivity emerges to the extent that higher property tax rates are levied in districts with above-average proportions of poor households and lower rates in districts with richer households. However, a different conclusion emerges for property tax rates that cover a broad geographic area like a large state. In this case, the new view would be more applicable, which would mean that the burden of an increase in the property tax rate is likely to be proportional or even relatively progressive. This observation suggests that a shift away from reliance on local property taxes (with their tax rate differentials that make the tax regressive) to a statewide property tax could well make the tax system fairer.

---

[2]This phenomenon of capitalization has implications not only for the equity of the existing system but also for changes in the system. Any policy that would change property taxes, such as increased reliance on alternative revenue sources, will generate windfall gains in housing values to those whose taxes fall and losses to those whose taxes rise. Similarly, the positive effects on poor people of equalizing aid that allows poor jurisdictions to lower tax rates or increase the quality of their education services could be offset in part by a rise in housing costs. However, if the low-income residents are homeowners, they also benefit from the higher value of their houses (see Wyckoff, 1995).

This discussion generates two conclusions about the fairness of the property tax. First, from an equity perspective, the administration of the property tax leaves a lot to be desired and inevitably leads to the unfair treatment of some taxpayers. The committee would support ongoing efforts to administer the tax as fairly as possible. As spelled out by Netzer and Berne (1995:39), a property tax system should be: (1) "transparent and straightforward," so that it is comprehensible to voters and property owners; (2) it should be "systematic," in the sense of having few internal contradictions; and (3) it should be "reasonably related to the policy objectives that animate the various provisions."

Second, the property tax is not so regressive—and hence unfair—a tax as some people make it out to be.[3] Its major failings are (1) the regressive elements that emerge because it is a local tax and (2) the inequities in spending that result from the wide variation across districts in the property tax base. However, these latter inequities result more from the fact that many states place such heavy reliance on local—in contrast to state—revenue sources rather than to the property tax itself.

This conclusion about regressivity implies that converting the local property tax with its variation in tax rates across jurisdictions to a statewide uniform-rate property tax could well improve the fairness of the revenue system. It would eliminate most of the regressive element that arises from the differential tax rates across jurisdictions and would eliminate the spending disparities that arise from the variation in local property tax bases.[4] A logical next question would then be whether further gains in equity could be obtained by shifting away from the property tax completely to other statewide taxes, such as income or sales taxes.

However, the committee is well aware that some people would argue that any gains in equity (either in the fairness of the revenue system or in the form of a more even pattern of spending across districts) from a shift to statewide taxes could come at a potentially large cost, namely the loss of local control and more efficient decision making that flows from local school districts having access to their own source of revenue. In light of the concern about local control and efficiency, it is worth examining first how the property tax stacks up against other local taxes that might be used by local school districts.

---

[3]Throughout this discussion we have defined regressivity with respect to a household's current income. An alternative approach would compare tax burdens across households as a proportion not of their current income but rather of their lifetime or "permanent" income. Such an analysis would make the property tax look less regressive and more proportional, given that household spending on housing is typically found to vary in line with a household's permanent income. It is worth noting, however, that if one is going to look at the incidence of property taxes in terms of permanent income, one must also examine the incidence of other taxes in similar terms. For a discussion of these issues in the context of excise taxes, see Poterba, 1989; Lyon and Schwab, 1995.

[4]At the same time, it should be noted that such a change in tax system could well lead to short run windfall gains and losses that could be quite arbitrary in their distributional effects. Hence, any change in tax structure would require attention to these arbitrary gains and losses.

SHOULD THE MIX OF LOCAL TAXES BE CHANGED?

The two major candidates to replace the local property tax are the local income tax and the local sales tax. Alternatively, one could imagine modifying the local property tax by applying it to residential property alone or by sharing the revenues across communities within a metropolitan area.

Local Income or Sales Taxes

A somewhat stronger case can be made for replacing the local property tax with a local income tax than with a local sales tax, but even here the argument is not compelling.

Strauss (1995) tries to make the case for a local income tax with particular reference to New York State. His starting point is that because education represents an important form of income redistribution, it should be financed out of broad ability-to-pay taxes, such as income or consumption broadly defined. The property tax is unfair, he argues, because it does not allocate burdens in line with any reasonable concept of ability to pay. For example, it often imposes heavy burdens on the elderly who are property wealthy but income poor, and it treats taxpayers in districts with a lot of business property favorably relative to those in districts that are primarily residential (with no reference, however, to the potentially offsetting impacts on housing prices that occur when differences in property taxes are capitalized). Few would disagree with the argument that the income tax is the superior tax judged in terms of ability to pay. Unlike the property tax, it applies directly to households and hence can be adjusted to take into account the circumstances of the family, such as the number of dependents. Furthermore, provided one accepts the view that current annual income is the appropriate measure of ability to pay, tax burdens will inevitably be more in line with household ability to pay than they would be with the property tax. Of course, in practice, in order to minimize administrative and compliance costs by taking advantage of the existing state administrative structure, the definition of income for a local income tax would most likely follow the state definition. Consequently, the fairness of any local income tax would depend on the fairness of the state income tax.

Although from an ability-to-pay perspective a local income tax could well be a fairer way to raise revenue within a district than the local property tax, the income tax may well be less desirable on other grounds. First, it could well lead to even greater disparities across school districts than those associated with the local property tax. This outcome would occur, for example, if the amount of business property (which is included in the property tax base but not the income tax base) were larger in areas with lower-income residents than in areas with wealthier residents, a pattern that would tend to mitigate the effects of large differences in household income or property wealth across districts. In practice, which tax base varies more is an empirical question and the outcome is likely to vary from one state to another. As Oates (1991) has pointed out, the unequal distribution of the tax base is likely to be a problem for *any* local tax whether it be a property, income, or sales tax, and the problem could well be less for the property tax than for other taxes.

Second, there are likely to be greater behavioral distortions with the income tax than with the property tax. If a redistributive local income tax and expenditure package is weighted toward lower-income individuals and families, then in-migration of the poor into the local jurisdiction raises the cost of redistribution and may cause out-migration of wealthier families. The property tax generates fewer distortions because the mechanism of tax capitalization through which differences in tax burdens are reflected in the prices of housing makes it more difficult for taxpayers to avoid the burden of the tax by movement from one jurisdiction to another.

Other possible advantages of the property tax over the income tax include the fact that it is potentially more stable over the business cycle because of the relative stability of housing values (but offsetting this is the possibility of increasing tax arrears during recessions) and its broader tax base, which includes business as well as residential property and means that tax rates can be lower for any amount of revenue. Finally, in contrast to the income tax, for which the marginal tax rate for a local income tax could be quite high because the same base is used by the federal government and most state governments, the property tax has the advantage of not being used by higher levels of government.

The local sales tax is an even less promising alternative than the local income tax. Shifting away from the local property tax to a local sales tax is unlikely to make the revenue system more fair. First, the sales tax itself is generally a very regressive tax. Although many states have moderated the regressivity of their state sales taxes to some extent by choosing not to tax food, the state sales tax typically remains quite regressive. There is no reason to believe that a local sales tax would be any less regressive. Whether it is more or less regressive than the property tax is a more complicated question, but one on which there is no clear presumption in favor of the sales tax.

Moreover the local sales tax has some other significant disadvantages. The disparities across districts in sales tax bases are likely to exceed the disparities in property tax bases because of the uneven distribution of large retail shopping centers across school districts. Local sales taxes are relatively easy for taxpayers to avoid and hence can distort the shopping behavior of local shoppers in significant ways. Revenue from sales taxes is typically quite unstable over the business cycle, and finally, sales taxes are not deductible under the federal income tax.

Thus, the property tax appears to dominate the other main alternative broad based local taxes—income and sales—as a revenue source for school districts based on standard evaluation criteria for revenue sources such as equity, efficiency, and stability. However, one final criterion remains—the effect of the tax on the willingness and ability of voters to raise funds for education.

Various constraints have recently been imposed by state governments on the local property tax, in the form of property tax caps and other limitation measures. Many of these constraints have been binding, and they would appear to be a serious indictment of the property tax as a source of revenue for education. Dye and McGuire (1997) and Rueben (1997) provide empirical evidence that these property tax limitation measures are effective at limiting the level and growth of property taxes. The evidence on the effects of these restrictions on school outcomes, such as student test scores, is more mixed. Downes et al. (1998) do not find strong evidence of a short-run effect of the Illinois tax cap on test scores, while Downes and Figlio (1997) find evidence that mathematics test scores are lower in states with binding limitation measures, and Figlio and Rueben (1997) find evidence that teacher quality is lower in states with strict property tax limitation measures. Typically, when tax limitation measures are imposed, the affected jurisdictions are allowed to circumvent the restrictions if they receive voter approval. The effectiveness of voter referenda as an escape valve for jurisdictions hard hit by limitation measures is in question.

However, one must be careful not to assume that taxpayers are revolting against the property tax per se. They may, instead, be concerned about the overall level of taxes and have chosen to protest against the one that is closest to them, the one at the local level. One particular characteristic of such a local tax provides some support for this view. In many jurisdictions, the local property tax is treated as the residual tax, in that its rate is the easiest one to increase when a jurisdiction finds that it has a shortfall between its planned expenditure and the revenue it will receive in the form of state or federal aid or from other tax bases subject to fixed tax rates. The rising property tax rates may well induce local voters to view the property tax as the culprit when the real problem is that expenditure demands are outstripping the growth in other sources of revenue. By this reasoning, one might expect to see limitations imposed on other forms of local revenues, should they become much more broadly used.

Possible Modifications to the Local Property Tax

Given that the reasons for shifting away from the local property tax to another broad based *local* tax are not compelling, it is worth considering whether various modifications of the local property tax might be desirable. The two most commonly discussed alternatives are shifting the taxation of nonresidential property to the state level and the introduction of local tax base sharing, as in Minneapolis-St. Paul.

The fact that the property tax applies not only to residential but also to business property raises a variety of policy issues for the financing of education. Ladd and Harris (1995) examine the case for shifting the nonresidential portion of the local property tax base to the state level, with the funds redistributed back to local districts for education. Such a shift might be justified on the following grounds. First, it would recognize the fact that it is residents who receive the primary benefits of locally provided education services, either directly in the form of education services or indirectly through the capitalization of education services into house values. In contrast, because they typically recruit workers from a region larger than the local school district, firms generally receive fewer benefits from local education than do residents. Second, the inclusion of business property in the local tax base could distort local spending by lowering the tax price of education to residents and thereby inducing districts with large amounts of local business property to overinvest in education, relative to the local benefits received by residents. Third, locally differentiated taxation of business property could distort firms' location decisions, as firms seek the districts with the lower tax rates, thereby creating inefficiencies in production. Fourth and more speculative is that shifting to statewide taxation of business property for education with the proceeds channeled back to school districts could generate a fairer pattern of education spending across the state. Whether this outcome would occur depends on the location of the business property and the formula by which the state distributed the revenue back to the local districts.

Ladd (1976) and Ladd and Harris (1995) observe that the impact on distribution as a result of statewide taxation of business property depends on the location of the business property and the structure of the aid system. Ladd (1976) simulates the results of this type of policy change on resource equity in Massachusetts. She concludes that the state would need to provide additional redistributive aid to poorer districts to make up for the lost revenue from the smaller tax base. If business property is disproportionately located in poorer school districts and the state aid system does not compensate, then equity would be reduced by such a proposal. Ladd and Harris (1995) consider the impact of this policy in New York State. They concluded that in order to improve the distribution of resources, the revenues would have to be distributed to the 75 percent of the school districts with the lowest income or property wealth. They noted, however, that such a redistribution program would drain a considerable amount of revenue from the New York City schools. The results from these studies highlight the limitations of these statewide property tax programs.

A variation of this approach is a system in which the tax base generated from new business investment within a metropolitan area is shared among the local communities. Such an approach has been used in the Minneapolis-St. Paul area for the financing of general public services since 1975 (Luce, 1998). Under that program, 40 percent of the new property tax base is put into a regional pool, which is then distributed among municipalities in line with their population and inversely with the market value of their property relative to the rest of the region. While this approach appears to have reduced fiscal disparities in the Minneapolis-St. Paul region, its failure to offset the higher costs of providing services in some areas has generated some anomalous outcomes, such as that the city of Minneapolis is a net loser under the program. Recent simulations for other areas such as Maryland, Milwaukee, and Chicago generate similar predicted impacts, including the anomalous results for specific cities (Luce, 1998).

WOULD STATE TAXES BE BETTER?

If a larger share of the financing for education were shifted to the state level, states would have to rely primarily on their individual income tax, on their sales tax, or possibly on a new statewide property tax. Alternatively they might try to generate additional revenue from lottery proceeds or selective sales taxes. In the following sections, we explore the equity and efficiency of each of these revenue sources.

Broad-Based State Taxes

The economic incidence of the state income tax is much better understood than that of the property tax, largely because of the typically unchallenged assumption that the burden of the tax is borne by the people who pay it. The typical state imposes a graduated-rate structure with a top rate of between 5 and 8 percent. A few states impose either a flat rate or a very compressed graduated-rate structure on incomes above a low threshold amount, so that the tax burdens in these states are distributed nearly proportionally. More than half of the states with an income tax have an optional standard deduction and most allow taxpayers to use the items reported as federal itemized deductions on their state tax form. Because of these characteristics, state personal income taxes are generally considered to be progressive, with the degree of each state's income tax progressivity based on the level of exemptions, number of deductions, and marginal tax rates.[5]

Since the state income tax rates are in addition to the federal income tax, they can impose significant efficiency costs. After all, it is the total tax rate that affects individuals' decisions about the trade-off between work and leisure, not simply the portion that is paid to one level of government rather than another. Moreover, such efficiency costs rise more than proportionately with an increase in the tax rate, since the further individuals move from what their preferred option would have been, the less well off they are. Hence, a 5 percent state tax rate on top of a 15 percent federal income tax rate would increase the efficiency loss by significantly more than 33 percent. However, working in favor of the income tax is the fact that compliance and administrative costs of the tax will be relatively low provided the state follows the federal definition of taxable income and uses employer withholding to collect the bulk of the revenue.

[5]This is consistent with Phares's (1980) calculations of the progressivity of each state's income tax.

The stability of the revenue source over the business cycle (short-run elasticity) and how the revenue source responds to economic changes over time (long-run elasticity) also need to be considered. A revenue source that is stable during short-run business cycle instabilities is important to local governments. In addition, revenue sources that grow with growth in the state and local economy are typically preferred to those that grow more slowly. Both of these effects affect the stability of the tax revenue both in the short run and the long run. Revenue growth is required because economic growth will probably increase demands on government services. It is generally believed that an important advantage of the property tax is its relative stability and, therefore, predictability. However, the state personal income tax also seems to perform well in terms of these attributes. Sobel and Holcombe (1996) found the personal income tax base to be fairly stable over the course of a business cycle. They also found that it is very responsive to state income growth.

As for general sales taxes, economists typically assume that they are shifted forward to consumers in the form of higher prices and consequently impose a regressive burden on taxpayers because low-income households devote a larger share of their income to taxable items than do households with higher income. This regressivity is mitigated somewhat in states that exempt various categories of purchases, such as food and drugs, which represent a larger share of spending in low-income households than in high-income households.[6] However, this improvement in equity is bought at a loss of tax revenue, since food for home consumption comprises a large share of total potentially taxable sales. Even when all these exclusions from the sales tax base are considered, Phares (1980) estimates the general sales tax to be regressive in each of the states that has one.

The state sales tax also imposes efficiency costs because of the lack of uniformity in the rates and tax bases and because the tax is applied to mobile consumers. These inefficiencies are most certainly larger than with the state income or property tax. Sales tax rates tend to range from 4 to 6 percent. These rates are low, but because some local governments often impose additional sales taxes on the same base, and because the base is narrowly defined, the inefficiencies of the tax are likely to be high, at least in some states.

The state sales tax is also not as stable over the short run or the long run as property or income taxes. The variability and growth of sales tax revenue depend on what items are included in the tax base. On one hand, according to Sobel and Holcombe (1996), retail sales taxes including food purchases have about the same short-run responsiveness as the personal income tax. On the other hand, short-run variability increases when food items are exempted (as they are in many states). Neither sales tax base (with or without food items) performs as well as personal income tax revenue with respect to long-run state income growth.

---

[6]See Due and Mikesell (1994) for a general discussion of state sales taxes and Poterba (1989) for an alternative view of the distributional consequences of general consumption taxes.

Revenue instability has become a concern in some of the states that have reformed their education finance systems. In states like California, and more recently Michigan, in which the state has become the primary financier of local school districts, local school districts find that their fortunes are tied to revenue sources that are arguably more sensitive to the business cycle than the property tax, and to revenue sources that they do not have control over. This is because of the restrictions placed on assessments as well as the difficulty (both actual and political) of accurately reevaluating property for tax purposes. In addition, in states that have shifted total financing to the state level, education spending competes for funding with other large state programs.

In part because of these revenue uncertainties, policies that were intended to shift from local to state spending have been partially undone. Arizona and California (and Massachusetts less dramatically) present interesting cases as each enacted major limitations on the local property tax in the late 1970s, which were reflected in large declines in their local shares between 1974-75 and 1984-85. Their local shares increased over the ensuing 10 years so that by 1994-95 Arizona's local share was right at the national average, and California's share was half again as large as it had been in 1984-85. This pattern results from either slowly growing state revenue sources for K-12 education, rising property values (and thus taxable property), or ineffective limitation measures.

In sum, any switch away from local financing of education to the state level will probably require a greater reliance on the state's income or sales tax. Although the sales tax fares less well by standard criteria, especially that of fairness, state legislators often seem to like it, perhaps largely because it is paid in such small amounts along the way and hence is relatively invisible. However, the income tax would be the fairest. Moreover, a recent analysis of the optimal combination of taxes to use at the state level by Gentry and Ladd (1994) shows that the state income tax dominates other state taxes on several key dimensions.

Alternative State Revenue Sources Such as Lotteries

Although income and sales taxes are the workhorses of state revenue systems and are currently the primary generators of state revenue for education, many states also rely on a variety of smaller revenue sources for education. Included among these sources are lottery revenues and selected sales taxes on items such as cigarettes. In some cases, these revenue sources contribute to the financing of education simply as part of a state's general fund. In other cases, they are specifically earmarked for education, as is frequently the case, for example, with lottery revenues.[7] Of course that earmarking does not ensure additional funds for

---

[7]By 1998, 37 states and the District of Columbia had introduced lotteries, with 17 of them earmarking the proceeds for education (LaFleur's Lottery World, 1998).

education since the earmarked funds may simply replace funds that otherwise would have been appropriated for that purpose.

Neither lottery revenues nor selective sales taxes are good sources of revenue for education in part because they are incapable of generating significant amounts of revenue relative to the amount spent on education and in part because they generally are quite regressive and often are unstable. Revenue from the lottery imposes a regressive burden because lower-income households on average spend much higher proportions of their income on the lottery than do higher-income households (Clotfelter and Cook, 1989). The regressivity of selected sales taxes varies with the particular item taxed but also can be quite significant for some items, such as cigarettes and alcohol (Poterba, 1989). In some cases, especially when they are first started, the revenue from lotteries may grow quite rapidly. However, over time, revenues level off and may well decline unless a state advertises aggressively and continually introduces new games.[8] The revenue from selective sales taxes will vary over the economic cycle to the extent the taxed goods are luxuries, the demand for which rises with income. Although spending on other goods, such as cigarettes, subject to selective sales taxation may be more stable over the cycle, that spending—and hence taxes from that source—may well decline over time as the number of smokers declines. In sum, none of these revenue sources represents a good substitute for a broad-based tax.

A Greater Role for State Property Taxes?

It would nearly be impossible for the country and most states to replace the property tax as the primary revenue source for education. Local governments provide almost 46 percent of all government revenue for primary and secondary public education and the local property tax accounts for over 95 percent of the local tax burden in those states served by independent school districts (see Tables 2-1 and 2-7). Hence, if for equity or other reasons, it made sense to expand the state role, state-level property taxes will undoubtedly have to play a significant role. State property taxes are probably as good or better than state sales taxes, but may be less desirable than state income tax financing. However, in light of the continued reliance on some form of property taxation, states should devote more attention to ensuring that the property tax is fairly administered. Nevertheless, statewide property taxes would be a fairer way to raise revenue than the current system of local property taxes for education. However, we emphasize that whether or not a shift to heavier reliance on state taxes, including state property taxes, is desirable raises many other issues—including the link between state

---

[8]Revenues from Pennsylvania's lottery nearly doubled each year for the first few years but than leveled off to a 4.5 percent growth a decade later. Revenue declines in some states have been as great as 50 percent in a particular year (Monk and Brent, 1997).

financing and overall spending levels, the relationship between financing and governance structures, and the effects on the productive efficiency of the system—which are discussed in the following section.

SHOULD STATES PLAY A BIGGER ROLE IN REVENUE RAISING?

An initial consideration for determining whether states should play a bigger role in revenue raising is the impact of such a strategy on the fairness with which revenues are raised. However, potential trade-offs between fairness in revenue raising and other criteria that are embedded in the other goals for a good finance system also need to be considered. In particular, if states were to play a bigger role in funding education, what impact might that have on the system's success in increasing student achievement in a cost-effective way (goal 1), and on its ability to reduce the nexus between family background and student achievement (goal 2)? To the extent that there are trade-offs among the goals, policy makers will need to decide which goal or goals they value most highly in making the decision about the appropriate role of state governments in revenue raising.

Implications for the Fairness of Revenue Raising

We have already argued that the local property tax is not a fair way to raise revenue for education when the relevant equity principle is an ability-to-pay standard. In particular, in a system of local property taxes the distribution of the tax burden across households will be more regressive than if a single statewide property tax were used. In addition, any system of local taxes is likely to give some districts significantly more capacity to generate revenue for education than other districts, and these disparities in turn will translate into spending inequities unless they are offset by carefully designed state aid programs.

Together these observations would seem to suggest that shifting more of the revenue-raising responsibility away from local school districts to the states will increase equity. However, two qualifications are worth noting. The first is that if the increase in state taxes is achieved through heavier reliance on state sales taxes (rather than state income or property taxes), fairness across households could be reduced. This conclusion follows because of the regressive nature of most state sales taxes. If reliance on such taxes is increased, low-income households could well end up bearing a larger portion of the education tax burden than they do with a local property tax. The second is that whether the increase in state financing offsets the inequities associated with reliance on local taxes will depend heavily on how the state distributes state aid for education among school districts. The more equalizing the state aid formula is, the greater the interdistrict equity that emerges from the shift from local to state funding.

In general, we conclude that, although the outcome is not guaranteed, a shift to greater reliance on state revenue sources could well increase the fairness with which revenues are raised for K-12 education. In addition, however, policy makers need to consider the extent to which this increase in fairness is bought at the cost of other goals for a good finance system or, alternatively, the extent to which it could be used as a way to promote those other goals.

Implications for Raising Achievement (Goal 1)

A larger state role in school finance could affect the education system's ability to raise overall student achievement and the efficiency with which it is produced in at least three ways. First, it could affect student achievement through its impact on the willingness of voters to support spending for education. Second, it could affect the stability of education revenues over the business cycle. Third, it could affect the efficiency with which education is provided.

Impact on the Level of Funding

Designing a finance system that is capable of generating an adequate level of funding for education is of primary importance. The question is the extent to which a shift to greater state financing of education would facilitate the objective of ensuring adequate revenue for education. This concern with the level of funding reflects the committee's view that money can matter—that is, money can affect student achievement if it is used wisely.

From a political economy perspective, one might predict that a shift toward a larger state role in revenue raising might reduce political support for education and thereby reduce the amount of funds available for education. One reason for this prediction is that education would have to compete with a broader array of services for funding at the state than at the local level. Especially in times of economic recession, that competition could potentially be detrimental to education, now that states have been given more responsibility for income support functions. In addition, this prediction reflects differing perceptions of the benefits of education. Voters making decisions about education spending in their local school district are likely to perceive greater benefits than when voters throughout a state make decisions about the level of state spending on education. In the case of the local decision, voters receive benefits in the form of higher-quality education for their own children or, alternatively, in the form of higher house prices associated with the increased desirability of the community to other families who value education. In contrast, for statewide decisions, the benefits to voters are much more diffuse and typically would not include the benefit of higher house prices. Consequently, political support for education could be lower when decisions were made at the state rather than the local level.

Silva and Sonstelie (1995) have developed a more formal political economy model that generates the same conclusion. The key to their model is the distinction between the median voter for local decisions and that for statewide decisions.

Under a decentralized system, the voters within each local school district choose their desired combination of taxes and expenditures. Each decision is the outcome of a majority-rule vote and, under certain assumptions, the relevant decisive voter in the school district is the one who prefers the median level of spending. This voter is generally identified as having the median income level in the school district. The weighted average of all school districts is the "state average" per-pupil spending level. With many different local districts available, families "vote with their feet" by moving to the school district with their preferred tax and expenditure combination. This migration creates relatively homogeneous school districts and, as they become more homogeneous, the weighted average of the school district medians will be approximately equal to the overall state average spending level or the amount desired by the individual with the state's mean income level. Under a centralized finance system, one tax and expenditure decision is made by the state's median voter or the individual with median income. Because for any typical distribution of income among households, the median is less than the mean, the amount chosen by the median voter at the state level will fall short of the average amount that would be chosen by the separate school districts in a decentralized system.

In addition to this income effect, Silva and Sonstelie identify a price effect of the change in revenue structure. This price effect is caused by the shift of the relevant tax base from the local property tax toward either a state income or a state sales tax. However, the size and direction of the price effect are unclear, since they depend on tax deductibility provisions (e.g., property and income taxes are deductible from the base of the federal income tax, but sales taxes are not) as well as the relative tax progressivity of the various taxes. The higher the progressivity of a tax, the lower would be the price to the median voter and the greater would be the willingness of that voter to support education. Because state income taxes are likely to be more progressive than local property taxes (yet both are deductible), this price effect could conceivably lead to greater support for education by statewide voters than by voters at the local level. Whether or not it does is an empirical question.

Also working to increase expenditures at the state level could be the economies of scale (described by Heise, 1998) gained by education lobbying groups under centralization as they are able to focus on a single state legislature rather than the far more numerous local school districts.

For empirical evidence, many observers have turned to California, where court-ordered reform eliminated most of the disparities in education spending across districts and increased the state role in financing. In that state, the subsequent change in spending was clear: it fell quite dramatically relative to what it otherwise would have been. However, for reasons we explain below, it would be a mistake to generalize from the California experience. In fact, we conclude that, in practice, a larger state role in education finance has led to higher spending in more states than it has led to lower spending.

The California experience (see Chapter 3) is worth describing because that state was the first to face successful court challenge to its system of education finance. In that case, *Serrano v. Priest*, the court severely restricted the degree of spending inequality across districts (to be less than $100 in 1971 dollars), allowing only for inflationary effects and variations in categorical aid. In effect, the state would determine the level of school district spending. The change in spending in California in the post-*Serrano* era has been dramatic. Rubinfeld (1995) showed that in 1971-72 California spending per pupil was 98 percent of the national average and that California ranked 19th among the states; by 1991-92, California spending was only 86 percent of the national average and the state's rank had fallen to 39th.

Silva and Sonstelie (1995) used regression techniques to attempt to measure for California the size of the price and income effects described above. They found that prior to *Serrano* in 1969-70, spending in California was similar to other states (after adjusting for differences in family income and tax prices). In 1989-90, however, they found that spending was significantly lower in California than they would have predicted. They estimate that roughly one-half of the decline in per-pupil spending in California can be attributed to *Serrano*. They attribute the remainder of the decrease to the growth of the California student population during the 1980s.

For a number of reasons, however, one should be careful about generalizing the California experience to other states. Most important is that, in 1978, California voters passed Proposition 13, which severely limited the level and rate of growth of local property taxes; they subsequently passed Proposition 4, which limited the rate of growth of state taxes. Together these changes rendered it extremely difficult to raise revenue in the state. While some authors (e.g. Fischel, 1996) attribute the passage of Proposition 13 to the *Serrano* decision, other plausible explanations are readily available. Those explanations start from the observations that prior to Proposition 13 housing values were rising very rapidly, that property tax assessments were rising almost as rapidly but in an uneven manner as only one-third of the residential properties were reassessed each year, that local public officials did not lower nominal property tax rates in proportion to the increases in property tax assessments, that the rapid rise in housing prices resulted in some shifting of the local tax burden away from business property onto residential property, and that the state had a large surplus with which it could have provided tax relief to local taxpayers. Together, these facts provided voters with plenty of reasons to be angry about their rising property tax burdens and to be frustrated with the local governments, the state government, or both.

Other changes make California unique as well. Because it was the first state supreme court decision in school finance, the *Serrano* court decision clearly did not involve the California legislature. After the *Serrano* decision, legislatures in other states may now view the court as a partner for the purpose of changing the education finance system. In addition, California experienced a large increase in its student population during much of the 1970s and the first half of the 1980s, while the rest of the country was still experiencing a decline in student enrollment.

At least one study (Joondeph, 1995) provides some evidence to suggest that the relative decline in California's spending after finance reform was not unique to that state. Comparing the growth rate in current expenditures for schools over a 20-year period in five states whose education systems had been found unconstitutional prior to 1984—California, Washington, Connecticut, Arkansas, and Wyoming—he found that, in four of the five states, spending on education grew at a slower pace than in the nation as a whole. His study also revealed that, with the exception of Connecticut, funding increased the least in those states that reduced interdistrict disparities the most (as measured by changes in the Gini coefficient). However, his analysis is based on simple correlations that do not capture the effects of alternative pressures on education spending. More sophisticated multivariate techniques are needed to sort out the causal impact on spending of the shift to a larger state role in the financing of education. In addition, his study focused roughly (depending on the availability of data) on the period from the time of the court case to the 1991-92 school year, giving him a somewhat different number of years to analyze across the five states.

Other researchers address more broadly the question of whether the California pattern is generalizable. Although the results from this literature are a bit mixed, on balance, the studies were somewhat more likely to find that finance reforms increased state spending than the reverse. For example, Downes and Shah (1995) document that the stringency of constraints on local discretion determines the effects of reforms on the level and growth of spending, and they used their results to estimate the effect of legislative and court-ordered reforms in California and Arkansas. They conclude that court-ordered reform in California reduced spending in real terms in 1990 by $640. In contrast, in Arkansas they concluded that court-ordered reform increased spending by about $40 above what they otherwise would have predicted.

Manwaring and Sheffrin (1997) examined similar issues in a dynamic model of state education spending between 1970 and 1990. In their model, successful litigation raised real per-pupil spending by $26 per year or 0.64 percent of expenditures, and education reform raised per-pupil spending by $106 per year or 2 percent of expenditures (in 1990 dollars). They used their empirical results to estimate the impact of legislative and legal reforms in individual states and find such reforms have raised real per-pupil spending in 14 states and reduced it in only 5 states. They note "our findings suggest that states do have some flexibility in choosing policies that move in the direction of equalizing spending per pupil without leading, inevitably, to an overall decline in per-pupil spending" (1997:123).

Similarly, Murray et al. (1998) concluded that successful state litigation increased state per-pupil primary and secondary education spending by $88 (in

1992 dollars) while decreasing significantly within-state spending inequality. Their results also suggest that the highest-percentage increase in spending would be in the poorest school districts and spending in the wealthiest districts would remain constant. Overall, they found that the state's share of total spending rose as a result of court-ordered reform, with funding for this increase in the poorest districts coming from higher taxes. Contrary to these results, Hoxby (1996b) estimated that the average level of per-pupil spending fell with more effective equalization, as a result of the large disincentives on high-demand school districts that are contained in these plans.

In light of this mixed evidence, the committee itself looked at the patterns of spending over time in all of the states that have had court-ordered reforms. Instead of following the Joondeph approach of picking a selected set of years, the committee examined annual average growth rates of spending in each state relative to the national average for specified numbers of years since the state's court case. We believe this approach better answers the question of how a court case affected spending, say, 5, 10, or 15 years after the court case. The results for all the states experiencing court-ordered reform are shown in Table 8-2. Up to three entries are provided for each state. The first one shows the difference in the average annual growth rate in per-pupil expenditures in that state from the U.S. average five years after the state's court case. The second entry for each state is the difference after 10 years, and the third is the difference after 15 years. The dates cited for the court cases are relatively straightforward except for California, for which we could use the 1971 date of *Serrano I* or the 1976 date of *Serrano II*,

TABLE 8-2 Annual Average Growth Rates (Relative to National Average) in Per-Pupil Expenditures Following Court-Ordered Reform

State and Case Year	Average Annual Growth Rate, 5 Years After Case	Average Annual Growth Rate, 10 Years After Case	Average Annual Growth Rate, 15 Years After Case
California, 1976	−0.0077	−0.0082	−0.0101
New Jersey, 1973	0.004	0.0068	0.0137
Connecticut, 1977	0.0268	0.0312	0.0189
Washington, 1978	0.0031	−0.0136	−0.005
West Virginia, 1979	0.0201	0.0035	0.0125
Wyoming, 1980	0.0276	−0.0101	−0.0103
Arkansas, 1983	0.0001	0.0052	NA
Kentucky, 1989	0.0294	NA	NA
Montana, 1989	−0.0002	NA	NA
Texas, 1989	0.009	NA	NA

NA = Not applicable.

NOTE: Calculations based on data from National Center for Education Statistics, *State Comparisons of Education Statistics: 1969-70 to 1996-97*, Table 39.

which led to the virtual equalization of spending across districts.[9] For the table we have used the 1976 starting date. Had we used the 1971 starting date for the California figures, the first entry for California would have been a positive number. That is, for the five years after the first *Serrano* case, per-pupil spending on schools in California grew faster than the national average.

The table shows that for the 10 states for which data are available five years after the court case, only two (California and Montana) experienced rates of spending growth that were below the U.S average growth rates. For the seven states with reforms early enough for there to be 10 post-reform years, the results are more mixed: spending in three states (California, Washington, and Wyoming) grew more slowly than the U.S. average, and spending in four states (New Jersey, Connecticut, West Virginia, and Arkansas) grew faster. Finally, after 15 years, three states exhibited faster spending and three states slower growth.

In summary, the committee believes that there is sufficient evidence to reject the conclusion that greater equalization of spending across local school districts will necessarily reduce spending on education. While spending in California did indeed fall relative to the spending in the nation (at least after 1976), the case for attributing that to the *Serrano* decision is not compelling. Moreover at least half of all states experiencing court-ordered reform have increased their spending relative to the national average over time. Greater equalization of spending is not incompatible with higher state spending for education.

Impact on the Responsiveness of the Tax Base

An additional consideration regarding a greater state role in education finance is what it will do to the stability of revenues over the economic cycle and to the growth potential for revenues over time as the economy grows. The flexibility of the base matters from a political perspective because it is politically much easier to raise revenue through growth in the tax base than through increases in tax rates. In general, the property tax base is quite stable over the business cycle and its growth over time depends heavily on assessment practices. Sobel and Holcombe (1996) find the personal income tax base to be fairly stable over the course of a business cycle and that, of all the main taxes, it appears to respond the most to growth in state income. This responsiveness is beneficial when a state's economy is growing but could be harmful during periods of slow state economic growth. According to Sobel and Holcombe (1996), the variability and growth of sales tax revenue depend on what items are included in the tax base. Retail sales taxes, including food purchases, vary over the business cycle in a manner similar to the personal income tax, but they vary much more when food

---

[9]*Serrano v. Priest (Serrano I)*, 487 P.2d 1241 (Cal. 1971), and *Serrano v. Priest (Serrano II)*, 557 P.2d 929 (Cal. 1976).

items are exempted. In general, sales tax bases (with or without food) are not as responsive to state income changes as the personal income tax, largely because they exempt spending on most services, which are the fastest growing part of the economy. Thus, in states like California, and more recently Michigan, where the state has become the primary financier of local school districts, local school districts find that their fortunes are tied to revenue sources that are arguably more sensitive to the business cycle than the property tax, and to revenue sources that they do not have control over.

This consideration is not inconsequential in weighing how best to design a financing system that raises revenues fairly but also generates sufficient revenue to foster the goal of facilitating high learning for all students. While a shift to a larger state role is likely to enhance equity, the increased responsiveness of the revenue system to changes in the economy could present serious problems in the event of an economic downturn. The absence of a serious economic downturn in the past 8-9 years provides little basis for prediction, but given that downturns in the economy are inevitable, one should not ignore their potential effects on the education finance system. The lesson from the research is that shifting away from a local property tax to a narrowly defined state sales tax (one with many exemptions including food) would put education revenues in the most jeopardy.

Impact on Cost-Efficiency and Student Outcomes

Independent of the impact on funding levels, would we predict that a larger state role in financing would increase or decrease student outcomes? At least two conceptual arguments can be made that a larger state role will decrease the cost efficiency of the system. Fischel (1996) and Hoxby (1996b) argue that because school quality is capitalized into higher home values, all homeowners (even those without children) are interested in improving their local schools when schools are financed locally. As a visible outcome of schools, test scores serve as a measure of school quality. Local homeowners can hold school administrators accountable for using higher property taxes (which will reduce housing values) effectively to improve local public schools (which will raise housing values) when improvement is measured by higher test scores. With a shift to a greater reliance on state revenue or if local control over spending is otherwise reduced, the incentives for this monitoring by all homeowners are removed and test scores may suffer.[10]

A second argument is that greater state involvement in financing will bring with it greater state control over the mix of inputs to be used by local school districts. For example, states may require districts to have certain class sizes, to

---

[10]We focus here on the cost-efficiency of production rather than the broader concept of overall efficiency discussed in Hoxby (1996b) because of the way we have stated goal 1. While goal 1 could be consistent with the economist's definition of efficiency, it need not be.

hire certain types of teachers, or to have libraries of a certain size. Given our conclusion in Chapter 5 that knowledge about the education production process is imperfect and that the effectiveness of certain inputs may vary with the specific context, such central directives might well keep schools from producing education in a cost-efficient manner.

Working in the other direction, however, is the possibility that the shift to a greater state role in financing could be accompanied by changes in school governance that give the state more authority to hold schools accountable for high achievement standards while giving them more flexibility to manage themselves. Such would be the case, for example, if the shift to greater state financing were part of an overall standards-based reform strategy. In that case, the greater state role (in financing and governance) could well lead to greater student achievement.

In practice, how much control states exert over local schools and the form of that control varies greatly from one state to another. Some states (such as California) control the total amount of spending by imposing spending restraints. A number of recent state education finance reforms have included some type of maximum per-pupil spending level or some type of limit on the growth rate of spending. Alternatively or in addition, state governments impose various regulations such as mandating a particular curriculum that students must complete, setting a minimum number of days and/or hours that students must spend in school, requiring specific treatments for some groups of students, granting teacher certification, imposing work rules for teachers and other school employees, setting standards for the provision of transportation and meals, and influencing or limiting capital investment decisions through controls on borrowing or debt. All of these regulations reduce the autonomy of local schools and, in most cases, influence the financial decisions of the schools. In evaluating the following evidence, it is important to bear in mind that to the extent that a larger state role is associated with more state control, it is difficult to sort out empirically the effects of centralizing finance from centralizing of governance.

Several researchers have investigated the relationship between the state role in financing and student outcomes by including various measures of centralization as explanatory variables in a standard educational production function regression. They typically find that a larger state share reduces student outcomes.

In two regression studies, Peltzman (1993) found that an increase in the state's share of education revenue lowered state SAT scores in the 1970s, but these variables were unrelated in the 1980s. In his examination of the performance of noncollege-bound students, Peltzman (1996) found that an increase in the state expenditure share was associated with a decline in scores on the Air Force Qualification Test. Fuchs and Reklis (1994) found that math scores are higher in states in which the state share in education revenues was lower. Hoxby (1996a) argues that the state revenue share is an inaccurate proxy for state control. For example, even though local governments in California collect property tax revenue, the *Serrano* decision took away local control over how much they spend. Irrespective of that lack of local control, California's state share in 1995 is listed at only 56 percent (Table 2-2). Rather than state share, Hoxby included a measure of the local government's tax price for an additional dollar of education expenditure (where the local tax price in California would be infinite since the spending of local districts is fully constrained). She found that an aggressive power equalization plan (i.e., higher tax price) had undesirable impacts on student outcomes in that it raised the student dropout rate by 3 percent and that a move to fully state-financed schools raised the dropout rate by 8 percent. Husted and Kenny (1998) included a measure of state education spending inequality in their educational production function and conclude that the mean SAT score is higher in those states with greater within-state variation in spending.

A second approach to exploring the relationship between a larger state role and student outcomes is to look at changes in outcomes that follow court-mandated reform. This second approach is more general in that it captures the effects not only of finance reform but also of any accompanying changes in governance. The disadvantage of this approach is that the effects of the finance changes cannot be separated from those of the governance changes. In some cases (for example, Kentucky after its recent court case that declared unconstitutional not only its school finance system but also its governance system), both changes were large. Downes (1992) looked at the California experience following *Serrano* and found that greater equality in spending was not accompanied by greater equality in measured student performance. Using individual-level data from the National Longitudinal Survey of the High School Class of 1972 (NLS-72) and the National Educational Longitudinal Survey (NELS), Downes and Figlio (1997) estimated that court-mandated school finance reforms did not result in significant changes in either the mean level or the distribution of student performance on standardized tests of reading and mathematics. They do find, however, those legislative reforms that are not a result of a court decision lead to higher test scores in general; the estimated effect was particularly large in initially low-spending districts.

In sum, there is no reason to think that a shift to a greater state share of funding (with no change in average funding level) will lead to greater achievement unless it is connected with policy changes designed to encourage that end. If state funding is not connected with such changes, the shift to a greater state share of funding may reduce the productive efficiency of the system, as local school districts may have less incentive to use their resources carefully given that fewer of those resources are coming directly from local taxpayers. The bottom line is that states that shift to more state funding in the name of fairness need to ensure that they do not inadvertently reduce the productivity of their education system in the process. Only with appropriate policy changes can they avoid that outcome.

Considerations Related to Goal 2: Breaking the Nexus

Many of the considerations related to how increasing the state role would affect goal 1 also apply to goal 2: breaking the nexus between family background and student achievement. Here we consider more directly the extent which a larger state role in financing can help ensure both equitable and adequate funding for disadvantaged students, particularly those who are concentrated in districts with limited resources relative to their educational needs.

One of the major justifications for a larger state role in education finance is that the state revenues can be used to offset what otherwise might be undesirable disparities in education spending across school districts. Court-ordered education finance reforms have frequently increased the state financial role and led to a more equitable distribution of spending than would have occurred in the absence of the reform. Assuming that money can make a difference in student achievement, this redistribution of resources to low-spending districts could potentially increase their students' achievement.

Current state aid is often not designed to compensate fully for the differences in the costs of providing education across school districts. This observation suggests that states that increase the role of the state in the financing of education must work hard to ensure that the funds are distributed across school districts in ways that take account as fully as is technically possible any differences in the costs of educating students. Failure to do so will be detrimental to the districts serving disproportionate numbers of difficult-to-educate children and will hinder efforts to reduce the nexus between family background and student achievement.

A second consideration is the political economy of grants-in-aid and its implications for the state's ability to ensure adequate funding for all districts, particularly those that are unable to supplement state funds from local sources. As Courant and Loeb (1997) describe, the extent to which centralization of school finance permits local districts to supplement the state funding has potentially significant implications for the likelihood that the state funding will be adequate for the poor districts. Consider a situation in which local districts are free to supplement the state funds in an unlimited way. One possible outcome is that many high-demand voters in rich districts will try to keep state spending on education relatively low. They do so out of their own self-interest. The higher the level of the state funding is, the greater is the proportion of their tax dollar that goes to pay for the education of children in other districts. Hence, they prefer a lower state amount so that they can direct their taxes to providing services in their own local district. According to Courant and Loeb, whether there is support for a state foundation grant at a level that would truly provide an adequate level of basic education depends on the number of voters in high-demand school districts and their political influence. This problem is alleviated when local supplementation is limited so that voters from high-demand school districts are restricted in their ability to substitute greater local revenue for general state grants.

A more extreme reaction by high-demand families who are restricted by state financing programs designed to equalize spending across districts is to opt out of the public school system altogether and send their children to private schools. As Brunner and Sonstelie (1997) explain, such equalization plans restrict the variation in public school spending across districts and they keep some families from obtaining their preferred level of education through the public sector. The only way for families to achieve their preferred level of education is by choosing a private school. Since these families no longer use the public school system and the statewide financing system eliminates benefits in the form of rising housing values, their support for the public education system is likely to shrink.

The empirical evidence on this question is mixed. Most of the research has focused, once again, on the experience in California after *Serrano*. The raw data suggest that *Serrano* has not led many families to choose private schools. Brunner and Sonstelie (1997) observe that about 9 percent of California schoolchildren were enrolled in private schools in 1973-74, compared with roughly 10 percent in the rest of the country. By 1992-93, private school enrollment had increased to about 10 percent in California and 12 percent in the rest of the country. They conclude that private school enrollment in California basically followed the national trend. Downes and Schoeman (1998), however, come to a different conclusion. They argue that even if the supply of private schools did not increase, *Serrano* could account for nearly half of the actual movement from public to private schools in California over the 1970-80 period.

These considerations highlight the importance of variation in individual demands for education and the fact that families with high demands for education are able to behave in ways that may be beneficial to them but potentially harmful to the goal of raising sufficient revenue to promote higher levels of achievement for all children, and particularly for disadvantaged students. To minimize the negative side-effects of the decisions of high-demand families on the overall level of support for education, states could (1) prohibit or severely limit local districts from supplementing state aid from local taxes (as was done in California) and (2) prohibit families from opting out of the public system in favor of private schools. However, such policies would run counter to some deeply rooted values in American education related to freedom of choice. Hence, the challenge is to design a system that ensures adequate funding for disadvantaged students but does not run roughshod over other values that people hold dear.

SHOULD A GREATER SHARE OF FUNDING FOR EDUCATION COME FROM THE FEDERAL GOVERNMENT?

A larger state role in financing primary and secondary education will only partially address education resource inequities in the United States. A case can also be made for a larger federal role in revenue raising for education, based on either an equity or an adequacy rationale. The two rationales lead to two alternative policy options for the federal government. (A third rationale for a larger federal role is reserved to Chapter 9 and Appendix A, which discuss research and data needs.)

Equity Arguments for a Greater Federal Role

Since enactment of the 1965 Elementary and Secondary Education Act (ESEA), the federal government has played a significant role in funding schooling for specific groups of at-risk students. The case for targeted support for such students rests largely on a redistributive or equity rationale. In such instances, the highest level of government is most appropriate as the source of revenues. In part, the argument for this is simply practical. It is much more feasible for the federal government to play that role than it is for lower-level governments because of the possibility of movement of households among subnational jurisdictions.

For example, consider a large city school district with a large percentage of economically and educationally disadvantaged students. Given that it costs more to provide a given level of education to those than to other students, the city would have to spend significantly more per pupil than other school districts. This condition is likely to lead to higher tax burdens. Those high taxes would provide an economic incentive for middle- and upper-income households as well as businesses to move out of the city (or to choose not to move there in the first place). Consequently, the city school district would become increasingly impoverished and unable to do much redistribution of funds away from wealthier residents to the disadvantaged students. In the extreme, there would be no nonpoor residents in the city to support educational services for the poor. This behavior is likely to occur at the state level as well as the local level, but is much less common at the federal level given that taxpayers would have to move out of the nation to avoid the burden of paying higher taxes to support needy students.

Related to this practical position is the ethical argument that poverty and its associated education characteristics are national problems that deserve national attention. While some districts would be wealthy enough to fund additional programs for disadvantaged students within the district, one can ask whether it is fair to make the people who happen to live in those districts or states bear the financial burden while others have opted out of such payments by moving to areas with low proportions of at-risk students. To the extent that poverty and other measures of educational disadvantage are national problems, the fair way to fund their alleviation is with a national tax, such as the federal income tax, which would spread the financing burden among all U.S. residents in line with their ability to pay, regardless of where they live.

This federal equity rationale is already reflected in categorical programs for specified groups of students, that is, students who need additional educational services in order to achieve to acceptable levels. Largely developed during the second half of this century, these programs often were initiated at the federal level in part because the students involved were not being served sufficiently by states and local school districts. Such programs include Title I, focused on low-achieving students from economically disadvantaged backgrounds; the Individuals with Disabilities Act (IDEA), concentrating on students with physical and mental disabilities; ESEA Title VII, directed at students whose native language is other than English; and several other related programs. Today, these programs for students with special needs permeate education strategies at the school, district, state, and national level, nearly always complemented by additional state and local funding. For most professionals in education today, these federally funded programs are simply a part of the infrastructure.

However, as discussed in Chapter 7, funding of these programs is still problematic. Although the federal government took the lead role in creating these programmatic emphases, it has never funded them at their fully authorized level. For IDEA in particular, this underfunding has created large financial burdens for states and local school districts. Thus one option for the federal government is to assume a larger share of this particular educational burden. Another would be to fund Title I at the full amount authorized by Congress, $24.3 billion annually (Independent Review Panel on the Evaluation of Federal Education Legislation, 1999:12). These additional federal funds could be used to expand school services for students with special needs and would free up state and local funds to expand the overall level of school services to all students.

Adequacy Arguments for a Greater Federal Role

A second argument for a greater funding role for the federal government emerges directly from analyses of funding inequities (Chapter 3). In their examination of 16,000 school districts, Evans et al. (1997) found that while within-state inequality fell slightly between 1982 and 1992, between-state inequality rose sharply. State government policies that are designed to improve intrastate inequality are not likely to improve interstate spending inequality. Only if education finance reform in states that is intended to reduce intrastate variation also raises the state average spending level and if the states pursuing such policies are those with relatively low per-pupil spending levels, would state-specific reform efforts reduce interstate differences. But these conditions are not always satisfied. Serious proposals to correct interstate inequality are most likely to require an increased federal role in financing education.

Thus, this second rationale leads to an alternative policy option for a larger federal role, namely ensuring that all states can adequately fund their schools. The federal government will face the same challenges (described in Chapter 4) in determining an adequate level of per-pupil revenues for a district or school with the typical mix of students. Nevertheless, there are proxy measures that could be used in the meantime. Odden and Busch (1998), for example, suggest the national median level of basic education revenues per pupil. Although whatever measure is used at this point would be imprecise, it would represent an acknowledgement that only an enhanced federal role can address interstate funding inadequacies. Especially in an era when the nationwide education goal is to teach students in *all states* to high standards, the time may have come to consider a new federal role in education on the basis of educational adequacy.

Such an approach would call for a new federal foundation program. An adequacy rationale at the state level leads to a foundation type of school finance structure; the state ensures that each district has an adequate level of education revenues so a district can educate an average student to specified performance standards and then would adjust this foundation amount by a factor that accounts for the higher costs of both students with special educational needs and geographic price differences for the educational inputs purchased. Each district would need to contribute financially to such a foundation base by making a required minimum tax effort. Districts that could not generate an adequate level of resources with the required tax effort would receive state aid to subsidize the difference.

A new federal role could be similar. First, federal policy makers would have to define a federal foundation level of spending that would be adequate for the state or district with the typical student. They would then need to adjust this base level by a factor that accounted for differences in pupil needs as well as in educational input prices across states. The federal government could ensure that each state could generate the foundation level of funding by giving each state federal aid equal to the difference between the foundation level and the revenue that the state would generate based on a minimum tax effort. Provisions would also be needed to ensure that states distributed revenues to districts and schools so that they too had an adequate amount of revenues per pupil. To be sure, considerable analysis would be needed to determine nationwide, cost- and price-adjusted revenue per-pupil amount for each state and district and how the minimum tax effort would be defined. Nonetheless, the basic approach should be clear.

Either of these policy options would require a substantial increase in federal revenues. Because of the existence of large federal surpluses at the current time, these ideas might have arrived at a fortunate time. Nevertheless, the politics for funding such new initiatives can be expected to be contentious.

CONCLUSION

Increasing the fairness with which revenues are raised for education will almost certainly require a greater revenue-raising role for states and the federal government. However, as with any change, there are trade-offs to be considered. The good news from our analysis is that, in some cases, the trade-offs are not so stark as some people have suggested. For example, the concern that increased centralization of financing at the state level will inevitably lead to lower state spending on education, an inference drawn from the California experience, is not supported by the evidence from other states. Nonetheless, some trade-offs remain. Of most importance for harnessing education finance to the broader goals of education policy is the need for policy makers to pay close attention to ensuring that changes in financing mechanisms do not weaken the incentives for districts or schools to be vigilant about the productive efficiency of the system and that intergovenmental aid programs are carefully designed to promote the goal of reducing the nexus between family background and student achievement.

9

Conclusion

Throughout this book, we have emphasized that the challenges of aligning the finance system with broader educational goals are large and that knowledge about how best to proceed is incomplete. Fortunately, as is evident from our discussion in the previous three chapters, good ideas about how finance systems can be better designed are available and are currently being implemented to various degrees in different states and districts. In this chapter we summarize broad conclusions that have emerged from our analysis and argue that experimentation with different approaches must continue and in some cases be expanded. Only systematic and comprehensive testing of a variety of strategies will provide policy makers with the knowledge needed to effectively harness education finance to the goal of improved performance.

BALANCING VALUES

The nation's existing education and education finance systems reflect underlying and hard-to-alter features of American education. These features include the decentralized and complicated federal structure of government in which American education is embedded and the long and revered tradition of local control, as well as certain values that Americans hold dear.

How to take account of those deeply rooted values as one tries to improve the system is a complicated task, given that many of them conflict with one another. For example, most Americans believe in equality of opportunity, but they also believe in the right of parents to choose to spend their money for the benefit of their own children. Most Americans believe that every child has a right to a good education in a publicly funded common school, but they also believe in freedom of mobility in a way that allows affluent Americans to live together in locales able to easily support good schools and that tends to concentrate poverty and disadvantage, often in urban areas. Most Americans believe that all children should be taught to high standards, but they also believe that schools should be local institutions governed by local preferences. None of these commitments is unworthy, and each has a claim for attention. But given these conflicting values, no model of either the finance system or of the education system as a whole could ever be consistent with all of them.

Despite these basic features of the U.S. education system and the competing values within which it is rooted, the committee concludes that the finance system can and should be changed in ways that will align it better with the broad objectives of fairness and school improvement. When making such changes, the challenge is to balance differing values in a thoughtful manner. The following sections highlight our conclusions about the major directions in which the system should be pushed.

FOCUSING ON ADEQUACY

In the committee's view, the emerging concept of funding adequacy, which moves beyond the more traditional concepts of finance equity to focus attention on sufficiency of funding for desired educational outcomes, is a useful step. At the same time, it poses risks. In addition, although adequate funding may be a necessary component of a finance strategy designed to promote goals of higher overall achievement and reducing the nexus between student achievement and family background, it must be combined with other strategies designed to increase achievement.

The concept of adequacy is useful first because it shifts discussion away from inputs to educational outputs and promotes discussion of how much money is needed to achieve selected ends. Thus, when policy makers determine education budgets, attention to adequacy should shift the discussion away from how much revenue is available to the educational outcomes that they are trying to achieve. Second, the adequacy concept could drive the education system to become more productive by focusing attention on the relationship between resources and outcomes. It will encourage policy makers and managers to ask whether existing resources are being used effectively toward the goal of higher achievement. Third, it could potentially drive the system to a more equitable pattern of educational outcomes by focusing attention on the current inadequacies at the bottom end of the resource distribution.

Nonetheless, the adequacy approach is not without challenges and pitfalls. The challenges include defining what is adequate, extending the concept to units smaller than the school district, and balancing adequate funding for education with demands to "adequately" fund other worthy objectives. Pitfalls include the risk that policy makers will overestimate the prospects for finding technical or mechanical answers to the question of how much adequacy costs. In fact, the meaning of educational adequacy will always be to some extent a matter of policy judgment, and the amount of funding required for any given level of educational adequacy cannot be determined with any precision given the absence of a well-defined production function and given the imprecision with which many educational outcomes are measured. At the most fundamental level, major questions remain regarding the meaning of adequacy. Is it a narrow, low standard or a wide, high standard? Does it focus attention on disadvantaged students, or does it contribute to improving achievement for all students? These are not technical questions for which scientific answers can be quickly provided. They require difficult political judgments and may be subject to public resistance.

Policy makers may also fail to recognize that any level of funding that is adequate for schools with a typical mix of students will need to be adjusted to account for the additional costs of educating students from disadvantaged backgrounds. Failure to make such adjustments could be detrimental to the goal of breaking the nexus between family background and student achievement. The problem, however, is that development of such cost indices is still in its infancy. In addition, failure to adjust figures for additional factors, such as geographically related cost-of-living differences, also could be detrimental to disadvantaged students to the extent that they live in cities with above-average costs of living, and hence with above-average employee remuneration related to factors outside the schools' control.

Finally, the definition of funding adequacy could be pegged so low as to trivialize the concept; alternatively, adjustments could be set so high for urban areas that such areas would have no incentive to use resources in a cost-efficient way. Although some researchers have been trying to incorporate differences in the efficiency with which districts operate into their estimates of need-based cost adjustments, much work remains to be done before that research can be used by policy makers.

On balance, however, the committee judges the new focus on adequacy of funding to be desirable and notes that efforts to ensure adequate funding will be necessary regardless of other changes that are made to the finance system.

PROMOTING FAIR SPENDING AND REVENUE RAISING

The new attention to the adequacy of funding does not eliminate concerns about disparities in funding across districts or schools. Indeed, the more successful strategies to make dollars effective in generating student achievement are, the greater will be the achievement consequences of any remaining disparities in cost- and need-adjusted funding levels.

However, reasonable people are likely to disagree about the extent to which efforts should be made to reduce or eliminate such disparities. One view is that disparities are acceptable provided that all districts or schools have access to at least an adequate level of funding (appropriately adjusted for the differential burdens associated with costs of educational inputs or with the mix of students served). To holders of this view, fairness relates only to the bottom end of the distribution of spending. Once the state has ensured that no district or school falls below the floor needed to provide an adequate education, it would not be deemed unfair for some schools or districts to spend more than the minimum. Indeed, enabling school districts to raise revenues in excess of those deemed to be adequate offers some potential benefits. Such behavior may induce greater local engagement with schools, and greater attention by local taxpayers to their performance, than would otherwise occur if the education system came to be viewed as a remote bureaucracy outside the sphere of influence by common citizens. It may also generate resources for education at levels that are more in line with consumer preferences, which vary across districts.

Others, however, may well take issue with the idea that funding levels could ever be adequate for all students if some districts or schools spend significantly more than other districts or schools. Moreover, a potential trade-off exists between the goal of ensuring fairness in spending levels and the deeply held values of consumer sovereignty and local control. One aspect of local control refers to control over the level of spending and the desire of local communities to make their own decisions about how much to spend on education. Here compromises will need to be made between the values of fairness and local control over spending. Another is control over how a given amount of money is spent within the school district. The magnitude of the trade-off between fairness and this second concept of local control depends in part on the extent to which any efforts by the state to ensure funding adequacy include controls over how local governments spend the money.

Further progress toward funding adequacy in spending and fairness in revenue raising will almost surely require an expanded role for states and the federal government. Only a larger state role in revenue raising can ensure that all schools and districts have sufficient funds to provide an adequate level of education, as defined through the state's political process, given the low fiscal capacity relative to educational needs of some school districts. In addition, a larger state role can reduce the potential regressivity arising from property taxation (although a shift to heavy reliance on a regressive state sales tax could offset some or all of such benefit). With respect to sources of local revenue, the property tax fares reasonably well in terms of standard criteria for evaluating taxes, although states have a clear role to play in ensuring that the local property tax is fairly administered.

There are several grounds on which a larger federal role might be justified: on the grounds of overcoming interstate disparities in spending that result from differences in state fiscal capacity; on the grounds of ensuring that all states can provide adequate funding should some national standard of adequacy be defined; or on the grounds that the federal government should take responsibility for providing educational support for poor, disabled, and otherwise disadvantaged students.

MAKING MONEY MATTER MORE

We have reviewed the literature on whether and how money matters. That review makes it clear that additional funding for education will not automatically and necessarily generate greater student achievement and in the past has not, in fact, generally led to higher achievement. Nevertheless, understanding of educational productivity is improving, both research and practice are increasingly informed by more sophisticated hypotheses about how to use resources effectively, and examples can be found of strategically chosen finance changes (sometimes involving reallocated funds, sometimes involving new monies, and frequently linked in a systematic way to other educational changes) that are making a difference.

While there is still much to learn about how to make schools better and how to deploy resources effectively, the committee is convinced that money *can* matter and that the lessons from research and practice make it increasingly possible to make informed school finance choices that make money matter for achieving educational objectives. The committee, as well as society, are less in agreement over the degree of confidence to have in particular strategies. While some are confident regarding which inputs make the best investments (for example, smaller class sizes or higher-quality teachers), others assert that what may be productive in one context may be less so in another. A key productivity challenge for the former group is how to ensure that those specific investments are made. For the latter group, a key challenge is to design incentives—either through administered mechanisms such as accountability or financial bonuses and penalties or through market mechanisms such as school choice or private contracting—to encourage each school to make the types of investments that will be best for it given its particular situation.

One of the greatest challenges is how best to induce a productive use of resources in large urban districts serving disproportionate numbers of disadvantaged students. The productivity problems in these areas differ in some significant ways from those of suburban areas, and there appear to be no easy or simple solutions.

NEW RESEARCH INITIATIVES FOR URBAN AREAS

Despite the nation's almost continuous attention to education reform, which has been especially intense in the last quarter century, much remains to be learned about how to use resources most effectively to foster higher levels of learning for all children. Another National Research Council panel on education research recently pointed out (National Research Council, 1999) that the benefits of reform efforts are not fully realized in part because education research has not been organized, funded, and utilized as well as has research in other important fields of public policy. That report calls for a large-scale and sharply defined program of research, demonstration, and evaluation aimed at a limited set of research questions aimed at strengthening schools and bringing about substantial improvement in student learning.

In the same spirit, this committee notes that the educational challenges facing urban districts and schools serving concentrations of disadvantaged students are particularly severe. Social science research currently provides few definitive answers about how to improve educational outcomes for these children. The failure of past piecemeal reforms to generate clear gains in achievement in these most troubled of U.S. schools highlights the urgency of more systematic experimentation with and evaluation of urban school reform. In part, this means more extensive evaluation of reform efforts currently under way, such as changes that link financing with performance standards and the expanding experience with charter schools. In addition, this means deliberate creation and evaluation of education experiments (both quasi-experiments and true experiments with random assignment of subjects to treatment and control groups[1]) that genuinely challenge business as usual in schools and districts with large numbers of low-performing students.

Since the benefits of experimentation and evaluation extend beyond any one district or state, the federal government is the most logical entity to finance some of this inquiry. It makes little sense for individual states or local school districts to invest in this research, the results of which benefit an entire nation. Thus, it is to the federal government that we look to mobilize the effort and generate sufficient resources to conduct such research to a high standard. This will require a significantly greater investment than the nation traditionally makes in education research, which is significantly underfunded compared with research in other areas of public policy and compared with what companies expect to invest in researching and developing their products (Consortium on Productivity in the Schools, 1995; Independent Review Panel on the Evaluation of Federal Educa-

---

[1]Researchers testing new programs in demonstration projects to find out what works employ both experimental and quasi-experimental methods. In true experiments, research subjects are randomly assigned to either a treatment group or to an untreated ("control") group. True experiments with random assignment are often thought to be the best approach to demonstration research in the field of public policy because random assignment controls for differences among treated and untreated groups that may be impossible to capture in other ways. Nevertheless, true experiments are not always possible or desirable. They are comparatively costly, for example, and there may be ethical or political constraints that preclude denying some individuals access to the treatment group. Therefore researchers also conduct quasi-experiments that rely on comparison groups (e.g., groups similar to treatment group but located in different sites) or statistical techniques that are applied to available datasets about people similar to those in the treatment group in order to assess the impact of the program design being tested (Nathan, 1988).

tion Legislation, 1999; National Research Council, 1999; President's Committee of Advisors on Science and Technology, 1997).

In setting priorities among major new experimental projects, the committee was faced with a basic difference in philosophical approach: between those who would focus reform efforts largely within the existing public school system and those who believe that reform requires a more dramatic break with traditional finance strategies, through something like publicly funded educational vouchers that could be used at either public or private schools.

Some committee members consider that the highest priority (especially for federally funded research) should be evaluating new approaches to building capacity in public schools and creating incentives for improved performance working within or on the edges of the existing system of school governance. This research effort might involve evaluating innovations that are already occurring or the initiation of quasi-experimental research projects to test ideas that do not occur naturally, or both.

Some committee members consider that the highest priority should be on testing a major alternative (i.e., vouchers) to the existing system of public education, especially in urban areas. To them, both the theory supporting vouchers and the limited evidence currently available about their effects warrant a major federally funded experiment on vouchers. Only with a large and ambitious experiment (employing a random-assignment research design) on the scale of those that have been conducted in housing and welfare policy would it be possible to give vouchers a true test. Moreover, given the large number of recent public proposals by elected officials for more use of vouchers and parental choice, they judge that an experiment of this type should be high on the priority list for major new research efforts. While acknowledging the potential value of such an experiment, other committee members object to the use of public funds for this purpose.

Underlying support for a voucher experiment is the view that improving education for at-risk children in cities with chronically poor schools requires dramatic change in school finance policies and the recognition that only a large-scale, random-assignment experiment can adequately address the many controversies that have surrounded the voucher idea since Milton Friedman (1962) popularized it nearly 40 years ago. The results of the small-scale efforts currently under way are often difficult to interpret, have been the subject of heated disagreements, and shed little or no light on how a large voucher program would affect the traditional public schools. These limitations arise because of the difficulties researchers have controlling for unmeasured differences among students, families, and schools and because none of the current experiments is large enough to have significant feedback effects on the regular public schools. According to this view, definitive lessons require a large-scale effort carried out with a strong research design and carefully controlled experimental conditions.

In summary, the committee proposes several new education experiments, without specifying the priority among them.

Research Project on Building Professional Capacity

A research project focused on building professional capacity would explore effects on student achievement of basic changes in conditions of professional learning and work. It would address the two-prong problem that many urban districts face in achieving high quality of teaching and learning: the inability to attract and retain an adequate supply of well-prepared educators and administrators and insufficient resources to provide the kind of intensive and on-site professional development needed to support significant improvements in practice. The project would seek to document the educational effects of an investment in professional capacity that is comparable in magnitude to that routinely made in American industry, on the order of 10 percent of operating budgets. It would be designed around current knowledge of effective approaches to developing professional capacity and would be evaluated as a system of coherent, interdependent strategies pursued by key stakeholders in public education.

The proposed project is grounded in evidence reported in Chapter 5 that large urban school systems face a constant challenge in recruiting and retaining teachers well qualified to teach in the content areas. Given the limited supply of well-prepared teachers seeking employment in such systems, the experiment would include incentives to attract well-prepared teachers to districts and schools serving the poorest and least academically successful students and investments in sustained professional development for individuals who teach in these settings. A capacity-building approach assumes that the supply problem will not be addressed by increased competition among urban schools for high-quality teachers and administrators, but needs to be addressed directly through economic incentives to attract teachers to these systems and through intensive preparation and support of teachers making their careers in these systems.

The project also is grounded in evidence from research on teacher learning cited in Chapter 6 and from successful teaching reforms like that of New York's District 2 (Elmore and Burney, 1997, 1998) that call for significantly greater and better investment in professional development at all levels of local school systems. The design for a capacity-building experiment would meet several criteria gleaned from this research: some relate to system conditions for implementing the strategy; other criteria relate to strategies for developing professional capacity. Necessary system conditions include: established state or district standards for student learning, student assessments aligned with the standards, adequate school safety and supports for students and families, teacher union collaboration in designing and supporting system strategies to enhance professional capacity, and the school board's commitment to a long-term project. The project should take place under conditions that fully reflect (and therefore test the possibilities for changing) the constraints that urban districts face, such as the rigidities in union contracts that restrict the options of school principals and district administrators to deal with teachers whose performance is regarded as poor.

Professional development strategies would build on several key design principles, such as: learning for teaching is focused on standards for student learning, beginning teacher education includes intensive support and mentoring during the first years of teaching, learning is built into the daily work of school professionals through inquiry and collaboration, administrators are partners in school learning communities and in communities examining administrative practice, and schools have authority to act on their learning of effective practice for the students they serve. The core of this strategy is establishing conditions of teachers' work that engender ongoing learning around shared responsibility and practice.

The capacity-building research project will need to address local political and cultural challenges, as well as financial demands, entailed in radically reframing the work of school professionals. Where is the locus of responsibility and authority to design structures for learning in daily professional work? What structures should be established at the system level and what should be tailored to the school? For example, is it desirable to follow models from abroad and expand teachers' work beyond the typical U.S. school day and year, with higher salaries; or to create incentive systems for individuals or schools to invest in professional development on- and off-site; or to mix and match such centralized and decentralized approaches? A bold federal experiment for reorganizing conditions of the profession will have the unique potential to minimize local politics and maximize wisdom in order to seriously test the capacity-building theory of improving the quality and equity of American education.

The key challenge for a capacity-building strategy is ensuring sufficient coherence in the vision, leadership, and incentives around professional learning to test this theory of educational reform. The potential is established by the progress that some states and districts have thus far made on standards-based, systemic reform. The missing piece of this broader reform strategy is establishing conditions for the kind of ongoing and collaborative learning among teachers and administrators that can sustain improved practice around shared standards for student learning. The time is ripe to test the theory through a federal investment in supporting and evaluating a sustained best-case effort to implement the new paradigm for developing professional quality. This experiment risks criticism that a selected state and district that meet the criteria of sufficient standards-based reform to warrant the investment will be privileged in funding for work under way. The capacity-building design therefore must be sufficiently bold and counter-normative to provide both a strong test of the theory and exception from such criticism of more money for business as usual. The district site of the experiment would be testing uncharted terrain in American education reform and would provide information to the nation on the value of continuing a course of systemic reform.

Evaluation of the experiment would focus on all facets of implementing the capacity-building design. Of particular interest will be gaining a better understanding of the balance of incentives that engender professionals' engagement in learning opportunities created by the experiment. Is increased emphasis on teachers' collective responsibility for student success and opportunities for their collective learning sufficient to motivate and sustain teachers' professional commitment and learning? How do individual incentives and systems, such as certification by the National Board for Professional Teaching Standards fit into the strategy for building local capacity? The ultimate purpose of the evaluation is to determine the impact of the project and its component parts on the learning outcomes of students. To isolate those outcomes, careful attention will have to be paid to the identification of appropriate comparison districts.

Incentives

There is also room for a great deal more systematic experimentation with incentives to motivate higher performance by teachers and schools. Economic theory based on free market principles suggests that incentives are an underutilized tool in education, but currently little is known about how best to apply these principles to schools, teachers, and students. Because people in organizations respond to rewards and sanctions, it is especially important that care be taken in designing such systems; establishing an incorrect or overly simple goal could result in distorted behavior or performance that proves to be counterproductive. Nevertheless, more attention needs to be paid than in the past to performance incentives in America's current education system.

This situation is beginning to change. Noneconomic incentives such as new and more rigorous graduation requirements are being implemented around the country. Financial rewards and sanctions for schools are also becoming more widespread (see Chapter 6). More systematic research is needed on these naturally occurring incentives.

Of particular interest would be a major investigation of various forms of pay systems that reward teachers for their knowledge and skills rather than simply for years of experience and graduate courses. Such an approach has significant conceptual appeal as a way to make money matter more for student achievement, but a large number of questions remain to be answered. Before such pay systems are introduced on a large scale, it would be desirable to learn more about their effectiveness in encouraging teachers to obtain the skills they need to increase student learning. Moreover, to the extent that the results of such research are positive, they could play an important role in making such an approach to teacher pay more palatable to teachers' unions than such changes might otherwise be.

Similarly, systematic research regarding the effects of performance accountability and the pressures of standards-based education reform on teacher recruitment, retention, and turnover would be beneficial. Anecdotal information suggests that such programs are increasing turnover and may be making schools that are identified as low performing less attractive to teachers. Thus, it would be desirable to determine how such programs affect the types of teachers who are attracted to and remain in an education system.

Research Project on School Vouchers

In contrast to the previous research investments, a voucher experiment is specifically intended to explore a major change in the system of education governance. A large-scale project employing a random-assignment research design can be justified in part based on the success of similar projects in other fields in answering important questions about major social programs. Housing, welfare, and medical policies have frequently been the subject of this kind of experimental research. Education has not, although the Tennessee STAR class-size experiment (see Chapter 5) represents a notable exception.

The purpose of a major experiment with school vouchers would be to determine whether a carefully crafted voucher program can bring about broad-based improvement in educational outcomes, especially for children in areas of concentrated disadvantage, without either significantly increasing costs relative to the current system or significantly worsening stratification by race and income.

The selection of schools and school districts is crucial for the experiment envisioned here. Many public schools serve their students well. Many suburban schools, for example, provide an excellent education to middle- and upper-income children and many urban schools succeed in very difficult environments. But some low-income and minority children, many of whom are concentrated in large urban school districts, are poorly served. Thus it would seem to make sense to focus the choice experiment on large urban districts. Middle-class families currently have many choices; they can choose to live in neighborhoods and school districts that offer their children the best possible education, and they can choose to send their children to private schools. Public schools in the suburbs face stiff competition from surrounding districts. The purpose of the experiment would be to explore the extent to which expanding choice, including the choice of private schools, in urban districts would have significant benefits to the children who otherwise would attend public schools in those districts.

The scale of such an experiment is crucially important. Choice advocates often argue that all children would gain if choice were expanded to private schools. Those students who attend private schools would be better off because private schools are more effective than public schools and those who remain in the public schools will be better off because the public sector will respond to increased competition by offering a better education to their students. This hypothesis can be tested only if a choice experiment is sufficiently large for public schools to perceive a growing private sector as effective competition. The experiment might, for example, offer vouchers to a significant fraction of students in several different school districts.

The experiment would need to continue for an extended period. For the experiment to be effective, parents need to know that their children will be able to continue in their new schools, those contemplating opening new private schools must know that the vouchers they depend on will continue, parents will need time to evaluate the new options available to their children, public schools must have the opportunity to respond to this change in their environment, and private schools must have time to learn from their inevitable mistakes at the outset of the experiment. A 10-year time frame seems sensible. Since we would not expect all efforts to extend choice to be suspended pending the outcome of this experiment, states or individual school districts moving forward with choice on their own could benefit from examining both the design of the experiment and any early findings from it.

Central to the experimental design should be features designed to ensure that low-income families will have an expanded set of schools from which to choose. This goal could be achieved in a number of different ways, and it might make sense to design the experiment so that the relative merits of these alternatives could be evaluated. These alternatives include scaling the size of the voucher to income so that the poorest families would face small, possibly zero, out-of-pocket costs to send their children to private schools. Alternatively, participating schools could be forced to set aside a fraction of the slots in their school for children from low-income families before they can cash vouchers from any children. In some circumstances, it might be essential to provide children from poor families with subsidized transportation. While the experiment could be structured in a number of sensible ways, to the extent possible it should avoid subsidizing upper-income families who would have sent their children to private schools even without a voucher program. At-risk children, including children in special education, should be given larger vouchers so that they can also effectively participate in the experiment.

Some difficult issues emerge related to admissions policy and tuition. If choice is to be effective, private schools should be given a great deal of flexibility; it would make no sense to initiate a large-scale choice experiment and then place such a broad range of constraints on private schools that they will, as a consequence, fail. This principle suggests that private schools be given flexibility, for example, in designing their curriculum and in hiring and promoting teachers. This principle also suggests that private schools should be given a good deal of freedom in setting admissions policy and tuition. But the dangers here are obvious. If they can pick and choose students, the advantages of a randomized experiment are reduced, and if they can set tuition so high that low-income children cannot afford to attend, the experiment will not reach the children who now are often poorly served by the public schools. It might be possible to mitigate some of these problems with means-tested vouchers. Nonetheless, these tough issues will require a great deal of careful thought.

With respect to accountability, at a minimum it would seem sensible to require schools receiving vouchers to provide information to the public on curriculum, admissions policies, staff, and student test scores. Schools that receive vouchers also should be required to have their students take specified standardized tests as part of the evaluation of the experiment. It would also make sense, however, to be somewhat cautious about establishing these accountability measures. The problem here again is one of providing sufficient flexibility to private schools. If private schools were required to meet a very long and detailed list of mandates, they would lose much of their freedom and the result of the experiment would be preordained.

The design will also need to specify which types of schools will be allowed to receive vouchers. Religious schools are an obvious issue. A recent court decision allowed religious schools in Milwaukee to participate in that city's choice experiment, but clearly this question raises some difficult issues in the separation of church and state. It might make good sense to allow students to use their vouchers to attend public schools outside their district.

Evaluation should be built into any such experiment from the start. It should focus largely on academic outcomes, but should look at other outcomes, such as school safety, as well. For a number of reasons, that evaluation will be far from straightforward. Suppose vouchers are offered to some of the children in a school district, with the intent of comparing the education outcomes of those who receive vouchers with those who do not. But now suppose that the public schools respond to expanded choice by offering their students a better education. In this case we might find that the control and experimental group have the same outcomes, but clearly it would be wrong to conclude that the choice experiment had been a failure. Suppose further that vouchers were offered randomly, but only to children whose parents agreed to participate in the experiment. This design would provide information about the children from families in which the parents care enough about their children to learn about the choice experiment and would be willing to have them be a part of the experiment, but very little about the rest of the students in the district. These evaluation challenges mean that setting up such a project will require significant planning by a team of experts in the field of research design.

References

CHAPTER 1

Blank, R.M.
   1997   *It Takes a Nation: A New Agenda for Fighting Poverty.* New York: Russell Sage Foundation.
Clark, K.B.
   1973   Critical issues in minority education: A policy program for the future. Pp. 121-134 in *When the Marching Stopped.* New York: National Urban League.
Coleman, J.S., E.Q. Campbell, C.J. Hobson, J. McPartland, A.M. Mead, F.D. Weinfeld, and R.L. York
   1966   *Equality of Educational Opportunity.* Washington, DC: U.S. Department of Health, Education, and Welfare.
Council of Economic Advisers
   1998   *Changing America: Indicators of Social and Economic Well-Being by Race and Hispanic Origin.* Prepared by the Council of Economic Advisers for the President's Initiative on Race. Washington, DC: U.S. Government Printing Office.
Cremin, L.A.
   1989   *Popular Education and Its Discontents.* New York: Harper and Row.
Elmore, R.F., and M.W. McLaughlin
   1988   *Steady Work: Policy, Practice, and the Reform of American Education.* Prepared for the National Institute of Education. Santa Monica, CA: RAND.
Jargowsky, P.A.
   1997   *Poverty and Place: Ghettos, Barrios, and the American City.* New York: Russell Sage Foundation.
Jencks, C., and M. Phillips, eds.
   1998   *The Black-White Test Score Gap.* Washington, DC: Brookings Institution Press.
Jencks, C., M. Smith, H. Acland, M.J. Bane, D. Cohen, H. Gintis, B. Heynes, and S. Michelson
   1972   *Inequality: A Reassessment of the Effect of Family and Schooling in America.* New York: Harper and Row.

Levin, H.M.
   1976   Education, life chances, and the courts: The role of social science evidence. Pp. 117-147
          in *Indeterminacy in Education,* J.E. McDermott, ed. Berkeley, CA: McCutchan Publish-
          ing.
Massey, D.
   1998   Residential Segregation and Neighborhood Conditions in U.S. Metropolitan Areas. Un-
          published paper presented at the National Research Council's Conference on Racial
          Trends, October 15-16, 1998.
Miller, L.S.
   1995   *An American Imperative: Accelerating Minority Educational Advancement.* New Haven,
          CT: Yale University Press.
Murnane, R.J., J.B. Willett, and F. Levy
   1995   The growing importance of cognitive skills in wage determination. *Review of Economics
          and Statistics* 77(2):251-266.
Ogbu, J.U.
   1978   *Minority Education and Caste: The American System in Cross-Cultural Perspective.*
          New York: Academic Press.
   1982   Cultural discontinuities and schooling. *Anthropology and Education Quarterly* 13(Win-
          ter):290-307.
Tyack, D., and L. Cuban
   1995   *Tinkering Toward Utopia: A Century of Public School Reform.* Cambridge, MA:
          Harvard University Press.
Wise, A.E.
   1976   Foreword. Pp. ix-xv in *Indeterminacy in Education,* J.E. McDermott, ed. Berkeley, CA:
          McCutchan Publishing.
Yergin, D., and J. Stanislaw
   1998   *The Commanding Heights: The Battle Between Government and the Marketplace that is
          Remaking the Modern World.* New York: Simon and Schuster.

CHAPTER 2

Advisory Commission on Intergovernmental Relations
   1995a *Significant Features of Fiscal Federalism, Volume 1: Budget Processes and Tax Sys-
          tems.* M-197. Washington, DC: Advisory Commission on Intergovernmental Relations.
   1995b *Tax and Expenditure Limits on Local Governments.* M-194. Washington, DC: Advisory
          Commission on Intergovernmental Relations.
Baumol, W.J.
   1993   Social Wants and Dismal Science: The Curious Case of the Climbing Costs of Health and
          Teaching. Unpublished working paper RR# 93-20, May 1993. C.V. Starr Center for
          Applied Economics. Faculty of Arts and Science, Department of Economics, New York
          University.
Berliner, D.C., and B.J. Biddle
   1996   Making molehills out of molehills: Reply to Lawrence Stedman's review of "The Manu-
          factured Crisis." *Education Policy Analysis Archives* 4(3). [Online]. Available: http://
          olam.ed.asu/epaa/ [September 16, 1998].
Blake, J.
   1989   *Family Size and Achievement.* Berkeley: University of California Press.
Blank, R.M.
   1997   *It Takes a Nation: A New Agenda for Fighting Poverty.* New York: Russell Sage
          Foundation.

Bureau of the Census
   1992   *Households, Families, and Children: A 30-Year Perspective.* Current Population Re-
           ports, P23-181. Washington, DC: Bureau of the Census, U.S. Department of Commerce.
   1995a *Public Elementary-Secondary Education Finances: 1994-95, Statistical Tables.* [Online].
           Available: http://www.census.gov/govs/school/95tables.pdf.
   1995b *State and Local Government Finance Estimates.* [Online]. Available: http://
           www.census.gov/govs/www/esti95.html.
   1997   *State Government Finances, 1997.* [Online]. Available: http://www.census.gov/govs/
           state.
   1998   *Statistical Abstract of the United States: 1998.* 118th edition. Washington, DC: Bureau
           of the Census, U.S. Department of Commerce.
Campbell, J.R., K.E. Voelkl, and P.L. Donahue
   1997   *NAEP 1996 Trends in Academic Progress.* Prepared by the Educational Testing Service
           under a cooperative agreement with the National Center for Education Statistics. NCES
           97-985. Washington, DC: U.S. Department of Education.
Chaikind, S., L.C. Danielson, and M.L. Brauen
   1993   What do we know about the costs of special education? A selected review. *Journal of
           Special Education* 26(4):344-370.
Chambers, J.G.
   1995   *Public School Teacher Cost Differences Across the United States.* NCES 95-758. Avail-
           able from U.S. Government Printing Office. Washington, DC: National Center for
           Education Statistics, U.S. Department of Education.
Coleman, J.S., E.Q. Campbell, C.J. Hobson, J. McPartland, A.M. Mead, F.D. Weinfeld, and R.L.
York
   1966   *Equality of Educational Opportunity.* Washington, DC: U.S. Department of Health,
           Education, and Welfare.
Consortium on Productivity in the Schools
   1995   *Using What We Have To Get the Schools We Need: A Productivity Focus for American
           Education.* New York: Institute on Education and the Economy, Teachers College,
           Columbia University.
Education Week
   1998   *Quality Counts '98: The Urban Challenge.* Prepared in collaboration with the Pew
           Charitable Trusts. *Education Week, Special Issue* 27(17).
Ellen, I.G.
   1999   Spatial stratification within U.S. metropolitan areas: A brief summary and analysis. Pp.
           192-212 in *Governance and Opportunity in Metropolitan America.* Committee on Im-
           proving the Future of U.S. Cities Through Improved Metropolitan Area Governance. A.
           Altshuler, W. Morrill, H. Wolman, and F. Mitchell, eds. Commission on Behavioral and
           Social Sciences and Education, National Research Council. Washington, DC: National
           Academy Press.
Elmore, R.F., and M.W. McLaughlin
   1988   *Steady Work: Policy, Practice, and the Reform of American Education.* Prepared for the
           National Institute of Education. Santa Monica, CA: RAND.
Finn, C.E.
   1991   *We Must Take Charge: Our Schools and Our Future.* New York: Free Press.
Gold, S.D., D.M. Smith, and S.B. Lawton, eds.
   1995   *Public School Finance Programs of the United States and Canada, 1993-94, Volume
           One.* Albany, NY: American Education Finance Association and the Nelson A.
           Rockefeller Institute of Government.
Grissmer, D.W., S.N. Kirby, M. Berends, and S. Williamson
   1994   *Student Achievement and the Changing American Family.* Santa Monica, CA: RAND.

Guthrie, J.W.
  1998   Reinventing education finance: Alternatives for allocating resources to individual schools. Pp. 85-107 in *Selected Papers in School Finance, 1996,* W.J. Fowler, Jr., ed. NCES 98-1217. Washington, DC: National Center for Education Statistics, U.S. Department of Education.
Hanushek, E.A., and Associates
  1994   *Making Schools Work: Improving Performance and Controlling Costs.* Washington, DC: Brookings Institution Press.
Hanushek, E.A., and S.G. Rivkin
  1996   *Understanding the 20th Century Growth in U.S. School Spending.* NBER Working Paper Series, Working Paper 5547. Cambridge, MA: National Bureau of Economic Research.
Heyns, B., and S. Catsambis
  1986   Mother's employment and children's achievement: A critique. *Sociology of Education* 59(3):140-151.
Howell, P.L., and B.B. Miller
  1997   Sources of funding for schools. *The Future of Children: Financing Schools* 7(3):39-50.
Itzkoff, S.W.
  1994   *The Decline of Intelligence in America: A Strategy for National Renewal.* Westport, CT: Praeger.
Jargowsky, P.A.
  1997   *Poverty and Place: Ghettos, Barrios, and the American City.* New York: Russell Sage Foundation.
Jencks, C., and M. Phillips, eds.
  1998   *The Black-White Test Score Gap.* Washington, DC: Brookings Institution Press.
Ladd, H.F., ed.
  1996   *Holding Schools Accountable: Performance-Based Reform in Education.* Washington, DC: Brookings Institution Press.
Lankford, H., and J. Wyckoff
  1995   Where has the money gone? An analysis of school district spending in New York. *Educational Evaluation and Policy Analysis* 17(2):195-218.
McMurrer, D.P., and I.V. Sawhill
  1998   *Getting Ahead: Economic and Social Mobility in America.* Washington, DC: Urban Institute Press.
Milne, A.M., D.E. Myers, A.S. Rosenthal, and A. Ginsburg
  1986   Single parents, working mothers, and the educational achievement of school children. *Sociology of Education* 59(3):125-139.
Murnane, R.J., and F. Levy
  1996   *Teaching the New Basic Skills: Principles for Educating Children to Thrive in a Changing Economy.* New York: Free Press.
Murnane, R.J., J.B. Willett, and F. Levy
  1995   The growing importance of cognitive skills in wage determination. *Review of Economics and Statistics* 77(2):251-266.
National Association of State Budget Officers
  1998   *1997 State Expenditure Report.* [Online]. Available: http://www.nasbo.org. [February 10, 1999]. Washington, DC: National Association of State Budget Officers.
National Center for Education Statistics
  1996   *Pursuing Excellence: A Study of U.S. Eighth-Grade Mathematics and Science Teaching, Learning, Curriculum, and Achievement in International Context.* NCES 97-198. Washington, DC: U.S. Department of Education.

1997   *Pursuing Excellence: A Study of U.S. Fourth-Grade Mathematics and Science Achievement in International Context.* NCES 97-255. Washington, DC: U.S. Department of Education.

1998   *Pursuing Excellence: A Study of Twelfth-Grade Mathematics and Science Achievement in International Context.* NCES 98-049. Washington, DC: U.S. Department of Education.

National Commission on Excellence in Education

1983   *A Nation at Risk: The Imperative for Educational Reform.* [Online]. Available: http://www.ed.gov/pubs/NatAtRisk/index.html. [February 18, 1998]. Washington, DC: U.S. Department of Education.

National Research Council

1999a   *Governance and Opportunity in Metropolitan America.* Committee on Improving the Future of U.S. Cities Through Improved Metropolitan Area Goverance. A. Altshuler, W. Morrill, H. Wolman, and F. Mitchell, eds. Commission on Behavioral and Social Sciences and Education, National Research Council. Washington, DC: National Academy Press.

1999b   *Grading the Nation's Report Card: Evaluating NAEP and Transforming the Assessment of Educational Progress.* Committee on the Evaluation of National and State Assessments of Educational Progress. J.W. Pellegrino, L.R. Jones, and K.J. Mitchell, eds. Commission on Behavioral and Social Sciences and Education, National Research Council. Washington, DC: National Academy Press.

Nelson, F. H., and K. Schneider

1997   *Survey and Analysis of Salary Trends, 1997.* Washington, DC: American Federation of Teachers.

Office of Management and Budget

1999   *Budget of the United States Government, FY 1999: Analytical Perspectives.* Washington, DC: U.S. Government Printing Office.

Orfield, M., S. Schley, D. Glass, and S. Reardon

1993   *The Growth of Segregation in American Schools: Changing Patterns of Separation and Poverty Since 1968.* Report of the Harvard Project on School Desegregation to the National School Boards Association. Cambridge, MA: Harvard Project on School Desegregation.

Parrish, T.B.

1996a   *Do Districts Enrolling High Percentages of Minority Students Spend Less?* Issue Brief, IB-2-96. Washington, DC: National Center for Education Statistics, U.S. Department of Education.

1996b   *Do Rich and Poor Districts Spend Alike?* Issue Brief, IB-1-96. Washington, DC: National Center for Education Statistics, U.S. Department of Education.

Parrish, T.B., C. Matsumoto, and W.J. Fowler, Jr.

1995   *Disparities in Public School District Spending: 1989-90.* NCES 95-300R. Washington, DC: National Center for Education Statistics, U.S. Department of Education.

Parrish, T.B., C.S. Hikido, and W.J. Fowler, Jr.

1998   *Inequalities in Public School District Revenues.* NCES 98-210. Washington, DC: National Center for Education Statistics, U.S. Department of Education.

Powell, B., and L. Carr Steelman

1996   Bewitched, bothered, and bewildering: The use and misuse of state SAT and ACT scores. *Harvard Educational Review* 66(1):27-59.

Rothstein, R.

1998   *The Way We Were? The Myths and Realities of America's Student Achievement.* New York: Century Foundation Press.

Rothstein, R., and K.H. Miles
1995   *Where's the Money Gone? Changes in the Level and Composition of Education Spending.* Washington, DC: Economic Policy Institute.

Rubenstein, R.
1998   Resource equity in the Chicago public schools: A school-level approach. *Journal of Education Finance* 23(4):468-489.

Stedman, L.C.
1998   An assessment of the contemporary debate over U.S. achievement. Pp. 53-122 in *Brookings Papers on Education Policy, 1998,* D. Ravitch, ed. Washington, DC: Brookings Institution Press.

Stiefel, L., R. Rubenstein, and R. Berne
1998   Intra-district equity in four large cities: Data, methods, and results. *Journal of Education Finance* 23(4):447-467.

Sykes, C.
1995   *Dumbing Down Our Kids: Why America's Children Feel Good About Themselves But Can't Read, Write, or Add.* New York: St. Martin's Press.

Tyack, D., and L. Cuban
1995   *Tinkering Toward Utopia: A Century of Public School Reform.* Cambridge, MA: Harvard University Press.

U.S. Department of Education
1994   *1994 NAEP Summary Data Tables.* [Online]. Available: http://nces.ed.gov/nations reportcard/ [October 6, 1998]. Washington, DC: U.S. Department of Education.
1996   *1996 NAEP Summary Data Tables.* [Online]. Available: http://nces.ed.gov/nations reportcard/ [October 6, 1998]. Washington, DC: U.S. Department of Education.
1997   *To Assure the Free Appropriate Public Education of All Children with Disabilities, Nineteenth Annual Report to Congress on the Implementation of the Individuals with Disabilities Education Act.* Available from the Superintendent of Documents, U.S. Government Printing Office. Washington, DC: U.S. Department of Education.
1998   *To Assure the Free Appropriate Public Education of All Children with Disabilities, Twentieth Annual Report to Congress on the Implementation of the Individuals with Disabilities Education Act.* Available from the Superintendent of Documents, U.S. Government Printing Office. Washington, DC: U.S. Department of Education.
1999a   *Digest of Education Statistics, 1998.* NCES 1999-036. Washington, DC: National Center for Education Statistics, U.S. Department of Education.
1999b   *Promising Results, Continuing Challenges: The Final Report of the National Assessment of Title I.* Washington, DC: Office of the Under Secretary, Planning and Evaluation Service, U.S. Department of Education.

U.S. Department of Health, Education, and Welfare
1972   *Digest of Education Statistics, 1971.* Washington, DC: National Center for Educational Statistics, Office of Education.

CHAPTER 3

Adams, J.E., Jr.
1997   School finance policy and students' opportunites to learn: Kentucky's experience. *The Future of Children: Financing Schools* 7(3, Fall):79-95.

Alexander, K.
1982   Concepts of equity. Pp. 193-214 in *Financing Education: Overcoming Inefficiency and Inequity,* W.W. McMahon and T.G. Geske, eds. Urbana: University of Illinois Press.

Barro, S.M.
1992   *Cost-of-Education Differentials Across States.* Revised Draft Report. Washington, DC: SMB Economic Research.

Baylis, E.A.
1997   The Oregon model: Education reform by public mandate. *Journal of Law and Education* 26(2):47-100.

Berne, R., and L. Stiefel
1984   *The Measurement of Equity in School Finance: Conceptual, Methodological, and Empirical Dimensions.* Baltimore: Johns Hopkins University Press.
1999   Concepts of school finance equity: 1970 to present. Pp. 7-33 in *Equity and Adequacy in Education Finance: Issues and Perspectives.* Committee on Education Finance. H.F. Ladd, R. Chalk, and J.S. Hansen, eds. Commission on Behavioral and Social Sciences and Education, National Research Council. Washington, DC: National Academy Press.

Bureau of the Census
various *Census of Government School System Finance File (F33).* Machine-readable data
years   files. Washington, DC: Bureau of Census, U.S. Department of Commerce and National Center for Education Statisitcs, U.S. Department of Education.

Card, D., and A.A. Payne
1997   *School Finance Reform, the Distribution of School Spending, and the Distribution of SAT Scores.* Working Paper #387. Princeton, NJ: Princeton University, Industrial Relations Section.

Carr, M.C., and S.H. Fuhrman
1999   The politics of school finance in the 1990s. Pp. 136-174 in *Equity and Adequacy in Education Finance: Issues and Perspectives.* Committee on Education Finance. H.F. Ladd, R. Chalk, and J.S. Hansen, eds. Commission on Behavioral and Social Sciences and Education, National Research Council. Washington, DC: National Academy Press.

Chambers, J.G.
1995   *Public School Teacher Cost Differences Across the United States.* NCES 95-758. Available from U.S. Government Printing Office. Washington, DC: National Center for Education Statistics, U.S. Department of Education.

Coleman, J.S., E.Q. Campbell, C.J. Hobson, J. McPartland, A.M. Mead, F.D. Weinfeld, and R.L. York
1966   *Equality of Educational Opportunity.* Washington, DC: U.S. Department of Health, Education, and Welfare.

Coons, J.E., W.H. Clune, and S.D. Sugarman
1969   Educational opportunity: A workable constitutional test for state financial structures. *California Law Review* 57:305-421.
1970   *Private Wealth and Public Education.* Cambridge, MA: Harvard University Press.

Courant, P.N., and S. Loeb
1997   Centralization of school finance in Michigan. *Journal of Policy Analysis and Management* 16(1):114-136.

Duncombe, W., J. Ruggiero, and J. Yinger
1996   Alternative approaches to measuring the cost of education. Pp. 327-356 in *Holding Schools Accountable: Performance-Based Reform in Education,* H.F. Ladd, ed. Washington, DC: Brookings Institution Press.

Edelstein, F.
1977   Federal and state roles in school desegregation. *Education and Urban Society* 9(3):303-326.

Enrich, P.
1995   Leaving equality behind: New directions in school finance reform. *Vanderbilt Law Review* 48:101-193.

Evans, W.N., S.E. Murray, and R.M. Schwab
1997   Schoolhouses, courthouses, and statehouses after Serrano. *Journal of Policy Analysis and Management* 16(1):10-31.
1999   The impact of court-mandated school finance reform. Pp. 72-98 in *Equity and Adequacy in Education Finance: Issues and Perspectives*. Committee on Education Finance. H.F. Ladd, R. Chalk, and J.S. Hansen, eds. Commission on Behavioral and Social Sciences and Education, National Research Council. Washington, DC: National Academy Press.

Feldstein, M.
1975   Wealth neutrality and local choice in public education. *American Economic Review* 61(1):75-89.

Fischel, W.A.
1998   School Finance Litigation and Property Tax Revolts: How Undermining Local Control Turns Voters Away from Public Education. Unpublished paper prepared for the Lincoln Institute of Land Policy, June 12, 1998.

Franklin, M.
1987   *The Constitutionality of the K-12 Funding System in Illinois*. Normal, IL: Center for the Study of School Finance.

Gold, S.D., D.M. Smith, and S.B. Lawton, eds.
1995   *Public School Finance Programs of the United States and Canada, 1993-94, Volume One*. Albany, NY: American Education Finance Association and the Nelson A. Rockefeller Institute of Government.

Guthrie, J.W.
1997   School finance: Fifty years of expansion. *The Future of Children: Financing Schools* 7(3):24-38.

Guthrie, J.W., W.I. Garms, and L.C. Pierce, eds.
1988   *School Finance and Education Policy: Enhancing Educational Efficiency, Equality, and Choice*. 2nd edition. Boston: Allyn and Bacon.

Heise, M.
1995   State constitutions, school finance litigation, and the "third wave": From equity to adequacy. *Temple Law Review* 68:1151-1176.
1998   Equal educational opportunity, hollow victories and the demise of school finance equity theory: An empirical perspective and alternative explanation. *Georgia Law Review* 32(2):543-631.

Horowitz, H.
1966   Unseparate but unequal: The emerging Fourteenth Amendment issue in public school education. *UCLA Law Review* 13:1147-1172.

Horowitz, H., and D. Neitring
1968   Equal protection aspects of inequalities in public education and public assistance programs from place to place within a state. *UCLA Law Review* 15:787-816.

Hubsch, A.W.
1992   The emerging right to education under state constitutional law. *Temple Law Review* 65(4):1325-1348.

Jencks, C., M. Smith, H. Acland, M.J. Bane, D. Cohen, H. Gintis, B. Heynes, and S. Michelson
1972   *Inequality: A Reassessment of the Effect of Family and Schooling in America*. New York: Harper and Row.

Johns, T.L.
1976   1975 school aid legislation: A look at three states. *Journal of Education Finance* 1(3,Winter):397-406.

Joondeph, B.W.
1995   The good, the bad, and the ugly: An empirical analysis of litigation-prompted school finance reform. *Santa Clara Law Review* 35(3):763-824.

Legislative Analyst, State of California
  1970   Progress Report: Fiscal Review and Analysis of Selected Categorical Aid Education
          Programs in California. Sacramento, CA.
McMahon, W., and S. Chang
  1991   *Geographical Cost-of-Living Differences: Interstate and Intrastate, Update.* MacArthur/
          Spencer Special Series, Number 20. Normal, IL: Center for the Study of Educational
          Finance.
McUsic, M.
  1991   The use of education clauses in school finance reform litigation. *Harvard Journal on
          Legislation* 28(2):307-340.
Minorini, P.A., and S.D. Sugarman
  1999   School finance litigation in the name of educational equity: Its evolution, impact, and
          future. Pp. 34-71 in *Equity and Adequacy in Education Finance: Issues and Perspec-
          tives.* Committee on Education Finance. H.F. Ladd, R. Chalk, and J.S. Hansen, eds.
          Commission on Behavioral and Social Sciences and Education, National Research Coun-
          cil. Washington, DC: National Academy Press.
Monk, D.H.
  1990   *Educational Finance: An Economic Approach.* New York: McGraw-Hill.
Murray, S.E., W.N. Evans, and R.M. Schwab
  1998   Education finance reform and the distribution of education resources. *American Eco-
          nomic Review* 88(4):789-811.
National Commission on Excellence in Education
  1983   *A Nation at Risk: The Imperative for Educational Reform.* [Online]. Available: http://
          www.ed.gov/pubs/NatAtRisk/index.html. [February 18, 1998]. Washington, DC: U.S.
          Department of Education.
Odden, A.
  1982   State and federal pressures for equity and efficiency in education financing. Pp. 312-323
          in *Financing Education: Overcoming Inefficiency and Inequity,* W.W. McMahon and
          T.G. Geske, eds. Urbana: University of Illinois Press.
  1999   *Improving State and School Finance Systems: New Realities Create Need to Re-Engineer
          School Finance Structures.* Philadelphia: Consortium for Policy Research in Education,
          Graduate School of Education, University of Pennsylvania.
Odden, A., and L.O. Picus, eds.
  1992   *School Finance: A Policy Perspective.* Boston: McGraw-Hill.
Poterba, J.M.
  1997   Demographic structure and the political economy of public education. *Journal of Policy
          Analysis and Management* 16(1):48-66.
Putterman, L., J.E. Roemer, and J. Silverstre
  1998   Does egalitarianism have a future? *Journal of Economic Literature* 36(2):861-902.
Reed, D.R.
  1997   Court-ordered school finance equalization: Judicial activism and democratic opposition.
          Pp. 91-120 in *Developments in School Finance, 1996,* W.J. Fowler, Jr., ed. NCES 96-
          535. Washington, DC: National Center for Education Statistics, U.S. Department of
          Education.
Roos, P.D.
  1974   The potential impact of Rodriguez on other school reform litigation. *Law and Contempo-
          rary Problems* 38(3):566-581.
Schwartz, M., and J. Moskowitz
  1998   *Fiscal Equity in the United States: 1984-85.* Washington, DC: Decision Resources
          Corporation.

Sinclair, B., and B. Gutman
  1996   State Chapter 1 Participation and Achievement Information, 1993-94: Summary Report. Washington, DC: Planning and Evaluation Service, U.S. Department of Education.
Sugarman, S.D., and E.G. Widess
  1974   Equal protection for Non-English-Speaking school children: Lau v. Nichols. California Law Review 62(1):157-182.
Tatel, D.
  1992   Desegregation versus school reform: Resolving the conflict. Stanford Law and Policy Review Winter:61-72.
Taylor, W.L., and D. Piche
  1991   Shortchanging Children: The Impact of Fiscal Inequity on the Education of Students at Risk. Serial No. 102-O. Prepared for the Committee on Education and Labor, U.S. House of Representatives, 102nd Congress. Washington, DC: U.S. Government Printing Office.
Thro, W.E.
  1990   The third wave: The impact of the Montana, Kentucky, and Texas decisions on the future of public school finance reform litigation. Journal of Law and Education 19(2):219-250.
  1993   The role of language of the state education clause in school finance litigation. West's Education Law Reporter 79:19-31.
Tyack, D., and L. Cuban
  1995   Tinkering Toward Utopia: A Century of Public School Reform. Cambridge, MA: Harvard University Press.
Underwood, J.K.
  1995   School finance adequacy as vertical equity. University of Michigan Journal of Law Reform 28(3):493-519.
U.S. Department of Education
  1979   Compilation of Studies and Reports Prepared Under Section 842. Projects as reported in state plans filed by January 1, 1979; compiled by Anne E. Just, January 15, 1979. Bureau of Elementary and Secondary Education.
  1994   Digest of Education Statistics, 1994. NCES 94-115. Washington, DC: National Center for Education Statistics, U.S. Department of Education.
  1999   Digest of Education Statistics, 1998. NCES 1999-036. Washington, DC: National Center for Education Statistics, U.S. Department of Education.
U.S. General Accounting Office
  1997   School Finance: State Efforts to Reduce Funding Gaps Between Poor and Wealthy Districts. GAO/HEHS-97-31. Washington, DC: U.S. General Accounting Office.
  1998a   School Finance: State and Federal Efforts to Target Poor Students. GAO/HEHS-98-36. Washington, DC: U.S. General Accounting Office.
  1998b   School Finance: State Efforts to Equalize Funding Between Wealthy and Poor School Districts. GAO/HEHS-98-92. Washington, DC: U.S. General Accounting Office.
Verstegen, D.A.
  1996   Concepts and measures of fiscal inequality: A new approach and effects for five states. Journal of Education Finance 22(2):145-160.
Verstegen, D.A., and T. Whitney
  1995   School Finance Reform Litigation: Emerging Theories of Adequacy and Equity. Unpublished paper. Presented at the American Public Policy and Management Association annual conference in Washington, DC, November 1995.
Williams, R.F.
  1985   Equality guarantees in state constitutions. Texas Law Review 63:1195-1224.

Wise, A.
  1968   *Rich Schools, Poor Schools: The Promise of Equal Educational Opportunity.* Chicago:
          University of Chicago Press.
Wyckoff, J.H.
  1992   The intrastate equality of public elementary and secondary education resources in the
          U.S., 1980-87. *Economics of Education Review* 11(1):19-30.

CHAPTER 4

Adams, J.E., Jr.
  1997   School finance policy and students' opportunities to learn: Kentucky's experience. *The
          Future of Children: Financing Schools* 7(3):79-95.
Augenblick, J.G.
  1997   Recommendations for a Base Figure and Pupil-Weighted Adjustments to the Base Figure
          for Use in a New School Finance System in Ohio. Report presented to the Governor's
          School Funding Task Force, Columbus, Ohio, July 17.
Augenblick, J.G., and J. Myers
  1994   *Determining Base Cost for State School Funding Systems.* Issuegram. Denver, CO:
          Education Commission of the States.
Augenblick, J.G., K. Alexander, and J.W. Guthrie
  1995   Report of the Panel of Experts: Proposals for the Elimination of Wealth Based Dispari-
          ties in Education. Report submitted by Ohio Chief State School Officer Theodore Sand-
          ers to the Ohio State Legislature.
Augenblick, J.G., J.L. Myers, and A. Berk Anderson
  1997   Equity and adequacy in school funding. *The Future of Children: Financing Schools*
          7(3):63-78.
Barker, R.C., and P.V. Gump
  1972   *Big School, Small School: High School Size and Student Behavior.* Stanford, CA:
          Stanford University Press.
Barro, S.M.
  1992   *Cost-of-Education Differentials Across States.* Revised Draft Report. Washington, DC:
          SMB Economic Research.
Berne, R., and L. Stiefel
  1999   Concepts of school finance equity: 1970 to present. Pp. 7-33 in *Equity and Adequacy in
          Education Finance: Issues and Perspectives.* Committee on Education Finance. H.F.
          Ladd, R. Chalk, and J.S. Hansen, eds. Commission on Behavioral and Social Sciences
          and Education, National Research Council. Washington, DC: National Academy Press.
Carr, M.C., and S.H. Fuhrman
  1999   The politics of school finance in the 1990s. Pp. 136-174 in *Equity and Adequacy in
          Education Finance: Issues and Perspectives.* Committee on Education Finance. H.F.
          Ladd, R. Chalk, and J.S. Hansen, eds. Commission on Behavioral and Social Sciences
          and Education, National Research Council. Washington, DC: National Academy Press.
Chambers, J.G.
  1995   *Public School Teacher Cost Differences Across the United States.* NCES 95-758. Avail-
          able from U.S. Government Printing Office. Washington, DC: National Center for
          Education Statistics, U.S. Department of Education.
Chambers, J.G., and T. Parrish
  1994   State level education finance. Pg. 45-74 in *Cost Analysis for Education Decisions: Meth-
          ods and Examples, Advances in Educational Productivity, Volume 4.* H.J. Walberg and
          W.S. Barnett, eds. Greenwich, CT: JAI Press.

Clune, W.H.
   1995   Accelerated education as a remedy for high-poverty schools. *University of Michigan Journal of Law Reform* 28(3):655-680.
Cubberley, E.P.
   1919a   *Public Education in the United States; A Study and Interpretation of American Educational History; An Introductory Textbook Dealing With the Larger Problems of Present-day Education in the Light of Their Historical Development.* New York: Houghton Mifflin.
   1919b   *State and County School Administration.* New York: Macmillan Company.
Downes, T.A., and T.F. Pogue
   1994   Adjusting school aid formulas for the higher cost of educating disadvantaged students. *National Tax Journal* 47(1):89-110.
Duncombe, W., and J. Yinger
   1997   Why is it so hard to help central city schools? *Journal of Policy Analysis and Management* 16(1):85-113.
   1999   Performance standards and educational cost indexes: You can't have one without the other. Pp. 260-297 in *Equity and Adequacy in Education Finance: Issues and Perspectives.* Committee on Education Finance. H.F. Ladd, R. Chalk, and J.S. Hansen, eds. Commission on Behavioral and Social Sciences and Education. National Research Council. Washington, DC: National Academy Press.
Duncombe, W., J. Ruggiero, and J. Yinger
   1996   Alternative approaches to measuring the cost of education. Pp. 327-356 in *Holding Schools Accountable: Performance-Based Reform in Education,* H.F. Ladd, ed. Washington, DC: Brookings Institution Press.
Education Commission of the States
   1997   *Determining the Cost of a Basic or Core Education.* Denver, CO: Education Commission of the States.
Fashola, O.S., and R.E. Slavin
   1998   Schoolwide reform models: What works? *Phi Delta Kappan* 79(5):370-379.
Glennan, T.K., Jr.
   1998   *New American Schools After Six Years.* Prepared for the New American Schools by RAND Education. Santa Monica, CA: RAND.
Gold, S.D., D.M. Smith, and S.B Lawton, eds.
   1995   *Public School Finance Programs of the United States and Canada, 1993-94, Volume One.* Albany, NY: American Education Finance Association and the Nelson A. Rockefeller Institute of Government.
Guthrie, J.W., and R. Rothstein
   1999   Enabling "adequacy" to achieve reality: Translating adequacy into state school finance distribution arrangements. Pp. 209-259 in *Equity and Adequacy in Education Finance: Issues and Perspectives.* Committee on Education Finance. H.F. Ladd, R. Chalk, and J.S. Hansen, eds. Commission on Behavioral and Social Sciences and Education, National Research Council. Washington, DC: National Academy Press.
Guthrie, J.W., G.C. Hayward, J.R. Smith, R. Rothstein, R.W. Bennett, J.E. Koppich, E. Bowman, L. DeLapp, B. Brandes, and S. Clark
   1997   *A Proposed Cost-Based Block Grant Model for Wyoming School Finance.* Report submitted to the Joint Appropriations Committee of the Wyoming Legislature by Management Analysis and Planning Associates, April 1997.
Gutmann, A.
   1987   *Democratic Education.* Princeton, NJ: Princeton University Press.

Haller, E.J., D.H. Monk, and A. Spotted Bear
1990   School size and program comprehensiveness: Evidence from High School and Beyond. *Educational Evaluation and Policy Analysis* 12(2):109-120.

Halstead, D.K.
1983   *Inflation Measures for Schools and Colleges.* Washington, DC: National Institute of Education, Office of Educational Research and Improvement, U.S. Department of Education.

King, J.A.
1994   Meeting the educational needs of at-risk students: A cost analysis of three models. *Educational Evaluation and Policy Analysis* 16(1):1-20.

Ladd, H.F., and J.M. Yinger
1994   The case for equalizing aid. *National Tax Journal* 47(1):211-224.

Lee, V.E., and J.B. Smith
1997   High school size: Which works best and for whom? *Educational Evaluation and Policy Analysis* 19(3):205-227.

Levin, H.M.
1989   Financing the education of at-risk students. *Educational Evaluation and Policy Analysis* 11(1):47-60.

McMahon, W., and S. Chang
1991   *Geographical Cost-of-Living Differences: Interstate and Intrastate, Update.* MacArthur/ Spencer Special Series, Number 20. Normal, IL: Center for the Study of Educational Finance.

Mishel, L., and R. Rothstein
1997   Measurement Issues in Adjusting School Spending Across Time and Place. Paper presented at Annual Data Conference, National Center for Education Statistics, August.

Monk, D.H.
1990   *Educational Finance: An Economic Approach.* New York: McGraw-Hill.

Moore, M.T., E.W. Strang, M. Schwartz, and M. Braddock
1988   *Patterns in Special Education Service Delivery and Cost.* Contract Number 3000-84-0257. Washington, DC: Decision Resources Corporation.

Murnane, R.J., and R.R. Nelson
1984   Production and innovation when techniques are tacit: The case of education. *Journal of Economic Behavior and Organization* 5:353-373.

National Research Council
1997   *Educating One and All: Students with Disabilities and Standards-Based Reform.* Committee on Goals 2000 and the Inclusion of Students with Disabilities. L.M. McDonnell, M.J. McLaughlin, and P. Morison, eds. Commission on Behavioral and Social Sciences and Education, National Research Council. Washington, DC: National Academy Press.

1999a   *Grading the Nation's Report Card: Evaluating NAEP and Transforming the Assessment of Educational Progress.* Committee on the Evaluation of National and State Assessments of Educational Progress. J.W. Pellegrino, L.R. Jones, and K.J. Mitchell, eds. Commission on Behavorial and Social Sciences and Education, National Research Council. Washington, DC: National Academy Press.

1999b   *High Stakes: Testing for Tracking, Promotion, and Graduation.* Committee on Appropriate Test Use. J.P. Heubert and R.M. Hauser, eds. Commission on Behavorial and Social Sciences and Education, National Research Council. Washington, DC: National Academy Press.

Northwest Regional Educational Laboratory, and the Education Commission of the States
1998   *Catalog of School Reform Models: First Edition.* Oak Brook, IL: Northwest Regional Educational Laboratory.

Odden, A.
1997   *How to Rethink School Budgets to Support School Transformation.* Arlington, VA: New American Schools.

Odden, A., and C. Busch
1998   *Financing Schools for High Performance: Strategies for Improving the Use of Educational Resources.* San Francisco: Jossey-Bass.

Odden, A., and L.O. Picus, eds.
1992   *School Finance: A Policy Perspective.* Boston: McGraw-Hill.

Orland, M.
1990   The demographics of disadvantage: Intensity of childhood poverty and its relationship to educational achievement. Pp. 43-58 in *Access to Knowledge: An Agenda for Our Nation's Schools*, J. Goodlad and P. Keating, eds. New York: College Entrance Examination Board.

Parrish, T.B., C. Matsumoto, and W.J. Fowler, Jr.
1995   *Disparities in Public School District Spending: 1989-90.* NCES 95-300R. Washington, DC: National Center for Education Statistics, U.S. Department of Education.

Parrish, T.B., C.S. Hikido, and W.J. Fowler, Jr.
1998   *Inequalities in Public School District Revenues.* NCES 98-210. Washington, DC: National Center for Education Statistics, U.S. Department of Education.

Peternick, L., B.A. Smerdon, W.J. Fowler, Jr., and D.H. Monk
1998   Using cost and need adjustments to improve the measurement of school finance equity. Pp. 149-168 in *Developments in School Finance, 1997,* W.J. Fowler, Jr., ed. NCES 98-212. Washington, DC: National Center for Education Statistics, U.S. Department of Education.

Rawls, J.
1971   *A Theory of Justice.* Cambridge, MA: Harvard University Press.

Reschovsky, A., and J. Imazeki
1998   The development of school finance formulas to guarantee the provision of adequate education to low-income students. Pp. 121-148 in *Developments in School Finance, 1997,* W.J. Fowler, Jr., ed. NCES 98-212. Washington, DC: National Center for Education Statistics, U.S. Department of Education.

Research Associates of Washington
1993   *Inflation Measures for Schools and Colleges, 1993 Update.* Washington, DC: Research Associates of Washington.

Rothstein, R., and L. Mishel
1997   Alternative options for deflating education expenditures over time. Pp. 159-182 in *Developments in School Finance, 1996,* W.J. Fowler, Jr., ed. NCES 97-535. Washington, DC: National Center for Education Statistics, U.S. Department of Education.

Rothstein, R., and J.R. Smith
1997   Adjusting Oregon Education Expenditures for Regional Cost Differences: A Feasibility Study. Report submitted by Management Analysis and Planning Associates to the Confederation of Oregon School Administrators. May 30, 1997.

Strayer, G.D., and R.M. Haig
1923   *Financing of Education in the State of New York.* New York: MacMillan.

Strike, K.A.
1988   The ethics of resource allocation. Pp. 143-180 in *Microlevel School Finance*, D.H. Monk and J. Underwood, eds. Cambridge, MA: Ballinger Publishing.

Stringfield, S., S. Ross, and L. Smith, eds.
1996   *Bold New Plans for School Restructuring: The New American Schools Designs.* Mahwah, NJ: Lawrence Erlbaum Associates.

CHAPTER 5

American Federation of Teachers
  1998   *Making Standards Matter, 1998: An Annual Fifty-State Report on Efforts to Raise Academic Standards.* Washington, DC: American Federation of Teachers.
American Institutes for Research
  1999   *An Educators' Guide to Schoolwide Reform.* Prepared by AIR for the American Association of School Administrators, American Federation of Teachers, National Association of Elementary School Principals, National Association of Secondary School Principals, and National Education Association. [Online]. Available: http://www.ers.org/. [February 18, 1999]. Arlington, VA: Educational Research Service.
Barzelay, M.
  1992   *Breaking Through Bureaucracy: A New Way for Managing in Government.* Berkeley: University of California Press.
Berg, I.E.
  1970   *Education and Jobs: The Great Training Robbery.* New York: Praeger.
Berndt, E.R.
  1991   *The Practice of Econometrics: Classic and Contemporary.* Reading, MA: Addison-Wesley.
Bimber, B.
  1993   *School Decentralization: Lessons from the Study of Bureaucracy.* Santa Monica, CA: RAND.
Bodilly, S.J.
  1998   *Lessons from New American Schools' Scale-Up Phase: Prospects for Bringing Designs to Multiple Schools.* Santa Monica, CA: RAND.
Brandl, J.E.
  1998   Governance and educational quality. Pp. 55-81 in *Learning from School Choice*, P.E. Peterson and B.C. Hassel, eds. Washington, DC: Brookings Institution Press.
Bryk, A.S., and M.E. Driscoll
  1988   *The School as Community: Theoretical Foundations, Contextual Influences, and Consequences for Students and Teachers.* Madison, WI: National Center on Effective Secondary Schools.
Burtless, G., ed.
  1996   *Does Money Matter? The Effect of School Resources on Student Achievement and Adult Success.* Washington, DC: Brookings Institution Press.
Chubb, J.E.
  1998   The performance of privately managed schools: An early look at the Edison Project. Pp. 213-248 in P.E. Peterson and B.C. Hassel, eds., *Learning from School Choice.* Washington, DC: Brookings Institution Press.
Chubb, J.E., and T.M. Moe
  1990   *Politics, Markets, and America's Schools.* Washington, DC: Brookings Institution Press.
Cohen, D.K.
  1995   What is the system in systematic reform? *Educational Researcher* 24(9):11-17, 31.
  1996   Rewarding teachers for student performance. Pp. 60-112 in *Rewards and Reform: Creating Educational Incentives that Work*, S.H. Fuhrman and J. O'Days, eds. San Francisco: Jossey-Bass.
Cohen, D.K., and H.C. Hill
  1998   *Instructional Policy and Classroom Performance: The Mathematics Reform in California.* CPRE Research Report Series, RR-39. Philadelphia: Consortium for Policy Research in Education, Graduate School of Education, University of Pennsylvania.

Coleman, J.S., E.Q. Campbell, C.J. Hobson, J. McPartland, A.M. Mead, F.D. Weinfeld, and R.L.York
    1966   *Equality of Educational Opportunity.* Washington, DC: U.S. Department of Health, Education, and Welfare.
Consortium for Policy Research in Education
    1998   *States and Districts and Comprehensive School Reform.* CPRE Policy Briefs. RB-24 (May). Philadelphia: Consortium for Policy Research in Education.
Darling-Hammond, L.
    1996   Restructuring schools for high performance. Pp. 144-192 in *Rewards and Reform: Creating Educational Incentives That Work,* S.H. Fuhrman and J.A. O'Day, eds. San Francisco: Jossey-Bass.
Darling-Hammond, L., and V.L. Cobb
    1996   The changing context of teacher education. Pp. 14-62 in *The Teacher Educator's Handbook: Building a Knowledge Base for the Preparation of Teachers,* F.B. Murray, ed. San Francisco: Jossey-Bass.
Elmore, R.F.
    1997a *Investing in Teacher Learning: Staff Development and Instructional Improvement in Community School District #2, New York City.* New York: Teachers College, National Commission on Teaching and America's Future.
    1997b The politics of education reform. *Issues in Science and Technology* 14(1, Fall):41-49.
Elmore, R.F., and M.W. McLaughlin
    1988   *Steady Work: Policy, Practice, and the Reform of American Education.* Prepared for the National Institute of Education. Santa Monica, CA: RAND.
Fashola, O.S., and R.E. Slavin
    1997   Promising programs for elementary and middle schools: Evidence of effectiveness and replicability. *Journal of Education For Students Placed at Risk* 2(3):251-307.
Ferguson, R.
    1991   Paying for public education: New evidence on how and why money matters. *Harvard Journal on Legislation* 28(2):465-498.
Ferguson, R.F., and H.F. Ladd
    1996   How and why money matters: An analysis of Alabama schools. Pp. 265-298 in *Holding Schools Accountable: Performance-Based Reform in Education,* H.F. Ladd, ed. Washington, DC: Brookings Institution Press.
Finn, J.D.
    1998   Class Size and Students At-Risk: What is Known? What is Next? Commissioned paper prepared for the National Institute on the Education of At-Risk Students. Washington, DC: Office of Educational Research and Improvement, U.S. Department of Education.
Glennan, T.K., Jr.
    1998   *New American Schools After Six Years.* Prepared for the New American Schools by RAND Education. Santa Monica, CA: RAND.
Goodlad, J.I.
    1984   *A Place Called School: Prospects for the Future.* New York: McGraw Hill.
Grissmer, D., and A. Flanagan
    1998   *Exploring Rapid Achievement Gains in North Carolina and Texas.* Washington, DC: National Education Goals Panel.
Guthrie, J.W.
    1976   Social science, accountability, and the political economy of school productivity. Pp. 253-308 in *Indeterminacy in Education,* J.E. McDermott, ed. Berkeley, CA: McCutchan Publishing.
Guthrie, J.W., W.I. Garms, and L.C. Pierce, eds.
    1988   *School Finance and Education Policy: Enhancing Educational Efficiency, Equality, and Choice.* 2nd edition. Boston: Allyn and Bacon.

Hanushek, E.A.
 1986   The economics of schooling: Production and efficiency in public schools. *Journal of Economic Literature* 24(13):1141-1177.
 1994   Money might matter somewhere: A response to Hedges, Laine, and Greenwald. *Educational Researcher* 23(4):5-8.
 1996   School resources and student performance. Pp. 43-73 in *Does Money Matter? The Effect of School Resources on Student Achievement and Adult Success,* G. Burtless, ed. Washington, DC: Brookings Institution Press.
 1997a Assessing the effects of school resources on student performance: An update. *Educational Evaluation and Policy Analysis* 19(2):141-164.
 1997b Outcomes, incentives, and beliefs: Reflections on analysis of the economics of schools. *Educational Evaluation and Policy Analysis* 19(4):301-308.
 1998   *The Evidence on Class Size.* Occasional paper number 98-1. Rochester, NY: W. Allen Wallis Institute of Political Economy, University of Rochester.
Hanushek, E.A., J.F. Kain, and S.G. Rivkin
 1998   *Teachers, Schools, and Academic Achievement.* NBER Working Paper Series, Working Paper 6691. Cambridge, MA: National Bureau of Economic Research.
 1999   *Do Higher Salaries Buy Better Teachers?* NBER Working Paper Series, Working Paper 7082. Cambridge, MA: National Bureau of Economic Research.
Hedges, L.V., R.D. Laine, and R. Greenwald
 1994a Does money matter? A meta-analysis of studies of the effects of differential school inputs on student outcomes. *Educational Researcher* 23(3):5-14.
 1994b Money might matter somewhere: A reply to Hanushek. *Educational Researcher* 23(4):9-10.
Hertert, L.
 1994   Systemic School Reform in the 1990s: A Local Perspective. Paper presented for The Policy Center, Consortium for Policy Research in Education, Rutgers University.
Hill, P.T., L.C. Pierce, and J.W. Guthrie
 1997   *Reinventing Public Education: How Contracting Can Transform America's Schools.* Chicago: University of Chicago Press.
Katzenbach, J.R., and D.K. Smith
 1993   *The Wisdom of Teams: Creating the High-Performance Organization.* Boston: Harvard Business School Press.
Kentucky Department of Education, Division of School Improvement
 no   *Results Based Practices Showcase, 1997-98.* Frankfort: Kentucky Department of
 date   Education.
Kirst, M.W.
 1995   Who's in charge? Federal, state and local control. Pp. 25-56 in *Learning from the Past: What History Teaches Us About School Reform,* D. Ravitch and M.A. Vinovskis, eds. Baltimore: Johns Hopkins University Press.
Kirst, M.W., D. Tyack, and E. Hansot
 1980   Educational reform: Retrospect and prospect. *Teachers College Record* 81(3):253-269.
Kroesen, K., D. Chin, R. Gallimore, G. Ryan, S. Subramanian, D. Takeuchi, B. Tucker, and T. Weisner
 1998   *Qualitative Tools for Multimethod Research: A Guide to the Literature.* Los Angeles: Division of Social and Community Psychiatry, Neuropsychiatric Institute, UCLA.
Krueger, A.B.
 1997   *Experimental Estimates of Education Production Functions.* Working Paper #379. Princeton, NJ: Princeton University, Industrial Relations Section.

Lawler, E.E., III
   1986   *High-Involvement Management: Participative Strategies for Improving Organizational Performance.* San Francisco: Jossey-Bass.
   1992   *The Ultimate Advantage: Creating the High-Involvement Organization.* San Francisco: Jossey-Bass.
   1996   *From the Ground Up: Six Principles for Building the New Logic Organization.* San Francisco: Jossey-Bass.

Lee, V.E., and J.B. Smith
   1997   High school size: Which works best and for whom? *Educational Evaluation and Policy Analysis* 19(3):205-227.

Levin, H.M.
   1974   Measuring efficiency in educational production. *Public Finance Quarterly* 2(1):3-24.

Malen, B., and R. Ogawa
   1988   Professional-patron influences on site-based governance councils: A confounding case study. *Educational Evaluation and Policy Analysis* 10(3):251-270.

Malen, B., R. Ogawa, and J. Kranz
   1990   What do we know about school-based management? A case study of the literature—a call for research. Pp. 289-342 in *Choice and Control in American Education, Volume 2: The Practice of Decentralization and School Restructuring,* W.H. Clune and J.F. Witte, eds. Bristol, PA: Falmer Press.

March, J.G., and J.P. Olsen
   1989   *Rediscovering Institutions: The Organizational Basis of Politics.* New York: Free Press.

Massell, D.
   1994   Achieving consensus: Setting the agenda for state curriculum reform. Pp. 84-108 in *The Governance of Curriculum,* R.F. Elmore and S.H. Furhman, eds. Washington, DC: Association for Supervision and Curriculum Development.

Massell, D., and S.H. Fuhrman
   1994   *Ten Years of State Education Reform, 1983-1993.* New Brunswick, NJ: Consortium for Policy Research in Education, Rutgers University.

Massell, D., M.W. Kirst, and M. Hoppe
   1997   *Persistence and Change: Standards-Based Reform in Nine States.* Philadelphia: Consortium for Policy Research in Education, University of Pennsylvania.

McDermott, J.E.
   1976   Introduction: Indeterminacy in education. Pp. 1-13 in *Indeterminacy in Education,* J.E. McDermott, ed. Berkeley, CA: McCutchan Publishing.

Meyer, J.W.
   1991   Centralization of funding and control in educational governance. Pp. 179-197 in *Organizational Environments: Ritual and Rationality,* J.W. Meyer and W.R. Scott, eds. Updated edition. Newbury Park, CA: Sage.

Meyer, J.W., and B. Rowan
   1978   The structure of educational organizations. Pp. 78-109 in *Environments and Organizations,* M.W. Meyer and Associates, eds. San Francisco: Jossey-Bass.

Miller, L.S.
   1995   *An American Imperative: Accelerating Minority Educational Advancement.* New Haven, CT: Yale University Press.

Mohrman, S.A.
   1994   High-involvement in the private sector. Pp. 25-52 in *School-Based Management: Organizing for High Performance,* S.A. Mohrman, P. Wohlstetter, and Associates, eds. San Francisco: Jossey-Bass.

Mohrman, S.A., P. Wohlstetter, and Associates, eds.
  1994   *School-Based Management: Organizing for High Performance.* San Francisco: Jossey-Bass.

Monk, D.H.
  1990   *Educational Finance: An Economic Approach.* New York: McGraw-Hill.
  1992   Education productivity research: An update and assessment of its role in education finance reform. *Educational Evaluation and Policy Analysis* 14(4):307-332.

Murnane, R.J., and R.R. Nelson
  1984   Production and innovation when techniques are tacit: The case of education. *Journal of Economic Behavior and Organization* 5:353-373.

Murphy, J., and L. Beck
  1995   Examining evidence from the current reform era. Pp. 131-161 in *School-Based Management As School Reform: Taking Stock.* Thousand Oaks, CA: Corwin Press.

National Commission on Excellence in Education
  1983   *A Nation at Risk: The Imperative for Educational Reform.* [Online]. Available: http://www.ed.gov/pubs/NatAtRisk/index.html. [February 18, 1998]. Washington, DC: U.S. Department of Education.

National Research Council
  1994   *Organizational Linkages: Understanding the Productivity Paradox.* Report of the Panel on Organizational Linkages. Committee on Human Factors. D.H. Harris, ed. Commission on Behavioral and Social Sciences and Education, National Research Council. Washington, DC: National Academy Press.
  1997   *Educating One and All: Students with Disabilities and Standards-Based Reform.* Committee on Goals 2000 and the Inclusion of Students with Disabilities. L.M. McDonnell, M.J. McLaughlin, and P. Morison, eds. Commission on Behavioral and Social Sciences and Education, National Research Council. Washington, DC: National Academy Press.
  1999   *How People Learn: Brain, Mind, Experience, and School.* Committee on Developments in the Science of Learning. J.D. Bransford, A.L. Brown, and R.R. Cocking, eds. Commission on Behavioral and Social Sciences and Education, National Research Council. Washington, DC: National Academy Press.

Newmann, F., and G. Wehlage
  1995   *Successful School Restructuring.* Madison, WI: Wisconsin Center for Education Research, University of Wisconsin-Madison.

Northwest Regional Educational Laboratory, and the Education Commission of the States
  1998   *Catalog of School Reform Models: First Edition.* Oak Brook, IL: Northwest Regional Educational Laboratory.

Nye, B.A., C.M. Achilles, J.B. Zaharias, B.D. Fulton, and M.P. Wallenhorst
  1993   Tennessee's bold experiment: Using research to inform policy and practice. *Tennessee Education* 22(3):10-17.

Odden, A., and C. Busch
  1998   *Financing Schools for High Performance. Strategies for Improving the Use of Educational Resources.* San Francisco: Jossey-Bass.

Ouchi, W.G.
  1980   Markets, bureaucracies, and clans. *Administrative Science Quarterly* 25:129-141.

Pritchard, R.D.
  1991   Organizational productivity. Pp. 443-472 in *The Handbook of Industrial and Organizational Psychology, Volume 3*, M.D. Dunnette and L.M. Hough, eds. 2nd edition. Palo Alto, CA: Consulting Psychologists Press.

Rowan, B.
  1981   The effects of institutionalized rules on administrators. Pp. 47-75 in *Organizational Behavior in Schools and School Districts,* S.B. Bacharach, ed. New York: Praeger.

Sanders, W.L., and J.C. Rivers
1996   *Cumulative and Residual Effects of Teachers on Future Student Academic Achievement.* Research Progress Report. Knoxville, TN: University of Tennessee Value-Added Research and Assessment Center.

Sink, S., and G.L. Smith, Jr.
1994   The influence of organizational linkages and measurement practices on productivity and management. Pp. 131-160 in *Organizational Linkages: Understanding the Productivity Paradox.* Report of the Panel on Organizational Linkages, Committee on Human Factors. D.H. Harris, ed. Commission on Behavioral and Social Sciences and Education, National Research Council. Washington, DC: National Academy Press.

Slavin, R.E., and O.S. Fashola
1998   *Show Me the Evidence: Proven and Promising Programs for America's Schools.* Thousand Oaks, CA: Corwin Press.

Smith, M.S., and J. O'Day
1991   Systemic school reform. Pp. 233-267 in *The Politics of Curriculum and Testing: The 1990 Politics of Education Association Yearbook*, S.H. Fuhrman and B. Malen, eds. New York: Falmer Press.

Smith, M.S., B.W. Scoll, and J. Link
1996   Research-based school reform: The Clinton administration's agenda. Pp. 9-28 in *Improving America's Schools: The Role of Incentives.* Board on Science, Technology, and Economic Policy. E.A. Hanushek and D.W. Jorgenson, eds. Commission on Behavioral and Social Sciences and Education, National Research Council. Washington, DC: National Academy Press.

Spillane, J., C. Thompson, C. Lubienski, L. Jits, and C. Reimann
1995   The Local Government Policy System Affecting Mathematics and Science Education in Michigan: Lessons from Nine School Districts. Unpublished paper, Michigan State University, East Lansing.

Steinberg, L.D.
1996   *Beyond the Classroom: Why School Reform Has Failed and What Parents Need To Do.* New York: Simon and Schuster.

Summers, A., and A.W. Johnson
1996   The effects of school-based management plans. Pp. 75-96 in *Improving America's Schools: The Role of Incentives.* Board on Science, Technology, and Economic Policy. E.A. Hanushek and D.W. Jorgenson, eds. Commission on Behavioral and Social Sciences and Education, National Research Council. Washington, DC: National Academy Press.

Tyack, D.
1974   *The One Best System: A History of American Urban Education.* Cambridge, MA: Harvard University Press.
1993   School governance in the United States: Historical puzzles and anomalies. Pp. 1-32 in *Decentralization and School Improvement: Can We Fulfill the Promise?* J. Hannaway and M. Carnoy, eds. San Francisco: Jossey-Bass.

Tyack, D., and L. Cuban
1995   *Tinkering Toward Utopia: A Century of Public School Reform.* Cambridge, MA: Harvard University Press.

U.S. Office of Technology Assessment
1990   *Worker Training: Competing in the New International Economy.* OTA-ITE-457. Washington, DC: U.S. Government Printing Office.

Wang, M.C., G.D. Haertel, and H.J. Walberg
  1997 *What Do We Know: Widely Implemented School Improvement Programs.* A special report issued by the Laboratory for Student Success, The Mid-Atlantic Regional Educational Laboratory at Temple University Center for Research in Human Development and Education. Philadelphia: Laboratory for Student Success, Center for Research in Human Development and Education, Temple University.

Weeres, J.G., and C.T. Kerchner
  1996 This time it's serious: Post-industrialism and the coming of institutional change in education. Pp. 135-152 in *The Politics of Education and the New Institutionalism, Reinventing the American School: The 1995 Yearbook of the Politics of Education Association,* R.L. Crowson, W.L. Boyd, and H.B. Mawhinney, eds. Washington, DC: Falmer Press.

Wohlstetter, P., and A. Odden
  1992 Rethinking school-based management policy and research. *Educational Administration Quarterly* 28(4):529-549.

Wolf, C., Jr.
  1993 *Markets or Governments: Choosing between Imperfect Alternatives.* A RAND Research Study. Cambridge, MA: MIT Press.

Wright, S.P., S.P. Horn, and W.L. Sanders
  1997 Teacher and classroom context effects on student achievement: Implications for teacher evaluation. *Journal of Personnel Evaluation in Education* 11(1):57-67.

CHAPTER 6

Ambler, J.S.
  1994 Who benefits from educational choice? Some evidence from Europe. *Journal of Policy Analysis and Management* 13(3):454-476.

Armor, D.J., and B.M. Peiser
  1997 Competition in Education: Interdistrict Choice in Massachusetts. Presented at the Conference on Rethinking School Governance, Kennedy School of Government, June 13. Available from the Taubman Center for State and Local Government and the Center for American Political Studies, Harvard University.

Ballou, D., and M. Podgursky
  1997 *Teacher Pay and Teacher Quality.* Kalamazoo, MI: W.E. Upjohn Institute for Employment Research.
  1998 Reforming teacher training and recruitment: A critical appraisal of the recommendations of the National Commission on Teaching and America's Future. *Opportunity* 2(1):4-5, 11-13.
  1999 Reforming teacher preparation and licensing: What is the evidence? *Teachers College Record* 101(1):5-26.

Bierlein, L.A., and M.A. Fulton
  1996 *Emerging Issues in Charter School Financing.* Policy Brief. Denver, CO: Education Commission of the States.

Bradley, A.
  1999 States' uneven teacher supply complicates staffing of schools. *Education Week* 18(26, March 10):1, 10-11.

Brandl, J.E.
  1998 Governance and educational quality. Pp. 55-81 in *Learning from School Choice,* P.E. Peterson and B.C. Hassel, eds. Washington, DC: Brookings Institution Press.

Brown, F., and R. Hunter
  1996 The privatization of public education: What do we mean? *School Business Affairs* 62(5):6-11.

Bryk, A.S., Y.M. Thum, J.Q. Easton, and S. Luppescu
  1998   *Academic Productivity of Chicago Public Elementary Schools: A Technical Report.* Chicago: Consortium on Chicago School Research.
Carr, M.C., and S.H. Fuhrman
  1999   The politics of school finance in the 1990s. Pp. 136-174 in *Equity and Adequacy in Education Finance: Issues and Perspectives.* Committee on Education Finance. H.F. Ladd, R. Chalk, and J.S. Hansen, eds. Commission on Behavioral and Social Sciences and Education, National Research Council. Washington, DC: National Academy Press.
Clotfelter, C., and H.F. Ladd
  1996   Recognizing and rewarding success in public schools. Pp. 23-64 in *Holding Schools Accountable: Performance-Based Reform in Education,* H.F. Ladd, ed. Washington, DC: Brookings Institution Press.
Cohen, D.K., and H. Hill
  1998   *State Policy and Classroom Performance: Mathematics Reform in California.* CPRE Policy Briefs. RB-23 (January). Philadelphia: Consortium for Policy Research in Education.
Cohen, D.K., M. McLaughlin, and J. Talbert, eds.
  1993   *Teaching for Understanding: Challenges for Policy and Practice.* San Francisco: Jossey-Bass.
Cohn, E.
  1996   Methods of teacher remuneration: Merit pay and career ladders. Pp. 209-238 in *Assessing Educational Practices: The Contribution of Economics*, W.E. Becker and W.J. Baumol, eds. Cambridge, MA: MIT Press.
Darling-Hammond, L.
  1990   Teaching and knowledge: Policy issues posed by alternate certification for teachers. *Peabody Journal of Education* 76(3):123-154.
  1997   *Doing What Matters Most: Investing in Quality Teaching.* New York: National Commission on Teaching and America's Future.
Easton, J.Q., and S.L. Storey
  1994   The development of local school councils. *Education and Urban Society* 26(3):220-237.
Echols, F.H., and J.D. Willms
  1995   Reasons for school choice in Scotland. *Journal of Education Policy* 10(2):143-156.
Edison Project
  1997   *Annual Report on School Performance: December, 1997.* New York: The Edison Project.
Educational Research Service
  1978   *Methods of Scheduling Salaries for Teachers.* Arlington, VA: Educational Research Service.
Elmore, R.F., C.H. Abelmann, and S.H. Fuhrman
  1996   The new accountability in state education reform: From process to performance. Pp. 65-98 in *Holding Schools Accountable: Performance-Based Reform in Education,* H.F. Ladd, ed. Washington, DC: Brookings Institution Press.
Evans, W.N., and R.M. Schwab
  1995   Finishing High School and Starting College: Do Catholic Schools Make a Difference? Department of Economics, University of Maryland, College Park.
Evans, W.N., S.E. Murray, and R.M. Schwab
  1999   The impact of court-mandated school finance reform. Pp. 72-98 in *Equity and Adequacy in Education Finance: Issues and Perspectives.* Committee on Education Finance. H.F. Ladd, R. Chalk, and J.S. Hansen, eds. Commission on Behavioral and Social Sciences and Education, National Research Council. Washington, DC: National Academy Press.

Ferguson, R.
  1991   Paying for public education: New evidence on how and why money matters. *Harvard Journal on Legislation* 28(2):465-498.
Ferguson, R.F., and H.F. Ladd
  1996   How and why money matters: An analysis of Alabama schools. Pp. 265-298 in *Holding Schools Accountable: Performance-Based Reform in Education,* H.F. Ladd, ed. Washington, DC: Brookings Institution Press.
Figlio, D.N., and J.A. Stone
  1997   Are Private Schools Really Better? Department of Economics, University of Oregon, December.
Fossey, R.
  1994   Open enrollment in Massachusetts: Why families choose. *Educational Evaluation and Policy Analysis* 16:320-334.
Fowler, F.C.
  1995   Participation in Ohio's Interdistrict Open Enrollment Option: An Investigation of the Supply-Side of Choice. Paper presented at the Annual Meeting of the American Educational Research Association, San Francisco, April.
  1996   Meaningful Competition? A Study of Student Movement under Interdistrict Open Enrollment in Ohio. Paper presented at the Annual Meeting of the American Educational Research Association, New York, April.
Glenn, C.L.
  1990   Parent choice in four nations. Pp. 63-93 in *Choice in Education,* W.L. Boyd and H.J. Walberg, eds. Berkeley, CA: McCutchan Publishing.
Goertz, M.E., and G. Natriello
  1999   Court-mandated school finance reform: What do the new dollars buy? Pp. 99-135 in *Equity and Adequacy in Education Finance: Issues and Perspectives.* Committee on Education Finance. H.F. Ladd, R. Chalk, and J.S. Hansen, eds. Commission on Behavioral and Social Sciences and Education, National Research Council. Washington, DC: National Academy Press.
Goldhaber, D.D., and D.J. Brewer
  1997   Evaluating the effect of teacher degree level on educational performance. Pp. 197-210 in *Developments in School Finance, 1996,* W.J. Fowler, Jr., ed. NCES 97-535. Washington, DC: National Center for Education Statistics, U.S. Department of Education.
Greene, J.P., P.E. Peterson, and J. Du
  1997   *Effectiveness of School Choice: The Milwaukee Experiment.* Cambridge, MA: Taubman Center for State and Local Government, John F. Kennedy School of Government, Harvard Univserity.
Grissmer, D., and A. Flanagan
  1998   *Exploring Rapid Achievement Gains in North Carolina and Texas.* Washington, DC: National Education Goals Panel.
Hambleton, R.K., R.M. Jaeger, D. Koretz, R.L. Linn, J. Millman, and S.E. Phillips
  1995   Review of the Measurement Quality of the Kentucky Instructional Results Information System, 1991-1994. A Report Prepared for the Office of Educational Accountability, Kentucky General Assembly.
Hannaway, J.
  1993   Political pressure and decentralization in institutional organizations: The case of school districts. *Sociology of Education* 66:147-163.
  1996   Decentralization in two school districts: Challenging the standard paradigm. Pp. 135-162 in *Decentralization and School Improvement: Can We Fulfill the Promise?* J. Hannaway and M. Carnoy, eds. San Francisco: Jossey-Bass.

Hanushek, E.A.
  1986   The economics of schooling: Production and efficiency in public schools. *Journal of Economic Literature* 24(13):1141-1177.
  1997   Assessing the effects of school resources on student performance: An update. *Educational Evaluation and Policy Analysis* 19(2):141-164.
Hanushek, E.A., and S.G. Rivkin
  1996   *Understanding the 20th Century Growth in U.S. School Spending.* NBER Working Paper Series, Working Paper 5547. Cambridge, MA: National Bureau of Economic Research.
Hanushek, E.A., J.F. Kain, and S.G. Rivkin
  1998   *Teachers, Schools, and Academic Achievement.* NBER Working Paper Series, Working Paper 6691. Cambridge, MA: National Bureau of Economic Research.
Hatry, H.P., J.M. Greiner, and B.G. Ashford
  1994   *Issues and Case Studies in Teacher Incentive Plans.* 2nd edition. Washington, DC: Urban Institute.
Hawk, P.P., C.R. Coble, and M. Swanson
  1985   Certification: It does matter. *Journal of Teacher Education* 36(3):13-15.
Heneman, H.G.
  1997   Assessment of the Motivation Reactions of Teachers to a School-Based Performance Award Program. Paper presented at the America Educational Research Association annual conference, Chicago, March, 1997.
Hess, G.A., Jr.
  1993   Race and the liberal perspective in Chicago school reform. Pp. 85-96 in *The New Politics of Race and Gender: The 1992 Yearbook of the Politics of Education Association,* C. Marshall, ed. Washington, DC: Falmer Press.
  1999   Comments on Bryk. Pp. 99-109 in *Brookings Papers on Education Policy.* D. Ravitch, ed. Washington, DC: Brookings Institution Press.
Hoxby, C.M.
  1995   *Do Private Schools Provide Competition for Public Schools?* NBER working paper 4978, revised. Cambridge, MA: National Bureau of Economic Research.
  1996   The effects of private school vouchers on schools and students. Pp. 177-208 in *Holding Schools Accountable, Performance-Based Reform in Education,* H.F. Ladd, ed. Washington, DC: Brookings Institution Press.
  forth- Does competition among public schools benefit students and taxpayers? Evidence from
  coming natural variation in school districting. *American Economic Review.*
Jacobson, S.M.
  1987   Merit pay and teaching as a career. Pp. 161-177 in *Attracting and Compensating America's Teachers,* K. Alexander and D.H. Monk, eds. Eighth Annual Yearbook of the American Educational Finance Association. Cambridge, MA: Ballinger.
Johnson, S.M.
  1986   Incentives for teachers: What motivates, what matters? *Educational Administration Quarterly* 22(3):54-79.
Kane, T.J.
  1996   Comments on chapters five and six. Pp. 209-217 in *Holding Schools Accountable, Performance-Based Reform in Education,* H.F. Ladd, ed. Washington, DC: Brookings Institution Press.
Karsten, S.
  1994   Policy on ethnic segregation in a system of choice: The case of the Netherlands. *Education Policy* 9(3):221-225.

Kelley, C.
1997   The Kentucky School-Based Performance Award Program: School Level Effects. Draft, paper prepared for the American Educational Research Association annual conference, Chicago, March 1997.

Kennedy, M.M.
1998   The Relevance of Content in Inservice Teacher Education. Paper presented at the annual meeting of the American Educational Research Association, April 1998, San Diego, CA.

Klein, S.P., and L.S. Hamilton
1999   *Large-Scale Testing: Current Practices and New Directions.* IP-182. Santa Monica, CA: RAND.

Kohn, A.
1993   Why incentive plans cannot work. *Harvard Business Review* 71(5):54-63.

Koretz, D.
1996   Using student assessments for educational accountability. Pp. 171-195 in *Improving America's Schools: The Role of Incentives.* Board on Science, Technology, and Economic Policy. E.A. Hanushek and D.W. Jorgenson, eds. Commission on Behavioral and Social Sciences and Education, National Research Council. Washington, DC: National Academy Press.

Koretz, D.M., and S.I. Barron
1998   *The Validity of Gains in Scores on the Kentucky Instructional Results Information System (KIRIS).* Santa Monica, CA: RAND.

Ladd, H.F.
1999   The Dallas school accountability and incentive program: An evaluation of its impacts on student outcomes. *Economics of Education Review* 18(1):1-16.

Ladd, H.F., and R.P. Walsh
1998   Valued-Added Measures of School Effectiveness: Can They Be Implemented Fairly? Unpublished paper. Sanford Institute of Public Policy, Duke University.

Lankford, H., and J. Wyckoff
1997   The changing structure of teacher compensation, 1970-94. *Economics of Education Review* 16(4):371-384.

Lewis, L., B. Parasd, N. Carey, N. Bartfai, E. Farris, and B. Smerdon
1999   *Teacher Quality: A Report on the Preparation and Qualifications of Public School Teachers.* NCES 1999-080. Washington, DC: National Center for Education Statistics, U.S. Department of Education.

Linn, R.L., and J.L. Herman
1997   *A Policymaker's Guide to Standards-Led Assessment.* Denver, CO: National Center for Research on Evaluation, Standards, and Student Testing (CRESST) and the Education Commission of the States.

Loeb, S., and M.E. Page
1998   Examining the Link Between Wages and Quality in the Teacher Workforce: The Role of Alternative Labor Market Opportunities and Non-Pecuniary Variation. Unpublished paper. Department of Economics, University of California, Davis.

Lord, B.
1994   Teachers' professional development: Critical colleagueship and the role of professional communities. Pp. 175-204 in *The Future of Education: Perspectives on National Standards in Education,* N. Cobb, ed. New York: College Entrance Examination Board.

Malen, B., and R. Ogawa
1988   Professional-patron influences on site-based governance councils: A confounding case study. *Educational Evaluation and Policy Analysis* 10(3):251-270.

Meyer, R.H.
  1996 Value-added indicators of school performance. Pp. 197-223 in *Improving America's Schools: The Role of Incentives.* Board on Science, Technology, and Economic Policy. E.A. Hanushek and D.W. Jorgenson, eds. Commission on Behavioral and Social Sciences and Education, National Research Council. Washington, DC: National Academy Press.

Molnar, A.
  1996 *Giving Kids the Business: The Commercialization of America's Schools.* Boulder, CO: Westview Press.

Monk, D.H., and S.L. Jacobson
  1985 The distribution of salary increments between veteran and novice teachers: Evidence from New York State. *Journal of Education Finance* 11(Fall):157-175.

Murnane, R.J., and D.K. Cohen
  1986 Merit pay and the evaluation problem: Why most merit pay plans fail and a few survive. *Harvard Educational Review* 56(1):1-17.

Murnane, R.J., J.S. Singer, and J.B. Willett
  1987 Changes in teacher salaries during the 1970s: The role of school district demographics. *Economics of Education Review* 6(4):379-388.

Nalbantian, H.R., and A. Schotter
  1997 Productivity under group incentives: An experimental study. *American Economic Review* 87(3):314-341.

National Research Council
  1991 *Pay for Performance: Evaluating Performance Appraisal and Merit Pay.* Committee on Performance Appraisal for Merit Pay. G.T. Milkovich and A.K. Wigdor, eds., with R.F. Broderick and A.S. Mavor. Commission on Behavioral and Social Sciences and Education, National Research Council. Washington, DC: National Academy Press.

  1999a *High Stakes: Testing for Tracking, Promotion, and Graduation.* Committee on Appropriate Test Use. J.P. Heubert and R.M. Hauser, eds. Commission on Behavioral and Social Sciences and Education, National Research Council. Washington, DC: National Academy Press.

  1999b *How People Learn: Brain, Mind, Experience, and School.* Committee on Developments in the Science of Learning. J.D. Bransford, A.L. Brown, and R.R. Cocking, eds. Commission on Behavioral and Social Sciences and Education, National Research Council. Washington, DC: National Academy Press.

  1999c *Testing, Teaching, and Learning: A Guide for State and School Districts.* Committee on Title I Testing and Assessment. R.F. Elmore and R. Rothman, eds. Commission on Behavioral and Social Sciences and Education, National Research Council. Washington, DC: National Academy Press.

Neal, D.
  1997 The effects of Catholic secondary schooling on educational achievement. *Journal of Labor Economics* 15(1):98-123.

Odden, A.
  1996 Incentives, school organization, and teacher compensation. Pp. 226-256 in *Rewards and Reform: Creating Educational Incentives That Work,* S.H. Fuhrman and J.A. O'Day, eds. San Francisco: Jossey-Bass.

Odden, A., and C. Busch
  1998 *Financing Schools for High Performance. Strategies for Improving the Use of Educational Resources.* San Francisco: Jossey-Bass.

Odden, A., and C. Kelley
  1997 *Paying Teachers for What They Know and Do, New and Smarter Compensation Strategies to Improve Schools.* Thousand Oaks, CA: Corwin Press.

Paine, L., and L. Ma
1993   Teachers working together: A dialogue on organizational and cultural perspectives of Chinese teachers. *International Journal of Educational Research* 19(8):675-697.

Peterson, P.E., D. Meyers, and W.G. Howell
1998   *An Evaluation of the New York City School Choice Scholarships Program: The First-Year.* Cambridge, MA: Program on Education Policy and Governance, Harvard University.

Rofes, E.
1998   *How Are School Districts Responding to Charter Laws and Charter Schools? A Study of Eight States and the District of Columbia.* Berkeley: Policy Analysis for California Education, Graduate School of Education, University of California.

Rouse, C.E.
1997   *Private School Vouchers and Student Achievement: An Evaluation of the Milwaukee Parental Choice Program.* NBER Working Paper No. W5964. Cambridge, MA: National Bureau of Economic Research.

Sander, W.
forthcoming   Private schools and public school achievement. *Journal of Human Resources.*

Schifter, D., and C.T. Fosnot
1993   *Reconstructing Mathematics Education.* New York: Teachers College Press.

Sebring, P.A., A.S. Bryk, M. Roderick, E. Camburn, S. Luppescu, Y.M. Thum, B. Smith, and J. Kahne
1996   *Charting Reform in Chicago: The Students Speak.* Chicago: Consortium on Chicago School Research.

Shipps, D., J. Kahne, and M.A. Smylie
1998   Legitimacy and Professionalism in Chicago's Layered School Reform or Been Down So Long, It Looks Like Up To Me. Paper presented at the Annual Meetings of the American Educational Research Association, San Diego, CA, April 1998.

Smith, M.L.
1991   Meanings of test preparation. *American Educational Research Journal* 28(3):521-542

Smith, S.S., and R.A. Mickelson
forthcoming   All that glitters is not gold: School reform in Charlotte-Mecklenburg. *Educational Evaluation and Policy Analysis.*

Strauss, R.P.
1998   Who should teach in New York's public schools? Implications of Pennsylvania's teacher preparation and selection experience. Pp. 137-175 in *Educational Finance to Support High Learning Standards: Final Report, State Board of Regents.* Albany, NY: New York State Board of Regents, State Education Department, University of the State of New York.

Summers, A., and A.W. Johnson
1996   The effects of school-based management plans. Pp. 75-96 in *Improving America's Schools: The Role of Incentives.* Board on Science, Technology, and Economic Policy. E.A. Hanushek and D.W. Jorgenson, eds. Commission on Behavioral and Social Sciences and Education, National Research Council. Washington, DC: National Academy Press.

Talbert, J., and M.W. McLaughlin
1994   Teacher professionalism in local school context. *American Journal of Education* 102:123-153.

UCLA Charter School Study
1998   *Beyond the Rhetoric of Charter School Reform: A Study of Ten California School Districts.* Los Angeles, CA: UCLA Graduate School of Education and Information Studies.

U.S. Department of Education
  1998a *A Back to School Special Report on the Baby Boom Echo: America's Schools Are Over-crowded and Wearing Out.* [Online]. Available: http://www.ed.gov/pubs/bbecho98/ [March 18, 1999]. Washington, DC: U.S. Department of Education.
  1998b *A National Study of Charter Schools, Second-Year Report.* Prepared by RPP International. Washington, DC: U.S. Department of Education.
Vandenberghe, V.
  1996 *Functioning and Regulation of Educational Quasi-Markets.* Nouvelle serie-No. 283, Louvain-la Neuve, Belgium: Faculte Des Sciences Economiques, Sociales et Politiques, Universite Catholique de Louvain.
Vanourek, G., B.V. Manno, C.E. Finn, Jr., and L.A. Bierlein
  1997 *The Educational Impact of Charter Schools.* Washington, DC: Hudson Institute.
Walsh, N.J.
  1995 Public schools, inc.: Baltimore's risky enterprise. *Education and Urban Society* 27(2):195-205.
Weiss, C., and J. Cambone
  1994 Principals, shared decision making, and school reform. *Educational Evaluation and Policy Analysis* 16(3):287-301.
Wells, A.S., and R.L. Crain
  1997 *Stepping Over the Color Line: African American Students in White Suburban Schools.* New Haven, CT: Yale University Press.
Wiley, D., and B. Yoon
  1995 Teacher reports of opportunity to learn: Analyses of the 1993 California Learning Assessment System. *Education Evaluation and Policy Analysis* 17(3):355-370.
Witte, J.F, T.D. Sterr, and C.A. Thorn
  1995 Fifth-Year Report: Milwaukee Parental Choice Program. Dissertation, University of Wisconsin-Madison and Wisconsin Department of Public Instruction, Madison, WI.
Wohlstetter, P., and A. Odden
  1992 Rethinking school-based management policy and research. *Educational Administration Quarterly* 28(4):529-549.
Wohlstetter, P., and N. Griffin
  1998 *Creating and Sustaining Learning Communities: Early Lessons from Charter Schools.* CPRE Occasional Paper Series, OP-03. Philadelphia: Consortium for Policy Research in Education, Graduate School of Education, University of Pennsylvania.
Wright, S.P., S.P. Horn, and W.L. Sanders
  1997 Teacher and classroom context effects on student achievement: Implications for teacher evaluation. *Journal of Personnel Evaluation in Education* 11(1):57-67.

CHAPTER 7

Annie E. Casey Foundation
  1995 *The Path of Most Resistance: Reflections on Lessons Learned from New Futures, 1995.* Baltimore, MD: Annie E. Casey Foundation.
Aspen Institute
  1997 *Voices from the Field: Learning from Comprehensive Community Initiatives.* Roundtable of Comprehensive Community Initiatives for Children and Families. Washington, DC: Aspen Institute.
Barnett, W.S.
  1995 Long-term effects of early childhood programs on cognitive and school outcomes. *The Future of Children: Long-Term Outcomes of Early Childhood Programs* 5(3):25-50.

Black, S.
1998 Do Better Schools Matter: Parental Valuation of Elementary Education. Research paper 9729, March. Federal Reserve Bank of New York.

Blank, M., and C. Steinbach
1998 Communities: Powerful resources for America's youth. Pp. 59-81 in *The Forgotten Half Revisited: American Youth and Young Families 1988-2008,* S. Halperin, ed. Washington, DC: American Youth Policy Forum.

Bloom, B.
1964 *Stability and Change in Human Characteristics.* New York: John Wiley.

Center for the Study of Social Policy
1995 *Building New Futures for At-Risk Youth.* Washington, DC: Center for the Study of Social Policy.

Chicago Magazine
1995 How do your high schools stack up? *Chicago Magazine* (February):77-98.

Coleman, J.M.
1983 Self-concept and the mildly handicapped: The role of social comparisons. *Journal of Special Education* 17:37-45.

Commission on Chapter 1
1992 *Making Schools Work for Children in Poverty: A New Framework Prepared by the Commission on Chapter 1.* Washington, DC: Commission on Chapter 1.

Council for Learning Disabilities
1993 *Concerns About the Full Inclusion of Students with Learning Disabilities in Regular Education Classrooms.* Washington, DC: National Joint Council on Learning Disabilities.

CSR Research Consortium
1999 *Class Size Reduction in California 1996-98: Early Findings Signal Promise and Concerns.* [Online]. Available: http://www.classize.org/ [August 9, 1999].

Dillon, S.
1994 Special education soaks up New York's school resources. *New York Times* (April 7):A16.

Duke, D.L.
1998 Does It Matter Where Our Children Learn? Unpublished paper commissioned by the National Research Council, February 18, 1998, Washington, DC.

Ehrenberg, R.G., and D.J. Brewer
1994 Do school and teacher characteristics matter? Evidence from "High School and Beyond." *Economics of Education Review* 13(1):1-17.

Elmore, R.F., and M.W. McLaughlin
1988 *Steady Work: Policy, Practice, and the Reform of American Education.* Prepared for the National Institute of Education. Santa Monica, CA: RAND.

Epple, D., and R.E. Romano
1996 Public School Choice and Finance Policies, Neighborhood Formation, and the Distribution of Educational Benefits. Working paper, July. Carnegie Mellon University.
1998 Competition between private and public schools, vouchers, and peer-group effects. *American Economic Review* 88(1):33-62.
1999 Educational Vouchers and Cream Skimming. Working paper, August. University of Florida.

Epple, D., D. Figlio, and R. Romano
1998 Stratification and Peer Effects in Education: Evidence Using Within and Between School Variation in the Data. Working paper, October. University of Florida.

Epps, S., and G. Tindal
1987 The effectiveness of differential programming in serving students with mild handicaps. Pp. 213-248 in *Handbook of Special Education: Research and Practice I,* M.C. Wang, M.C. Reynolds, and H.J. Walberg, eds. Oxford, England: Pergamon Press.

Fashola, O.S.
   1998   *Review of Extended Day and After-School Programs and Their Effectiveness.* Report no.
          24. Baltimore, MD: Center for Research on the Education of Students Placed at Risk,
          Johns Hopkins University and Howard University.
Ferguson, R.F.
   1991   Paying for public education: New evidence on how and why money matters. *Harvard
          Journal on Legislation* 28(2):465-498.
   1998   Can schools narrow the black-white test score gap? Pp. 318-374 in *The Black-White Test
          Score Gap,* C. Jencks and M. Phillips, eds. Washington, DC: Brookings Institution
          Press.
Ferguson, R.F., and H.F. Ladd
   1996   How and why money matters: An analysis of Alabama schools. Pp. 265-298 in *Holding
          Schools Accountable: Performance-Based Reform in Education,* H.F. Ladd, ed. Wash-
          ington, DC: Brookings Institution Press.
Fuchs, D., and L.S. Fuchs
   1995   Sometimes separate is better. *Educational Leadership* 52(4):22-26.
Gerald, D.E., and W.J. Hussar
   1995   *Projections of Education Statistics to 2005.* NCES 95-169. Washington, DC: National
          Center for Education Statistics, U.S. Department of Education.
Hayes, C.D., E. Lipoff, and A.E. Danegger
   1995   *Compendium of Comprehensive, Community-Based Initiatives, A Look at Costs, Benefits,
          and Financing Strategies.* Washington, DC: Finance Project.
Honeyman, D.S.
   1990   School facilities and state mechanisms that support school construction: A report from
          the fifty states. *Journal of Education Finance* 16:247-272.
Hoxby, C.M.
   1996   Are efficiency and equity in school finance substitutes or complements? *Journal of
          Economic Perspectives* 10(4):51-72.
Independent Review Panel on the Evaluation of Federal Education Legislation
   1999   *Measured Progress: An Evaluation of the Impact of Federal Education Legislation En-
          acted in 1994.* April, 1999. Washington, DC: U.S. Department of Education.
Kain, J.F., and K. Singleton
   1996   Equality of educational opportunity revisited. *New England Economic Review* (May/
          June):87-114.
Kakalik, J.S., W.S. Furry, M.A. Thomas, and M.F. Carney
   1981   *The Cost of Special Education.* A RAND Note. Santa Monica, CA: RAND.
Karoly, L.A., P.W. Greenwood, S.S. Everingham, J. Hoube, M.R. Kilburn, C.P. Rydell, M. Sanders,
and J. Chiesa
   1998   *Investing in Our Children: What We Know and Don't Know About the Costs and Benefits
          of Early Childhood Interventions.* Santa Monica, CA: RAND.
Kavale, K.
   1990   The effectiveness of special education. Pp. 868-898 in *The Handbook of School Psychol-
          ogy,* 2nd edition, T.B. Gutkin and C.R. Reynolds, eds. New York: Wiley.
Kavale, K., and G.V. Glass
   1982   The efficacy of special education interventions and practices: A compendium of meta-
          analysis findings. *Focus on Exceptional Children* 15(4):1-14.
Kavale, K.A., D. Fuchs, and T.E. Scruggs
   1994   Setting the record straight on learning disability and low achievement: Implications for
          policy making. *Learning Disability Research and Practice* 9(2):70-77.
Keller, B.
   1999   School construction in U.S. tops $15 billion. *Education Week* 18(23, February 17):6.

Keltner, B.R.
1998   *Funding Comprehensive School Reform. RAND Issue Paper.* Santa Monica, CA: RAND.
Kritek, W.J.
1996   Introduction. Pp. ix-xxv in *Coordination Among Schools, Families, and Communities: Prospects for Educational Reform,* J.G. Cibulka and W.J. Kritek, eds. Albany: State University of New York Press.
Ladd, H.F.
1998   Hoe school districts respond to fiscal constraint. Pp. 35-59 in *Selected Papers in School Finance, 1996,* W.J. Fowler, Jr., ed. NCES 98-217. Washington, DC: National Center for Education Statistics.
Lankford, H., and J. Wyckoff
1996   The allocation of resources to special education and regular instruction. Pp. 221-257 in *Holding Schools Accountable: Performance-Based Reform in Education,* H.F. Ladd, ed. Washington, DC: Brookings Institution Press.
Lyon, G.R.
1996   Learning disabilities. *The Future of Children: Special Education for Students with Disabilities* 6(1):54-76.
Martin, E.W., R. Martin, and D.L. Terman
1996   The legislative and litigation history of special education. *The Future of Children: Special Education for Students with Disabilities* 6(1):25-39.
Melaville, A.
1998   *Learning Together: The Developing Field of School-Community Initiatives.* Flint, MI: Charles Stewart Mott Foundation.
Millsap, M.A., M. Moss, and B. Gamse
1993   *Chapter 1 in Public Schools: The Chapter 1 Implementation Study.* Washington, DC: Planning and Evaluation Service, U.S. Department of Education.
Mitchell, A., C. Ripple, and N. Chanana
1998   *Prekindergarten Programs Funded by the States: Essential Elements for Policy Makers.* New York: Families and Work Institute.
Monk, D.H.
1990   *Educational Finance: An Economic Approach.* New York: McGraw-Hill.
Moore, M.T., E.W. Strang, M. Schwartz, and M. Braddock
1988   *Patterns in Special Education Service Delivery and Cost.* Contract Number 3000-84-0257. Washington, DC: Decision Resources Corporation.
Murnane, R.J.
1981   Interpreting the evidence of school effectiveness. *Teachers College Record* 83(1):19-35.
Murnane, R.J., and F. Levy
1996   Evidence from fifteen schools in Austin, Texas. Pp. 93-96 in *Does Money Matter? The Effect of School Resources on Student Achievement and Adult Success,* G. Burtless, ed. Washington, DC: Brookings Institution Press.
National Joint Committee on Learning Disabilities
1993   *A Reaction to Full Inclusion: A Reaffirmation of the Right of Students with Learning Disabilities to a Continuum of Services.* Washington, DC: National Joint Committee on Learning Disabilities.
National Research Council
1997   *Educating One and All: Students with Disabilities and Standards-Based Reform.* Committee on Goals 2000 and the Inclusion of Students with Disabilities. L.M. McDonnell, M.J. McLaughlin, and P. Morison, eds. Commission on Behavioral and Social Sciences and Education, National Research Council. Washington, DC: National Academy Press.

1998 *Preventing Reading Difficulties in Young Children.* Committee on the Prevention of Reading Difficulties in Young Children. C.E. Snow, M.S. Burns, and P. Griffin, eds. Commission on Behavioral and Social Sciences and Education, National Research Council. Washington, DC: National Academy Press.

1999 *How People Learn: Brain, Mind, Experience, and School.* Committee on Developments in the Science of Learning. J.D. Bransford, A.L. Brown, and R.R. Cocking, eds. Commission on Behavioral and Social Sciences and Education, National Research Council. Washington, DC: National Academy Press.

Natriello, G., E.L. McDill, and A.M. Pallas

1990 *Schooling Disadvantaged Children: Racing Against Catastrophe:* New York: Teachers College Press.

Odden, A., and C. Busch

1998 *Financing Schools for High Performance. Strategies for Improving the Use of Educational Resources.* San Francisco: Jossey-Bass.

Organisation for Economic Co-operation and Development

1996 *Education at a Glance: OECD Indicators.* Centre for Educational Research and Innovation. Paris: Organisation for Economic Co-operation and Development.

Orland, M.E., and E. Foley

1996 *Beyond Decategorization: Defining Barriers and Potential Solutions to Creating Effective Comprehensive, Community-Based Support Systems for Children and Families.* Washington, DC: Finance Project.

Orland, M., and S. Stullich

1997 Financing Title I: Meeting the twin goals of effective resource targeting and beneficial program interventions. Pp. 1-26 in *Implementing School Reform, Practice and Policy Imperatives,* M.C. Wang and K.K. Wong, eds. Philadelphia: Center for Research in Human Development and Education, Temple University.

Orland, M.E., A.E. Danegger, and E. Foley

1995 *Creating More Comprehensive, Community-Based Support Systems, The Critical Role of Finance.* Washington, DC: Finance Project.

Parrish, T.B.

1995 What is fair? Special education and finance equity. *CSEF Brief* 6(Fall). Palo Alto, CA: Center for Special Education Finance, American Institutes for Research.

1997 *Special Education in an Era of School Reform.* Washington, DC: Regional Resources and Federal Center Network, Federal Resource Center.

Parrish, T.B., and J.G. Chambers

1996 Financing special education. *The Future of Children: Special Education for Students with Disabilities* 6(1):121-138.

Parrish, T.B., C. Matsumoto, and W.J. Fowler, Jr.

1995 *Disparities in Public School District Spending: 1989-90.* NCES 95-300R. Washington, DC: National Center for Education Statistics, U.S. Department of Education.

Pelavin Research Institute and American Institutes of Research

1997 *Investing in School Technology: Strategies to Meet the Funding Challenge.* Washington, DC: Office of Educational Technology, U.S. Department of Education.

Peterson, P.E.

1983 Background paper. Pp. 23-174 in *Making the Grade: Report of the Task Force on the Federal Elementary and Secondary Education Policy.* New York: Twentieth Century Fund.

President's Committee of Advisors on Science and Technology, Panel on Educational Technology

1997 *Report to the President on the Use of Technology to Strengthen K-12 Education in the United States.* Washington, DC: Executive Office of the President.

Puma, M.J., N. Karweit, C. Price, A. Ricciuti, W. Thompson, and M. Vaden-Kiernan
  1997   *Prospects: Final Report on Student Outcomes.* Prepared by Abt Associates for the Planning and Evaluation Service, U.S. Department of Education. Washington, DC: U.S. Department of Education.
Renick, M.J., and S. Harter
  1989   Impact of social comparisons on the developing self-perceptions of learning disabled students. *Journal of Educational Psychology* 81:631-638.
Reschly, D.J.
  1996   Identification and assessment of students with disabilities. *The Future of Children: Special Education for Students with Disabilities* 6(1):40-53.
Reynolds, A.J., E. Mann, W. Miedel, and P. Smokowski
  1997   The state of early childhood intervention: Effectiveness, myths and realities, new directions. *Focus* 19(1):5-11. Newsletter of the Institute for Research on Poverty, University of Wisconsin-Madison.
Rotberg, I.C., and J.J. Harvey
  1993   *Federal Policy Options for Improving the Education of Low-Income Students.* Santa Monica, CA: RAND.
Rothstein, R., and K.H. Miles
  1995   *Where's the Money Gone? Changes in the Level and Composition of Education Spending.* Washington, DC: Economic Policy Institute.
Shapiro, J., P. Loeb, and D. Bowermaster
  1993   Separate and unequal. *U.S. News and World Report* December 13:46-50, 54-56, 60.
Slavin, R.E., N.L. Karweit, and N.A. Madden, eds.
  1989   *Effective Programs for Students At Risk.* Boston: Allyn & Bacon.
Sommerfeld, M.
  1994   Pew abandons its ambitious 10-year children's initiative. *Education Week* (April 6) [Online]. Available: http://www.edweek.org [April 7, 1997].
Stern, J.D., ed.
  1994   *The Condition of Education in Rural Schools.* Washington, DC: Office of Educational Research and Improvement, U.S. Department of Education.
Turnbull, H.R.
  1993   *Free Appropriate Public Education: The Law and Children with Disabilities.* 4th edition. Denver, CO: Love Publishing.
U.S. Department of Education
  1996   *Mapping Out the National Assessment of Title I: The Interim Report.* Washington, DC: Planning and Evaluation Service, U.S. Department of Education.
  1997   *To Assure the Free Appropriate Public Education of All Children with Disabilities, Nineteenth Annual Report to Congress on the Implementation of the Individuals with Disabilities Education Act.* Available from the Superintendent of Documents, U.S. Government Printing Office. Washington, DC: U.S. Department of Education.
  1998   *To Assure the Free Appropriate Public Education of All Children with Disabilities, Twentieth Annual Report to Congress on the Implementation of the Individuals with Disabilities Education Act.* Available from the Superintendent of Documents, U.S. Government Printing Office. Washington, DC: U.S. Department of Education.
  1999a   *Digest of Education Statistics, 1998.* NCES 1999-036. Washington, DC: National Center for Education Statistics, U.S. Department of Education.
  1999b   *Promising Results, Continuing Challenges: The Final Report of the National Assessment of Title I.* Washington, DC: Office of the Under Secretary, Planning and Evaluation Service, U.S. Department of Education.
  1999c   *The Condition of Education, 1999.* NCES 1999-022. Washington, DC: National Center for Education Statistics, U.S. Department of Education.

U.S. Department of Education and U.S. Department of Justice

1998   *Safe and Smart: Making After-School Hours Work for Kids.* Washington, DC: U.S. Department of Education.

U.S. General Accounting Office

1994   *Remedial Education: Modifying Chapter 1 Formula Would Target More Funds to Those Most in Need.* GAO/HRD-92-16. Washington, DC: U.S. General Accounting Office.

1995a   *School Facilities: Accessibility for the Disabled Still an Issue.* GAO/HEHS-96-73. Washington, DC: U.S. General Accounting Office.

1995b   *School Facilities: America's Schools Not Designed or Equipped for 21st Century.* GAO/HEHS-95-95. Washington, DC: U.S. General Accounting Office.

1995c   *School Facilities: Condition of America's Schools.* GAO/HEHS-95-61. Washington, DC: U.S. General Accounting Office.

1995d   *School Facilities: States' Financial and Technical Support Varies.* GAO/HEHS-96-27. Washington, DC: U.S. General Accounting Office.

1996   *School Facilities: America's Schools Report Differing Conditions.* GAO/HEHS-96-103. Washington, DC: U.S. General Accounting Office.

1998   *School Finance: State and Federal Efforts to Target Poor Students.* GAO/HEHS-98-36. Washington, DC: U.S. General Accounting Office.

Verstegen, D.A., T.B. Parrish, and J.M. Wolman

1997   A look at changes in the finance provisions for grants to states under the IDEA amendments of 1997. *The CSEF Resource:* Newsletter of the Center for Special Education Finance. Palo Alto, CA: Center for Special Education Finance, American Institutes for Research.

Wall Street Journal

1993   Special education's special costs. *Wall Street Journal* October 20:A14.

Wolman, J.M., and T.B. Parrish

1996   Escalating special education costs: Reality or myth? *The CSEF Resource:* Newsletter of the Center for Special Education Finance. Palo Alto, CA: Center for Special Education Finance, American Institutes for Research.

Woods, T.

1996   *Building Comprehensive, Community-Based Support Systems for Children and Families, A Review of Legislative Examples.* Washington, DC: Finance Project.

Zigler, E., and S. Muenchow

1992   *Head Start: The Inside Story of America's Most Successful Educational Experiment.* New York: Basic Books.

CHAPTER 8

Brunner, E., and J. Sonstelie

1997   School Finance Reform and Voluntary Fiscal Federalism. Unpublished working paper, November. Department of Economics, San Diego State University.

Citrin, J.

1979   Do people want something for nothing: Public opinion on taxes and government spending. *National Tax Journal* 32(2, supplement):113-129.

Clotfelter, C.T., and P.J. Cook

1989   *Selling Hope: State Lotteries in America.* Cambridge, MA: Harvard University Press.

Courant, P.N., and S. Loeb

1997   Centralization of school finance in Michigan. *Journal of Policy Analysis and Management* 16(1):114-136.

Downes, T.A.
  1992   Evaluating the impact of school finance reform on the provision of education: The Cali-
          fornia case. *National Tax Journal* 45(4):405-419.
Downes, T.A., and D.N. Figlio
  1997   *School Finance Reforms, Tax Limits, and Student Performance: Do Reforms Level Up or
          Level Down?* Discussion Paper No. 1142-97. Insitute for Research on Poverty, Univeristy
          of Wisconsin-Madison. [Online.] Available: //www.ssc.wisc.edu/irp/ [June 14, 1999].
Downes, T.A., and D. Schoeman
  1998   School financing reform and private school enrollment: Evidence from California. *Jour-
          nal of Urban Economics* 43:418-443.
Downes, T.A., and M.P. Shah
  1995   The Effect of School Finance Reforms on the Level and Growth of Per Pupil Expendi-
          tures. Unpublished paper. Department of Economics, Tufts University.
Downes, T.A., R.F. Dye, and T.J. McGuire
  1998   Do limits matter? Evidence on the effect of tax limitations on student performance.
          Journal of Urban Economics 43(3):401-417.
Due, J.F., and J.L. Mikesell
  1994   *Sales Taxation: State and Local Structure and Administration.* Washington, DC: Urban
          Institute Press.
Dye, R.F., and T.J. McGuire
  1997   The effect of property tax limitation measures on local government fiscal behavior. *Jour-
          nal of Public Economics* 66(3):469-487.
Evans, W.N., S.E. Murray, and R.M. Schwab
  1997   Schoolhouses, courthouses, and statehouses after Serrano. *Journal of Policy Analysis and
          Management* 16(1):10-31.
Figlio, D.N., and K. Rueben
  1997   Do Tax Limits Affect Teacher Quality? Working paper, Public Policy Institute of Cali-
          fornia, San Francisco.
Fischel, W.A.
  1992   Property taxation and the Tiebout model: Evidence from the benefit view from zoning
          and voting. *Journal of Economic Literature* 20(March):171-177.
  1996   How Serrano caused Proposition 13. *The Journal of Law and Politics* 12(4):607-636.
Fuchs, V.R., and D.M. Reklis
  1994   *Mathematical Achievement in Eighth Grade: Interstate and Racial Differences.* Work-
          ing Paper No. 4784. Cambridge, MA: National Bureau of Economic Research.
Gentry, W.M., and H.F. Ladd
  1994   State tax structure and multiple policy objectives. *National Tax Journal* 47(4):747-772.
Gramlich, E.M., and D.L. Rubinfeld
  1982   Micro estimates of public spending demand functions and tests of the Tiebout and me-
          dian-voter hypotheses. *Journal of Political Economy* 90(3):536-560.
Hamilton, B.
  1975   Zoning and property taxation in a system of local governments. *Urban Studies* 12(2):105-
          111.
Heise, M.
  1998   Equal educational opportunity, hollow victories and the demise of school finance equity
          theory: An empirical perspective and alternative explanation. *Georgia Law Review*
          32(2):543-631.
Hoxby, C.M.
  1996a   All School Finance Equalizations Are Not Created Equal: Marginal Tax Rates Matter.
          Working paper, March, Harvard University.

1996b Are efficiency and equity in school finance substitutes or complements? *Journal of Economic Perspectives* 10(4):51-72.

Husted, T.A., and L.W. Kenny
   1998 Evidence from the States on the Equity and Efficiency Tradeoff in Education. Unpublished working paper, October. Department of Economics, University of Florida.

Independent Review Panel on the Evaluation of Federal Education Legislation
   1999 *Measured Progress: An Evaluation of the Impact of Federal Education Legislation Enacted in 1994.* April 1999. Washington, DC: U.S. Department of Education.

Joondeph, B.W.
   1995 The good, the bad, and the ugly: An empirical analysis of litigation-prompted school finance reform. *Santa Clara Law Review* 35(3):763-824.

Ladd, H.F.
   1976 State-wide taxation of commercial and industrial property for education. *National Tax Journal* 29(2):143-153.

Ladd, H.F., and E.W. Harris
   1995 Statewide taxation of nonresidential property for education. *Journal of Education Finance* 21(1):103-122.

Ladd, H.F., and J.B. Wilson
   1982 Why voters support tax limitations: Evidence from Massachusetts' Proposition 2 1/2. *National Tax Journal* 35(2):121-148.

LaFleur's Lottery World
   1998 U.S. lotteries' government profits earmarking. *LaFleur's Lottery World 1998—Fast Facts, Supplement to LaFleur's Lottery World Magazine* October.

Luce, T.
   1998 Regional tax base sharing: The Twin Cities experience. Pp. 234-254 in *Local Government Tax and Land Use Policies in the United States,* H.F. Ladd, ed. Cheltenham, UK: Edward Elgar Publishing.

Lyon, A.B., and R.M. Schwab
   1995 Consumption taxes in a life-cycle framework: Are sin taxes regressive? *Review of Economics and Statistics* 77(3):389-406.

Manwaring, R.L., and S.M. Sheffrin
   1997 Litigation, school finance reform, and aggregate educational spending. *International Tax and Public Finance* 4(2):107-127.

McLure, C.E., Jr.
   1977 The 'new view' of the property tax: A caveat. *National Tax Journal* 30(1):69-75.

Mieszkowski, P., and G.R. Zodrow
   1989 Taxation and the Tiebout model: The differential effects of head taxes, taxes on land rents and property taxes. *Journal of Economic Literature* 27(September):1098-1146.

Monk, D.H., and B.O. Brent
   1997 *Raising Money for Education: A Guide to the Property Tax.* Thousand Oaks, CA: Corwin Press.

Murray, S.E., W.N. Evans, and R.M. Schwab
   1998 Education finance reform and the distribution of education resources. *American Economic Review* 88(4):789-811.

National Center for Education Statistics
   1998 *State Comparisons of Education Statistics: 1969-70 to 1996-97.* NCES 98-018. Washington, DC: National Center for Education Statistics, U.S. Department of Education.

Netzer, D., and R. Berne
   1995 Discrepancies between ideal characteristics of a property tax system and current practice in New York. *Journal of Education Finance* 21(1):38-56.

Oates, W.E.
    1991   The theory and rationale of local property taxation. Pp. 407-424 in *State and Local Finance for the 1990s: A Case Study of Arizona,* T.J. McGuire and D.W. Naimark, eds. Tempe: Arizona State University.

Odden, A., and C. Busch
    1998   *Financing Schools for High Performance: Strategies for Improving the Use of Educational Resources.* San Francisco: Jossey-Bass.

Peltzman, S.
    1993   The political economy of the decline of American public education. *Journal of Law and Economics* 36(1):331-383.

    1996   Political economy of public education: Non-college-bound students. *Journal of Law and Economics* 39(1):73-120.

Phares, D.
    1980   *Who Pays State and Local Taxes?* Cambridge, MA: Oelgeschlager, Gunn, and Hain.

Poterba, J.M.
    1989   Lifetime incidence and the distributional burden of excise taxes. *American Economic Review* 79(2):325-330.

Rubinfeld, D.L.
    1995   California Fiscal Federalism: A School Finance Perspective. Unpublished working paper, June.

Rueben, K.
    1997   Tax Limitations and Government Growth: The Effect of State Tax and Expenditure Limits on State and Local Government. Working paper, Public Policy Institute of California, San Francisco.

Silva, F., and J. Sonstelie
    1995   Did Serrano cause a decline in school spending? *National Tax Journal* 48(2):199-215.

Sobel, R.S., and R.G. Holcombe
    1996   Measuring growth and variability of tax bases over the business cycle. *National Tax Journal* 49(4):535-552.

Strauss, R.P.
    1995   Reducing New York's reliance on the school property tax. *Journal of Education Finance* 21(1):123-164.

Tiebout, C.M.
    1956   A pure theory of local expenditures. *Journal of Political Economy* 54(October):416-424.

Wyckoff, P.G.
    1995   Capitalization, equalization, and intergovernmental aid. *Pubic Finance Quarterly* 23(4):484-508.

CHAPTER 9

Consortium on Productivity in the Schools
    1995   *Using What We Have To Get the Schools We Need: A Productivity Focus for American Education.* New York: Institute on Education and the Economy, Teachers College, Columbia University.

Elmore, R.F., and D. Burney
    1997   *Investing in Teacher Learning: Staff Development and Instructional Improvement, Community School District #2, New York City.* CPRE/NCTAF Joint Report. New York: National Commission on Teaching and America's Future, and Consortium for Policy Research in Education.

1998   School Variation and Systemic Instructional Improvement in Community School District #2, New York City. Unpublished manuscript, University of Pennsylvania, Consortium for Policy Research in Education.

Friedman, M.
1962   *Capitalism and Freedom.* Chicago: University of Chicago Press.

Independent Review Panel on the Evaluation of Federal Education Legislation
1999   *Measured Progress: An Evaluation of the Impact of Federal Education Legislation Enacted in 1994.* April 1999. Washington, DC: U.S. Department of Education.

Nathan, R.P.
1988   *Social Science in Government: Uses and Misuses.* New York: Basic Books.

National Research Council
1999   *Improving Student Learning: A Strategic Plan for Education Research and Its Utilization.* Committee on a Feasibility Study for a Strategic Education Research Program. Commission on Behavioral and Social Sciences and Education, National Research Council. Washington, DC: National Academy Press.

President's Committee of Advisors on Science and Technology, Panel on Educational Technology
1997   *Report to the President on the Use of Technology to Strengthen K-12 Education in the United States.* Washington, DC: Executive Office of the President.

APPENDIX
A
Data Needs

The challenge to school finance policies to become more closely aligned with improved student learning presents a new challenge to data collection efforts, one final area the committee was asked to address. Traditionally, finance data collected by federal and state education statistics agencies have served primarily to answer questions about how education funds are distributed. Much less attention has been directed to collecting finance and related data needed to understand in a sophisticated way how financial resources are linked to particular educational programs and to the performance of schools and students. For example, we have come to understand how much revenue each school district receives from various local, state, federal, and philanthropic sources. We understand what proportions of these revenues are expended for such things as teacher salaries, fringe benefits, and textbooks and supplies. However, we have virtually no understanding of what these budget "objects" are intended to accomplish. In short, what is missing is a linkage between the objects of expenditure and their educational purposes.

This situation is beginning to change as state and federal statistical officials respond to increased public interest in school reform and accountability and to growing demands for information about what education dollars buy. The committee was not able to explore in depth the demands on the education statistics system. We did hold a one-day workshop to discuss with 25 invited experts what the new challenges for school finance might mean for the data collection efforts of the National Center for Education Statistics (NCES).

NCES, the statistical arm of the U.S. Department of Education, is in a unique position to serve as a catalyst in improving both national and state efforts to obtain education finance data related to the important question of how funding and school improvement policies intersect, as well as continuing to improve understanding of the distributional consequences of school finance policies. Through its national surveys, procedural handbooks, national outreach and professional communication efforts, and technical assistance, the agency already plays an essential role in fostering the availability and comparability of education data on a nationwide basis, and it has even now begun a number of innovative activities designed to enhance the usefulness of its school finance information. For example, the NCES school-finance Internet web site is a remarkably advanced high-tech effort in data distribution.

We divide our suggestions for additional improvements in school finance data into four topics: types of data collected, the level of education about which data are collected, methods of data collection, and the usefulness of data. We conclude with some thoughts about the resources NCES will need to follow through on these suggestions.

TYPES OF DATA COLLECTED

The core of the NCES current school finance data program is information on revenues and expenditures for every state and school district, collected annually from state administrative records. Although it is often assumed that NCES itself collects data from school districts, this is not the case. The agency has always depended on state-collected data, which in turn reflect the fact that state administrative records were developed mainly for the purpose of financially auditing school districts for the appropriate receipt and spending of education funds.

The federal government has so far not chosen to require that state and district data be reported to Washington using a uniform accounting standard, nor is there any nationwide requirement that school districts follow generally accepted accounting principles. Instead, NCES permits flexibility and diversity within an overall standard, which each state can interpret and to which it can align its data for purposes of reporting to NCES. The standard involves a function and object accounting approach[1] using common definitions, rather than an approach based on programmatic categories. State and district data from the fiscal surveys are linked in the database called the Common Core of Data (CCD) to nonfiscal education data on states, districts, and schools. Through development and refine-

---

[1] In school finance accounting parlance, an "object code" refers to the subject of the expenditure, what was purchased with the money. This can be a teacher's salary, fringe benefits, a computer, food for the cafeteria, or fuel for school buses, for example. "Function" codes refer to the broad purposes for which such objects of spending were made. The conventional function codes are so large and amorphous as to be of little use to researchers. The conventional function codes are broad areas, such as instruction, administration, pupil services, food service, maintenance, and transportation. They may assist fiscal auditors, but they do not build a link to instructional or school effectiveness.

ment of the CCD surveys, NCES has been instrumental in improving the availability and comparability of education revenue and expenditure data on a nationwide basis and in enabling these data to be linked to basic characteristics of states and districts as reported in the nonfiscal surveys. Until recently, virtually no finance data were included in other parts of the NCES data collection program, such as the longitudinal surveys and international comparative studies.

NCES can help meet the new challenge of linking school finance more closely to educational performance by adding productivity concerns to its traditional emphasis on revenues and expenditures. (Revenue and expenditure data continue to be important as well, and we suggest some improvements in these statistics at the end of this section.) Giving more attention to data linking finances and performance requires attention to the level of education for which data are collected as well as to how data are collected, topics which are addressed in the next two sections. But interacting with those issues are questions about the types of finance data that will be needed.

We were not able to undertake detailed analysis of the feasibility, trade-off, and cost considerations that NCES will need to address before making decisions about additional data to be sought; rather, we suggest some key areas that should be explored as instruments are developed to link finance data more closely to issues of student and school performance.

Outcome Data

Outcome data are clearly central in evaluating school performance and its connection with finance. It is also clear that developing appropriate outcome indicators will be a complex and expensive task with great potential for inappropriate use of available measures, for all the reasons discussed in this report. Not only in data reporting, but in state and local administrative structures as well, there has been a sharp separation between those who are concerned with fiscal information and those who are concerned with curricular and assessment issues, and so we have little experience with bringing these separate universes together in a common reporting framework.

State-level policy makers, however, are beginning to demand that outcome data be included in routine fiscal reporting; and the Government Accounting Standards Board (GASB) has for several years been involved in research efforts that in the foreseeable future could result in requirements that performance measures be included in annual financial reports for all governmental entities, including those responsible for elementary and secondary education.[2] NCES should be

---

[2] Information about the board's government performance measures project can be found on the its web site: http://www.rutgers.edu/Accounting/raw/gasb/seagov/SEARR1.htm. Examples of input, output, outcome, and explanatory factors under consideration are shown at: http://www.rutgers.edu/Accounting/raw/gasb/seagov/E&S EducRR1.htm.

a major player in efforts to think about what performance measures might be appropriate to link with finance, given its knowledge about the availability and quality of outcome data and its experience in cooperating with state and district officials to develop standard and comparable reporting categories. The agency has already begun to respond to requests from states about how to meet new demands for performance measures; the demand for more and improved measures seems sure to grow in the foreseeable future.

Programmatic and Service Data

The traditional function and object categories that were developed to track revenues and expenditure data for fiscal auditing purposes do not represent a particularly useful lens on educational activity when the focus shifts to what schools strive to do instructionally and how they do it. Programmatic or service categories have the potential for revealing much more about how resource use relates to performance. (Program reporting, for example, might seek to allocate school resources across major areas of activity, such as regular education, special education, Title I or other remedial education, and so forth. Resource reporting attempts to identify the direct services being delivered and the resource mix being devoted to them.) Past efforts to develop program and resource reporting, however, indicate the dilemmas involved; for example, program reporting requires difficult decisions about allocating activities such as staff time across multiple programs; resource reporting, which tends to build from the micro-level of the classroom up, is extremely data-intensive and expensive. Such problems will need to be addressed and overcome, nonetheless, to find out what patterns of resource use are in educationally relevant ways.

"Off Budget" Data

To link school finance to educational performance, and not just track the appropriate use of public funds, requires new attention to counting all the financial resources that may be available to schools. Traditional school finance data collection instruments will not be sufficient for this task, as nontraditional streams of revenue become increasingly available to schools. For example, local foundations in California were established in the wake of the *Serrano v. Priest*, 487 P.2d 1241 (Cal. 1971), decision to funnel privately raised funds to schools as a way of circumventing state-imposed limits on public spending. Likewise, it appears that some districts in Wyoming are responding to that state's takeover of school finance in the wake of an adequacy-based court suit by moving some items conventionally funded through school budgets to municipal budgets. Furthermore, charter schools, which are public schools, may in some cases receive significant funds from parents or others in addition to their publicly provided revenues.

School Organization Data

Many new forms of school organization are being tried in the name of improving school performance, including charter schools, outsourcing of both auxiliary and instructional activities, schools-within-schools, site-based management, and others. None of these distinctions are captured by traditional school finance reporting categories. Data collection programs must allocate attention to gathering new kinds of information about school structure so that questions regarding possible differences in patterns of resource use and their effects, and how these differences might be connected to organizational differences and instructional outcomes, can be addressed.

Data on Quality of Inputs

While NCES surveys have historically attempted to gather basic information on school inputs, we are beginning to understand that traditional input measures do not capture quality so much as quantity. For example, research is providing evidence that conventional measures of teacher inputs, such as teacher experience, tell us too little about the underlying trait of teacher quality (see Chapter 5). It is the quality of resources, not just their amount, that is important in terms of understanding how the way money is spent affects school and student performance. This new concern for educational productivity and its determinants poses an important challenge for NCES in developing input measures that address new rather than old policy concerns. Better measures of productivity will be dependent on improved understandings from research on how educational inputs affect outcomes.

Equity-Related Data Issues

While many of the demands for new school finance data arise from the need to link finance more closely to educational productivity, NCES statistics are also vital for continued monitoring of the distribution of education resources. One avenue for new data development is taxable wealth and tax rates; it is at present impossible on a national basis to link school spending to the ability and effort of state and local governments to provide educational revenues. Such data have not been collected in the past largely because of the variation across states and localities in how closely they adhere to true market value in the assessment of property. Any effort to collect information on the property tax base by school district would have to take into account the differing assessment-to-sales ratios across districts. We recognize that in some states, these adjustments would be difficult, if not impossible, for a federal agency to make. In other states, the task has already been completed by a state agency. Analysts seeking to evaluate the wealth neutrality of school finance policies are forced to use personal income data as an imperfect proxy for taxable wealth. Another avenue for further data development relates to cost adjustments in school finance formulas (discussed in Chapter 7).

LEVEL OF EDUCATION ABOUT WHICH DATA ARE COLLECTED

In the past, school finance data, especially on a national basis, have been collected almost exclusively at the state and school district level. Growing concern about educational performance, however, has heightened the demand for all kinds of data, including finance data, to be collected at the school level, as efforts to decentralize decision making to principals, teachers, and parents move forward. Scholars interested in probing productivity questions would even like to study resource levels in individual classrooms and for individual students. Increasing awareness of intradistrict disparities in resource allocation has also spurred demand for better measures of school-to-school differences in spending. Finally, policy makers concerned about accountability and about how to determine proper funding levels for schools (like charter schools) that may operate outside district budgets need improved information on expenditures at the individual school level.

School-level finance data development is, in most states, in its infancy, although there are notable exceptions. Florida, Ohio, Oregon, and Texas are among states that have or are developing school-based financial reporting systems; and New York City does school-based reporting for its approximately 1,000 schools. By all accounts these are massive and time-consuming undertakings, especially since policy makers may (as in Oregon) accompany requirements for new financial accounting with mandates that school-level financial data be combined with school-level information about staffing, student demographics, school processes, and student outcomes and be available to the public and to policy makers via the Internet. Such efforts require major investments in standardizing accounting procedures across districts and schools, developing new accounting categories to capture new data elements of policy interest, automating record-keeping and data transmission, and providing training for district and school personnel.

While state policy makers, auditors, and business leaders are often behind the push for school-level information on performance, supporters of school-level accounting also hope that these new systems will encourage a more data-oriented climate at the local level, with principals, teachers, and parents beginning to ask new questions about their own schools and how they compare with others. In this way, better information might become an engine of school reform, increasing community pressures for improvement that may be more successful than top-down mandates.

While the big investments that are necessary to develop school-based accounting systems may indeed pay off in data that are particularly useful and used for improving education, this outcome is by no means certain. The political climate undoubtedly has become much more supportive of performance measurement in public agencies (witness such developments as the GASB performance measurement project mentioned above and the Government Performance and Results Act of 1993 mandating federal agencies to focus on measuring the results of their programs and services). Herrington (1996), however, provides a useful reminder that the mere existence of data on school expenditures and student performance does not ensure that they will be used to explore the relations between dollars and learning. Florida created a school-level fiscal system, along with a sophisticated and comprehensive assessment system, over two decades ago. Herrington (1996:246-248) found, however, that the additional data did not have the desired effects on school improvement efforts, for several reasons:

1. State political interests do not necessarily support the development of a capacity for systematic inquiry that is necessary to convert school-level fiscal data into knowledge useful for policy.

2. Educator professional norms do not support the development of a capacity for systematic inquiry that is necessary to convert school-based fiscal data into knowledge useful for management.

3. The publication and dissemination of data on school-level finance do not necessarily stimulate public interest in or public pressure for school improvement.

The primitive state of school-level data in many states, along with questions about how useful these data will eventually be, suggest that the time is not yet ripe for NCES to undertake nationwide school-level data collection. Instead, the appropriate agency role at this time is to catalyze and assist states in their school-level data development efforts. NCES can play an important role in helping states learn from one another's efforts, in developing standards for states to use if they wish, and in supporting the development of school-based data collection software, which is not cost-effective for individual states or private companies to create.

At the same time, NCES can use data collection instruments other than its national census surveys to explore the feasibility and usefulness of gathering financial resource data at the school, classroom, and individual student level for use in illuminating educational productivity questions. One example of how the agency has already begun moving in this direction involves the new Early Childhood Longitudinal Survey. Designers are attempting to insert measures of the relative resources behind individual children from kindergarten through sixth grade, eventually enabling researchers to study the impact of these resources on their performance over time. Teacher resources are the focus: base salary, merit pay, benefit rate, and full- or part-time status of the specific teachers to which each child is assigned. Earlier NCES longitudinal studies have been important sources of data for scholars studying productivity in education, but until now they have lacked explicit information on the financial resources available to individual students. The early childhood study is an important first step in overcoming that deficiency.

METHODS OF DATA COLLECTION

NCES finance data have in the past been collected through the agency's nationwide, census-type surveys of all states and school districts. While these surveys continue to be important for tracking revenue and expenditure data, they are not the only or even the best way of gathering the kind of statistics that will help illuminate productivity issues. We have also indicated how NCES is beginning to use the longitudinal studies for this purpose, and we support continued investment in the developmental work necessary to devise and test fiscal measures that can be included in those surveys.

We also urge NCES along with the Office of Educational Research and Improvement (OERI, the Department of Education's research arm) to provide support for analysis and dissemination of the school-level information available from individual states. There is no reason to believe that a full 50-state census of schools is necessary to explore what school-level data can tell us about how instructional effectiveness might be improved. Fully exploiting state-generated data for productivity purposes, however, will require many years of sustained research and development effort, something states have no track record in supporting. The federal government rather than state government has generally been the locus of public support for research and development efforts. Herrington's (1996) history of Florida's experience with a school-based data system confirms the absence of political interest in the research necessary to learn about improved delivery of instruction; Florida's school-based data system eventually focused on holding individual students accountable for performance rather than on ways to improve schools and foster their accountability. NCES and OERI could augment the analysis states are likely to do of their own data and make the results generally available for others to learn from rather than directly undertaking national data collection.

At the classroom level, NCES has already been experimenting with innovative techniques for illuminating instructional processes and developing methods for making data about these processes available for analysis. In particular, the classroom videotape studies and accompanying software programs utilized in the Third International Mathematics and Science Study provide fascinating new information (sometimes at odds in interesting ways with information gathered through traditional survey instruments) about what actually goes on inside the classroom. Video studies appear to be a promising addition to the traditional arsenal of data collection instruments; for example, more such studies might help illuminate what it is about how instruction proceeds in smaller classrooms that contributes to higher levels of student learning, and under what conditions.

Finally, we suggest that NCES consider increased use of samples to augment its nationwide census surveys. Many important questions can be addressed without obtaining information on the whole population by relying on the behavior that can be inferred from appropriately chosen samples. For example, with regard to the issue of how much money might be flowing from private sources to schools whose public revenues are capped, useful information on this subject could come from careful sample surveys much more quickly than from nationwide data collection efforts. NCES's existing quick-response survey program is a very appropriate mechanism for using samples to get information on such topics. We understand, however, that funding for quick-response surveys is limited and that school finance topics have to compete with the many other data demands on NCES.

USEFULNESS OF DATA

Data are valuable only to the extent that they match the needs of potential users. Timeliness is a perennial concern, particularly of policy makers. Researchers yearn for additional education and demographic variables that will let them test more refined and sophisticated hypotheses about student learning. Suppliers of data are apt to be unenthusiastic about providing information unless they can see some immediate benefits to themselves, yet in many cases they do not have the capacity for sophisticated data manipulation or analysis. All data users are concerned about comparability of education data across 50 states, 15,000 school districts, and 80,000 schools.

Technological advances offer options for addressing many of these concerns. NCES has been innovative in exploiting these opportunities, and we urge that even more attention be given to them.

Concerns over timeliness, for example, might be alleviated by making survey data available on the Internet as soon as it has been checked for accuracy, even before all relevant units have been heard from. The publication of data is frequently delayed because some jurisdictions are slow in returning surveys and because NCES does not want to publish incomplete or inaccurate statistics. An interim solution would be to make partial (but accurate) information, with appropriate caveats, available on line.

Researchers' needs for more data could be addressed in several ways, even within the confines of the available survey instruments. NCES could invest more resources in merging its own data with related data from other agencies; demographic data from the Census Bureau is one key target of opportunity. Demographic data provide crucial mediating variables in the quest to understand how school finance is linked to school performance, but until recently we have been dependent on the decennial census for demographic data, which is thus outdated almost as soon as it becomes available. The Census Bureau is currently developing the American Community Survey (ACS) to identify rapid changes in population and provide annual estimates of housing, social, and economic characteristics every year for all states, as well as for cities, counties, metropolitan areas, and population groups of 65,000 persons or more. This annual data collection should be fully implemented in 2003; estimates for smaller areas and population groups will also be made available on a more frequent (but not annual) basis beginning in 2008. As ACS data become available, NCES should position itself to create links to education data and to make merged databases available to researchers.

NCES can also expand the universe of variables available to researchers by serving as a clearinghouse for information about merged datasets that scholars have developed to support their analyses. NCES should not disseminate these merged datasets itself; it is not in a position to exercise quality control over individual researchers' efforts and the reputation of its own data hinges on the high statistical standards to which it holds itself. NCES is currently working with Inter-University Consortium for Political and Social Research (ICPSR) at the University of Michigan to contribute its own data to the ICPSR Internet-accessible archive of international education statistics. The agency could expand this effort to include helping researchers lodge their own datasets there and disseminating information about the data variables that these datasets contain.

Through its Internet web site on education finance (http://nces.ed.gov/edfin), NCES is already taking innovative steps to make education statistics more usable to practitioners. A good example is the peer search feature, which allows web users to select a school district and see how its finances compare with a group of peer districts, on the basis of characteristics such as enrollment, student/teacher ratio, median household income, district type, and metro status. Current per-pupil expenditures, core instructional expenditures, student/teacher ratio, administration ratio, and revenue sources can be compared with peer districts as well as with state and national averages. As states improve their own district and school-level databases, there will be increasing opportunities for NCES to develop web-based search functions providing valuable and instant information to policy makers and the public.

STAFFING AND RESOURCES AT NCES

For almost a decade, the Department of Education has been operating under a congressionally imposed personnel ceiling, which has had the effect of capping staff levels at NCES while the agency's overall budget was increasing roughly threefold. Data gathered by the committee[3] indicate that NCES now manages a $116 million budget with a staff of 115 (a ratio of roughly $1 million per staff member). Budget-to-staff ratios are noticeably lower in other statistical agencies

[3]Estimates for FY 1999 funding come from the Office of Management and Budget (1998); staff estimates are based on raw data gathered from various statistical agencies and the Office of Management and Budget.

we examined: National Center for Health Statistics ($86 million budget; 528 staff; ratio of $163,000 per staff member); Bureau of Justice Statistics ($31 million budget; 65 staff; $477,000 per staff member); Bureau of Economic Analysis ($48 million budget; 520 staff; ratio of $92,000 per staff member); and Bureau of Labor Statistics ($399 million budget; 2,642 staff; ratio of $151,000 per staff member.)

The only way in which NCES could begin to comply with the added expectations for education that have evolved over the last decade is through the creative construction of the Education Statistics Services Institute and by relying heavily on outside contract vendors. As a consequence, NCES personnel have been converted from statisticians and researchers into contract managers. Even so, their capacity to oversee the ever-enlarging world of education statistics accumulation, compilation, and distribution is seriously strained. Moreover, heavy reliance on outside contractors, while not necessarily detrimental to the quality of data collected, does detract from the agency's ability to develop in-house talent and expertise that can be helpful in analyzing data and using findings from current surveys to help plan future activities (see remarks by the executive director of the Council of Professional Associations on Federal Statistics, reported in Rothman, 1992). It will not be possible the for nation to undertake the data collection efforts required to address important questions of education equity, adequacy, and productivity unless NCES is accorded the necessary budget and professional staff.

REFERENCES

Herrington, C.
    1996   The politics of school-level finance data and state policy making. Pp. 236-252 in *Where Does the Money Go? Resource Allocation in Elementary and Secondary Schools*, L.O. Picus and J.L. Wattenbarger, eds. Sixteenth Annual Yearbook of the American Education Finance Association, 1995. Thousand Oaks, CA: Corwin Press.
Office of Management and Budget
    1998   *Statistical Programs of the United States Government, Fiscal Year 1999*. Washington, DC: Office of Management and Budget.
Rothman, R.
    1992   Desire for better picture of schools ups NCES's standing. *Education Week* (September 23) [Online]. Available: http://www.edweek.org [1999, April 26].

Biographical Sketches

HELEN F. LADD *(Cochair)* is professor of public policy studies and economics at the Terry Sanford Institute of Public Policy at Duke University, where she also directs the graduate program in public policy. Her current research focuses on education policy, particularly performance-based approaches to reforming schools and public school choice. She is editor of *Holding Schools Accountable: Performance-Based Reform in Education* and coauthor (with Edward B. Fiske) of the forthcoming *When Schools Compete: A Cautionary Tale.* In addition, she has published extensively in the areas of education finance, property taxation, state economic development, and the fiscal problems of U.S. cities; she is the author of *Local Government Land Use and Tax Policies in the United States: Understanding the Links* and (with John Yinger) *America's Ailing Cities: Fiscal Health and the Design of Urban Policy.* She has been a visiting scholar at the Federal Reserve Bank of Boston, a senior fellow at the Lincoln Institute of Land Policy, a visiting fellow at the Brookings Institution, and a Fulbright lecturer/researcher in New Zealand. She has a Ph.D. in economics from Harvard University.

THOMAS SOBOL *(Cochair)* is Christian A. Johnson professor of outstanding educational practice at Teachers College, Columbia University. As the Johnson professor, he leads Teachers College in efforts to merge academic research and educational practice. He served as the commissioner of education in New York State for 8 years and as superintendent of schools in Scarsdale, New York, for 16 years. He has chaired the board of the New Standards Project and has served on the executive committee of the Council of Chief State School Officers. As a practitioner and scholar, his research interests include education reform, public school governance and finance, and the development of reflective education practice. He has an A.M. in teaching from the Harvard Graduate School of

Education; and an Ed.D. in curriculum and teaching from Teachers College, Columbia University. He was the 1996 recipient of the Harvard Graduate School of Education award for outstanding contribution in education and a 1997 award from Teachers College for excellence in teaching.

ROBERT BERNE is vice president for academic development at New York University, where he has been a faculty member since 1976. His primary research interests involve educational policy research issues, such as school finance equity and school-level budgeting. In addition to numerous published articles, he is the coauthor (with Leanna Stiefel) of *The Measurement of Equity in School Finance* and the coeditor (with Lawrence Picus) of *Outcome Equity in Education*. He chaired the Outcome Equity Study Group for the New York State Commissioner of Education, served as executive director of the New York State Temporary Commission on New York City School Governance from 1989 to 1991, and was the director of policy research for New York State's Temporary Commission on the Distribution of School Aid in 1988. He has an M.B.A. in finance and a Ph.D. in business and public administration from Cornell University.

ROSEMARY CHALK (*Senior Program Officer*) is study director of the Committee on Immunization Finance Policies and Practices at the Institute of Medicine. Formerly, she was a senior program officer at the National Research Council with the Commission on Behavioral and Social Sciences and Education. She has directed several projects at the National Research Council since 1987, including studies on family violence, child abuse and neglect, and research ethics. Prior to that time, she was a consultant for science and society research projects in Cambridge, Massachusetts. She was the program head of the Committee on Scientific Freedom and Responsibility of the American Association for the Advancement of Science from 1976 to 1986. She has a B.A. in foreign affairs from the University of Cincinnati.

DENNIS N. EPPLE is Thomas Lord professor of economics at the Graduate School of Industrial Administration at Carnegie Mellon University and a research associate at the National Bureau of Economic Research. His research interests include the economics of education, public economics, industrial organization, and applied econometrics. He has published in the areas of education finance and policy, state and local public finance, and urban economics. He is a former coeditor of the *American Economic Review*. He has an M.P.A. from the Woodrow Wilson School of Public and International Affairs, Princeton University, and a Ph.D. in economics from Princeton University.

NEAL D. FINKELSTEIN (*Senior Program Officer*) is a research coordinator with the University of California, Office of the President, evaluating the university's outreach efforts to primary and secondary schools. Before his work with the committee, he was the assistant director of Policy Analysis for California Education and a research associate with the National Center for Research in Vocational Education. He has conducted research on numerous education policy issues, including public school finance, school governance, school-to-work programs, and early childhood education. He has a Ph.D. in education policy from the University of California, Berkeley.

ANNE MARIE FINN (*Research Associate*) is a research associate at the National Research Council with the Division on Education, Labor, and Human Performance. Previously, she was a policy analyst at the Laurel Consulting Group (Laurel, Maryland), where she contributed to projects examining child abuse and neglect, family violence, youth development, and health care issues. She has an M.A. in applied anthropology from American University.

SUSAN H. FUHRMAN is the dean and George and Diane Weiss professor of education at the Graduate School of Education, University of Pennsylvania. She is also chair of the management committee of the Consortium for Policy Research in Education. She has written widely on education policy and finance. Among her edited books are *Designing Coherent Education Policy: Improving the System*, and *Rewards and Reform: Creating Educational Incentives that Work* (coedited with Jennifer O'Day). She serves on the Policy Council of the Association for Public Policy Analysis and Management and the congressionally mandated Independent Review Panel for Title I. She is also a vice president of the American Educational Research Association and a consultant to the Shanghai Municipal Education Commission. Her research interests include state policy design, accountability, deregulation, intergovernmental relationships, and standards-based reform. She has a Ph.D. in political science and education from Columbia University.

EDMUND W. GORDON is the John M. Musser professor of psychology (Emeritus) at Yale University and a visiting scholar at the College Board. He also serves as a member of the National Research Council's Committee on Early Childhood Pedagogy and is a past member of the National Research Council's Board on Testing and Assessment. He was one of the founders and the first national director of research of Head Start. He has conducted research on children living in poverty, cultural diversity and multicultural education, educational policies for socially disadvantaged children, and cognitive development and schooling. He has published numerous books, including *Educational Resilience: Challenges and Prospects* (with Margaret Y. Wang), *Education and Social Justice: A View from the Back of the Bus*, and *Handbook of Equal Educational Opportunity*. He has an Ed.D. in child development and guidance from Teachers College, Columbia University.

JAMES W. GUTHRIE is professor of education and public policy at Peabody College, Vanderbilt University, and director of the Peabody Center on Education Policy. Previously, he was codirector of Policy Analysis for California Education and professor of education at the University of California, Berkeley. He has worked for the California and New York State education departments, served as an education specialist for the U.S. Senate, and was a special assistant to the assistant secretary of the U.S. Department of Health, Education, and Welfare. He has been honored as an Alfred North Whitehead postdoctoral fellow at Harvard University, has been a visiting fellow at the Department of Educational Studies of Oxford University, and in 1990 was named as the American Education Research Association's first senior fellow. He is president of a private management consulting corporation, Management Analysis and Planning Inc., which specializes in education finance and litigation support. He has a Ph.D. in education policy from Stanford University.

JANET S. HANSEN *(Study Director)* is a senior program officer at the National Research Council. She has managed several projects related to education and training, international comparative studies in education, and civilian aviation careers. Prior to joining the NRC staff, she was director for policy analysis at the College Board. She has written and lectured widely on issues relating to higher education finance, federal and state student assistance programs, and how families pay for college. She also served as director for continuing education and associate provost at Claremont College and as assistant dean of the college at Princeton University. She has a Ph.D. in public and international affairs from Princeton University.

THOMAS A. HUSTED *(Senior Consultant)* is associate professor of economics at American University. His research interests include public economics and applied microeconomics, and he has written on such issues as educational efficiency and productivity and student achievement. He has a Ph.D. in economics from the University of North Carolina, Chapel Hill.

STEPHEN P. KLEIN is a senior research scientist with the RAND Corporation, where he directs policy research studies in the fields of education, health, and criminal justice. At RAND he has examined alternative assessments of student achievement in science, the relationship between various types of teaching practices and student ability in mathematics and science, and the utility of delivering computer-adaptive tests over the Internet. He serves as a member of the NRC's Committee on Assessment and Teacher Quality and is a past member of the NRC's Committee on Appropriate Test Use. He also serves as a consultant to several professional licensing boards on matters relating to testing and assessment. Before joining RAND, he was a research psychologist with the Educational Testing Service in Princeton, New Jersey, and an associate professor in residence at the University of California, Los Angeles. He has a Ph.D. in industrial psychology from Purdue University.

DIANA LAM is superintendent of the Providence Public School District in Providence, Rhode Island. She has also served as superintendent of the San Antonio Independent School District in San Antonio, Texas; superintendent of the Dubuque Community School District in Dubuque, Iowa; and was the first superintendent named under the partnership between the Chelsea School District and Boston University in Chelsea, Massachusetts. Since 1992, she has also served as a senior adviser and consultant with Expeditionary Learning Outward Bound. As principal designer of this program, she has been a consultant to school sites implementing Expeditionary Learning in Boston, Denver, New York City, and San Antonio. She is also a senior fellow of the Annenberg Institute for School Reform and is a member of the board of directors for numerous charitable and educational organizations. She has an M.Ed. in bilingual education from Boston State College.

LAURENCE E. LYNN, JR., is the Sydney Stein, Jr., professor of public management at the School of Social Service Administration (where he was dean from 1983 to 1988) and the Irving B. Harris Graduate School of Public Policy Studies, University of Chicago. He is also director of the Center for Urban Research and Policy Studies at the University of Chicago. Formerly, he was professor of public policy and chairman of the public policy program at Harvard University's John F. Kennedy School of Government. He has held senior positions with the federal government, including deputy assistant secretary of defense; director of program analysis at the National Security Council; assistant secretary, Department of Health, Education, and Welfare; and assistant secretary, Department of the Interior. He has also chaired the National Research Council's Committee on Child Development Research and Public Policy and the Committee on National Urban Policy. He has a Ph.D. in economics from Yale University.

PAUL A. MINORINI (*Senior Consultant*) is a director of Boys Hope Girls Hope, a national residential and college preparatory program for at-risk, yet academically capable, youth, headquartered in Bridgeton, Missouri. Prior to joining the National Research Council, he was an attorney at Hogan & Hartson in Washington, D.C., where he represented school districts in efforts to obtain greater education funding equity and program adequacy through policy reform and litigation. He has published several articles related to school finance equity and adequacy legal cases. He has a J.D. from the University of Pennsylvania Law School.

GARY NATRIELLO is professor of sociology and education at Teachers College, Columbia University. He is also a senior research scientist at the Institute for Urban and Minority Education and editor of the *Teachers College Record.*

His current research interests include the impact of evaluation processes on students, the needs of at-risk students, and the impact of school finance reform on school districts and students. He has worked with at-risk students projects at The Johns Hopkins University National Center for Research on Effective Schooling for Disadvantaged Youth. Among his numerous publications, he is coauthor (with Edward McDill and Aaron Pallas) of *Schooling Disadvantaged Children: Racing Against Catastrophe* and *From Cashbox to Classroom: The Impact of the Quality Education Act in New Jersey* (with William Firestone and Margaret Goertz). He has a Ph.D. in the sociology of education from Stanford University.

ALLAN R. ODDEN is professor of educational administration at the University of Wisconsin at Madison. He is also codirector of the Consortium for Policy Research in Education and director of its teacher compensation project. Previously, he was professor of education policy and administration at the University of Southern California and director of Policy Analysis for California Education. He worked with the Education Commission of the States for a decade, serving as assistant executive director, director of policy analysis and research, and director of its educational finance center. He has also served as a research director for several state education finance projects and served as a consultant to federal, state, and local education officials and policy makers. He has written extensively in the areas of education policy, public school finance, teacher compensation, and decentralized school management. He has a Ph.D. in educational administration from Columbia University and an M.Div. from Union Theological Seminary.

TED SANDERS is president of Southern Illinois University. He has extensive experience with state-level education departments. Previously, he served as superintendent of public instruction for the Ohio Department of Education. He also served as superintendent of education for the Illinois State Board of Education and the Nevada Department of Education, and as assistant state superintendent for the New Mexico Department of Education. At the federal level, he served as deputy secretary of education and acting secretary of education, U.S. Department of Education. Active in many educational organizations, he is an executive board member of the National Council for Accreditation of Teacher Education and board member of the Institute for Educational Leadership. He is past president of the Council of Chief State School Officers and the Illinois-based North Central Regional Educational Laboratory. He has an Ed.D. in education administration and higher education from the University of Nevada at Reno.

ROBERT M. SCHWAB is professor and director of graduate studies at the Department of Economics, University of Maryland, College Park. His primary field of research is public economics with an emphasis on state and local government. He has published numerous articles on education finance; his most recent research focuses on education finance reform, the distribution of education resources, and education productivity, with a particular emphasis on the relative efficiency of public and private schools. He has a Ph.D. in economics from The Johns Hopkins University.

KENNETH A. STRIKE is professor of education at Cornell University. His research interests include the philosophical and political aspects of school reform, professional ethics in education, as well as social and legal educational issues. He has authored numerous books and papers on the ethics of teaching, educational policy, and school administration. His published work includes *Educational Policy and the Just Society* and *The Ethics of Teaching* (with Jonas Soltis). He is a past president of the Philosophy of Education Society and is a member of the National Academy of Education. He has a Ph.D. in philosophy of education from Northwestern University.

STEPHEN D. SUGARMAN is the Agnes Roddy Robb professor of law at the University of California, Berkeley, School of Law. His published scholarship in the field of educational policy and the law covers topics such as school finance reform, school choice, and the legal rights of public schoolchildren. Among his many publications, he is coauthor (with John Coons and William Clune) of *Private Wealth and Public Education* and (with John Coons) of *Education by Choice*, *Scholarships for Children*, and *Making Choice Work for All Families*. He is also coeditor (with Frank Kemerer) of *School Choice and Social Controversy: Politics, Policy and Law*. He has participated in school finance litigation in several states, and on behalf of children from low-wealth school districts argued the case of *Serrano* v. *Priest* before the California Supreme Court. He has a J.D. from the Northwestern University School of Law.

JOAN E. TALBERT is senior research scholar at Stanford University and codirector of the Center for Research on the Context of Teaching. The center's research investigates education outcomes of various school reform initiatives. She specializes in organizational sociology, the sociology of occupations, and survey research methods and is interested in effects of education policy and school organization on teaching and learning. Her publications include *Teaching for Understanding: Challenges for Practice, Research, and Policy* (coedited with David K. Cohen and Milbrey W. McLaughlin) and *The Contexts of Teaching in Secondary Schools: Teachers' Realities* (coedited with Milbrey W. McLaughlin and Nina Bascia). She is a council member of the American Educational Research Association. She recently served on an advisory panel for the National Academy of Education and the Office of Educational Research and Improvement, U.S. Department of Education, charged with recommending directions for research on teacher professional development. She has a Ph.D. in sociology from the University of Washington.

AMY STUART WELLS is professor of educational policy at the Graduate School of Education and Information Studies, Department of Education, University of California, Los Angeles. Her research interests include the sociology of education and qualitative policy analysis. Of special interest are educational policy issues pertaining to the politics of race and culture, including school desegregation, school choice, and "de-tracking" in racially mixed schools. She has recently completed a study of charter school reform in 10 school districts in California. Among her many publications, she is the author of *Time to Choose: America at the Crossroads of School Choice Policies* and coauthor (with Robert L. Crain) of *Stepping Over the Color Line: African American Students in White Suburban Schools*. She has a Ph.D. in the sociology of education from Teachers College, Columbia University.

Index

S